Nurses' Medication Er
An Interpretative Study of Ex

Marianne Arndt

Nurses' Medication Errors

An Interpretative Study of Experiences

PETER LANG
Frankfurt am Main · Berlin · Bern · New York · Paris · Wien

Die Deutsche Bibliothek - CIP-Einheitsaufnahme

Arndt, Marianne:

Nurses' medication errors : an interpretative study of experiences / Marianne Arndt. - Frankfurt am Main ; Berlin ; Bern ; New York ; Paris ; Wien : Lang, 1994
Zugl.: Edinburgh, Univ., Diss., 1993
ISBN 3-631-47209-9

ISBN 3-631-47209-9

Printed in Germany 1 2 3 5 6 7

TABLE OF CONTENTS

PART III - DATA ANALYSIS - THEMES AND KEY ISSUES

PART IV - MAKING A MEDICATION ERROR - THE MEANING OF THE EXPERIENCE

CHAPTER 9 - Subjection and Power, Identification and Change

Chapter 10 - Guilt and Shame - Reconciliation with Human Precariousness

Chapter 11 - Learning from Mistakes, Teaching Ethics in Nursing Education

Concluding Interpretive Remarks

FOREWORDS

This book makes a significant contribution to the nursing literature. It illuminates an aspect of nursing which, though crucially important, has remained unhealthily obscure, possibly because of its sensitivity. My nursing colleagues are sure to join me in welcoming this candid, helpful and challenging analysis with its potential for continued learning.

Edinburgh, November 1993 Lisbeth Hockey

This is an innovative book of many facets. It is indeed about the hazards of therapeutic practice and the professional conduct of nurses, but it is also a fine development in the doing of Ethics. If Carol Gilligan shook up the traditional male oriented scientistic study of morals, Arndt further advances the paradigm of an egalitarian, interactive, integrative and feminist orientation. So the book will be of interest and more importantly, of use, to all kinds of social scientists and philosophers.

It is in the philosophical discussions that the continental background of Arndt's work comes to the fore. Her modifications of Althusser's ideas on subjection and power and in particular her application of Pecheux's theory of identification, counteridentification and disidentification, show what we gain from her scholarship and her fluent explication of their use for us here.

She has gone into dangerous territory. Mistakes, as we have to confess them, are always a fraught matter, and mistakes in medical treatment especially are surrounded not only by embarrassment and shame, but also by guilt and professional punishment. Yet as we see,

Arndt has tackled the matter very simply. Without elaborate psychometrics, she has respected the integrity of her nurse informants; asked them good straight questions and been rewarded by their confidence and exemplary openness. By this means we have the lived experiences of the nurses, not just the facts of the cases.

Although she labels the study 'interpretive', this does not imply any psycho-dynamic second-guessing, instead her sophistication is used in the analysis of the discourse of justification for actions which were difficult to reconsider, complex for even the actor to understand, and which have consequences which were sometimes very painful.

I myself had initially grave doubts about the degree to which nurses would be willing to discuss their past mistakes with an unknown stranger in the name of the social science enterprise, but the book demonstrates how Arndt's skill and her obvious constructive and empathic interest, allowed her informants to show their own hard-won understanding of what happened and what did follow, or should have done... And this involved the whole structure of mistake, revelation, and procedures that come into play not only to repair the error but to 'deal with' the perpetrator. Sometimes this led constructively and smoothly to new learning and reparation, other times not so.

The reader must end the book with an increased respect for the nurses, who whatever their human error, spoke out with such moral courage and are obviously good people, better than their institutions sometimes seem to deserve....

Halla Beloff

University of Edinburgh, November 1993

ACKNOWLEDGEMENTS

Writing about mistakes, about nurses' medication errors? This project is not about mistakes, it is about learning and about change. Many people have helped me to learn and to understand better.

First of all I want to thank those nurses who have shared their experiences with me, both, in Germany and in Scotland. They talked about their feelings and provided me freely with their knowledge. That was the basis for this study.

I am deeply indebted to my supervisors, Kath Melia, formerly Senior Lecturer, now Head of the Department of Nursing Studies, University of Edinburgh whose cogent thinking prevented me from going astray; and to Halla Beloff, Senior Lecturer in the Department of Psychology, who never failed to give me warm encouragement. Both listened patiently to me. Their suggestions and comments were much appreciated especially when I got stuck!

My thanks go to the Department of Nursing Studies, University of Edinburgh; especially to Helen Sinclair, former Head of the Department, who gave me a good start, advice and practical help through three years of thinking, reading and writing. Rosemary Weir and Steve Tilley, both Lecturers at the Department of Nursing Studies, showed interest in my project and helped me to widen my horizon.

It is also to my fellow students, that I owe thanks. Martha MacLeod opened the doors to phenomenology for me, and Bill Gilroy and Jonathan Klein listened patiently during the later stages to what I thought I knew. Innumerable cups of coffee and office lunches were shared with Ilana Kadmon, Therese Mazer, Jean Lugton, and Rebecca Strachan. We worked out complicated arguments and had exhilarating discussions.

Annie Altschul and Ruth Schröck were valuable sources of information. Both were liberal with their time and shared their knowledge and experience. Lisbeth Hockey was a special friend. I would not have missed the intellectual stimulation through discussions and the physical sustenance through good food.

The library staff and the staff of the computer support team never faltered in giving time, expert advice and practical help. I am grateful that Margaret Peach took on the task of proof-reading and Linda Morris was ready to help with the final production of the thesis.

A thesis grows and takes shape with the help of many who have no direct interest in academic work. Comfortable lodgings and friendly talks are a necessity which brighten up life. I want to thank Nessie and Ben Farrell, landlady and landlord during the first eighteen months, and the Sisters of St. Anne's Convent who housed me during the second half of my stay in Scotland. Their interest in my work helped me to keep in touch with reality. Living at Ru'A Reidh Lighthouse during the final stretches of writing was amazingly helpful. The wind and storms gave me, body and mind, a new alertness. Chris Barnett and Fran Cree made sure that physical needs were met. Their humour, their empathy, and their knowledge (not only at 'Trivial Pursuit'), made those last weeks a special experience.

Throughout the time of working on this project, my family and friends in Germany were near, and supported me. Telecommunication and the postal services ought to be thanked for maintaining technical and organisational means for these contacts across the channel.

Finally I want to make acknowledgements to the Commission of the European Council, The World Health Organisation, and especially to the Robert Bosch Stiftung in Stuttgart, Germany, who gave financial support to make it possible to conclude this project without undue anxiety.

Edinburgh, Januar 1993 Marianne Arndt

Preface

The meaning that nurses assign to their experiences with medication errors is at the centre of this study. Using discourse analysis within a framework of an interpretive research design, the phenomenon of a not all too uncommon occurrence in nursing practice is examined. The decisions made in such situations have moral implications on a personal, an institutional, and a professional level.

Insight into nurses' involvement with medication errors was gained from various data sources. Twelve senior nurses were interviewed and asked about their experiences. In two group discussions, one in Germany, the other in Scotland, ward sisters shared their knowledge and their feelings. Six senior nurses provided written self reports. The participants were asked to talk and write about what helped and what hindered in the situations they had lived through. These interviews, group discussions and self reports provided data on retrospectively recounted experiences. Furthermore, six documents of disciplinary proceedings where the Professional Conduct Committee of the United Kingdom Central Council for Nursing, Midwifery and Health Visiting has dealt with incidents of medication errors supplemented the data.

The literature on medication errors provided a fertile backdrop to the study as did the literature on ethics in nursing and on the teaching of ethics in basic and post-basic nurse education.

Three key issues are discussed in this study as they evolved from the analysis of the data: The first issue deals with identification and change. Identification, in its various forms, with the image of nursing, with the nursing hierarchy and with the social reality of the health care services, either result in the perpetuation of prevailing practices, or lead to changes in and development of the same. Guilt and reconciliation with human precariousness is addressed as the second issue. Personal failure and the limits of an imperfect world can be come to terms with by regaining professional confidence and by seeing the value basically inherent in nurses' work. The third issue is taken from the areas of teaching and learning. The moral courage that is needed to learn from mistakes can be enhanced through honest dealings with the situation.

Where the attention is shifted from the person involved onto the problem at hand, fair judgement may be advanced and the fear of owning up to a mistake be diminished. Not only do the deontological arguments of an ethic of justice have to be pursued, but in addition a teleological line of argument is asking for attention that takes into account the need of carers, to be cared for.

Only when reflected upon, can personal experience merge into the stream of development and progress. This study makes a contribution to such reflection.

"I have made a mistake."

"Listen, it has happened to me,

-I know how you feel. I do know how you feel!"

INTRODUCTION AND OVERVIEW

THE CONCEPT OF THE THESIS

Our societies are moving into a new age of integration and relation as modern philosophers and scientists have pointed out. This can be perceived vividly by looking at the latest political developments especially in central Europe.

Political and social ideology is being re-examined and re-stated. Capra talks about a "new vision of reality" that is dependent on understanding:

> ...the essential interrelatedness and interdependence of all phenomena - physical, biological, psychological, social and cultural (Capra 1982 p. 285).

Words like 'holistic' and 'integrative' rather than 'discerning and separating' have a high value in modern thinking and perception. Capra understands this integration as applicable to the individual as well as to society as a whole: "What is unhealthy for the individual is generally also unhealthy for the society and for the embedding ecosystem" (Capra 1982).

In nursing literature 'holistic health models' are being described of late (e.g. Travelbee 1971; Roy 1970, 1981; Rogers 1970; King 1976, 1981, 1983). They supersede the traditional medical model of health care that features an organic, reductionistic approach. The focus is on the whole human being as well as on the human interaction with the environment (Donnelly et al 1980; Meleis 1985).

Within these models a new emphasis is placed on the integrative approach of the 'health care team' rather than on a strictly hierarchical structure.

Capra states:

> The natural balance of living organisms includes a balance between their self-assertiveness and integrative tendencies (Capra 1982 p. 355).

He understands this integrative approach as a systems approach where life is not structured by a hierarchical order. Capra envisages a development that goes "beyond the conventional disciplinary distinctions". "Communication" and "co-operation" are the key-words in the development he foresees.

Within these changing concepts the nursing profession is asserting itself more and more in its new position. Nurses have pledged themselves to the promotion of health; the prevention of illness; the restoration of health; and the alleviation of suffering (International Code of Nursing Ethics, 1973). Within the context of their work nurses have begun to develop their own sense of moral awareness. Neither general aspects of medical ethics, nor broad perspectives of moral philosophy provide the ethical baselines for the profession. These do have their place within the discussion specific for the nursing profession, but ethics in nursing has its own themes and centres of gravity. Ethics in nursing acquires an ever increasing interest. Topics specifically relevant to nursing practice, nursing theory and nurse education which embrace varying aspects of moral philosophy are legion.

In this project I focus on ethical issues that stem from direct involvement in nursing practice and are linked with the changing awareness regarding an integrative rather than separating development of the profession. The vast field of ethics in nursing obviously cannot be dealt with as a whole, thus the topic of making moral decisions in specific situations of nursing practice is focused on as the centre of attention.

Being responsible for one's actions, dealing with success and failure is a feature of life in general. This feature also includes dealing with errors. A variety of mistakes can be encountered during the professional life of a nurse. These may include medication errors, mistaking patients' names or violating rules of procedures. Mistakes can lead to life threatening situations or be of little consequence to a patient; but any kind of mistake is likely to have great importance for the nurses involved.

This study focuses on the situation of medication errors. The administration of medication provides a setting of common nursing experience. The giving of drugs is considered at once an everyday nursing activity and a highly responsible task.

The very word 'medication' stems from the Latin word *mediare,* to be in the middle, and connotes the intermediate position from which the giver of medication operates. The word 'medicine' in turn goes back to the Latin word *mederi,* to heal. Both words are tied to the Latin word *medius,* middle. Thus, it takes no wonder to appreciate the importance allocated by nurses to the task of giving out medications. It has a central position, in the concrete act of contributing to the alleviation of suffering, the restoration and promotion of health, and also in the prevention of illness, when nurses interact with patients, and for the perception of a professional identity of nurses. Mistakes in this area take on an existential meaning, be they serious ones, harming patients, or be they negligible ones. It is not surprising that nurses speak of *'being devastated'* after having made a medication error.

Decisions to be made in a situation of medication error then pertain to the personal value system of the nurses involved. They are made against the background of their professional education and formation. Making decisions in this situation, nurses have to take into account the institutional structure of their work setting, the immediate situation concerning staffing levels and work load, and the interpersonal relations with patients and other health care workers.

Campbell speaks about "two attitudes which are fundamental to all moral decision-making". He addresses the "*willingness to be self-critical* and the *readiness to communicate openly with others*" (Campbell 1979, italics in the original). The experience of nurses as they have been involved in situations of medication errors is being examined in this thesis. Self critique and communication formed the basis which made this study possible. Only because nurses were willing to speak critically about their experiences, about themselves, and about others was it possible for me to gain insight into the meaning the phenomenon of medication errors has for nurses.

This study in itself represents an effort to be critical and self-critical; it is a contribution to open communication within the nursing profession. And it is also a contribution to the communication of nursing science with other social sciences.

THE STRUCTURE OF THE THESIS

The project is presented in four parts. In the first two parts the project is described and in the third and fourth parts the findings are presented and discussed.

Part one: The project

The content of the three chapters of the first part provide the backdrop for this research project. In chapter one the concept of medication errors is defined and the administration of medication is addressed. The practice of giving out drugs as is customary in Britain is described and discussed. Chapter two offers a comparative element between Britain and Germany as far as policy-making in nursing is concerned. The practice of drug administration in Germany differs a great deal from British practice. It is described and compared to the British one. This comparison illuminates the British situation and offers a wider spectrum of comprehension as to the ways medication errors are handled.

The title of Chapter Three is 'Ethics in nursing'. This chapter provides an outline of ethical aspects as they pertain to the baseline of this thesis. Professional autonomy, and rules and regulations feature in this chapter, as well as personal and professional development. In the conclusion of this chapter the research question is defined and formulated.

Thus, the first part sets the scene for the scope of this study. In these chapters appraisals of respective literature are included.

Part two: The method - an interpretive design

In the three chapters of the second part the methodological approach to this study is delineated. The research tools are defined and a description is offered as to the use of these tools. The theoretical and practical aspects of the research design are described and unfolded in this part.

In Chapter Four a discussion is offered on qualitative research. Here a focus is given to phenomenology as a basis for all qualitative research. The method-combination for this study is outlined, giving credit to discourse analysis as the method of choice informing the research design of this study.

Chapter Five features an overview and a description of the data sources. The data for this study were derived from group discussions, interviews, written self reports, and from documents pertaining to cases where the Professional Conduct Committee has dealt with medication errors. Some theoretical aspects of data collection are discussed and practical and technical issues concerning the collection of data for this study are reiterated.

In Chapter Six the process of data analysis is described. Three levels of analysis are detailed and discussed. The first level can be referred to as the organising level. The second level of analysis was a phase when the themes emerging from the data were structured and contextualised in a model that provides an overview of the phenomena connected with medication errors. At the third level of analysis three key issues were isolated from the themes. They provide the content of the three chapters comprising the fourth part of the project.

The steps involved in the three levels of analysis are described in detail, illuminating the understanding of parts three and four of this thesis.

Part three: Themes and key issues

Five main themes emerged from the data as a result of analysis at the first level. They are addressed in Chapter Seven of this part. The themes featuring in this chapter are: *'The procedure of dealing with medication errors'; 'The role of the medical staff'; 'The image of the nurse and of nursing'; 'The situation of student nurses';* and *'Support in the situation of medication errors'.* These themes also appear in the literature that was addressed in the first part of this thesis.

An overview over the way all themes interconnect is provided by a model. This empirical model represents the second level of analysis and features in Chapter Eight. It shows how experiences of medication errors are part of a dynamic process of change. The cornerstones of the model are: *'Influential factors (givens) for the acquisition of meaning in the situation of medication errors'; 'Reactions to the occurrence of medication errors';* and *'Ultimate effects of medication errors, of the reactions to them and of the consequences that followed their occurrence'.* The overview which is provided by this model helps to understand the many-faceted reality that is underlying nurses' experience of medication errors.

Connected with the themes are three key issues each of which in turn links up in one way or another with each of the themes. These key issues represent the cornerstones of the empirical model. The three key issues that I chose to address as of foremost importance and interest are: *'Subjection and power - identification and change'; 'Guilt and reconciliation';* and *'Learning from mistakes'.* The key issues are unfolded in the three chapters of Part IV of this thesis. There, they are dealt with in an in-depth manner.

Part four : Making a medication error - The meaning of the experience

In this part the main objective of the study culminates. The key issues are explored at the third level of analysis, and this exploration provides insight into the meaning of the experience of being involved in a medication error. A chapter is allocated to each of these issues.

The *'Givens' or 'Influential factors for the acquisition of meaning'* are elucidated in Chapter Nine by addressing the key issue of *'Subjection and power'* in the context of moral decision-making in the situation of medication errors. This issue is seen against a background of identification with the role of nurses and related to the notions of an ethic of justice and an ethic of care. In this context the connection between structural changes and role identification is addressed.

'Reactions to the occurrence of a medication error' are (amongst others) certainly those of guilt and shame. In Chapter Ten the perceptions of *'Guilt and shame* are explored and various perspectives that are helpful for the process of reconciliation with the experience of failure are discussed on the basis of the available data.

The third cornerstone of the empirical model *'Ultimate effects of a medication error, of the reactions and consequences'* is represented in Chapter Eleven which deals with teaching and learning and especially with the notion of *'Learning from mistakes'*. The experience of medication errors is explored in its relation to affective learning. Learning in practice by reflection is highlighted as a central issue of this thesis. The internalisation of what is learned provides new givens for the acquisition of meaning and thus a new basis for subsequent experiences.

SUMMARY

The themes I found as having emerged from the data and the key issues that are discussed may well not be the only themes and key issues of importance when addressing experiences surrounding medication errors. Nevertheless, they appear to tie in with the concept of integration rather than separation. Whenever a mistake in nursing practice occurs or is about to occur, it will be the way it is handled and reflected upon that provides the meaning that is inherent in such an experience, and not the fact of having made a mistake as such. Learning from mistakes involves personal change of attitude and practice and does not of course exclude cognitive learning. It can also be part of a process of change in the organisational structure of practice, and it could effect changes in the understanding of hierarchy and the execution of power. The willingness to be self-critical and the readiness to communicate as the two attitudes fundamental to all moral decision-making empower nurses to develop a perception of professional and personal integrity that includes traditional values as well as heeding the problems encountered in a changing world.

In this study I try to make sense of the meaning that is expressed in nurses' discourse about their experiences of medication errors. Of qualitative research it is sometimes said that it is unwieldy and of little practical use. However, I hope that the exploration of nurses' experiences of medication errors in this interpretive study contributes to the understanding of such situations. It may help nurses to understand themselves as well as colleagues; and it may provide nurse teachers with new insights where they address topics connected with the administration of medicines and where the transmission of ethical content is concerned.

PART I
THE PROJECT

THE USELESS TREE

Hui Tzu said to Chuang:
I have a big tree,
The kind they call a "stinktree."
The trunk is so distorted,
So full of knots,
No one can get a straight plank
Out of it. The branches are so crooked
You cannot cut them up
In any way that makes sense.

There it stands beside the road.
No carpenter will even look at it.

Such is your teaching-
Big and useless.

Chuang Tzu replied:
Have you ever watched the wildcat
Crouching, watching his prey-
This way it leaps, and that way,
High and low, and at last
Lands in the trap.

But have you seen the yak?
Great as a thundercloud
He stands in his might.

Big? Sure,
He can't catch mice!

So for your big tree. No use?
Then plant it in the wasteland
In emptiness.
Walk idly around,
Rest under its shadow;
No axe or bill prepares its end.
So no one will ever cut it down.

Useless? You should worry!

(Thomas Merton: The way of Chuang Tzu)

CHAPTER 1
MAKING A MISTAKE IN THE ADMINISTRATION OF DRUGS

INTRODUCTION TO THE CHAPTER

The purpose of this first chapter is to provide a picture of the phenomenon of making medication errors. A fairly large body of literature has accumulated. Various aspects connected with medication errors are addressed. They cover causative circumstances, means to prevent medication errors, and the manner in which medication errors are handled. The literature includes journal articles, text books or text book chapters, and research projects. Some of this literature is evaluated here.

The chapter includes three sections, the first of which deals with definitions of medication errors as offered in the literature. In the second section the drug routine is described. Knowledge, skills and responsibilities as they pertain to the administration of medications are outlined. The routine procedures of giving out medicines and the occurrence of medication errors are focused on. A diagram is used to illustrate the interdependencies of the drug routine, the various factors that may cause its disturbance and breakdown, and the consecutive occurrence of a medication error. In the last section the reduction of medication errors is addressed focusing on guide-lines for the prevention of medication errors, on organisational aspects relevant to the administration of medications, and on disciplinary measures after a medication error has occurred.

Definition and Classification of Medication Errors

An error, at first sight, is an inaccuracy or deviation from an accepted norm. Where nurses contribute to the treatment of sick people, accuracy is of paramount importance. However, a variety of factors have to be taken into account when describing the nature of medication errors. In order to convey a comprehensive picture of what medication errors refer to, a classification of medication errors is presented which includes causative factors contributing to the occurrence of errors.

The literature surveyed and represented here, accounts for only a small part of the material available and concentrates on articles and research reports published in North America and in Britain. No distinction is made between the different national sources as the topics discussed apply generally and on a supranational level to problems in relation to the administration of medication.

Medication errors have been defined on varying levels of abstraction. According to Fuqua and Stevens

> A medication error is a dose of medication that deviates from the physician's medication order on the patient's chart (Fuqua and Stevens 1988 p. 10).

Downie, MacKenzie, and Williams give the following definition:

> A drug error can be defined broadly as an act of commission or omission that militates against the achievement of the therapeutic objective, that is of benefit for the patient (Downie et al 1987 p. 171).

This is further exemplified by Wolf. She distinguishes between errors of commission and errors of omission that are either intentional or unintentional. Wolf further offers a typology of medication errors which classifies them according to the consequences they have for patients. These consequences are: Death, disability, no effects, or beneficial effects (Wolf 1989 p. 9).

Brandt et al define medication errors as:

> Incorrect medication or solution; incorrect route; medication or solution not given at scheduled time or ordered interval; medication or solution given twice or omitted; discontinued medication or solution given; outdated medication or solution given and administration of allergic medication or solution (Brandt et al 1988 p. 80 i).

Other authors enumerate similar points (Fuqua and Stevens 1988; Cushing 1986).

These definitions do not take the various causes into account which may be instrumental in the occurrence of medication errors. They focus only on the administering nurse.

Instead of trying to define medication errors, some authors give lists of causative circumstances against which drug administration policies are developed in order to arrive at safe practice. Often, after a damaging incident has occurred, causing harm to a patient, a strict policy is enforced to prevent similar situations from happening in the future.

Such causative circumstances may be: the condoned practice that in certain circumstances nurses administer drugs without written prescription (Jones 1988); unclear, even incorrect prescription (Turton 1984; Fuqua and Stevens 1988); faulty dispensing or packaging (Davis and Cohen 1989; Fuqua and Stevens 1988). A further hazard that is not included in the above cited definitions, may be a patient's allergic reaction to a prescribed and correctly administered drug (McGovern 1988; Fuqua and Stevens 1988). Long (1982) reports in a study on medication errors that omission was the most frequently occurring instance of medication errors. This was followed by administering the wrong dosage and/or the wrong medication. The latter is often found to be due to failure of correctly checking the patient's identity so that medication intended for one patient is not given to another (Fuqua and Stevens 1988).

Fuqua and Stevens (1988) classify medication errors within the responsibility of those concerned with the manufacture, prescription, dispensing and administration of drugs. They see the responsibility:

With the nursing staff; here they list medication errors due to inadequate knowledge or medication administration skills, failure to comply with required policy or procedure, and failure in communication;

with the physician; here medication errors are found to be due to incorrect, vague or ambiguous orders, over-reliance on nursing staff, and unsafe practice or malpractice (e.g. not taking a complete patient history, failing to discover known allergies);

with the pharmacist; in this category medication errors may be due to dispensing problems, labelling problems (mostly misreading or misinterpreting physician's orders);

with the drug manufacturers; medication errors in this sphere may be due to labelling practices (e.g. illegibility of inprints on ampoules) or badly defined colour-coding. (The responsibilities of Pharmacists and drug manufacturers are further exemplified by Davis and Cohen, 1989);

with the nursing administration; in this area medication errors are accorded to work stress and insufficient staffing.

Fuqua and Stevens report that "failure to comply with required procedures for the safe administration of medications" was recognised as a major source of error. "Failure to check instructions or procedures" being the predominant cause here (Fuqua and Stevens 1988).

In addition Johnson (1987) ascribes a large number of medication errors due to lack of clear policy, for example the permission of telephone orders. Turton (1984) mentions how medication errors still persist in spite of 'fool proof' procedures.

In summary medication errors can be described as actual or potential mistakes made by nurses within their own sphere of responsibility:

- the wrong preparation may be given to a patient,
- the wrong doses of the correct medicine may be given to a patient,
- the wrong manner of application may be chosen,
- the medication may be given at the wrong time (or speed in the case of i.v. application),
- the medication is given to the wrong patient.

As has been mentioned, mistakes may be due to wrong labelling or due to wrong preparations - which is the pharmacists responsibility, or they may be due to wrong prescription - where the doctor is accountable.

However in these circumstances the nurses' vigilance and experience is called upon and the question arises whether or not she acted in good faith and cannot be made responsible for a third party's negligence.

A further problem situation may arise, where doctor and nurse do not agree about the medication for a patient and the knowledge and experience of the nurse stands against the question of obedience within a hierarchical structure. A nurse may carry out the act of giving a drug correctly as to all aspects of the routine procedures of medication administration and for the benefit of a patient. If the drug was not prescribed by a doctor, this would amount to professional misconduct.[1]

In order to understand how medication errors happened in the context of nurses' work, in the next section all factors that comprise the administration of medication are addressed.

---

[1] An example for this situation see in UKCC Document Four, the case of Nurse C. as described in the summaries of all medication errors in the appendix.

THE DRUG ROUTINE

(YOU SHOULD NEVER MAKE A MISTAKE IF YOU FOLLOW THE DRUG ROUTINE!)

General remarks

The administration of medicines is considered at once an everyday nursing activity and a highly responsible task. It provides the setting of a common nursing experience. In British nursing various formal safeguards are employed in order to prevent mistakes. On the basis of primary legislation concerning the administration of medicines which is the Medicines Act of 1968 and the Misuse of Drugs Act of 1971 the United Kingdom Central Council for Nursing, Midwifery and Health Visiting (UKCC) has issued an advisory paper that deals with the administration of medicines.[2] This Advisory paper provides a framework to assist the development of local policies and guide-lines. Local health authorities as well as individual hospital groups have subsequently set up rules and guide-lines to regulate the practice of drug-prescription, storage and administration.[3] They are constantly updated to safeguard patients and nurses alike where the administration of medicines is concerned. Furthermore the Royal College of Nursing (RCN), Department of Policy and Practice issued

---

[2] UKCC Advisory paper on the administration of medicines (1986) 'A framework to assist individual and professional judgement and the development of local policies and guide-lines.' (This paper was replaced by a new set of guidelines in October 1992 "Standards for the Administration of medicines".)

[3] for example: Lothian Health Board (1981) Standard Procedures for safe Handling, Administration, Storage and Custody of Medicinal Products. Edinburgh: Lothian Health Board (this paper is in the process of being updated).

Wessex Health Authority (1984) Drugs - policies and practices in Wessex. Bath: The Group.

several papers on drug administration and the nurses' role in this task.[4] Most hospitals and wards in Britain are subjected to formulated policies of drug administration which basically refer to these documents. Yet, no matter what policies and guide-lines regulate the administration of medicines or what routines are followed, actual or potential mistakes occur time and again.

The administration of medication by various routes and differing procedures are part of the recognised duties of nurses. In order to safeguard patients' welfare nurses adhere to an established routine of drug administration. This routine is taught during nursing training and is composed of various elements that concentrate on the avoidance of the above enumerated possibilities of erroneous drug administration.

The drug routine, which comprises all aspects connected with the administration of medications, consists of four main components: Pharmacological knowledge; knowledge of the administration procedure; skills applying pharmacological knowledge and knowledge of the administration procedure; and patients' participation in the responsibilities connected with medication administration.

The drug routine

Pharmacological knowledge

Nurses must have an adequate knowledge of the medications they handle. This includes pharmacological knowledge as well as the knowledge of how drugs are prescribed, stored and handled. It also includes knowledge of the normal therapeutic dosages. Apart from knowing the actions and effects as well as the correct means of administration and application, the side effects and dangers in connection with any specific drug are also to be known by the nurse.

---

4 Royal College of Nursing (1987) Drug administration - a nursing responsibility. London: Royal College of Nursing.

Knowledge of the procedure

In order to administer medications correctly, certain procedures have to be known. These procedures are generally laid down in drug administration policies on local, regional and national levels.

They are part of the drug routine that is addressed here and they include certain steps which will ensure the correct administration of medicines. These steps consist in the checking of:

- patient identity,
- the prescription,
- the drug to be given, (name and dosage)
- expiry dates and strength of the preparation,
- the route to be used to administer the drug.

The drug policy on a given level may also state whether one or two nurses are to carry out these procedures. In this context it is laid down that generally only medical practitioners may prescribe drugs and have to do this in writing. Possible exceptions will be addressed individually in local hospital drug administration policies. Thus nurses may under certain circumstances exercise their own discretion if this is previously agreed upon. This may apply to changing dosage or time of certain medications. In some settings it is usual practice that certain routine drug regimen employed in emergency situations, need not immediately be written up by a doctor but may be initiated by a specially prepared nurse.

Skills applying pharmacological knowledge and knowledge of the procedure

The acquisition of skills in the administration of medications is not to be equated with the cognitive aspects of drug administration. Pharmacological knowledge and the knowledge of drug administration procedures do not mean that a nurse is able to, and will actually give drugs according to the procedures she has learned about and knows. Practical skills have to be acquired.

These skills not only include the safe handling of oral medications, but also those needed to apply drugs by various other routes such as hypodermically, intramuscularly or intravenously by injection or by infusion; rectally by way of suppositories or enema; locally in the form of lotions, drops or poultices. They also include the skills needed to safely handle the appropriate technical equipment needed for such administrations.[5] One important aspect of a nurses' responsibility is the constant updating of knowledge and skills in drug administration.

Patient's participation in the responsibilities connected with medication administration

This fourth component of the drug routine is a feature not necessarily recognised and understood as of importance in connection with drug administration. Nearly every person in the Western world from time to time handles drugs bought at the chemist or prescribed by the general medical practitioner. In these situations the individual takes the responsibility for the correct administration.

Also in the clinical setting, if in the position of taking a responsible part in their treatment, patients should be encouraged to do so. Responsibility does not have to rest with the health care workers alone. This of course applies only insofar as the patient is conscious and physically and mentally able to share in this responsibility.

If this aspect of patients taking responsibility for their medication in the clinical setting as they do at home, is seen as an important component of the drug routine, nurses will have to listen carefully to what patients say, and take patients' claims seriously.

---

5 Examples for medication errors in these areas see in UKCC Documents Two, the case of Nurse B., and Document Six, the case of Nurse P. and Nurse M.

It confers a different kind of responsibility on to the nurse: that of ensuring a patient's right to exercise his or her own responsibility.

Drug routine and medication errors

> *...if you had followed procedure, as it states you should .. you would never have made the error!*

This, or similar statements are generally used when the pitfalls of drug administration are being addressed.

The drug routine as outlined above, provides many safeguards that should assure the correct administration of medication. The relationship between a break down of the drug routine and the occurrence of medication errors is depicted in the diagram below.

Figure 1: The drug routine

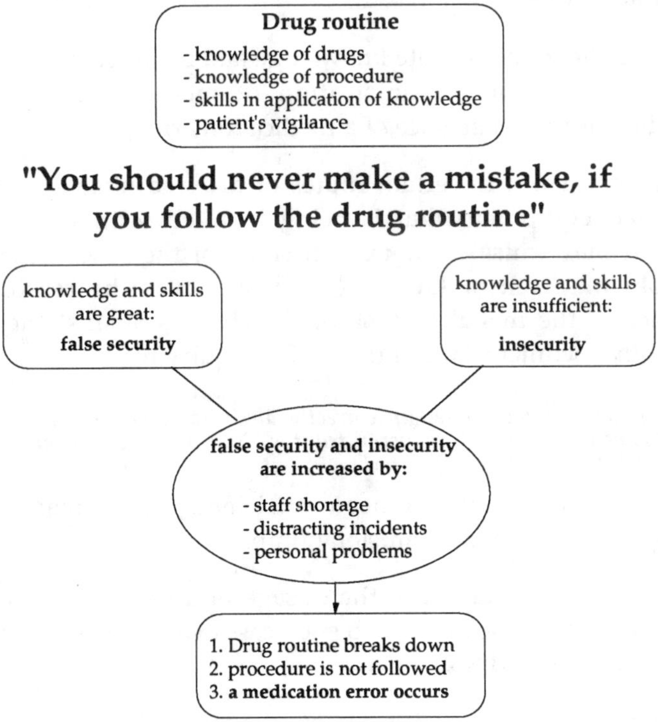

inct sources for the breakdown of the drug routine can be . They in turn have several ramifications which are addressed below.

Very experienced nurses, whose knowledge and skills regarding drug administration were great, confessed that their medication error occurred, because they felt too secure and did not follow the identification procedure for their patients. Several nurses in this study admitted that sometimes the checking is not carried out exactly as the procedure prescribes, especially if the patients on a given ward have been there for a lengthy period of time. The familiarity with the patients on the ward and, having carried out the routine countless times expose a nurse to making an error.

On the other hand inadequate knowledge and insufficient skills causing an insecurity in the administration of medication may also be responsible for the occurrence of a medication error.

Being inexperienced in certain routes of drug administration or with complicated equipment that is being handled without appropriate instruction may cause mistakes. In some of the cases heard by the UKCC obvious lack of knowledge or skill was the reason for the occurrence of the mistake. One of the charges against the midwife Nurse B., in Document Two of the UKCC inquiry read:

> *...That you did fail to set up correctly an intravenous infusion of the drug Syntocinon, which failure permitted the patient to receive an unregulated dose of the said drug, (DOC2 p. 1).*

Here the midwife had not been sufficiently conversant with the handling of an intravenous infusion pump.

Mistakes in the calculation of the dosage of a drug are also frequent causes of medication errors. Two such cases were dealt with in UKCC Documents Three and Six.

False security and insecurity are often increased by accompanying circumstances such as staff shortage or too great a work load. Often emergencies or other distracting incidents while doing a drug round were mentioned by the respondents of this study for being partly responsible for the occurrence of medication errors.

Also personal distractions which preoccupy a nurse may increase false security or insecurity and add to the chances of a medication error occurring. This was the case with one nurse in the Scottish Group Discussion. She had just returned to nursing after some years of raising a family. On her first day she made a drug-error. A similar situation was mentioned in Self Report Two.

If for any of the aforementioned reasons the drug routine breaks down and the procedure for drug administration is not followed correctly a medication error will occur.

In this thesis questions related to the drug routine are not addressed any further. The drug routine and its disruptions are not the topic to be examined. Insofar as they connect to the themes depicted later however, a better understanding can be gained if the facts mentioned here are kept in mind.

To Minimise Medication Errors

Guide-lines for the prevention of medication errors

In this section a further survey of relevant literature is presented. This survey takes into account some of the points made in the section above. It gives an overview of possible measures that can be taken, in order to minimise medication errors.

The occurrence and possible prevention of medication errors have been studied, using quantitative methods (Ley, Jain and Skilbeck 1976; Long and Johnson 1981; Long 1982; Betz and Levy 1985; Wieser and Dann 1987; Poster and Pelletier 1988). In addition a large number of descriptive articles has been produced (e.g. Vincent 1989; Cohen 1987, 1988, 1989a, 1989b; Fuqua and Stevens 1988; Williams 1990). Some of the above mentioned articles also deal with the procedures of reporting medication errors and with disciplining the responsible person(s).

Arising from close scrutiny of the possible causes for medication errors, check-lists and rules for safe medication administration have been developed (eg.: McGovern 1988, 10 Golden Rules for Administering Drugs Safely). Also Fuqua and Stevens (1988) present recommendations for reducing medication errors. Similarly Williams (1990) sets up a list equating sources of errors with possible actions to reduce them.

Davis and Cohen advise for the minimisation of medication errors the following guide-lines:

- Always follow drug administration procedures according to the stated routine.
- Plan staff development programmes on new drug information.
- Whenever you must calculate and prepare your own infusions, always check the accuracy of your work with another health care professional.
- Use premixed I.V. drugs and standard concentrations whenever possible.
- Insist that supervisors test new graduate nurses returning to work after a time off, and inexperienced new hires on their administration drug competencies (Davis and Cohen 1989 p. 51).

Most procedures focus on minimising or eliminating medication errors. However, policies may be agreed upon, but they can only be a guide to action.

Checking and double checking

In this context the practice of double checking can fittingly be discussed. Aspects of control on the one hand, and professional confidence and autonomy on the other are closely linked with this issue. Whether two nurses do the drug rounds and check the distribution of medication or one nurse does it alone is often discussed in connection with the advisory paper of the UKCC on the administration of medicines. This states:

> The UKCC is of the view that practitioners whose names are on the first level parts of the register, and midwifes, should be seen as competent to administer medicines on their own, and responsible for their action in so doing. The involvement of a second person in the administration of medicines with a first level practitioner need only occur where that practitioner is instructing a learner or the patient's condition makes it necessary or in such other circumstances as locally determined. Where two persons are involved responsibility still attaches to the senior person (UKCC 1986 p. 8).

The guide-lines of the UKCC suggest that it can be considered safe for the first level nurse to give drugs on her own, and to accept full responsibility for this (see also Johnson 1987). However, in most ward settings in Britain this is not practised so far. Instead, generally two nurses do the 'drug round', one of whom is mostly a senior nurse, one a student or even a nursing auxiliary. This has in the past been cause for many controversies (Johnson 1987; Callaghan 1990).

In an article reporting on a trial period of single-nurse administration of drugs, Callaghan, who was responsibly involved with this project wrote that "many employers still apparently feel safer with two-nurse drug administration" (Callaghan 1990). Thorough discussion with senior as well as junior staff members preceded the trial period which was to last for one week and included enrolled nurses as well as registered nurses. In a brief questionnaire involving 20 nurses Callaghan elicited that most nurses thought it to be a good idea if only one nurse gave out medications. Most participants felt, however that an update on drug administration policies and legal aspects of the same as well as a general update on drugs would be beneficial.

There was a certain disparity as to checking intravenous and intramuscular medications, as well as Insulin with two nurses. Most nurses felt that prescription charts should be printed in order to avoid difficulties in reading doctors' handwriting. Some nurses expressed a certain reluctance giving out medicines when they were "tired, hurried or harassed" (Callaghan 1990). Callaghan summarises:

> The data collected demonstrated a general willingness among the nurses for the new drug administration procedure - only one of the nurses was unwilling to administer any drugs, under any circumstances, on her own (Callaghan 1990 p. 37).

This trial period or pilot study, as it was called was aimed at easing the transition from a two-nurse policy of drug administration to a one-nurse policy. It was evaluated as having been "very successful" (Callaghan 1990).

One problem connected with the policy of student nurses checking drugs with senior nurses was addressed by Turton (1984). This may be defined as the dichotomy in the learner's role of the student having to act as a colleague and equal to a senior staff in a hierarchical setting.

Uys (1988) states from the perspective of the South African Nursing Council that student nurses "... are legally responsible for their own actions". This, too is certainly the case in most continental nursing settings. Therefore the student may only be given responsibilities for which she can safely be made accountable. The role of supervised learner and the role as an equal to a senior staff are not compatible. It is obvious that given too much responsibility the role of the learner is violated. Turton states:

> We may conclude that the main objective of the double checking procedure, safeguarding the patient, is based on an unrealistic expectation of the junior nurse's ability to 'make a stand'. It places the student in the contradictory position of being on the one hand legally responsible for her actions, therefore, in an equal relationship with her senior nurse, and on the other hand in the role of the 'learner' and consequential in an unequal relationship ... One solution would be to reconsider the possibility of trained nurses becoming legally responsible for the administration of drugs (Turton 1984 p. 19).

Learning experience must be clearly defined as such and the nurse giving clinical instruction will have to acknowledge her part of the responsibility for the actions carried out by the student. Students do take part in drug-rounds in the practical setting as part of their training. The involvement of students in drug rounds however, is to be understood as a learning experience. Thus their participation in a drug round changes the normal routine from a nursing task into a teaching measure.

Organisational aspects

The question of work stress and understaffing needs some further discussion. Often medication errors are reported as being due to unsafe staffing levels causing too high a workload (Jones 1988; Johnson 1987; Campbell 1984). In this context it is quite common that a nurse may give a prescribed medication correctly but forgets to sign for it or intends to do this later in order to attend to more urgent aspects of work. In several cases recounted in the interviews, another nurse subsequently gave the medication again. This apparently is a common type of medication error. By reducing the workload and the stress connected with it, a great number of errors could be avoided. Faddis (1939 quoted in Fuqua and Stevens 1988), points out that teachers and administrators of nursing are responsible for errors to the extent that they allow conditions to exist that are conducive to making mistakes.

By implementing individual care systems the risk of medication errors may also be reduced. Long addresses this issue in her study on medicine delivery systems and nursing care methods. She examines unit dose systems, individual prescription order, and the complete floor stock system and evaluates them in combination with function (task) allocation of nursing care, total patient care allocation and primary care. It was found that functional nursing and floor stock systems in combination provide the greatest error chance. All systems are shown to have strengths and weaknesses. Certain systems provide better means to monitor medications given, and this applies to medicine delivery systems as well as to care giving systems. Long concludes that it is the administrator's responsibility to make adaptations in both systems in order to bring about good co-ordination for the sake of the patient's medication therapy (Long 1982).

Disciplinary measures - on reporting and disciplining

Once it is known that a medication error has occurred, generally steps are taken to follow it up. These steps may range from dealing with a medication error in a low key manner on ward level, assessing it within the nursing hierarchy, or on hospital or Health Board levels, to opening disciplinary actions against the persons responsible. (Situations where medication errors led to civil or criminal court proceedings are not dealt with in this study).

On a local level generally four choices of disciplinary actions may be used: informal warning; written warning; final written warning; dismissal (Johnson 1987). However, nurses may also be suspended for a limited time from giving the type of medication with which the error has occurred. They may also be suspended altogether from giving out drugs for a time; and they may be suspended from duty until the incident has been dealt with (Carlisle 1991).

It is suggested that disciplinary measures are used and understood as instruments of punishment rather than as tools of correction. The fear of punitive action does prevent errors from being reported (Carlisle 1991). Carlisle states:

> The fact that practitioners who have made mistakes ... and are open and honest about those mistakes to their manager are often made the subject of disciplinary action must simply encourage dishonesty and be to the potential detriment of patients (Carlisle 1991 p. 31)

An unnamed nurse, writing about her experience concerning the way her minor medication error was handled remarks:

> This was clearly a necessary process both for protection of patients and standards of nursing. But the feelings of guilt and self-doubt that these (responses of senior nursing staff) induced should have been used to encourage additional vigilance while accepting there is always the risk of human fallibility ... Is it really necessary to make an error such a degrading, destructive experience? (Nursing Times, October 25, 1989 p. 41)

Several incidents appear in the literature that was surveyed where nurses were dismissed or suspended from their jobs according to unclear strategies which were employed to deal with their medication errors (Jones 1988; Cushing 1986). Inconsistency of evaluation in the event of medication errors has caused undue severity as Johnson (1987) and Turner (1988) point out.

The UKCC has changed the "disciplinary hearing" where professional misconduct of nurses in Britain was investigated and dealt with, to a "professional conduct hearing". Herewith showing that professional guidance is to be the main objective when disciplinary action is to be decided on in the case of error (Campbell 1984). The UKCC has dealt with these cases often with more benevolence than health authority managers, whose purpose seemed to be "to establish the grounds of misconduct" by measuring an incident against existing rules and guidelines. (Johnson 1987). The unnamed nurse referred to above asks, why a mistake is considered misconduct? (Nursing Times, October 25 1989). Also Johnson mentions that "most drug errors have nothing to do with misconduct or general incompetence", and that often "the disciplinary system is inappropriate to deal with them" (Johnson 1987).

In order to reduce medication errors emphasis is to be placed on a non-punitive error-reporting system (Fuqua and Stevens 1988). This should cause an increase of errors reported. Thus means can be employed to eliminate causative factors, which may be the lack of pharmacological knowledge, or insufficient skills in the administration of certain medications. In many hospitals it is routine practice that nurses have to undergo further training after they have been involved in a medication error. Fuqua and Stevens maintain that by simply updating knowledge in training programmes for nurses who have encountered medication errors, an improvement of error rates does not seem to be attained. Indeed, training sessions could be "interpreted as selective or punitive" (Fuqua and Stevens 1988). Fuqua and Stevens advise routine training sessions for all staff.

Johnson (1987) points out that medication errors should be dealt with in such a way that they are minimised and subsequently prevented. When evaluating medication errors several factors should be taken into account: "the drug dispensing, administration and documentation systems"; "the circumstances surrounding the error"; "the person responsible for the error" (Carr 1989). Measures taken after the occurrence of a medication error should take into account whether "carelessness, ignorance or negligence" were responsible for the mistake.

Cobb discusses this issue and states that "... the severity of the error is a critical factor in determining disciplinary action" (Cobb 1986). For her study a tool was developed to assess medication errors' severity on the grounds of "type of error, route of administration, classification of drug, and time elapsed after the error, that the report is initiated". The main objective was to develop this tool "for supervisor's use with staff nurses". Cobb reports that "staff nurses have responded favorably toward the tool because it ensured objectivity, fairness and clarity of expectation". Furthermore "consistency among supervisors" in judging medication errors was achieved (Cobb 1986). Evaluating medication errors according to severity, and taking into account the actual context of the occurrence, not only focuses on assisting, counselling, and updating training for the nurses concerned, but also ensures fair dealing with matters of negligence and incompetence.

The assessment and evaluation of medication errors has been included into the quality assurance of patient care. Several studies have addressed the possibilities of reducing medication errors by way of monitoring errors and reporting incidents (e.g. Francis 1980; Long and Johnson 1981; Long 1982; Hodgin 1984; Wieser and Dann 1987; Brandt et al 1988; Carr 1989; Pearlson 1988; Poster and Pelletier 1988;). Brandt et al (1988) are certain that "controlled monitoring of medication incidents promotes quality patient care". These authors introduce three categories relating to the severity of incidents. These three categories are:

1) Incidents that require minimal or no medical or nursing intervention;

2) Incidents that produce a systematic or localised response requiring interventions to counteract medication or flow rates;

3) Incidents that are potentially life threatening with immediate medical and nursing intervention mandated to counteract reactions.

The authors report that medication error incident reports are reviewed on a monthly basis, followed up and evaluated. The incidents are reported by the professionals concerned, and brought to the attention of the head nurse and medical officer as well as the hospital administration. The situation is assessed in order to discover learning needs, or to bring about further action in improving the minimisation of medication errors concerning all parties involved; like pharmacy, medical service, and nursing service. As a result policy changes were effected at the hospital where the said study was carried out. Through the "trending of incidents", attention could be focused on areas that required further education (Brandt et al 1988).

In order to deal with medication errors it is not sufficient to set standard rules, to establish comparable means as to organisational and disciplinary dealing with medication errors, and to devise training programmes in order to ensure the updating of knowledge. Appropriate medication delivery systems, safe staffing levels and care systems, prescription routines and regular practice revisions, are suggested to reduce the occurrence of medication errors.

SUMMARY

The administration of medication in its various forms is a main nursing task. In order to be aware of the risks involved and of the consequences erroneous administration may have, nurses are educated in the understanding of pharmacology, namely the effects and side effects that various medications in therapeutic use may have. Furthermore nurses are trained in reading and interpreting physician's prescriptions; they are trained in routine procedures of medication administration; in the ordering, handling and storing of medicines; as well as in organisational matters regarding the policies in dealing with the administration of medication. The educational objective for nurses is to attain an awareness of the responsibilities they have as regards to patient's safety as well as an awareness of the responsibilities for their own personal and professional development. Professional conduct, codes of ethics and nurses accountability are touched upon in the course of lectures and practical exercises.

In spite of careful theoretical learning and practical training, mistakes of varying severity consistently do occur. Research at different levels has sought to understand and describe the nature of medication errors in order to provide insight into factors relating to them and to offer means of action to be taken in order to prevent or minimise medication errors. It appears that medication errors cannot be accorded to the incompetence of the one person concerned with the immediate delivery and administration of medication, but that multiple causation has to be taken into account. Chain reactions and combinations of factors have to be considered as shown above.

In this chapter the interdependence between the breakdown of the drug routine and medication errors has been examined. This examination provides the basis for the analysis of the phenomenon of medication errors.

CHAPTER 2
COMPARING BRITISH AND GERMAN NURSING PERSPECTIVES

INTRODUCTION TO THE CHAPTER

This study is not a comparative one between the health care systems of Germany and of Britain. It focuses on the experiences of nurses in relation to medication errors. All experiences are embedded in a social reality. The writing of this study happens to take place in the British situation. The main body of data were gathered in Scotland. However, my own reality is strongly influenced by my German cultural and professional background. My own general education has taken place in Germany, my nursing training and education, in Britain. I have experienced British as well as German nursing, even though in recent years I was mainly concerned with German perspectives of nursing. I cannot thus eliminate the German cultural and specific professional elements from my thinking, as they provide the backdrop against which my writing takes place.

Therefore at this point a comparative element is not amiss. As my personal situation made it easy to gather data from German nurses, as well as offering easy access to information about the German Health Service and about the nursing perspective within it, I used some of the available sources to complement the British perspective. It seemed worthwhile to highlight some of the specific differences between Germany and Britain regarding the administration of medicines. The inclusion of a contrasting element brings about a better understanding of the issues addressed and about the position from which I write.

These elements provide the factual contents of this thesis. By comparing and contrasting them within a different world of perception, an interpretative understanding may be gained.

POLICY MAKING IN BRITAIN AND IN GERMANY

General remarks

In Britain as in Germany the legislation of the Council of the European Commission has of late made a fair impact on many aspects of nursing and on nurse education.

The Council Directives from 1977 address the

> '... mutual recognition of diplomas, certificates and other formal qualifications of nurses responsible for general care, ...' (Directive 77/452/EEC); they also deal with '... the co-ordination of provisions laid down by law, regulation or administrative action in respect of the activities of nurses responsible for general care' (Directive 77/453/EEC).

The two directives concern mainly the areas of practice to be included in the training schedules, as well as the number and content of theoretical lectures. They also regulate the proportion between theoretical and practical course content. One important feature is stated in Article One of Directive 453, where it says that nurse training is to provide:

> ... adequate clinical experience; such experience which should be selected for its training value, should be gained under the supervision of qualified nursing staff and in places where the number of qualified nursing staff and equipment are appropriate for the nursing care of the patients (Directive 77/453/EEC).

Even though abidance by written rules and regulations does not guarantee the quality of training and education, more attention has been given to the learner status of British students as compared to German ones. In Germany the EEC Directives were not implemented until 1985. This was reflected in some of the data I collected. It bore especially on the supervision of students where the administration of medications was concerned. As can be seen from the demographic data of the participants, most British nurses underwent their training at a time when these legislative points had already made a great impact on nursing education.

The British perspective

In Britain the General Nursing Councils (GNC), which were the predecessors of the UKCC, stipulated the implementation of the European directives within the UK during 1978. For instance the GNC for Scotland issued 'Schemes of Training for the Register of Nurses' in 1978. Here is stated:

> With respect to training for the General part of the Register, Council is responsible for ensuring that all courses of training satisfy the requirements imposed by the E.E.C. Directives on nursing coming into force on 29th June, 1979. The new scheme of training is compatible with these requirements (GNC for Scotland, 1978 Schemes of Training for the Register of Nurses. Section 1/19 p. 3).

Recent changes in British nurse education [1] include supernumerary status to be guaranteed for students while in their practical placements in clinical and community nursing.

In Britain, nursing affairs are first and foremost in the hands of nurses, who are represented in policy making bodies on local, regional, and national levels. The government has delegated administrative powers to the UKCC in the Nurses, Midwives, and Health Visitors Act of 1979:

> The Council is charged by Parliament with the duty to establish and improve standards of training and professional conduct for nurses, midwives and health visitors (UKCC 1990).

The register of the different kinds of nurses are a part of this. To be struck off the register is an immanent fear of all practitioners in Britain.

> ... The right to practise is conferred by the Council by registration and this right may be removed only by the Council (UKCC 1990).

---

[1] Project 2000, a new education programme for nurses which is currently being introduced in Britain, grants student status to student nurses.

Herewith safe practice is to be controlled. The UKCC has issued various guide-lines regarding professional conduct. The 'Code of Professional Conduct for the Nurse, Midwife, and Health Visitor', as well as an advisory paper on the administration of medicines regulates the various aspects of professional responsibilities in the area of drug administration (See Footnote 2, Chapter 1). A Professional Conduct Committee is appointed to consider allegations of misconduct by nurses. As to medication errors, disciplinary procedures are clearly defined.

The Nurses, Midwives, and Health Visitors Act of 1979 has been amended in 1992 and changes in the structure of the UKCC will take effect as from April 1993. Under the old Act members of the UKCC and the four National Boards for England, Scotland, Wales and Northern Ireland were appointed by the Secretary of State (Hand 1992).

The new Act requires that 40 of the 60 Central Council members will be directly elected by the profession and 20 members will be appointed by the Secretary of State. The National Boards will be smaller executive bodies with administrative functions whose members are appointed by the Secretary of State. The majority of Board members will be registered nurses, midwives, or health visitors. Changes also affect the Council's Professional Conduct Committee (PCC). In Future the PCC will deal directly with cases of alleged professional misconduct. Up to now the National Boards carried out the initial investigations and referred a case to the PCC if deemed necessary. The PCC will now carry out investigations and will have powers, not only to remove the name of a nurse from the register, but it can also caution a nurse about future conduct, or it can suspend a nurse for a specified period (Nursing Times, March 25, 1992). This makes for greater "flexibility to deal effectively with lesser offences " (Hand 1992).

In future the PCC will also have a different composition. As well as council members, professionals will be appointed according to the practice area from which a nurse comes against whom allegations are made. In addition non-nurses, such as consumer representatives will be allowed to sit on a panel (Nursing Times, March 25, 1992; Hand 1992).

The UKCC Code of Professional Conduct was subsequently revised in 1992 and supplemented by a paper called 'The Scope of Professional Practice'. Here principles are laid down that are to 'govern adjustments to the scope of professional practice' (UKCC 1992). In this paper the traditional 'certification' of certain techniques is superseded by 'principles'. According to these principles nurses are held to acknowledge:

> ...any limits of personal knowledge and skill and take steps to remedy any relevant deficits in order effectively and appropriately to meet the needs of patients and clients (UKCC 1992).

This clearly emphasises autonomy and accountability as well as personal responsibility of individual nurses. Whether the traditional certification of certain tasks can be abolished remains to be seen. However, it is important to point out that reference in this thesis to the UKCC and its Professional Conduct Committee is made in its context of the 1979 Act.

Additionally in Britain also the Royal College of Nursing (RCN) safeguards and upholds professional standards as an independent professional organisation. About 75 % of all nurses (including students) are members of the RCN. [2] The department of Nursing Policy and Practice within the RCN advises on various practice matters. The department has issued a paper on drug administration which addresses nursing responsibilities in this field. Another function of the RCN is to provide concrete help and advice in cases of professional conduct allegations. A representative of the College will undertake to represent a nurse at a professional conduct hearing of the UKCC.

Complementary to the RCN some Trade Unions have taken up the responsibility to look after nurses' interests. They balance the role of the RCN and generally nurses who are not members of the RCN are a member of one of the unions. In conclusion it may be said that the

---

[2] Telephone information from Press Officer, External Relations Department, RCN London, 7.1.1993.

nursing profession in the United Kingdom has a fair degree of self-regulation.

The German perspective

In Germany nursing is regulated by a rather general Federal law. Current nursing legislation is devised by the German Government in collaboration with the Federal Minister for Education and Science. The law on nursing that implemented the European Directives from 1977 was not passed until 1985. It replaced the previous Nursing Law from 1965. The 'Krankenpflegegesetz' (Nursing Law) puts the responsibilities for the recognition of schools of nursing into the hands of the local health authorities which employ medical officers for administrative services.

All schools of nursing are attached to a hospital or a hospital group. The directorship of a school of nursing is in the hands of a qualified nurse teacher, sometimes in co-operation with a medical doctor or a nursing administrator. Within this setting the schools of nursing have a relatively free hand to organise nurse training as long as it complies with the basic requirements of the Federal law. In Germany hospitals have a directorial board which consists of a senior doctor, a qualified nurse manager and an administrator. The directorial board is responsible to the governing agency of the hospital. A governing agency may be the regional health administrative authority; a private trust or charity; or one of the church agencies which run about 50% of all health care institutions in Germany.

Churches in Germany, therefore, have a powerful voice regarding matters of health care and regarding the structure of education for those health care professionals whose training institutions are linked with hospitals. There is no professional statutory body for nursing in Germany. Together with the directors of the individual schools of nursing the medical officers of the health authorities are also responsible for the conduct of the state examination of nurses. They issue the certificates and diplomas to nurses after their training is completed and the examinations are successfully passed.

As there is no registration for nurses, they cannot be struck off a register. However, the law does make provision for the official approbation of nurses. This approbation is certified by permit after successfully completing the appropriate training in a recognised school of nursing and after passing the required examinations. The approbation of nurses extends solely to the right to be called 'nurse'. The execution of nursing tasks is not covered by any law. The Nursing Law states:

> 1 Whoever wants to hold one of the designations 1. "Nurse" or "Male Nurse", 2."Children's Nurse", or "Male Children's Nurse" or 3. "Nursing Assistant", or "Male Nursing Assistant" needs permission to do so.
>
> 2 A permit is to be granted after application, if the applicant has absolved the time of training prescribed by this law and has passed the state examination, ...[3]

The approbation can be withheld or withdrawn under certain circumstances. These as a general rule have to be of a severe nature, preventing a person to be employed as a nurse. Illness, physical disability or addiction as well as proven untrustworthiness may be reasons to withdraw the approbation. However, this is an extremely rare action.

Only recently for the first time in German nursing history a trade union for nurses has been founded. The membership is very small as yet and its role is ambivalent as it seems to be in competition with the traditional Union movements in Germany which are relatively powerful. The Trade Union for Public Services, Transport and Traffic (ÖTV); the German Employees Trade Union (DAG); and the German

---

[3] Krankenpflegegesetz, mit Ausbildungs- und Prüfungsverordnung für die Berufe in der Krankenpflege. Stuttgart, Verlag Kohlhammer:

1 Wer eine der Berufsbezeichnungen 1. "Krankenschwester" oder "Krankenpfleger", 2. "Kinderkrankenschwester" oder "Kinderkrankenpfleger" oder 3. "Krankenpflegehelferin" oder "Krankenpflegehelfer" führen will, bedarf der Erlaubnis.

2 Eine Erlaubnis (...) ist auf Antrag zu erteilen, wenn der Antragsteller die durch dieses Gesetz vorgeschriebene Ausbildungszeit abgeleistet und die staatliche Prüfung bestanden hat, ...(my translation).

Trade Union Federation (DGB) run courses on professional development and sponsor about half of all institutions for the education of nurse teachers and nurse administrators of which there are about 25 in total. The other half of these institutions is under the auspices of the churches or the local governments and two or three are run privately.

There is as yet no possibility of basic nurse education at University level. However, preparations are under way to institute nurse teacher education and the preparation of nurse managers in German universities. One polytechnical college already offers a degree course for nurse managers.

Germany has many nurses' associations which represent the various religious denominations or the various nursing specialties. Their functions are similar to the functions of the RCN. Unlike the public role the RCN plays in the UK, the efforts of the various nursing associations in Germany are often diversive and sometimes contradictory. They do not have the same political influence that can be exercised by the RCN and the UKCC. In the past the associations have tried to work together in issuing statements on policies regarding nursing education and nursing practice. Such statements are noted by the law-giving bodies in Germany. In the past they had a certain public influence but no decisive political function. Representatives of the associations or the trade unions may be involved by their members in protecting a nurse against unjust treatment; by supplying expert opinion; or by providing an advocate in a court case, should need arise, for instance in a situation of medication error.

Most problems regarding nurses' professional misconduct are dealt with internally at ward or hospital levels. If an incident occurs, it is at first dealt with by the ward sister or charge nurse. It may be brought to the notice of the nursing managers or hospital directors. A nurse may be reprimanded verbally or in writing. Dismissal can only occur if a series of grave events has been noted in writing and these have been brought to the attention of the hospital directors. In such cases the employees representatives play an important role in the decision whether or not a nurse will be dismissed.

A nurse can however, gain appointment again in a different hospital without much difficulty, providing no civil or criminal allegations have been proven and the nurse has not been convicted by a court. In any case such a conviction very rarely includes the withdrawal of the nurses' approbation.

I do not know of any official measures or procedures concerning the way medication errors are dealt with in Germany. It is a feature of recent years that German nurses and nurse managers in a process of democratic negotiation formulate policies applicable to their own fields of activity. Especially private hospitals or hospitals and hospital groups under the auspices of the churches or other charities have begun to negotiate guide-lines of practice that are based on individual or religious convictions.

MEDICATION ADMINISTRATION IN GERMANY

Basically, medication administration in Germany and in Britain embrace the same elements. People feel unwell or are ill; they submit themselves to the care of health professionals and pharmaceutical remedies are ordered by a medical doctor. In hospitals or community care generally nurses will administer the medication according to the doctor's prescription.

In Germany the possession, handling, prescription, storage and administration of pharmaceutical products, and administrative and legal matters connected with this, as well as the general classification of drugs is regulated by Federal laws.[4] The Federal Health Office is ultimately responsible for the enforcement of these laws.

Like in Britain, drugs are classified according to their action, potential addictiveness, and the need for prescription by a medical practitioner. Medication for a patient in hospital may only be prescribed by a medical

---

[4] Gesetz über den Verkehr mit Betäubungsmitteln (1981). In March 1992 the "Medicinal Products: Prescription by Nurses etc Act" was passed by the British Parliament. It permits nurses under certain circumstances to prescribe "certain products" (UKCC, Oct. 1992; UKCC Register 1992).

doctor. As a rule nurses may not hand out to patients any medications that have not been prescribed by a doctor. Generally, only one nurse gives out medications. What is given is noted in the patient's case notes, but not signed for. Only recently various forms of Kardex-systems[5] have been introduced in some hospitals, were the administration of drugs can be marked individually. Addictive drugs and opiates are accounted for in special records. The nurse who administers them signs with her/his name in these records. It is the responsibility of the senior doctor and the pharmacist to check the records.

The ordering of pharmaceutical products from pharmacy is the responsibility of the nurse in charge of a ward and is geared to the needs of the medical practitioners. All orders have to be countersigned by a doctor. In many hospitals this also applies to nursing equipment and materials used in nursing such as dressings, feeding cups, or incontinence sheets.

Just like their British counterparts nurses in Germany also have to acquire basic knowledge in pharmacology. The Federal law on nursing (1985) states that out of 1600 lectures in all, 60 lectures have to be allocated to contents regarding pharmacology and the administration of medications. [6]

Thus, during their training nurses in Germany are familiarised with the appropriate laws and with individual hospitals' policy regarding ordering, storing, handling and administering pharmaceutical products. These policies, if in existence, are often issued by senior pharmacists. Apart from the obvious precautions of giving out the prescribed medications to the right patient, there are no general rules for nurses, regarding the administration of medications.

---

[5] Kardex is a Brand-name for an organising system employing cards and special folders to note care and treatment-plans for patients in health care institutions or in community care. It has been in use in Britain for about 30 years. In Britain the name has become synonymous for written documentation of nursing notes.

[6] Krankenpflegegesetz, op. cit., p. 31.

In Germany, as in Britain it is the responsibility of qualified nurses to give out medications. In Germany varying systems prevail. Medications are prepared in the duty room of a given ward, directly from the medicine cupboards. Medicine trolleys and drug rounds are unknown.

Medications may be put in containers with compartments for morning, midday and evening drugs, for individual patients for a whole day which are given to each patient in the morning; or may be dispensed and set up on trays in little plastic cups for a whole ward. These are labelled for each patient. Trays for morning, midday, and evening drugs are prepared in the late afternoon for the next day. Sometimes the night staff takes on this duty. The trays are then left in the medicine cupboard until the time for their distribution comes. Still, in some hospitals or some wards trays are prepared immediately prior to giving them out at the scheduled times.

It is quite usual for a nurse to give out medications prepared by a colleague from another shift on the previous day. However, it will be the individual nurse's responsibility to check and compare the medication with the patient's case notes prior to handing them out. Medications are not checked by a second nurse.

In Germany the personal responsibility of a nurse is the major issue in all matters concerning professional conduct. In the case of medication administration this starts with the fact that a nurse is personally responsible for the medicines she gives to a patient. In Britain the practice of two nurses doing the drug round is very common, though not a standing rule. German nurses already have to learn to understand and accept their personal responsibility when students. Control here is self control. In Germany a nurse can not rely on the checking and controlling by another nurse.

In some few hospitals student nurses are not allowed to give out medications. They may be allowed to assist a qualified nurse in order to learn the necessary techniques. In most hospitals students are encouraged to prepare medication containers or trays. In some hospitals this may not be done until a certain stage of training has been reached. Often students are supervised by a qualified nurse. There are however, occasions were students are entirely responsible for a session of drug administration. Charge nurses accept this and allocate these tasks only to students whom they personally trust. Students understand their responsibilities and are expected to ask for assistance or control if they are not absolutely sure of what they are doing.

NURSES' AUTONOMY AND THE LAW

To sum up the main differences between the German and the British system, the following points may be noted. Nursing in Germany is far more than in Britain subject to influences from outside the nursing community. In Germany non-nursing government officers, medical officers, and church officials have strong administrative powers regarding professional issues in nursing. Theoretically doctors have the final responsibility for patient's treatment, and therefore all nurses' actions are subject to a doctor's approval. As administrative policies regarding nursing and nurse training are defined on a high legislative level, a great deal of freedom ensues for nurses in the practical field. This applies to nurse education as well as to nursing practice.

In Britain, all matters of nurse education and of nursing practice, including matters of professional misconduct are subject to clearly defined policy. A much tighter set of rules, regulations, and procedures leaves less room for action for the individual nurse than is the case in Germany. However, issues regarding professional policies are clearly defined from within nursing. This gives nurses in Britain a higher degree of professional autonomy.

Nurses' professional autonomy and doctors' responsibility are at times subject to controversial opinion, but medical doctors' ultimate responsibility for a patient's treatment is, in any case, also accepted by British nurses.

I have addressed the regulative nature of the British nursing culture as well as aspects of the situation of nursing in Germany. Here few generally binding regulations exist. This has resulted in the fact that in Germany a great deal of responsibility is put on decision making at an individual level. This leaves nurses more vulnerable. Where clear rules and regulations govern practical procedures as well as professional relationships, nurses are less subject to arbitrariness.

A certain lack of professional autonomy on an official level may however, be seen as a positive aspect in German nursing. Not being subjected to as stringent an organisational format as British nurses, procedural decisions can easily be made as the need arises.

In Germany, as well as in Britain, the 'International Code of Ethics for Nurses' as accepted by the International Council of Nurses in 1973, is the basis for professional conduct. Rules and regulations or policies, whatever background they are made against, are measured by the standards of this code.

However, professional codes of conduct, policies of drug administration, as well as individual rules and regulations have either a prohibitive or an imperative character, and they incorporate punitive measures if perpetrated. As far as can be seen, the stringent disciplinary procedures of the UKCC have the sole purpose of safeguarding the public from professional misconduct of nurses. This of course is necessary, but leaves no or little room for a nurse who has for example the misfortune to be involved in a medication error, to overcome her or his inadequacy.

It is the objective of this study to examine how nurses experience medication errors, how they deal with their own precariousness and how they overcome the trauma of being confronted with their own failure. The regulative nature that surfaces especially in British nursing is not only restorative. In Germany, a certain lack of stringent regulations offers more flexibility but no guarantee for institutionalised support. One goal of dealing with medication errors, even if they are minor ones, should be to help nurses to address the reality of their own fallibility.

In this study these aspects are explored and addressed by looking further and more deeply than laws, rules and regulations. Their reality has to be seen and understood however, to conceive of and to understand nurses' actions and reactions in situations of medication errors.

CHAPTER 3

ETHICS IN NURSING - THE RESEARCH QUESTION

INTRODUCTION TO THE CHAPTER

In this study the meaning which the experience of being involved in a medication error has for nurses is explored. Decisions which have to be made in such a situation have moral relevance. The literature on medication errors refers to questions of moral philosophy only implicitly. Still, the topic of medication errors warrants the discussion of various aspects of ethics. Therefore an examination of the literature pertaining to ethics in nursing is undertaken with the aim to deliberate on various aspects of ethics in nursing as they appear of relevance to the experience of being involved in medication errors as addressed in this study. These aspects represent only a small fraction of what may be discussed in the field of ethics in nursing and what at the same time may be relevant to the content of this study. I discuss texts mainly written by North American and British nurse scholars, as well as descriptions of some research projects and studies carried out in Britain or North America. In the discussion of this literature I do not remark on the different countries of origin as most subjects relating to ethics have a supranational character. Sometimes the terminology points to the source as either American or British.

The chosen aspects are highlighted in five main sections. The first section pertains to the general perception of what ethics mean to nurses, it differentiates between what nurses understand to be ethical problems, and ethics as of relevance in everyday situations. Telling the truth, honesty, as well as reporting or not reporting a colleague fall under this aspect. They do not represent major points of ethics in nursing, but they are of undisputed importance in situations of medication errors. In the second section an outline is given of how ethical content and ethical principles are addressed in the nursing literature. This is relevant as definitions are given of ethical baselines which are referred to throughout the study. In the third section caring for the carers is emphasised. In this section an ethic of justice versus an ethic of care are compared and related to nursing as a profession which is mainly taken up by women. It is a logical step, to discuss the issue of professionalisation in the fourth section. The debate on autonomy for nurses has political, social as well ethical implications. The ethicality of the political and social imperatives connected with this category is closely linked with policy making in the health care services and is reflected in the microcosm of situations where medication errors are being dealt with. In the final section ethics in nursing practice is discussed, as it involves the role conception of nurses; values and value clarification; and the educative transmission of ethical content.

HOW NURSES SEE MORAL ISSUES

(THE 'BIG QUESTIONS OF ETHICS' AND ETHICAL IMPLICATIONS OF EVERYDAY SITUATIONS)

Most nurses who are practising today have not had a formal ethical education during their training that would address and focus upon moral decision-making in everyday situations of nursing practice (Crisham 1981 and many others). Throughout their work, nurses are however confronted with questions that pertain to ethical issues. These issues concern not only matters regarding life and death. Giving or withholding information, telling the truth, deciding on the distribution of institutional and personal resources, encountering practice in colleagues with which a nurse does not agree, having to submit to doctors' orders that personal experience and professional knowledge reject, are understood as moral dilemmas and identified as such by nurses (Johnstone 1989; Wilkinson 1988; Crisham 1981).

Davis carried out a survey amongst Canadian nurses, one feature of which was to identify the types of moral dilemmas nurses encounter (Davis, quoted in Johnstone 1989).

Dilemmas were experienced for example:

- when the nurse's principles and beliefs conflicted with those of other nurses, supervisors, physicians, or the institution;
- when conflicts arose between the physician and the patient;
- when the nurses' idea of what was necessary for good care and the institution's budget or legal restrictions prevented the access;
- when no obvious right or wrong choice existed such as the rights of the patient and the obligations of the institution;
- when someone's conduct was considered emotionally based instead of rationally based;
- when life was sustained without regard for quality of life.

Further dilemmas were defined as existing in specific situations amongst which the reporting of peer or physicians errors was listed (Johnstone 1989). Medication errors may be placed as morally relevant issues among these perceptions.

Schröck however, found that many nurses did not perceive some of the above mentioned issues as being connected with morality (Schröck 1980). In her study among Scottish nurses moral issues were mainly defined as problems concerned with abortion, resuscitation, organ transplantation and euthanasia. She found that issues connected with authority, patient's property, fellow nurses, patient care and relatives, if seen at all as relevant ethical issues, were mentioned by undergraduate nursing students but not by registered nurses and postgraduates.

The mention of 'everyday moral issues' was registered as almost totally absent where nurses were asked to list topics or issues that might be relevant to a forthcoming series of discussions on moral aspects of nursing.

Schröck enumerates every-day moral issues as:

> ... telling the truth, keeping promises, respecting privileged information, defining the limits of obedience owed to formal professional authority, and balancing justifiable self-interest against that of the patient (Schröck 1980 p. 139).

Schröck states that nurses connect these "lesser" issues with "what might be more appropriately called social-organisational contexts" (Schröck 1980 p. 139). It emerges that medication errors were not necessarily seen as issues that nurses recognise as having ethical relevance.

Medication errors however, have been experienced by most nurses (Long 1982; Wolf 1988, 1989). Wolf maintains that medication errors are part of the clinical reality of nurses (Wolf 1989). She states that "Mistakes (in medication administration) happened (on a certain ward) as they do when humans are involved in any activity", and "... hospital personnel make mistakes randomly as other humans do" (Wolf 1988).

In the context of experiences with medication errors nurses will have to understand the ethical implications inherent in the decisions to be made in these situations. They most often do not relate to the major ethical problems concerning life and death. But they pertain to interaction and communication, to honesty and truth-telling. These subjects clearly have their place in the discussion of ethics.

Ethical Principles Addressed in the Nursing Literature

In this section I give an overview of general texts and research reports that are relevant to ethical principles as they relate to nursing. This overview outlines the scope within which the discussion regarding medication errors and their moral relevance must be placed.

Some of the textbooks on ethics written for nurses depict foundations of ethical reasoning (e.g. Davis and Aroskar 1978; Tschudin 1986; Thompson, Melia and Boyd 1988). They draw on several sources, namely on the 'classical' literature of moral philosophy like the works of Aristotle, Kant, Maritain, Thomas of Aquin, Spinoza, and Bentham.

They also regard modern general texts on ethics and moral philosophy, and they include writers who focus specifically on medical ethics (e.g. Frankena 1973; Kay 1975; Illich 1977; Beauchamp and Childress 1983; Campbell 1975, 1979; Downie 1971; Vaux 1974; Duncan, Dunstan and Welbourne 1981).

In various articles on ethical issues in nursing journals the authors summarise ethical principles in order to substantiate their arguments (Davis and Slater 1988; Fry 1988, 1989; Liffrig 1989; Johnstone 1989). These texts are helpful additional sources or valuable alternatives to general textbooks when summaries of ethical principles are looked for. In this section I draw on the texts mentioned above and discuss their relevance as it applies to nursing generally. This section has no direct connection with medication errors but it provides the foundation upon which further arguments rest and to which frequent recourse is taken.

Davis and Slater provide a short and precise picture of concepts, ethical rules and principles. They define *normative ethics* as raising questions of what is right and what is wrong, or what ought to be done in a situation that calls for a moral decision. *Descriptive ethics* is seen as a concern of sociology, focusing on what really happens. This would be the area in which the present study is anchored. Regarding the field of health care Davis and Slater refer to *bioethics.* They address basic ethical principles such as autonomy, doing no harm, and truth telling; and they discern between *deontological* and *utilitarian* models of ethical reasoning (Davis and Slater 1988).

Thompson and Thompson (1985) classify ethics into *utilitarianism, deontology* and *natural law.* The latter is to be viewed as a combination of the first two. Roach differentiates between the *deontological position* (from Greek: *deon*, duty) and the *teleological position* (from Greek: *telos*, end, goal, aim, purpose). Thus, Roach only defines the duty based and the outcome based stances. She states:

> In deontological positions the rightness or wrongness of actions are totally independent of goodness or badness of consequences (Roach 1987 p. 70).

In opposition to the deontological approach, teleological arguing finds its position from the perspective of the consequences or the outcome of actions. Teleological arguing in its classical form was presented by Aristotle. A modern but extreme version of teleological thinking is the *position of utilitarianism* (Thompson, Melia and Boyd 1988). The three modern exponents of utilitarianism as a normative ethical doctrine were J. Bentham (1748 - 1832); J.S. Mill (1806 - 1873), and H. Sidgwick (1838 - 1900).

Of this position Roach says that it

> ... discerns rightness and wrongness of actions as exclusively a function of the goodness or badness of consequences (Roach 1987 p. 71).

Benjamin and Curtis (1981) have categorised several approaches to describe ethical principles. First they attend to *utilitarian theories,* stating that

> ... the rightness and wrongness of an act is always a function of the extent to which its being performed or omitted will contribute to the goal of maximizing the overall good, which is construed variously as the total or average happiness or welfare (Benjamin and Curtis 1981 p. 30/31).

A conflict between patients' rights and nurses' responsibility for instance will be resolved or decided upon "by appeal to the utilitarian principle" (Benjamin and Curtis 1981).

Secondly Benjamin and Curtis turn to *duty based theories.* Here "a particular duty or a set of duties is fundamental" (Benjamin and Curtis 1981). The ten commandments or codes of professional conduct embody such duties. Kant's first formulation of the categorical imperative *'Act only on that maxim that you can will to be a universal law'* (cited according to Benjamin and Curtis 1981) finds its place here. Problems however, may arise where "conflicting duties make it impossible to uphold each one" (Benjamin and Curtis 1981). Circumstances may make decisions necessary that recourse to the utility of the outcome. The classical example here is the principle of 'Triage' where in a situation of catastrophe rescue and medical resources are allocated according to the survival chance of the individual.

A third approach within the classification of ethical principles Benjamin and Curtis describe as *right based theories.* This approach is similar to duty based theories but it centres on the individual rights of the person. Kant's second formulation of the categorical imperative would apply here: *Act so as to treat all persons as ends-in-themselves and never as means only* (cited according to Benjamin and Curtis 1981).

In order to differentiate duty based theories and right based theories Benjamin and Curtis state:

> Societies that are characterized by a great deal of agreement on social, metaphysical, and religious beliefs may be said to provide the appropriate background conditions for a duty-based ethical framework. Where such agreement cannot be presupposed, however - where the conception of the human condition and of the human well-being is pluralistic rather than monistic - right based frameworks may seem more plausible (Benjamin and Curtis 1981 p. 34).

Applied to health care the centre of right-based theories is the patient's right

> ... to do or receive something *as he or she sees fit* and in a way that flows *from his or her values and life plan* (Benjamin and Curtis 1981 p. 34, emphasis in the original).

As a last category *intuitonist theory* is mentioned by Benjamin and Curtis. Here "no prior ordering of basic social goals, duties, and rights" is made (Benjamin and Curtis 1981). Therefore in the intuitonist fashion conflicts are not resolved by appeal to basic principles but by

> ... appeal to *intuition* or some sort of moral faculty that directly informs (the person that has to make a decision) of what on balance is the right thing to do (Benjamin and Curtis 1981 p. 36, emphasis in the original).

A helpful and short description of ethical principles can be found in a paper by Ericksen:

> Throughout the ages philosophers have pondered the weighty question, What is right? Or more specifically, What is our responsibility to others in society? Several broad ethical principles have emerged, of which the more common are beneficence, autonomy and justice (Ericksen 1989 p. 23).

Differently expressed but meeting basically the same intention, Packard and Ferrara name the moral key ideas as *goodness; justice; freedom; equality; and respect for human beings;* and they refer to *veracity; integrity;* and *honesty* as moral qualities (Packard and Ferrara 1988). They also mention knowledge and talents in the context of moral behaviour as nursing skills.

At this point I offer a short definition of what is meant by 'ethics' and how I differentiate it from the use of 'moral'. Ethics (from Greek: *ethos;* or Latin: *ethicus* custom) refers to the teaching of standards of behaviour, also termed 'moral philosophy'. This connotes the theoretical content of a moral system. By moral (from Latin: *mos* custom) is meant the actual behaviour of people on the basis of ethical teaching.

A comparison and critical appraisal of the two main concepts of morality (the deontological and the teleological positions) as they can be applied in nursing is undertaken by Van Hooft. He maintains that the Kantian deontological position is shown to be insufficient. Van Hooft refers to Kant, saying:

> He (Kant) taught persons act morally well only when they act out a sense of duty without regard to their inclinations, and that their duty consisted in treating all persons with the respect that arose from seeing them as autonomous rational agents rather than as a means to be used (Van Hooft 1990 p. 212).

Instead of empowering the moral agent for free decision-making, the deontological approach makes him obedient. "Knowing what morality dictates is knowing what to do" (Van Hooft 1990). Van Hooft asserts that reason occupies the central part in Kantian ethics:

> Even when we move from the justification of particular actions to discourse about norms and principles, the motivation of actions is left mysterious while reason is given the task of justifying what these motivations lead us to (Van Hooft 1990 p. 212).

Thus, logical argument is reduced to a simple tool for "justifying and codifying our pre-existing moral intuitions" (Van Hooft 1990). To Van Hooft

> The basis for moral decision-making remains a mysterious mix of emotion, knowledge, determination, commitments, ideals, thought and the agent's character (Van Hooft 1990 p. 213).

It is true that a lack of motivation will prevent us from acting well. Cognition of the rightness of an act still lacks "the courage and determination to do it" (Van Hooft 1990). Teleological arguing as proposed by Aristotle, on the other hand can help to "act in a way that fulfilled oneself as a person" (Van Hooft 1990).

Van Hooft argues:

> For Aristotle, human agents were many faceted and their actions invaded their emotions and desires as well as their pure reason. Morally sensitive practical reason leads one not only to think rightly about ones actions, but also to feel rightly (Van Hooft 1990 p. 213).

It is not only the cognitive approach in regard to moral reasoning, it is just as important to develop "sensitivity and caring which would motivate nurses to act well" (Van Hooft 1990).

CARING FOR OTHERS AND CARING FOR SELF

In the context of medication errors it seems to be taken for granted that a deontological approach dictates how such situations are handled. This is so especially in Britain. Rules and regulations seem to attract the primary attention, be it where medication administration is concerned or be it where the focus is on the procedure of dealing with a medication error. From what has been unfolded in the above section however, it is apparent that in situations of medication errors rules and regulations cannot be the sole basis upon which decisions are made. Nursing as a developing profession is spelling out its own ethical foundations where the imperative of caring for others is argued for and grounded in what repeatedly is termed an 'ethic of care' (Huggins and Scalzi 1988; Fry 1988, Johnstone 1989; Crowley 1989). The full understanding and development of an ethic of care presupposes that nurses are aware of themselves. In order to care for others, care has to be taken of the self. Caring is said to be a feminine quality and as a profession nursing is mainly chosen by women. Being however socialised in a male dominated society, an integrating understanding of caring has been neglected by many women in nursing.

The theme that regards the integrative personal development as 'care for the carers' has appeared in social science and nursing literature in the recent past (e.g. Paine 1982; Richardson 1989; Firth and Britton 1989; Powel 1989; Cook 1989; Manthey 1989; Lunn 1991).

Gilligan (1982), has pointed out that the hitherto well accepted stages of moral development as described by Kohlberg (1958, 1972, 1978) represent a one-sided comprehension of morality which neglects this caring-for-self aspect. Kohlberg has chosen 'justice' as the central principle of moral judgement which has been shown by Gilligan to be a typically male attribute. Kohlberg bases his research regarding moral development on the assumption that a cognitive developmental view:

> ... starts philosophically from a different view of morality than either common sense or personality psychology. It claims that, at heart, morality represents a set of rational principles of judgement and decision, valid for every culture, the principles of human welfare and justice. ... The principle central to development of moral judgement, ... is that of justice (Kohlberg 1972 p. 14).

By looking how Freud, Piaget, Erikson, and Kohlberg among others in the field of social sciences arrived at their theories, Gilligan found that most studies included male participants only. This was the case with various life-cycle descriptions of developmental psychology where the exclusion of women "generated a perspective from which women insofar as they differ, appear deficient in their development" (Gilligan 1982). The fact that women are different from men, that they have different conceptions of life has not been sufficiently recognised in the generation of theories. Women give different priorities to values.

Kohlberg asks the initial question "Are there universal values that children should develop?" (Kohlberg 1972), but only boys were included in his research of 1958 (Kohlberg 1984). Kohlberg describes a scale of moral development in relation to cognitive development, (studied by Piaget from 1932-1948) which is based on testing the moral judgement of 72 boys aged 10-16 by asking them questions involving moral dilemmas (Kohlberg 1972). His studies culminate in his description of the *pre conventional*, the *conventional*, and the *post conventional* levels, which a person attains by stages.

On the pre conventional level, moral guidance is gained by at first simply referring to authority, then by considering the satisfaction of personal needs and later also by considering the needs of others. Guidance through the approval of others and later social conformity mark the conventional level. At the post conventional level the association of morality with socially approved of values and rights is attained. At the highest stage of moral development the ability to apply the universal principle of justice is said to emerge (Kohlberg 1972, 1984; Gilligan 1982; Meyers and Kittay 1987).

For Kohlberg moral autonomy is paramount. The individual in the justice tradition is self-governing in such away that "each person is the source of the moral and political principles they obey" (Meyers and Kittay 1987).

Justice being only one element in the development and application of moral decision-making, Gilligan shows how the 'ethic of care' is neglected in Kohlberg's research. In contrast to Kohlberg's perception she speaks of

> ... moral maturity ... (that) can be based on general injunctions to give care, to sustain interpersonal relationships and to serve one's own integrity (Gilligan 1982).

If in the execution of a nurse's duty a mistake occurs it is not difficult to see that the principle of justice is not enough to deal with the situation. It is questionable if by adhering to this principle only, interpersonal relationships can be sustained or personal integrity can be served.

In her 'abortion study', where she looked at the way women came to make their decisions for or against an abortion, Gilligan finds that a shift from self-centredness to self-abandoning and finally a self and others integrating 'ethic of care' marks the moral development of women. In her research the concept of integration is largely sustained.

Not solely autonomy, but "self, others, and the relationship between them" are the organising elements of moral judgement (Gilligan 1987).

Gilligan speaks of the same three levels of moral development Kohlberg has described. But she sees a different sequence and weight in the development of moral judgement in women. The initial concern with survival or egocentricity is replaced by a focus on "goodness" where the "other" and not the self is the centre of concern. Moral judgement eventually matures into a reflective understanding of care as the most adequate guide to the resolution of conflicts in human relationships. This includes the care for self as well as for others (Gilligan 1982).

Kohlberg, in a reply to Gilligan's critique summarises her descriptions of the three levels of moral development as follows:

> ... a preconventional level which is primarily egocentric; a conventional level which is primarily concerned with caring for others; a postconventional level which balances care for self and care for others (Kohlberg 1984 p. 344).

Gilligan however, does not describe justice and care as in polar opposition or as "mirror images"; nor as "better or worse representations of a single moral truth" (Gilligan 1987). She understands them as "different concerns", as "two moral versions - one of justice and one of care". The moral injunctions, not to act unfairly toward others, and not to turn away from someone in need, capture these different concerns" (Gilligan 1987).

The importance of these different concerns emerge throughout the present study. Gilligan's understanding of the feminine element seems of great importance in the understanding of the development and inclusion of moral judgement in nursing as a profession. Gilligan states her case for an integrated development of moral judgement that takes into account the elements of justice as well as caring. She pleads for an awareness that justice does not need to exclude care, nor care justice. Gilligan speaks of "two disparate modes of experience that are in the end connected" (Gilligan 1982). She refers to the themes of relating and of separating; the ethic of care which is relating; and the ethic of justice which is separating, dissecting and analysing. She details:

> With a shift in perspective from justice to care, the organizing dimension of relationship changes from inequality/equality to attachment/detachment, reorganizing thoughts, feelings, and language so that words connoting relationship like "dependence" or "responsibility" or even moral terms such as "fairness" and "care" take on different meanings (Gilligan 1987 p. 22).

Inherent in all men and women are qualities of care and of justice, of connection and of separation. However, in order to strive for an integrative understanding of life, work and relationships it is necessary to understand the importance of a dialectical tension between these poles. Both are to be valued, care as well as justice; connection as well as separation. Only in their dialectical relation a viable tension can bring about development. This applies to the individual, to a profession, as well as to societies.

The nursing profession is learning to integrate personal needs into professional demeanour. What applies to the development of the individual nurse applies to the development of the profession. But an integrative development of the profession will have its base in the development of its members as persons and as professionals.

To establish and to live a professional life that is truthful and furthering to the members of the profession and to others, nurses will need their own vision of the outcome. And that could well be the serious concern about their fellow men and women, not in the sense of various groups of caregivers pouring nursing, medicine, surgery, occupational-, psycho-, and physiotherapies, pastoral, and other care over the needy, and competing with each other, developing 'professional images' and demonstrating no more than the urge for power. A serious concern for others will start with the ability to care for self and to accept being cared for. Such a self may then reach out and establish contact with, communicate with, and open up spaces for patients and clients, for colleagues and students to live, work and develop in.

PROFESSIONALISATION

In this section the social role of nursing and nurses is brought into context with the discussion on autonomy and professionalisation. Merits and pitfalls of this discussion are outlined. Ethical values in nursing and their foundations derive from social values which harbour, protect and generate individual values, these being respect for the well-being of individuals, peoples and societies, and the free development of all personal and collective contingencies. In the literature reviewed here, the political dimension of nursing is discussed and brought into context with ethical issues concerning the development of professional autonomy of nurses. The dependency of nursing on societal systems, and ethical implications as they derive from this dependency are focused on. Aroskar points out:

> To promote decision-making that takes explicit account of ethics, the political/power dimension must also be taken into account (Aroskar 1987 p. 268).

Ethics does not only present problems on the personal interactive level, but is to be seen as closely associated with the power structures in a given society. Aroskar advocates that we have to look at

> ... politics as public or social ethics or as a branch of ethics concerned with the state as a whole rather than the individual person (Aroskar 1987 p. 268).

In her article 'The interface of ethics and politics in nursing' Aroskar unfolds three dimensions of this aspect. First, the ethical concern between the nurse and the patient; second, the ethical concern between the nurse and the institution; third, the ethical concern that stems from the second dimension, which is the ethical concern between the nurse and the decision-making bodies which appears in the conflict that may arise out of individual or group needs and interests that are incompatible with each other or with the interest, as well as the means a state health care system can provide.

This question is addressed also by Johnstone who argues that by moving away from the reductionist medical model the question arises whether patients *must* be cared for in Hospitals and *must* be treated by doctors. And as to the professional autonomy of nurses she asserts that "it is also open whether the doctor's orders *must always* be carried out" (Johnstone 1989). Johnstone presents the case of a nurse who was dismissed from her job on the grounds that she refused to dialyse a terminally ill patient. Johnstone states that

> ... it is intolerable that nurses are expected to *obey doctor's orders* on the one hand, and yet are held *independently accountable* on the other! (Johnstone 1989 p. 89, Johnstone's italics).

Here questions arise concerning the allegiance nurses owe to their employing institutions or to doctors and other members of the health care team, as well as to their personal and professional value systems. These issues have to be argued out on a general professional level as well as within the personal sphere of each nurse as they apply to everyday work.

Gaze enlarges on this aspect by saying that questions of ethics and moral decision-making in nursing cannot be solved by the nursing profession alone, but must be addressed within the socio-political context of health care.

She suggests:

> Nurses, of course have less freedom than doctors, to make decisions. A nurse's moral dilemmas must be solved within the context of the nursing hierarchy, the health care team and her responsibility to the profession (Gaze 1987 p. 19).

Yarling and McElmurry also relate the situation of nursing to the social context. They view the role of nurses to be dependent on the structure of the hospital they work in:

> ... nurses are often not free to be moral because they are deprived of moral agency by the repressive character of the hospitals in which they practice (Yarling and McElmurry 1986 p. 65).

For nurses to act as free moral agents, Yarling and McElmurry maintain, "the emergence of a strong sense of professional autonomy" is needed; as well as "a shift in the locus of accountability from the physician to the patient" (Yarling and McElmurry 1986). They understand ethics in nursing as a "social ethic" and they claim an ethical obligation that "must seek reform of the policies and structures" of health care institution (Yarling and McElmurry 1986.

Packard and Ferrara challenge this position in their own discussion of professionalisation. They maintain that it is not the concept of autonomy which gives rise to moral values in nursing, but "an understanding and acceptance of certain principles of action that relate to the value of human life" (Packard and Ferrara 1988). They come to the conclusion that moral ideas such as goodness, justice, freedom, equality and respect for human beings form the basis of values in nursing. But they emphasise that "nurses do not operate in isolation from others" (Packard and Ferrara 1988) and even though autonomy is to be striven for in an attempt to professionalise nursing, they make it clear that it is misleading to think that "increased and high-toned professionalisation should serve as the moral foundation of nursing" (Packard and Ferrara 1988).

Campbell too criticises the concept of professionalisation as it is often presented today, by showing that professionalisation is not purely sought out of altruistic motives.

He states:

> To be recognized as a profession (especially if this can be achieved through a legal process which leads to state registration) is undoubtedly a prime objective for numerous occupational groups. ... the high-sounding ideals on the basis of which these occupational groups make claim to reliability and social usefulness may not be all that they first appear (Campbell 1988 p. 2).

He suggests that the claim to be disinterested helpers of the clients/patients may be part of what has been called "the rhetoric of self-advancement" (Campbell 1988).

An integrative aspect of moral understanding and learning is advocated by Packard and Ferrara when they touch on the developmental model of Gilligan by stating:

> ... a moral foundation of nursing, properly conceived, will show how a nurse's commitment to self is altogether compatible with the nurse's commitment to others, whether they be patients in the usual sense or people in the broadest sense (Packard and Ferrara 1988 p. 69).

Such an integrative understanding has been put forward by Bishop and Scudder (1987, 1990). They take into account the reality of the position nursing holds in the present social systems. Bishop and Scudder do not advocate autonomy for the nursing profession and then despair at the impossibility of achieving it. They see a "moral sense" in the position of nurses between the proponents of medical science, the hospital bureaucracy, and the patient. Nurses in this perception are not seen as facilitators of compromise, but rather as

> ... advocate(s) of communal decisions that bring together expert medical advice and treatment, sound hospital policy and procedure, and the realizable hopes and aspirations of the patient ... (Bishop and Scudder 1987 p. 43).

How communal decisions are made without compromise, Bishop and Scudder do not address. However, they speak of the "special in-between-position" of nurses regarding their role as experts in health matters as well as nurses being knowledgeable as to the requirements of hospital policy and administrative necessities. This puts nurses "in a more privileged position for fostering the communal decisions that the moral sense requires" (Bishop and Scudder 1987).

Bishop and Scudder derive a moral sense of nursing from its practical expert application. They argue for an applied science that rests on the value of its "professional and technical expertise (which is) incorporated into the moral sense" of nursing (Bishop and Scudder 1990). On the basis of the results of a qualitative research project in which nurses gave examples as to experiences from practice that were either most fulfilling or least fulfilling Bishop and Scudder speak of the confirmation of a moral sense of nursing that was found in practice. They state:

> This deeply felt confirmation of the moral sense of being a nurse occurred when the intentionality of benevolence embedded in the practice of nursing became manifest in a personal relationship in which an ill person was helped. Then the professional sense of being a nurse and the moral sense of being a nurse converged in a practice which integrated personal and professional care (Bishop and Scudder 1990 p. 104).

This is easily overlooked in the lengthy discussions about ethics in nursing which too frequently "focus on the technical aspects of ethics and miss the moral sense already inherent in nursing". Thus, Bishop and Scudder claim the moral sense of nursing as an "ethic of practice" which "in concrete nurse-patient relationships is what makes nursing fulfilling" (Bishop and Scudder 1990).

Both authors also criticise the position of Yarling and McElmurry, who, they feel, "stress structural and conceptual moral issues to the neglect of moral issues in everyday practice" (Bishop and Scudder 1990). They argue:

> ... policy is not changed only in the way Yarling and McElmurry advocate but often by the gradual change of practice which then becomes hospital policy. Certainly nurses should seek reform which would allow them to exercise their legitimate authority, but in the meantime, they have a moral responsibility to change policy by changing practice in desirable ways (Bishop and Scudder 1990 p. 134).

The striving for autonomy can be seen as an expressively male way of thinking. Bishop and Scudder refer to Gilligan who has "attacked this view ... in contrast to a feminine ethic which is much more situational and relational".

In accord with Gilligan they argue:

> Regardless of the significance of gender designation, our contention is that the situational, relational ethic is the one required in health care as practised (Bishop and Scudder 1990 p. 136).

Enlarging on the special in-between position of nurses, Bishop and Scudder make it clear that this position does not free nurses from the responsibility of making moral decisions, but that it provides a realistic context in which to make them.

It is not simply the achievement of greater autonomy for nurses which will answer questions concerned with nurses' professionalisation. The political and social aspects have to be weighed against practical implications of nursing. In this area however, the research that has been undertaken generally addresses the relationship between nurses and patients. Even though the various nursing scholars argue different aspects related to an ethic of care, the meaning that such an ethic of care has for the personal development of a nurse is seldom discussed. The focus on the topic of nurses' experiences of medication errors in this study, allows for the exploration of this meaning

ETHICS IN NURSING PRACTICE

Role conception and moral dilemmas

The research on nursing ethics that is referred to in this section deals with the role conception of nurses and with the effectivness of educational endeavours. Several studies have been conducted to uncover some of the underlying issues regarding the discrepancy between theoretical knowledge about ethical content and moral practice.

Ketefian has conducted several studies regarding the role conceptions of nurses. She examined the relationship between role conceptions and role discrepancies and moral behaviour as a selected dimension of professional practice.

As a result of one of her studies she says:

> Nurses studying for a master's degree had higher professional normative scores and higher bureaucratic discrepancy scores than other nurses (Ketefian 1985 p. 252/253)

She found that role discrepancy was negatively related to role conception in nurses with a professional role conception and that nurses with a bureaucratic role conception demonstrated a higher degree of role discrepancy and role conception.

The socialising effect of higher education brought about a better professional orientation and caused nurses to be aware of role discrepancies. The findings of the study suggest that "the higher the professional categorical score, the higher the moral behaviour" (Ketefian 1985). In a study cited by Ketefian (Kramer and Baker 1971), it has been found that nurses leaving the profession generally had a high professional role conception.

This may reveal that nurses who identify their independent and professional role within the health care system, suffer from conflicts between their ideal role perception as professionals and the reality that presents itself in the various settings of nursing activities. If the gap between beliefs held, and perceived reality could be closed, the experience of conflicts could be reduced. Ketefian, therefore, suggests that nurses need to "cultivate loyalty to both professional and bureaucratic values" (Ketefian 1985).

Cassidy and Oddi studied the effects of teaching ethics and moral choice made by nurses. They wanted to determine in this study whether there were

> ... differences in perceptions of ethical dilemmas in practice and attitudes toward autonomy/patient advocacy, patients' rights and traditional nursing role limitations among four groups of students (Cassidy and Oddi 1988 p. 406).

The students were of different ages and took part in post graduate nursing programmes on different academic levels. Some of the findings are summarised here. It was found that younger students scored higher on autonomy and the rejection of traditional role limitations, the first of which applied to registered nurses as well when compared to non-registered nurses. Non-registered nurses however, scored higher on patients' rights and on the rejection of traditional role limitations. For autonomy the associate degree and generic baccalaureate students scored higher than degree completion and master's students. 38.0 % of the students had completed a course in ethics, and 49.2 % had completed a seminar dealing with ethics. Students who had taken a course in ethics scored higher on autonomy and rejection of traditional role limitations. Students who had not attended an ethics seminar scored higher on autonomy only. As to the findings Cassidy and Oddi state:

> This finding may be related to age and status as a registered nurse, in that continuing education offerings are attended by practising nurses. On the other hand, a rather superficial exploration of ethical issues in a seminar as opposed to more in-depth analysis in a course taught over a period of time may render learners less confident about exercising their autonomy in ethical dilemmas (Cassidy and Oddi 1988 p. 410)

Overall significant differences were found on perception of idealistic and realistic moral behaviour, but there was a consensus on the perception of ethical decision making. The study has shown "the need for nurse educators to question their assumptions about the ways in which students learn to address ethical aspects of practice" Cassidy and Oddi 1988). Cassidy and Oddi state that it is imperative to prepare nurses in such away that society is assured that

> ... members of the profession are exercising high standards of self-regulation and are worthy of autonomy and the authority to make clinical decisions (Cassidy and Oddi 1988 p. 405).

Swider, McElmurry and Yarling conducted a study which tried to answer the following questions:

- What are the values of the nursing profession?
- How do nurses respond to ethical dilemmas?
- Why do nurses respond the way they do to ethical dilemmas? (Swider, McElmurry and Yarling 1985).

705 generic nursing students and 70 students who were registered nurses, completing a baccalaureate degree were divided into small groups of about five students in each group. The participants were asked to read a case presentation and to discuss steps they would take to resolve the dilemma. They were then asked to assume that the steps were not successful and to continue to decide what was to be done next until all reasonable possibilities were exhausted. The same case was

used with all groups and they were allowed one and a half hours to come to an agreement on the solution of the dilemma.

The categories of nursing responsibilities for classifying responses were pre-selected and answers that did not fit these categories were subsumed under 'other'. The categories were: a) patient-centred decisions; b) physician-centred decisions; c) bureaucratic-centred decisions. The results showed that the groups varied widely in the number of steps they chose to take in order to resolve the presented dilemma (3-17 steps). Furthermore, the bureaucratic approach to a solution of the dilemma seemed to be favoured by most groups. This shows that

> ... the students first sought to work within the system ... Even though the groups seemed to agree on the first steps to be taken there was little endpoint consensus as to when the nurse (in the presented dilemma) had fulfilled her responsibilities in this case (Swider, McElmurry and Yarling 1985 p. 111).

The study itself seems to feature a rather artificial set-up. The intricate analysis of the study is not presented here, but turning to peers for assistance did not seem to range high in the presented solutions, rather an overall sense of confusion seemed to show up in the responses. Thus, it was shown that the "conflicting loyalties and responsibilities of nurses create problems in trying to arrive at clear, crisp answers (Swider, McElmurry and Yarling 1985).

The relationship between critical thinking, educational preparation and level of moral judgement was examined in a study by Ketefian which built on Kohlberg's stages of moral development (Ketefian 1981a). Ketefian found that the greater the nurses' ability in critical thinking, the higher was their ability for moral reasoning. Further, nurses who had a professional education as opposed to nurses with a technical preparation exhibited a more advanced level of moral reasoning (Ketefian 1981a).

This, however, leaves open the question of practical application. Moral reasoning does not guarantee moral behaviour. Nurses who have been exposed to moral theory still tend to have difficulties in applying what they learned (Cragg 1988). In her study on moral reasoning and moral behaviour Ketefian examined "the relationship of the way nurses reason about moral choice and the content of decisions they make in ethical dilemmas" (Ketefian 1981b) Ketefian poses the question of relationships between moral reasoning and the perception of realistic moral behaviour in nursing dilemmas. Ketefian found that even though professionally prepared nurses have higher levels of moral reasoning than nursing technicians, there is no difference in their perception in what would actually be done in a situation of conflict. This suggests that "nurses' knowledge and values do not seem to be translated into reality" (Ketefian 1981b).

A more concrete practical component as far as autonomous decision-making in nursing is concerned seems to be inherent where the nursing process is adopted. The introduction of the nursing process has made quite an impact facilitating nurses' ability in autonomous decision-making in the implementation of care. (Kratz 1984; Roper, Logan and Tierney 1985; Arndt 1988; and many others). Crisham states:

> As nurses participate in decision-making about patient care, they make moral judgements that have influence on others (Crisham 1981 p. 105)

Crisham also maintains that certain value commitments "are inherent in this problem solving process (the nursing process)" (Crisham 1981). This underpins Bishop and Scudder's understanding of a moral sense of nursing that comes out of practice expertise.

Values and ethics in nursing

The topic of values in nursing pertaining to nursing ethics is addressed in a multitude of texts written by nursing scholars (e.g. McFarlane 1982; Fry 1986; Self 1987; Reilly 1989; Johnstone 1989). One main text written by Steele and Harmon (1983) offers a comprehensive picture of the general issues of moral philosophy and relates them to nursing, but furthermore it depicts techniques and procedures that help nurses to check out and clarify their own values in order to act upon them in an autonomous and informed manner.

Good decisions can only be made on the basis of sound knowledge and a well balanced value system. In her discussion of teaching nursing ethics in continuing education Cragg defines the process of value clarification as a first step of a strategy to promote ethical practice in the practical work setting (Cragg 1988). For the teaching of ethics in nursing programmes the process of understanding and discerning values prevalent in society, in the profession, and for the student herself, is seen as a prerequisite before deeper issues of moral philosophy can be touched upon (Sternberg 1979).

But it is not enough to include cognitive ethical content into curricula applying to nurse education. An internalisation on the deeper affective level is to be sought. "Values ... aren't learned from books" (Lyneham 1988). The emotional or affective side has to be taken into consideration.

Wilkinson sees the 'context' of learning experience as a further variable:

> Cognitive ability, affective considerations and context are all variables that affect the outcome of a decision (Wilkinson 1988 p. 18).

Adding to the three areas of learning (cognitive, psychomotor, and affective) as described by Bloom (1956, 1964), Ericksen makes the destinction of five areas of knowledge which are basic for informed moral decision-making:

- knowledge of oneself and ones' values,
- knowledge of the facts of a situation,
- knowledge of the profession's values,
- legal knowledge,
- knowledge of moral philosophy (Ericksen 1989).

These five areas only indicate a different than the cognitive domain insofar as they encompass values of oneself and of the profession.

The immanent importance of values and attitudes is addressed in this study where the affective considerations of learning from situations of medication errors are taken into account.

Learning to act morally

A large variety of studies has been carried out to determine the link between moral education and concrete moral decision-making in nursing and to explore the situation in which nurses are to apply their knowledge of ethics (e.g. Crisham 1980; Clamp 1980; Self 1987; Scanlon and Fleming 1987; Ketefian 1987; Sietsema 1987; Felton and Parsons 1987; Garritson 1988; Mustapha and Seybert 1989; and many others). In this section some texts are mentioned and two research projects are discussed which focus on educative endeavours on a post qualification level.

MacKenzie (1985), describes a model that could help nurses in the primary health care team to promote moral decision-making in their own practical setting. This model is based on Curtin's model of critical analysis (Curtin 1978). In the situation of primary health care autonomy and individual decision- making play a greater part than in the hospital setting; but co-operation and collaboration are of great importance here too. One feature of the described learning experience is the team approach. To learn with and from each other, to draw on each others' resources of knowledge and experience and not to feel isolated is a possibility to be used in a more pronounced manner in all areas of nursing activities.

It is a point repeatedly addressed by the nurses participating in the present study on medication errors and appears to be the most natural way of solving moral conflicts.

In MacKenzie's project during workshops and study days for all team members not only ethical issues were addressed theoretically, but the project included the discussion of case studies that were part of the team members' concrete experience. The nurses reflected in their groups on situations they had lived through or were experiencing at the time, and they learned to apply models of moral decision-making and ethical theory to these situations.

Five stages of identifying the teams' learning needs were followed in order to arrive at concretely improved decision-making skills:

1) Learning how to select and gather information about a concrete situation by using interviewing-skills, role play and simulation;

2) deciding on theoretical input if a lack of theoretical knowledge is perceived by the team;

3) discussing each member's professional role in order to gain a greater acceptance within the team;

4) applying problem-solving techniques which should help to practice and develop skills in generating alternatives and assessing consequences (in a given case study);

5) clarifying values within the group in order to understand and accept each other. Hearing about each others' experiences in this context in order to clarify individual values (MacKenzie 1985).

One important feature of this model is that theory is only fed into the sessions to underpin ethical components of personal experience as need arises. Thus, relevant theory closely related to immanent experience is offered in accordance with the needs of the group members and is linked to the affective and emotional reality of each nurse.

Further approaches of a similar nature found to be of practical value for nurses were shown to be ethical discussion groups, ethics rounds, or ethical support groups (Davis and Slater 1988; Cragg 1988; Wilkinson 1988).

Cragg emphasises the need for continuing education in ethics for nurses that does not stop short at the transmission of ethical theory content. She states "Nurses, like other professionals need to learn skills in dealing with ethical dilemmas" (Cragg 1988). Cragg maintains that caring has a clear moral component that must be recognised in each concrete situation:

> Seeing a familiar situation from a new perspective can raise awareness of inherent moral questions and allow staff to examine these insights to determine more ethical courses of action (Cragg 1988 p. 267)

This addresses again the point made by Schröck, which was raised above, that nurses' perception of what counts as a moral dilemma is not always clear. Cragg emphasises the value of the discussion of experiences among nurses. She calls for ethics committees where nurses, jointly with other members of the health care team, raise ethical questions occurring within their sphere of practice. She accentuates that "the deliberations of ethics committees can be a powerful means of providing practical education for health care practitioners" (Cragg 1988).

Also Scanlon and Fleming propose a model of ethical decision-making that is based on concrete practice. They describe three phases in the activity of a nursing ethics group:

1) exploration of feelings and issues;

2) consideration of an ethical decision-making model;

3) values clarification (Scanlon and Fleming 1987).

Going through these steps will increase an awareness of the ethical dimension of nursing practice, facilitate communication among nurses, and familiarise nurses with ethical principles and components of the decision-making process.

Similar approaches for in service training or for basic nurse education are described and advocated by Sternberg 1979; Stanley 1980; Woodruff 1985; Baker 1987; Thompson and Thompson 1989; Hedin 1989; Ryden et al 1989a, 1989b; Waithe et al 1989; Crowley 1989; Van Hooft 1990; and others.

The discussion of and work on critical incidents in connection with ethics in nursing was explored in a research project by Clamp (1980). This pilot study focused on post basic nursing education and was aimed at evaluating the use of a teaching method that utilises critical incidents. The study was described as follows:

> The project's aim is to study, promote and assess attitude development in nursing education, using critical incidents as a basis for analysis and discussion (Clamp 1980 p. 1756).

The use of critical incidents as a research method in the social sciences was first described by Flanagan (1954). In Clamp's study critical incidents as 'snapshot' views "of the daily work of the nurse" were used to examine "the effects of care on patients ... and interactions between colleagues" (Clamp 1980). Again a team approach was shown to be of importance. Nurses discussed and shared their views on everyday occurrences in the hospital which encompassed 'critical situations' such as patients gaining confidence in walking and reacting favourably to the helpful attitude of a nurse, or a rude remark by a nurse that upset a patient, or a thoughtless way of giving information to a junior nurse. The discussions involved the following dimensions:

> ... the activity/problem was identified; each person's point of view was examined; the functioning of the team was explored; possible action/solutions were (sic) suggested; plans of action were devised where appropriate (Clamp 1980 p. 1756).

During sessions, which were conducted over a period of four months a teacher was present in each group helping and facilitating the discussion. As for an evaluation of the teaching method an assessment tool was developed which measured the following objectives:

The nurses are to

> ... analyse their work in a more detailed way; identify problems and make decisions about nursing care; discuss how an increased understanding of patients, relatives and colleagues as individuals can be achieved; demonstrate an increased ability to empathise; explore the concept of a harmonious team; assist peers and colleagues more positively; identify and describe their own behaviour; demonstrate intellectual skills - the ability to think clearly and critically (Clamp 1980 p. 1758).

Nurses assessed and evaluated their own progress and found that they had

> ... gained an increased awareness and understanding of themselves and colleagues; they appreciated how attitudes contribute to good nursing care; they had increased their ability to participate in discussion groups; (however,) they experienced difficulties associated with differentiating incidents from everyday happenings (Clamp 1980 p. 1758).

Even though the focus of this study was directed at nurses' attitudes and the labels 'ethics', 'moral development', and moral decision-making' were not used it is felt that in this project a main feature of ethical education was addressed and operationalised. Again it was shown that apart from teaching moral philosophy content; the discussion of everyday occurrences in nursing, the acquisition of problem-solving skills, and the promotion of team interaction facilitate moral awareness.

This is shown as an important feature of the present study on the meaning, the experience of making medication errors has for a nurse. Here, too, the aspects of communication and interaction play a decisive role in how such a situation is managed. The promotion of skills in interpersonal communication assists in putting into practice what theoretical teaching aims at.

CONCLUSION: THE RESEARCH QUESTION

In this chapter the topic of ethics has been discussed as it seems to be of relevance to the present research project. A framework is defined and unfolded within which experiences of medication errors can be explored. In the previous two chapters the administration of medication and medication errors have been addressed, and the British and the German perspectives of policy making have been outlined to provide a further aspect of the setting for this study.

The studies or research projects that have been carried out in the field of ethics in nursing, some of which were discussed in this chapter addressed a variety of topics, for instance, the role perception of nurses in relation to moral awareness, moral decision-making, the development of moral maturity or issues of learning ethical content and its application in practice (Ketefian 1981a, 1981b, 1985, 1987; Swider, McElmurray and Yarling 1985; Cassidy and Oddi 1988).

The studies undertaken in the field of medication administration mostly refer to the causes of medication errors, the question of how to prevent them, or how to organise the administration of medications in the best possible ways (Ley, Jain and Skilbeck 1976; Francis 1980; Long and Johnson 1981; Long 1982; Hodgin 1984; Betz and Levy 1985; Wieser and Dann 1987; Brandt et al 1988; Poster and Pelletier 1988; Pearlson 1988; Carr 1989; Callaghan 1990).

In the present project the situation where a medication error has occurred is examined. Its qualitative and interpretive approach focuses on the meaning, the experience has for the nurses concerned. This has not been dealt with in depth by any of the studies mentioned.

The guiding question for this project is:

What does the experience of having made a medication error mean to a nurse?

When medication errors occur decisions have to be made about admitting the error or concealing it. Nurses indirectly involved in such a situation may have to decide about reporting such an incident in the context of possible disciplinary consequences. Decisions in this area will pertain to the personal value system of the nurses involved; to their professional education; to the institutional structure of their work setting; and the interpersonal relations to other health care workers. These aspects clearly are of ethical concern. Underlying ethical principles have to be discerned and understood in order to place everyday situations in an appropriate context.

A moral decision has to be made after the occurrence of an error has been noted either by the acting nurse herself or by another person involved. The decisions made hereafter and the way the situation is handled by peers and superiors will have a bearing on the future personal and professional development of those involved.

The dealing with a mistake may be marked by sympathetic and understanding demeanour of colleagues and superiors, still safeguarding the security of the patient involved. The nurses may be encouraged to own up to mistakes and given opportunities to rectify possible damage. Nevertheless, if even small mistakes or errors are dealt with harshly and in an undignified manner, nurses may learn to conceal mistakes and under all circumstances try to preserve the image of the competent nurse practitioner who is never subject to mistakes. These points are dealt with as they emerge from the discourse of nurses.

In the situation of medication errors nurses are in a position of dichotomy as far as the care that they owe to self is concerned. Should a nurse own up to a mistake or conceal it, especially if no harm has come to the patient? Reporting a mistake might cause more harm to the nurse herself. Accepting self, caring for self and accepting the care and support offered, are examined in the light of the development of moral decision-making, but also the way 'justice' is understood and carried out in the situation of medication errors is scrutinised in this thesis.

Professional identity and the possibilities of structural changes are addressed as seen and understood from the perspective of experiences of medication errors. The questions of guilt and shame and how to come to terms with the actuality of human precariousness are discussed in detail, as well as the possibilities of teaching and learning in the areas of attitudes and values.

The research question can be detailed by asking:

a) What does it mean to a nurse when she/he discovers that a mistake has been made in the administration of medicine? What does it mean to the nurse who has made the mistake? What does it mean to nurses being involved in the situation?

b) What decisions are made by the nurses concerned in such a situation? What is it like to make these decisions? What guides the decision-making process?

c) What results does the experience have for the nurse who made such an error? What does it mean to personal and professional development? How are the other nurses affected, who are also involved in the situation?

The analysis of nurses' accounts of their experience aims to identify supportive and furthering means of action that can be made fruitful in clinical practice as well as in the clinical and theoretical teaching of nurses. However, it is not a set of suggestions or guide-lines that evolve from this project. It is the discourse of nurses about their experiences that is to be made heard. Listening to what nurses have to say in and about situations of medication errors is the communicative endeavour of this study.

PART II
THE METHOD -
AN INTERPRETIVE DESIGN

THREE IN THE MORNING

When we wear out our minds, stubbornly clinging to one partial view of things, refusing to see a deeper agreement between this and its complementary opposite, we have what is called "three in the morning."

What is this "three in the morning?"

A monkey trainer went to his monkeys and told them:

"As regards your chestnuts: you are going to have three measures in the morning and four in the afternoon."

At this they all became angry. So he said: "All right, in that case I will give you four in the morning and three in the afternoon." This time they were satisfied.

The two arrangements were the same in that the number of chestnuts did not change. But in one case the animals were displeased, and in the other they were satisfied. The keeper had been willing to change his personal arrangement in order to meet objective conditions. He lost nothing by it!

This is called following two courses at once.

(Thomas Merton: The way of Chuang Tzu)

CHAPTER 4
THEORETICAL AND PRACTICAL ASPECTS OF THE RESEARCH DESIGN

INTRODUCTION TO THE CHAPTER

In this chapter methodological questions are dealt with as they pertain to this study. I look at theoretical issues of methodological importance and their practical applications. The reasons for using a qualitative approach in this project are spelled out, and the components of the method employed are outlined.

The chapter comprises four sections. In the first section the theoretical approach of the study is presented and some aspects regarding qualitative and quantitative research are discussed. In the second section, phenomenology is discussed as the perspective that informs the methodological background of the study. Here, phenomenology is addressed as a basis for qualitative research. By tracing the origins of qualitative research to the phenomenological method as applied in philosophy, I establish the matrix for my approach. In this section the epistemological grounding of the present study is delineated. In the third section an overview over discourse analysis as a qualitative research method is presented. The presumptions for the employment of discourse analysis as a main analytic instrument for the study is discussed here. Phenomenology as a 'research method' and discourse analysis are contrasted and the use of the latter method is described as it finds its place in this study. In the last section some practical aspects of this research are described. This section sets the present project into context with the reasoned choice of method. It also deals with the reality value of interview situations and finally focuses on the different perspectives from which participants in this study chose to view their involvement in medication errors.

Research Methods - Previous Research - Quantitative and Qualitative Approaches

The questions posed in chapter three have repeatedly been subject to investigation. Most studies, as has been addressed earlier, have been undertaken in realisation of a positivist perception. Quantitative research methods were generally employed.

The studies in the field of moral development built on talk about a person's projected moral behaviour. Vignettes were used to elicit judgement on possible moral action and moral development (e.g. Kohlberg 1958, 1984; Ketefian 1981a, 1981b; Swider, McElmurray and Yarling 1985; Cassidy and Oddi 1988; and many others).

Also in the field of research on medication errors most frequently quantitative methods have been used (e.g. Long and Johnson 1981; Francis 1980; Poster and Pelletier, 1988; and many others). Medication errors have been counted and their occurrence has been related to external circumstances or to the disposition of the nurses concerned. The institutional structure of health care settings has been scrutinised and analyses of medication errors have resulted in new concepts of medication distribution and administration.

Contextual and narrative methods could not be traced in research that offers a combination of the issues such as addressed in the present study. As far as could be ascertained, the intrinsic meaning which a medication error has for the nurse who is responsible for it, has not been subject to research. Also the experience of nurses who are involved in such a situation, having to make decisions about reporting the incident and about ensuing disciplinary action, has not been explored. The implications that arise for nurses' moral development from a situation of medication errors has not been examined.

Looking at the meaning that is derived from the experience of having made an error in the administration of medicines may well call for a qualitative, interpretive research design. A qualitative research approach using an interpretive mode of data analysis is suited to investigate the processes nurses go through when being involved in a medication error. In this study the personal experiences of nurses is drawn upon. It is not a "generalized other" (Benhabib 1987), whose voice is listened to in order to understand the experience of being involved in a medication error. It is the voice of the nurse who has lived through this experience that is listened to.

PHENOMENOLOGY AS A BASIS FOR QUALITATIVE RESEARCH

Various research approaches have been used to arrive at a fuller understanding of the construction of social reality. It appears that all 'methods' of qualitative research contain 'techniques' that follow certain rules in order to collect, organise, and analyse data. In the various qualitative research methods employed by social scientists a basic phenomenological background can be traced.

Phenomenological thinking provides a basis for frameworks of interpretive modes of analysis as used in the social sciences. This applies to the grounded theory approach, described by Glaser and Strauss (1967); or ethnomethodology as first used by Garfinkel (1967); as well as discourse analysis as understood by Potter and Wetherell (1987).

Phenomenology however, emerged from Husserl's intention of forging a new method of philosophical inquiry that has its focus on the essences of the things themselves.

Spiegelberg (1982) summarised phenomenology in such a way that he described it as a methodological approach to philosophy that originated from the psychologist Brentano (1838-1917), who was a teacher of Husserl (1858-1938). Opposing the hitherto unquestioned stance of Cartesian positivism, Husserl hoped to develop phenomenology into a science of the "intuition of essences and essential structures" (Enc. Brit. 1974). "Back to the things themselves!" was Husserl's battle-cry. He wanted to discern phenomena as they appeared in their own right. He said about phenomenological idealism:

> ... its sole task and service is to clarify the meaning of this world, the precise sense in which everyone accepts it, and with undeniable right, as really existing

(Husserl 1931 p. 21).

Stein, at first Husserl's student, then his assistant, states very aptly:

> With the phenomenological school (that is the school of E. Husserl) I share the view that the method of philosophy differs in principle from that of the positivist sciences. Philosophy has its own functions of knowledge, which enables it to do what is necessary for the foundation of the other branches of scholarship and what these latter cannot do themselves, namely to define the domain of their subject and to reveal the means and methods of knowledge adapted to it. Phenomenology has called this peculiar function of knowledge intuition or *Wesensanschauung*. (Stein 1956 p. 131/132, italics in the original).

Husserl did not want to devise a theory as an answer to the historical problem of idealism. He stated that the phenomenological method

> ... is a science founded in itself, and standing absolutely on its own basis; it is indeed the one science that stands absolutely on its own ground ... (Husserl 1931 p. 20).

With Husserl, a movement started in philosophy that now appears to be rather divergent and not easily captured. It may be said that there are as many phenomenologies as there are phenomenologists.

Apart from informing the interpretive understanding of the various qualitative research methods within the social sciences, phenomenology has come to be understood as a research approach in its own right. Various social scientists and social philosophers have written about it and established its place in social research (e.g. van Kaam 1959; Schutz 1970; van Manen 1978, 1983, 1984, 1986, 1989, 1990; Burch 1989; Giorgi 1979, 1985; Linschoten 1979; Packer 1985; Langeveld 1983a, 1984,).

As a 'method' for qualitative research however, phenomenology is not easily placed within the tool box of social science research. It can neither be clearly differentiated from ethnomethodology, which investigates co-ordinated interaction and social organisation as it presents itself to the researcher on the basis of "what everybody knows" (Mann 1983), nor from the reflexive process of ethnography which by participant observation gains insight into the issues people are concerned with (Hammersly and Atkinson 1983), or from the grounded theory method, which aims at establishing low level theory from plausible explanation of interview data.

The phenomenologist in social research claims to discover the 'essence' of a social phenomenon by distilling stories of real life experience in order to get at the meaning they have for the person or persons living these experiences. By discriminating "meaning units" from a story, this is retold and restated in order to arrive at a better understanding of the reality of an experience (Giorgi 1985; van Manen 1984).

Where quantitative research claims to be objective, factual and replicable, the analysis of discourse according to the so called phenomenological approach reconstructs the life experience of the subject. It is said to be personal, never replicable and strictly speaking does not explain objectively social reality (Bergum 1989). This approach looks for "the subjective meaning in the interpretation of social action". Knowledge is sought "directly through immediate human experience" (Davis 1973). Here, the experience of people in their everyday world is explored as to the meaning it has for them. The basic question asked in 'phenomenological research' is: What does it mean? This question can be diversified into:

> What practices occur?
> What are the situations/contexts of such practices?
> What aspects of situations are salient from the informant's point of view?
> What meanings do informants attach to their lived experience? (Wilson 1990 p. 491)

Within nursing science many scholars have engaged in phenomenological research; used it as a 'method' for investigation or have extensively written about it (e.g. Davis 1973; Oiler 1982, 1986; Omery 1983; Knaack 1984; Benner 1985; Morse 1991). A number of projects have been conducted using the phenomenological approach. In these projects experiences in nursing have been examined from the perspectives of nurses or patients. For instance the essential structure of a caring interaction was looked at (Riemen 1986); the experience of giving care to a patient dying of cancer (Gray-Snelgrove 1982); or the experience of dying (Paige 1980). Other studies included topics such as the acquisition of excellence in nursing practice (Benner 1984); or the nurses' experience of problem patients (Mayberry 1980). These are but a few examples.

Omery (1983) asserts as to the use of the 'phenomenological method' in nursing research that its implementation is virtually infinite. She writes:

> As long as an experience has meaning, the potential is there for the phenomenological method (sic) to be utilized (Omery 83 p. 59).

The 'phenomenological method' employed as a research approach in nursing does not seek to analyse or to explain phenomena. "...analysis and explanation are excluded" as Oiler contends. Oiler states further "It is the perceived world that is studied, not subjective phenomena" (Oiler 1986).

Oiler gives an example which explains the use of phenomenology in nursing research:

> It is the experience, for example of loving and doubting or of the phantom limb that calls for description in phenomenology, not an analysis of what love is or an explanation of what causes the phantom limb to appear (Oiler 1986 p. 71).

Bishop and Scudder conclude as to the place of phenomenological analysis in nursing:

> The purpose of phenomenological analysis is to bring to consciousness what we already know from practice but have not yet articulated, rather than to develop new and novel ways of understanding and engaging in practice. This bringing to consciousness improves practice directly by fostering enlightenment (Bishop and Scudder 1990 p. 176).

These intentions are honourable but lead to the question of how concretely nursing practice will be improved by an enlightened consciousness. Wolf (1988), in her Book Nurses' work, The sacred and the profane, for example describes nurses' work in great detail but fails to draw any conclusions from her descriptions that further nurses' practice in a concrete way. Still, even a purely descriptive study may give explanations. It does so implicitly. Therefore, an elucidation and pronunciation of what could improve nursing practice would not be amiss in such a study. Conclusions need not be left to the imagination of the reader. However, studies which were conducted under the name of 'phenomenological research' did in fact analyse, interpret and explain the phenomena they addressed.

Phenomenology as understood from its philosophical origin I maintain, provides a basis to all qualitative research, but as a research approach it cannot lay claim to answering philosophical questions in a philosophical manner. Kikuchi and Simmons address this dilemma of nursing research. They state:

> Disillusioned with the positivistic approach to science, many nurse researchers, following the social scientists, have turned to other approaches and, in so doing, have stretched the scope of science as traditionally understood. (...) In attempting to move beyond traditional scientific methods, nurse researchers have not held squarely in view the kind of questions science is capable of answering and have, at times, unwittingly moved into the realm of questions that only philosophy can answer (Kikuchi and Simmons 1992 p. 5/6).

Kikuchi and Simmons hold that nurses "have used the scientific mode of inquiry inappropriately" thus confusing scientific and philosophical questions. This is due, they say to a "lack of understanding" of the real nature of philosophical and scientific questions (Kikuchi and Simmons 1992).

Kikuchi claims that science has been misused in studies "being conducted using the grounded theory method (à la Glaser and Strauss) to answer philosophical questions such as 'What is the nature of nursing?' ... " (Kikuchi 1992, parenthesis in the original). Kikuchi does however credit such studies with the attribution 'scientific'.

Kikuchi claims that "adequate answers" to this kind of questioning are not attainable "until they are recognized as philosophical in nature and are pursued philosophically, not scientifically" (Kikuchi 1992).

Philosophical inquiry is needed to find answers to ethical, epistemological, and ontological questions regarding nursing. It is evident that such issues must be addressed on a philosophical basis. Such a basis however, cannot be attained by using the phenomenological mode of inquiry as a research method. What Kikuchi rightly perceived as a misuse of the grounded theory method, in the same sense applies to the use of phenomenology as a 'research method' too. Phenomenology is to be understood as a rigorous method of philosophical investigation and according to Husserl, it is "a science founded in itself... " (Husserl 1931).

Still, Simmons states:

> Science is investigative, and philosophy is not; science depends on special experience, philosophy on common experience - for engendering their concepts, and for the falsificability of their propositions and theories (Simmons 1992 p. 16).

This presupposes that questions of an ontological nature are raised and explored in the context of 'special' experience. In order to render the 'special' experience accessible as a basis for philosophical inquiry, qualitative research can well aim at making 'special' experience intelligible as 'common' experience.

Van Maanen asserts that "Qualitative research involves ontological inquiry" (van Maanen 1983). Most questions in nursing research that address their topics in a non positivistic way must needs be of an ontological nature. This means that qualitative research really occupies a position between quantifiable science and philosophical inquiry.

This position is most marked in the so called 'phenomenological method' of social research which truly has its roots in philosophy. It is possibly the naming of such research designs that is misleading. There does not seem to be a real problem in positing a question that investigates special experience in order to answer a common problem. This kind of investigation will be of a rich nature, not shunning philosophical elements. In fact, in such studies an interface between positivistic and philosophical inquiry is attained.

It is a different undertaking to philosophise or to arrive at answers to questions which have an ontological, ethical or epistemological background by using certain qualitative research methods. Non-empirical, philosophical studies may well fall back on empirical studies like the present one which covers part of the hitherto untilled ground between philosophy and practice. Empirical studies will be able to provide the facts for questions which philosophical enquiry may answer. As Sherlock Holmes aptly pronounces:

> Still, it is an error to argue in front of your data. You find yourself insensibly twisting them around to fit your theories (Doyle 1891/1991 p. 692).

In this study a claim to philosophical inquiry is not made. Rather, questions are asked whose style advertise the so called phenomenological mode of enquiry. Looking at details of the experience after a medication error has occurred complies with this research approach as undertaken in the social sciences and in nursing respectively. In this study however, I focus on meaning to be discerned in order to inform nursing practice and a humanistic approach to nurse education. This conforms with the basic understanding ethnomethodology has protracted.

> The ethnomethodologist pictures the skilled member who is constantly attending to the particular, indexical qualities of situations, giving them meaning, making them knowledgeable, communicating this knowledge to others and constructing a sense and appearance of order (Haralambos 1985 p. 558).

Furthermore I use the concept of discourse analysis, which has grown out of Garfinkel's method of interpreting social reality (Garfinkel 1967).

DISCOURSE ANALYSIS

Discourse analysis is a further development in socio-psychological research. It is based on the philosophical work of J.L. Austin (1911-1960). He examined contemporary English discourse identifying speech acts in their performative characteristics. Discourse analysis starts from the assumption that every utterance has a specific meaning and is said with a certain performative force. Both of these, meaning and force, will have effects or consequences. Effects and consequences however, are independent of the truth and general validity of what is said (Austin 1961, 1962). It can be assumed that people use language as a tool to get things done (Potter and Wetherell 1987).

Potter and Wetherell describe discourse analysis as a new style of socio-psychological research erected on the foundations of speech act theory, ethnomethodology and semiology. It provides a "radically new perspective with implications for all socio-psychological topics" (Potter and Wetherell 1987). Language is used to give accounts, to explain, to justify or to excuse action.

Contrasting the approach of the so called phenomenological interpretation with discourse analysis as described by Potter and Wetherell, the actual words used are examined here as to their functional properties. The story is not retold and thus subject to misinterpretation, but discourse is taken at its face value. Rather, the social and political implications of text can emerge as "the entirety of anyones' understanding of the social world, mediated by discourse "(Potter and Wetherell 1987). It is the discourse about experiences which represents their reality and their transforming power. Althusser drew attention to the fact that it is through our discourse we are perpetuating or changing the social world we live in. What we are and how we relate to each other is "spoken into existence" (Davies 1992). Davies maintains:

> Our selves and our human nature are not the causes of what we do but the products of the discourses through which we speak and are spoken into existence (Davies 1992 p. 64).

The aim of discourse analysis "is to move from an analysis of language to an understanding of an internal, causal mechanism - the person's social competence" (Potter and Wetherell 1987).

Thus, discourse analysis in opposition to Oiler tries to gain an understanding by analysing experiences and by explaining their meaning within a given social context. The difference between the so called phenomenological method and discourse analysis mirrors the difference in the perception of the term 'hermeneutics'. In an objectivist perception hermeneutic interpretation of text looks at the 'correct' meaning. In this sense phenomenological investigations study "perceived world" objectively (Oiler 1986). A subjectivist approach stresses "the interaction between interpreter and text" in order to gain an understanding of what the text may mean in the life experience of the producer of the text and therefore for the reader or interpreter (Mann 1983). Discourse analysis uses this subjectivist approach by a careful analysis of structure and function of text.

THE PRESENT PROJECT

In my study I aim to get at the meaning of text according to discourse analysis employing a matrix of ethnomethodological inquiry. That is, I analyse text at its own level.

In the course of this analysis the function and consequences of the discourse employed by the participants is discerned (Potter and Wetherell 1987). On the basis of detailed scrutiny and appraisal of the language used, I try to understand the meaning that nurses accord to their experiences. I utilise data from different sources. This variety of data sources should contribute to the possibility of seeing the phenomenon of medication errors from different perspectives.

It seems a logical step of epistemological congruence with the research questions and the interpretive approach of this study to obtain and examine data from personal accounts of nurses. Official documents, that deal with disciplinary proceedings against nurses involved in medication errors, supplement these accounts. I can thus study the experience of nurses having made a medication error from the "particular perspective" of the actors. Knaack suggests that phenomenological "research techniques are open-ended and suggestive rather than definite" (Knaack 1984). This justifies the choice of discourse analysis, and its application in this study.

Truth and reality

The question arose, would my respondents tell the truth? Would they openly talk about their own failure, or would they emphasise how unjustly they have been treated, would they dwell on unfavourable circumstances that led them to making the error?

The subject of my investigation is not so much the 'reality' of what happened, but rather the manner how what happened was perceived, and how it was represented in my participants' discourse. Thus, the accounts reflect people's "own (...) situations and perception of problems at hand" (Silverman 1985). By looking at texts derived from different data sources, I have investigated the meaning the experience of having made a medication error had for nurses. These texts contain nurses' discourse about their experiences. But furthermore the texts represent the reality of nurses' experience. They are the centre of my investigation and not preliminary to it. "...they are reality in their own right" (Silverman 1985).

The interview situations, and for that matter the situations of the group discussions, writing a report and speaking at a UKCC hearing, each contain the participants' present emotional state as well as objective aspects of the incident related.

Dean and Whyte reveal:

> *The informant's statement represents merely the perception of the informant, filtered and modified by his cognitive and emotional reactions and reported through his personal verbal usages.* Thus, we ... are getting merely the informant's picture of the world as he sees it. And we are getting it as he is willing to pass it on to us in *'this particular investigation'* (Dean and Whyte 1969 p. 105/106, italics in the original).

To be taken into account for the analysis of the data provided by the participants, according to Dean and Whyte are a) the current emotional state; b) the informant's opinions; c) the informant's attitudes; d) the informant's values; e) the informant's hypothetical reactions; f) the actual tendencies of the informant to behave or feel (Dean and Whyte 1969). They rightly state:

> ...the informant may have conflicting opinions values, attitudes or tendencies to act (Dean and Whyte 1969 p. 106).

Discrepancies here, are in fact what discourse analysis wants to reveal. The inconsistencies of talk and action are what make up the subjective truth of a situation. This can be elicited by careful analysis.

For instance, one participant talked about being an approachable manager, easy going and open to the problems of his team. Describing his actions when dealing with the mistake of a colleague, he revealed that he overrode these values in that he seemed to be eager to report any drug error that had come to his notice. In doing so, he diverted his responsibilities to people senior to himself, thus avoiding difficult decisions and the need to be approachable and easy going.

It is, therefore, not a question of whether the participants tell the truth in their accounts, but as Dean and Whyte say:

> Instead the researcher will ask, "What do the informant's statements reveal about his feelings and perceptions and what inferences can be made from them about the actual environment or events he has experienced?" (Dean and Whyte 1969 p. 114).

Here lies the thrust of this study. The texts derived from the interviews, group discussions, self reports and documents revealed information about the situation of medication errors as they were experienced by the participants.

Different perspectives

To avoid the danger of representing only the perceptions and problems as experienced by "the underdog" (Silverman 1985), I chose senior nurses to participate in my study. They talked about their experiences from the varying perspectives of their own changing positions throughout their careers. Thus, it was not only nurses talking about their experience of having made a mistake in the administration of medications and how they were dealt with by senior management. It was not only the story of the underdog I listened to and represented in a one-sided fashion. All data include the perspective of having made a medication error as well as having to deal with the mistakes made by colleagues or by juniors.

The discourse, representing the reality of medication errors, consiststs of my participants' talk about their own past errors, talk about others' (colleagues, seniors, friends) reactions to the mistake, talk about medication errors colleagues have made, and the participant's reactions to their own or to others' experiences, as well as possible future reaction of self or of others.

It had to be taken into account that the past and past attitudes of the respondents would

> ... modify a recollection of past feelings in a selective way that fits them more comfortably into (our) current point of view Dean and Whyte 1969 p. 107).

Again, discourse analysis leaves room to explore how past feelings were integrated into a present situation and how a current point of view came into existence.

Such a use of the data material has to take into account that not only personal experiences and 'lived through' decisions and actions are presented by the participants but also projected decisions and imagined actions on projected decisions. This is carefully differentiated in the analysis of the data.

CHAPTER 5
THE DATA SOURCES

INTRODUCTION TO THE CHAPTER

This chapter provides some insight into the process of data collection. It has four sections, in the first of which arguments are put forward for the use of interviews in qualitative research. Further discussed in this section are reasons for a combination of different data sources.

Then follows a section in which the different data sources of this study are dealt with. The procedures of gaining access and of data collection are described for each data source. A further section addresses questions of reliability and validity as they apply to qualitative research. This includes 'sampling' and the quality and quantity of data. Each data source is examined in turn in relation to these questions.

In the last section of this chapter practical and technical issues are discussed. Here, confidentiality and voluntary participation feature, as well as the role of the researcher. A demographic overview provides a picture of the participants who supplied the data. The value of including quantitative data in a qualitative study is touched upon. A brief account of the practical means employed to handle and secure the data material concludes this chapter.

DATA SOURCES - OVERVIEW

The positivist tradition of research relies on "uncontaminated" data that are "neutral, unbiased and representative". They are secured from surveys and structured interviews. Such "artificial settings" are criticised by qualitative researchers such as ethnomethodologists as "purely external concepts" (Silverman 1985). Silverman argues for the use of data derived from interviews in qualitative studies. To him, it is the method of analysis which accounts for the difference in qualitative or quantitative research. He contends:

> ... that interview data display cultural realities which are neither biased nor accurate, but simply 'real' (Silverman 1985 p. 157).

This reality revealed itself in the discourse of nurses about their experiences and in the texts derived from this discourse.

Silverman argues that even though interviews represent artificial settings they "reproduce and rearticulate cultural particulars grounded in given patterns of social organisations" (Silverman 1985).

A further point made by Silverman is that too narrow an understanding of social structures, represented in micro or macro studies, "precludes a proper understanding of the process of interpretation through which (social structures) are reproduced and, sometimes changed". He reflects on the relation between the macro level of social realities - that is the institutional context in which phenomena occur - and the micro level which encompasses the actors and their actions (Silverman 1985).

In order to avoid a reductionist view in my study, I am addressing the system - the institutional context in which the administration of medication takes place - as well as the reality of the participants experience with medication errors. This is at the heart of my study.

Apart from open ended, unstructured interviews I use group discussions and self reports as my data sources as well as documents from proceedings where the UKCC officially dealt with cases of medication errors. A multidimensional approach to gain data about the experience of medication errors will give better access to the true nature and essence of this experience. Oiler states:

> The people who live the experience are the source, but the ways in which experience is presented to others must be established. What people say or write about their experience is important as are their actions, their gestures and expressions in art, humour and so on. (Oiler 1982, p180).

A multiple nature of data sources also meets the concept of 'triangulation'. The idea of standing somewhere in the landscape, looking at another point and by locating a third prefixed and known point, determining the position I am standing at, is rather compelling. Bulmer (1977), addresses the questions of validity and reliability in the context of a discussion about data collection. Citing Galtung, he proposes that a "much higher degree of confirmation (is attained) when multidimensional approaches to the data problem are made use of" (Bulmer 1977).

Fetterman describes the importance of using different data sources, maintaining that "Triangulation always improves the quality of data...". In order to grasp the value of information offered for instance in documents, interviews may be helpful to place this information into a wider context (Fetterman 1989).

Hammersley and Atkinson also understand the use of different data sources as a possibility to validate research results. They propose that "if ... diverse kinds of data lead to the same conclusion, one can be a little more confident in that conclusion" (Hammersley and Atkinson 1983). The triangulation of different techniques of data collection may increase the validity of the results derived from the data.

Hammersley and Atkinson however, caution that the triangulation of data "is not the combination of different kinds of data per se, but rather an attempt to relate different sorts of data in such a way as to counteract various possible threats to the validity of our analysis". They maintain that data from different sources will not necessarily add to the production of a more complete picture. They point out that the "difference between sets or types of data may be just as important and illuminating" (Hammersley and Atkinson 1983).

As for discourse analysis, the use of different data sources is advocated by Potter and Wetherell. They advise that by "using documents from many sources it is possible to build up a much fuller idea of the way participants' linguistic patterns are organised compared to one source alone" (Potter and Wetherell 1987).

However, Potter and Wetherell do not see triangulation as a method to arrive with more certainty at a correct version of events. They find rather that the use of a variety of accounts compounds the variability between participants' claims and descriptions. This, in their view, is not a negative aspect as discourse analysis does not try to resolve variation, but is a way of analysis which can bring about an understanding of what is achieved by different accounts (Potter and Wetherell 1987).

To use a variety of data sources then, is in line with the general idea of interpretive studies. By hearing in single interviews what nurses have to say about their experience regarding medication errors, their personal ways of comprehension are being disclosed to me in a spontaneous way, depending on the rapport I have with each of my interview partners. By getting a group of nurses together, talking about the same matter, a different angle emerges. Here, nurses share their views with peers. The discussion is shaped by argument and counterargument from within the group, giving the researcher less control over what is being said, but assuring that what is being said corresponds more to nurses' normal talk on the subject. By having some nurses anonymously write about their experiences of medication errors, emphasis is being placed differently. Here, the respondents have the opportunity to reflect on their experience and concentrate on what is of importance to them as to their own mistakes. Taylor and Bogdan mention the non-directive element inherent in group discussions. I felt that this element would be far greater than in the one to one setting of an interview or in the situation of nurses writing a self report according to guide-lines I had drawn up (Taylor and Bogdan 1984).

In addition to direct accounts I use documents where the disciplinary bodies of the profession dealt with situations of medication errors. These documents supply an official and institutionalised aspect of what otherwise might only be seen as nurses' private opinions.

In the context of methods of data collection, questions on validity and reliability are raised by various authors. Leininger, for instance, states that

> ... validity in qualitative research refers to gaining knowledge and understanding of the true nature, essence, meanings, attributes, and characteristics of a particular phenomenon under study ... knowing and understanding is the goal. (Leininger 1984 p. 68)

The four data sources were combined in order to provide differing perspectives and to ascertain a vivid picture of the reality of having been involved in the experience of dealing with medication errors. They provide knowledge and understanding of the phenomenon under study.

I chose to address ward sisters and senior nurses for the participation in group discussions, interviews and self reports. As for the UKCC documents I had communicated these requirements to the secretary of the Disciplinary Committee of the UKCC. Unlike student nurses or newly qualified staff whose experiences might be limited and who would possibly talk or write from hearsay, senior nurses were more likely to have moved into a more settled position as to their involvement with medication errors. Their experiences might still date from their own student days, but they will at least have had plenty of time to reflect them, compare and share them with colleagues, friends, and relatives.

Description of the Data Sources

Group discussions

I was giving a series of lectures in pedagogy in two middle-line management courses for senior nurses in Germany in September 1990. This opened up a first opportunity to collect data at a relatively early point during my study. The German Group Discussion provided me with some hints as to the points of issue likely to be addressed when senior nurses talk about medication errors. It proved to be a helpful primary 'hands on' research experience. The main specifications that were addressed provided me with a structuring element for the schedule for the interviews that followed in Scotland. Also the Scottish Group Discussion, conducted after the interviews were finished, profited from this experience.

The students came from different Roman Catholic hospitals in Northern Germany. All of them held ward sister's posts or were deputy ward sisters. They had started the course in March 1990 and knew each other from their study-days and study-blocks. In joint learning endeavours an atmosphere of trust and mutual understanding had been created, which is usual in these courses. The nurses utilised their study-days to share experiences of day to day work and support each other in discussing difficulties that arose from their work. These factors enhanced the ease with which a discussion on medication errors could be conducted.

Permission to organise a group discussion was readily granted by the convenor of the course.[1] During one of my lectures I had cause to touch upon nursing research and I used this situation to convey the content of my study to the students. The response was enthusiastic. More nurses than I needed volunteered to participate in the group discussion. In Germany, research in nursing is a fairly new feature in the profession. The possibility, actually to participate in a nursing research project was therefore seen by the nurses as a novelty.

In order to recruit participants for the Scottish Group Discussion, contact was established with a regional College of Nursing and Midwifery during May 1991. A fairly comparable situation to the German Group Discussion presented itself. The course convenors asked me to talk about my project to a group of nurses during one of their lectures. Thereafter, I invited the students to participate in my project.

Even though possible, it did not seem appropriate to recruit the participants from the nurses who volunteered for the interviews. Especially where the sensitive issue of medication errors was concerned I thought it more prudent not to bring nurses together who worked in the same clinical setting. This would have been the case with the interview participants who all came from the same hospital. Morse states:

---

[1] All correspondence and information for the participants regarding the group discussions can be found in Appendix One.

> Awkward situations are created when the individuals have first confided possible discordant views to the researcher and then find themselves in a position of having to conceal the earlier position (Morse 1991 p. 134).

Most nurses participating in the group discussions, came from different hospitals. Both the German and the Scottish group included members who knew each other and who worked/had worked together. But joining the discussion group was entirely the personal choice of the participants and no personal communication with me regarding medication errors had preceded the discussion.

The German Group Discussion took place in September 1990 and the Scottish one in May 1991. In the introduction with the German group I touched on the following points:

- Medication errors do happen in every day practice. We all know the situation when a nurse realises that a medication error has been made.
- The situation of a medication errors calls for reactions. How did you (or the nurses involved) react? How did other members of the team react? What was it like? What decisions were made? Why? How do you feel about a situation like that retrospectively?

The same schedule governed the Scottish discussion only here, two key questions were added which had emerged during the interviews as being of importance:

- What helped, and what hindered in dealing with the situation of medication errors?

Seven female nurses and one male nurse agreed to offer some time of their lunch break for the German Group Discussion; and five female nurses and one male nurse agreed to join the Scottish Group Discussion which was to take place during the last lecture period of the same day. The other students of the Scottish group were given the opportunity of writing a self-report.

In the German Group Discussion I had felt that it was not easy for eight participants to relate well to each other in discussion, so six Scottish participants seemed to be an ideal number.

Before the discussions started, time was given for questions. Both discussions were recorded. In both groups a lively exchange of experiences took place. The nurses talked openly about mistakes they had made themselves and about the reactions they had encountered as well as about experiences they had witnessed and about their own feelings as to situations of medication errors.

The Scottish and the German Group Discussions were not intended as a basis for comparative analysis of data. However, some of the information gathered supplied material to be contrasted and compared. In using group discussions as data sources I could listen to nurses sharing their experiences. In so doing they opened personal experiences to the comments of their colleagues, thus agreeing, even reinforcing opinion and attitude or contradicting each other on the grounds of their experiences. By sharing their experiences, incidents were remembered which might not have come up in an interview or in a written report. In some instances nurses also corrected one another as to actual facts of the medication errors they jointly knew about.

Interviews

The appropriate authorities were contacted to gain access to a research site where I could recruit my interview participants.[2] The following arrangements were finally made with the nursing and midwifery managers of a general hospital in Scotland.

An information-sheet covering the general aspects of the project was distributed to the wards of the hospital. Two weeks later, the nursing managers showed me round their departments and introduced me to various charge nurses and ward sisters.

---

[2] All correspondence and information for the participants regarding the interviews as well as the interview schedule can be found in Appendix Two.

I then addressed potential participants personally explaining my project. There was a marked difference in reception on the different wards. For some nurses, it went without question that mistakes in the administration of medicines are made. These nurses generally responded favourably to my request for an interview appointment. Some were actually prepared to start their accounts there and then. Any hesitation I met, was either due to allegedly never having been involved in a medication error, which was stated quite emphatically several times, or the lack of time or other commitments. I talked to five or six nurses out of a total of eighteen, who felt that they really could not help me.

Some comments made during my visits to the wards were:

> *"Mistakes - of course, everyone has made mistakes, if someone says it never happened, you can be sure they are not honest about it."*
>
> *"Sure, you can interview me, I don't know if I have anything really interesting to tell you, but there were little things ...for instance...*
>
> *"Yes, something really grave happened to me, I'll never forget it and I would like to talk to you about it."*
>
> *"Oh, yes, there was something, ehm .. and I really would like to talk to you about it."*

Several times ward sisters referred me immediately to their staff nurses:

> *"Yes, I know, its a very interesting project, maybe one of the staff nurses..." (calls to a passing by staff nurse).*
>
> *"This is something Staff can deal with, I'm sure she will be happy to talk to you."*

Negative responses included:

> *"Hmm, ... yes, but I never made a mistake, it never happened to me, touch wood, no, I wouldn't have anything to tell you."*
>
> *"No, it never happened to me, sorry, I can't help you." (exit quickly)*
>
> *"Thanks goodness, it never happened to me, I am very conscientious."*
>
> *"I'm going to be moved away from this ward, so it will be difficult.."*

All the ten main interviews were conducted between the end of February and the end of April 1991. I used an interview schedule that had been tested and amended during two pilot interviews in the beginning of February 1991. The volunteers for the pilot interviews were recruited from the 'Master of Nursing' course in a Scottish university. Three main objectives guided the pilot-interviews:

- to gain personal experience in conducting research interviews;
- to discuss the interview schedule with the participants;
- to get feedback on my interview style.

The evaluative discussion after each of the pilot interviews reassured me as to my interview style. The participants said that they felt at ease talking. Minor changes were made to the interview schedule.

I have included the pilot interviews into the body of data because both compare well with the main interviews. Some issues were discussed in depth which provided valuable additional data material that otherwise would have been lost.

Self Reports

Encouraged by a German colleague who spontaneously sent me her 'story' after I had talked to her about my project I asked for participants in my study through a small advertisement in the Nursing Times. It appeared in January 1991 and in April 1991 under the rubric 'Information wanted'.[3] The advertisements brought three replies from interested nurses. Three further participants were recruited from the regional College of Nursing and Midwifery during the contacts I had made regarding the Scottish Group Discussion.

The nurses who had declared interest in the study were supplied with a short description of my project and guide-lines for the writing of a self

---

3 All correspondence regarding the advertisments, the advertisment, the description of the project and the guide-lines for the writing of a self report can be found in Appendix Three.

report which would help with structuring the written account. The self reports were ready at my disposal by the end of May 1991.

UKCC Documents

A letter to the chairman of the UKCC Professional Conduct Committee explaining my study and asking for access to case proceedings which dealt with the situation of medication errors opened up contact with the UKCC.[4] By December 1991 I had been provided with 6 transcripts of Committee proceedings. They were selected by the chairman as to their representativeness in the occurrence of allegations made against nurses involved in medication errors and fitted the requirements I had stated in my letter.

SAMPLING

Participants and samples

I have chosen to use the term 'participants' for the nurses who consented to take part in the group discussions, to be interviewed and to write self reports. Even though they provided me with information, I did not simply see them as 'informants' or interviewees in the case of the interviews. Occasionally, for the sake of readability, I refer to them, as respondents. I use 'group discussion' rather than 'group interview' because the interactive nature is better expressed by this term.

In the following section I address some aspects that would be termed reliability and validity in quantitative research as they apply to the selection of samples. In the context of this project, they are simply to be understood as an elaboration on some aspects concerning the participation of the nurses who shared their experiences of medication errors. When I use the term 'sample', again this is not to be understood in terms of quantitative research. As it is referred to in the literature on

---

[4] All correspondence regarding the UKCC Documents can be found in Appendix Four.

qualitative research projects (Morse 1991; Potter and Wetherell 1987) I include it in my vocabulary.

Knowledge and personal experience

Discussing the question why a certain group of people is chosen to be addressed in order to take part in a research project, Morse mentions "knowledge" of the issue at hand, personal "experience", and the "willingness" to share this experience and "to reflect" on it (Morse 1991). These criteria were fulfilled insofar as the nurses I had addressed were senior nurses and all had been directly or indirectly involved with medication errors. Also all potential participants had time to think about their possible involvement in my project and discuss it with peers, friends or partners before deciding to join. Thus a certain degree of reflection was presupposed when the decision to be interviewed or to take part in the group discussion was made. The willingness and ability to reflect on their personal experience were even more marked with the nurses who wrote the self reports During the hearings of the UKCC Disciplinary Committees, the ability to reflect was certainly elicited by the fact that several examiners questioned the nurses against whom allegations were made. In addition to this these incidents had been thoroughly investigated at local levels beforehand.

Recruiting participants

Morse refers to four types of samples in qualitative research. The "purposeful", the "nominated", the "volunteer", and the "total population" samples (Morse 1991). The four data sources fulfilled to a greater or lesser extent the criteria Morse set in her description of samples. Ward sisters and senior nurses were addressed purposefully and all participants volunteered to take part in the study.

The 'snowball principle' which guides the nominated sample as described by Taylor and Bogdan (1984) came into action specifically during the recruitment of the interview participants. Here, one nurse who was willing to talk to me introduced me to the next one, and so forth. Some of my respondents were thus 'nominated' by their peers. I did not utilise the possibility of a total population sample in the development of my project. To address the complete team of a given unit or ward, did not seem to provide a broad enough perspective for the research question. The guiding element in the sample selection was to get a good representation of nurses from varying areas of practice. Insofar as all volunteers who responded to my requests were either interviewed, took part in the group discussions or wrote the self reports, my data material could be termed "primary" (Morse 1991). The data sources and the method of obtaining samples proved to be 'appropriate' (Morse 1991).

The fact that the choice of the documents was not within my sphere of decision-making, helped to create an independent data source which could be used to render the written and spoken word more reliable.

Quality and quantity of data

Morse mentions "adequacy of quality and quantity" of data for qualitative studies (Morse 1991). The data I secured seemed to be adequate with respect to the quality of the information they yielded and with respect to their quantity. One criterion for data quality is their overall relevance to the research question. Most data met this criterion.

This was especially marked in the self reports which gave concentrated information very much to the point of my project. In the group discussions lengthy passages appeared to be irrelevant but they were of importance to further the discussion. During the pilot interviews childhood experiences were discussed, which later on proved to be irrelevant. In the interviews I learned to focus progressively on emerging aspects as I grew more conversant with the themes the participants addressed. Those themes were for example support, helpful or unhelpful behaviour in dealing with medication errors, the disciplinary procedure and the routine of medication administration.

Potter and Wetherell deem "ten interviews" as an adequate source for "valid information" (Potter and Wetherell 1987). The twelve interviews including the two pilot ones were adequate in the present study as no more "new themes" came up during the later interviews (Taylor and Bogdan 1984).

Holding the Scottish Group Discussion as a last activity for data collection proved to be helpful as I could enter this field with the experience of the German Group Discussion and the interviews. The aspect of having to report a mistake another nurse has made, featured as a dilemma here. This aspect had been mentioned in the interviews but did not appear to present a problem. Had my attention been drawn to this point at an earlier stage, I would have followed it up in a more concentrated manner.

In the UKCC documents a great deal of material irrelevant to the present study had to be distinguished from passages of importance. The statements nurses made about circumstances which accompanied the incidents were of great value. As they were elicited by cross-questioning during the disciplinary procedures they helped to illustrate the context of a given medication error. This provided a means of better understanding how and why errors happened.

The total amount of data was just manageable in the given time. Two group discussions, 12 interviews, 6 self reports and 6 UKCC documents provided ample work for the year during which data collection took place. Collecting, transcribing, coding and analysing more data would probably not have added to their fruitfulness.

Practical and Technical Issues

Confidentiality and voluntary participation

Consent to tape-record the group discussions and the interviews was obtained initially at the beginning of each event and I reassured the participants that everything they said would be treated confidentially.

In transcribing the taped group discussions, the interviews and the self reports, I disguised the locations and identities of institutions. I wrote about 'a Scottish Regional Health Board'; a Scottish General Hospital'; or ' a hospital in Britain'; and a group of nurses from hospitals in 'Northern Germany'.

The interview situations came about by personal contact which continued for some time during one year. I became quite familiar with most of the participants and with the exception of four participants we addressed each other by first names. Therefore, I used fictitious Christian names for all interview participants in the data analysis. Occasionally I referred to respondents as to 'sister' or 'staff nurse'. In the analysis of the group discussions and the self reports I referred to the respondents according to their status, 'sister', 'charge nurse', staff nurse'. As for the UKCC documents I used fictitious abbreviations (e.g. Nurse A.).

The prospective self report writers had been asked not to disclose their identity. Confidentiality was already assured in the advertisement. In the data analysis they are therefore referred to as 'writer of self report'.

As the hearings of the UKCC Council are public hearings, the typescripts thereof are accessible to the public. No problems were encountered in obtaining these case proceedings which were sent to me as complete photocopies. By December 1991 all data were at my disposal.

Time and locations for group discussions and interviews

For the German Group Discussion a small room within the educational institution was readily found. The discussion took place during the lunch hour. Grouped around a table the participants first listened to my short introduction before entering into the discussion. It lasted about 90 minutes.

The Scottish Group Discussion was held in the students' classroom which was arranged for our needs. The tables were removed and we sat in a circle. The discussion took place after lecture time and lasted for about 60 minutes.

As for the location of the interviews I suggested that the participants could come to an office at the university. One nursing manager felt that her office would be a convenient place for the interviews, as she was going to be on holiday. I declined this offer as there might be interruptions by telephone or visitors and as the nursing manager's office is the place where a nurse is questioned, counselled or disciplined when problems arise. I did not want to be associated with the hospital hierarchy, and thus, preferred a more neutral location for the interviews. Some charge nurses or sisters found quiet places within their own wards. Their interviews took place during their duty time. On one occasion we used the rest room of the delivery ward. On two occasions empty side wards were used. Four interviews took place in an office in the Department of Nursing Studies at the University. These participants came during their off duty time.

Demographic data about the participants

For the participants of the Scottish Group Discussion, the interviews and the self reports I prepared a short questionnaire asking for sex, age, nursing qualifications and practical nursing experience.[5] I could thus capture roughly the nursing background of the participants. I extracted comparable details about the nurses involved in the medication errors dealt with by the UKCC, from the documents. The nurses participating in the German Group Discussion had been provided with a consent form which included questions as to their sex and age, their educational background and the year of final nursing exam. An overview as to the nurses participating in the project follows.

German Group Discussion:

Seven women and one man aged between 26 and 39 participated in the discussion. Two participants had a high school certificate (Abitur), four had finished intermediate school (Mittelere Reife) and two had a basic school education (Hauptschulabschluß). All German nurses had undergone a hospital based training lasting three years. They qualified as nurses between 1973 and 1984. At least three had a post-qualification course in intensive care/therapy of two years duration. Three of the German participants held ward sisters' posts and five were deputy ward sisters.

Scottish Group Discussion:

---

[5] see Appendix One.

Amongst the six Scottish participants was one male nurse. The age range was between 26 and 49 years and they had gained their general nursing qualification between 1964 and 1984. All participants had done some further training courses; two had done their midwifery training, one had done training as a mental nurse; and one had followed a degree course in nursing. Four participants worked as ward sisters or charge nurses and three as staff nurses.

Interview participants:

Of the twelve Scottish respondents four were male nurses, the age-range was between 27 and 55. They qualified as general nurses between 1976 and 1987. All had undertaken post basic courses, four had qualified as midwives, four had qualified as mental nurses, one had obtained a bachelor of arts degree. Five of the participants worked as ward sisters or charge nurses and seven as staff nurses.

Respondents writing the self reports:

The six respondents included one male nurse and their age range was between 23 and 55. They qualified as general nurses between 1956 and 1987. All had undergone further qualifications. Three were nurse educators, one an orthopaedic nurse, one an obstetric nurse, and one a community health nurse, one had obtained a masters degree. Three worked as sisters or charge nurses and three as tutors or lecturers in nursing education.

Demographic data regarding the nurses against whom allegations were made by the UKCC:

I had access to six case proceedings of the UKCC Professional Conduct Committee. Four cases dealt with allegations against one nurse respectively and two with joint allegations against two nurses. All eight nurses were women. Their age could not be discerned but they qualified as general nurses between 1967 and 1983. All had gained further qualifications or taken part in post registration courses. Of two nurses it was mentioned that they had additionally to their general training, qualified as midwives and of one that she qualified as a mental nurse. Four worked as ward sisters and four as staff nurses. One nurse had retired after the drug incident.

It appeared that all participants had a considerable amount of post-basic experience as well as post basic training. Together they can be said to represent an average of the nurses currently employed in Britain and in Germany. However, it was notable that the Scottish sample included a number of middle aged women whereas the oldest German nurse was 39.

Of the 39 participants in my study, seven were men. The representation of men amongst nurses in Britain is 10 %, in Germany it is 7%.

These demographic data were not obtained for any kind of quantitative investigation. They simply helped to convey a picture of the nurses who supplied the discourses for my study. It is only in the light of each participants' personal life history and in the light of each one's learning and working experiences that meaning as to medication errors can be interpreted.

Silverman speaks for the inclusion of quantitative data in qualitative studies, but warns that "quantitative data produced in the research can play no more than a suggestive role" (Silverman 1985).

I approached all nurses as individuals and as individuals they told their stories. The problems addressed and discussed however, are of general concern to the profession. This demographic overview can therefore serve as an assurance that all data were taken from the life world of nursing today.

Securing the data

The group discussions and the interviews were recorded on a small unobtrusive battery tape recorder on high quality tapes.

To keep track of the turns of speech during the group discussions, I had in both groups allocated a number to each nurse and marked each contribution on a prepared sheet of paper keeping a continuous count. When a new topic was introduced I noted the key words of the speaker. On transcribing however, I did not always find it easy to identify the speaker. Especially in the Scottish group this was difficult when more than one nurse spoke at the time. This discussion was extremely lively and animated.

Unfortunately during the Scottish discussion I had placed the microphone on the floor in the middle of the circle and one participant who related important aspects, speaking very softly, was not audible.

Of the German discussion I produced a verbatim German transcript. Passages quoted in this thesis were translated and presented to a bilingual colleague who verified the translations.

The group discussions and the interviews were transcribed immediately after their occurrence. At first I carefully listened to the tapes again before starting to transcribe. After the first draft of the transcriptions had been completed I again listened to the tape, comparing the spoken with the written word. This helped me to eliminate mistakes or to ascertain at first inaudible passages. Transcribing the interviews and the Scottish Group Discussion proved to be difficult in some cases because of the Scottish accent. Generally, audibility of the tapes was good. Where indiscernible utterances occurred ' (... ? ...) ' was inserted or the utterance was put in brackets and ' ? ' was added in the transcript. Pauses and hesitations were marked by '..' or '... ...' according to the lengths of hesitation in speech. Sounds like 'Ehm', 'Aha', 'Ach', and words like 'and', 'well' and 'I think..', 'you know..' were included as they occurred. Interceptions like 'mmh' or 'hmm' were noted within the turns of speech whenever they occurred, with the according abbreviation of the speaker (MA: mmm).

A first copy of the transcript was sent to the participants with an accompanying letter as soon as the transcription was finished. Some respondents sent the copies back with minor corrections which were then checked against the tape and included into the transcript where appropriate.

Of the UKCC documents only selected passages were transcribed.

I arranged the transcripts in hanging files in a filing cabinet which was kept locked. As analysis progressed I added notes and information to the respective files.

Excerpts of the data in the text of this thesis

An interpretative study following the method of discourse analysis is highly dependent on the representation of data extracts. To supply a flavour of the texts that provide the basis for this study, abundant use is made of the data in order to illustrate lines of argument.

Quotations from the data are taken from the original transcripts. They have however, been 'tidied'. That is, some of the interceptions mentioned above were removed. The extracts can be identified as to their source as follows:

INT 1-12 refers to the interviews 1-12. These include the two pilot-interviews. GD-D refers to the group-discussion in Germany, and GD-SC refers to the group-discussion in Scotland. REP 1-6 refers to the six self-reports, and DOC 1-6 to the six UKCC Documents. EX.. denotes the example which provides the context in which a quotation occurs. Numbers after these abbreviations indicate the line numbers of the transcript. Thus, (INT1 EX2 154-155) means that this is a quote from interview one, and refers to the second example mentioned by the interviewee; the quote includes the lines 154 and 155. At times nurses talked without referring to a specific example, in such a case only the data source and the text-line numbers are given.

CHAPTER 6
DESCRIPTION OF DATA ANALYSIS

INTRODUCTION TO THE CHAPTER

In this chapter the process of data analysis is described. I refer to the way I progressively gained an understanding of the data. In the first place I was led by my own intuition, but I also took advantage of the suggestions made by the authors of the handbook that accompanies The Ethnograph programme for qualitative data analysis. Furthermore, I took recourse to Cormack (1991); Strauss (1987); Parker (1990), and Potter and Wetherell (1987).

This description will open up to scrutiny the "disciplinary practice" (Pollock 1991) which I engaged in, in order to arrive at a systematic treatment of my data. The analysis was conducted on three levels and is described in detail in the three sections of this chapter.

THE FIRST LEVEL OF ANALYSIS

Using The Ethnograph

From the time the first data were obtained I immediately started with the process of analysis. Beginning with the German Group Discussion, I employed The Ethnograph, which is a computer programme for the analysis of qualitative data. Here I had found a relatively simple way to organise, structure and handle my data. The Ethnograph is described as an

> ... interactive, menu driven computer program designed to assist the ethnographic/qualitative researcher in some of the mechanical aspects of data analysis (Seidel et al 1988 p. 1-2).

The Ethnograph makes it easy to number text lines and to code and re-code data. Text can be printed out either as a completely numbered and coded file, or according to codes across files. The programme is organised to display text and coded text segments on the computer screen according to the code words assigned to lines of text. The task of 'cutting and pasting' which is a major task in organising qualitative data is mechanised and thus, access to the sense the data will reveal is simplified. Furthermore, The Ethnograph can either show on the screen or print out, lists of code words that have been applied to a file. The lists can be given alphabetically or by the frequency of their appearance.

Data files can be sorted into groups of files. The programme allows for the possibility of codes overlapping or of creating codes within codes. Changes can easily be made in texts already analysed. This assures flexibility when new codes need to be inserted or code names are changed in texts already analysed. The initial step of coding is understood as "an analytic preliminary preparation for the deeper analysis to follow (Potter and Wetherell 1989). The authors of the User's Guide to The Ethnograph too, feel that the coding of texts is a preliminary step for deeper analysis. They prefer to call it "tagging" or "indexing" rather than coding. They state:

> The analysis of qualitative data is a progressive and iterative process that generally proceeds from a concrete to a more analytical or theoretical level (Seidel et al 1988 p. 7-7).

The verbatim transcripts of the taped material in this study were produced on a personal computer. I created individual files for each group discussion, interview, self report, and UKCC document.

Figure 2 shows a page of transcribed text from Interview One before being formatted:

Extract from Interview One

and I was absolutely sure that I had given it to the wrong person, and she said, well you realise we'll have to tell ... the boss, and this will have to be reported and I said yes, of course ...

MA: Who was the boss?

H: Well, the boss was our midwifery manager from the maternity unit (MA: ja, mm) and I said, yes of course, I realise that..I accepted my fate, quite stoically, I mean I knew I was for the chop, and so ...

+Ex dropped tablets

I had during my nurse training a friend ... a colleague had given .. I think she dropped a load of tablets on the floor (laughs) and picked them up and put them back in the bottle .. and of course she got a real telling off (laughs) she got disciplined and counselled and god knows what else (...?...) I mean, I think that's stuck in my mind and... and eh...

+Ex Anti-D

I wrote the report and Sister wrote something. But the next day she actually said to me, I am not going to report this ... because .. I feel that you know exactly what you have done, why you have done it, I am actually responsible as well, and we've both learned from this and I am not going to take it any further. She had taken advise from one of her peers, another sister, I think, and they

Figure 3 shows the same text from Interview One formatted and numbered by the Ethnograph

Numbered version of INT1 5/6/91

and I was absolutely sure that I 231
had given it to the wrong person, 232
and she said, well you realise 233
we'll have to tell ... the boss, 234
and this will have to be reported 235
and I said yes, of course ... 236

MA: Who was the boss? 238

H: Well, the boss was our midwifery 240
manager from the maternity unit 241
(MA: ja, mm) and I said, yes of 242
course, I realise that..I accepted 243
my fate, quite stoically, I mean I 244
knew I was for the chop, and so 245
... 246

+Ex dropped tablets 248
I had during my nurse training a 249
friend ... a colleague had given 250
.. I think she dropped a load of 251
tablets on the floor (laughs) and 252
picked them up and put them back in 253
the bottle .. and of course she 254
got a real telling off (laughs) 255
she got disciplined and counselled 256
and god knows what else (...?...) 257
I mean, I think that's stuck in my 258
mind and... and eh... 259

+Ex Anti-D 261
I wrote the report and Sister wrote 262
something. But the next day she 263
actually said to me, I am not 264
going to report this ... because .. 265
I feel that you know exactly 266
what you have done, why you have 267
done it, I am actually responsible 268
as well, and we've both learned 269
from this and I am not going to 270
take it any further. She had taken 271
advise from one of her peers, 272
another sister, I think, and they 273

Figure 4 shows the same page after coding

Coded Version of INT1 5/6/91

#-ACT/PASS

and I was absolutely sure that I	231	-#		
had given it to the wrong person,	232	-#		

#-PROCED

and she said, well you realise	233	-#		
we'll have to tell ... the boss,	234	ö		
and this will have to be reported	235	ö		
and I said yes, of course ...	236	ö		
MA: Who was the boss?	238	ö		
H: Well, the boss was our midwifery	240	ö		
manager from the maternity unit	241	ö		
(MA: ja, mm) and I said, yes of	242	ö		

$-CONSEQ

course, I realise that..I accepted	243	ö	-$	
my fate, quite stoically, I mean I	244	ö	ö	
knew I was for the chop, and so	245	-#	-$	
...	246			
+Ex dropped tablets	248			

#-EX-DROPTAB

I had during my nurse training a	249	-#		
friend ... a colleague had given	250	ö		

$-COUNSEL

.. I think she dropped a load of	251	ö	-$	
tablets on the floor (laughs) and	252	ö	ö	
picked them up and put them back in	253	ö	ö	
the bottle .. and of course she	254	ö	ö	
got a real telling off (laughs)	255	ö	ö	

%-DISCI %-LEARN

she got disciplined and counselled	256	ö	ö	-%
and god knows what else (...?...)	257	ö	-$	ö
I mean, I think that's stuck in my	258	ö		ö
mind and... and eh...	259	-#		-%

%-PROCED *-COVERUP *-REACTOTH

+Ex Anti-D	261			-% -*

#PROCED $-COVERUP

I wrote the report and Sister wrote	262	-#	-$	ö	ö
something. But the next day she	263	-#	ö	-%	ö
actually said to me, I am not	264		ö		ö
going to report this ... because ..	265		ö		ö

#-LEARN

I feel that you know exactly	266	-#	ö		ö
what you have done, why you have	267	ö	ö		ö

$-RESPONSIB

done it, I am actually responsible	268	ö	ö		ö
as well, and we've both learned	269	ö	-$		ö
from this and I am not going to	270	ö			ö
take it any further. She had taken	272				ö
advise from one of her peers,	273				ö
another sister, I think, and they	274				ö

Figure 5 shows an example of the codeword 'responsib' across some interviews. The relation to other codes is also shown:

SORTED OUTPUT FOR FILE INTI 5/6/91
SORT CODE: RESPONSIB
INT1 +Ex anti-D

E: *-COVERUP *-REACTOTH
E: #-LEARN

SC: RESPONSIB
$-RESPONSIB

:	done it, I am actually responsible	268	ö	-$
:	as well, and we've both learned	269	ö	-$

INT1 +Ex Diamorphine
SC: RESPONSIB
$-RESPONSIB

:	because . . if people find it hard	881	-#	ö
:	to understand me now, and if they	882	#	ö
:	have any respect for what I do . .	883	#	ö
:	(MA: hmm) it will just . . .	884	#	ö
:	dissipate, if they think ehm . . if	885	#	ö
:	they think I'm a coward or a . . I	886	#	ö
:	don't know what words you use . .	887	#	ö
:	but I think part of it is to do	888	#	ö
:	with facing up to your	889	#	ö
:	responsibility, being accountable	890	#	
:	that's what its all about, being	891	#	ö
:	accountable for what you do, and I	892	#	ö
:	do believe, very strongly, that	893	#	ö
:	you should be accountable for what	894	#	ö
:	you do, and if one of those things	895	#	ö
:	is making a mistake, you should	896	#	ö
:	account for it.	897	-#	-$

INT2
SC: RESPONSIB
$-ACT/PASS $-RESPONSIB

:	know, if, if we made a mistake	262	-ö	-$
:	then we'll have to . . be	263	ö	$
:	accountable for it and you have to	264	ö	$
:	be able to stand up (MA: mmh), and	265	ö	$
:	. . . say, well . . I did it, it was	266	ö	$
:	my fault . . (MA: mmh), ehm . .	263	ö	$

INT2
SC: RESPONSIB
#-RESPONSIB #-OWNUP

:	(MA: mmh), . . but, because I had	669	-#

:	done the drug error, I was	700	#			
:	responsible for my own actions,	701	#			
:	and . . I was willing to stand up	702	#			
:	and . . you know, say that I've done	703	#			
:	it, and take the consequences . .	704	#			

INT3
SC: RESPONSIB
$-RESPONSIB

:	afterwards. But I have actually	64	ö	-$		
:	been involved in . . giving the	65	ö	$		
:	dose . . (MA: mmh), the second	66	ö	$		
:	time, so . . no matter wether the	67	ö	$		
:	other dose hadn't been signed for,	68	ö	$		
:	they were at fault, but I was	69	ö	$		
:	still . . involved, and I'm the	70	ö	$		
:	one, you know, who would be held	71	ö	$		
:	. . say it had been something a bit	72	ö	$		

%-REACTRESP *-MISTAKE

:	more . . eh . . potent, would be held	73	ö	$	-%	
:	responsible. And you feel very . .	74	#	-$		ö

E: $-REACTRESP
E: #-EX-SYTRON
SC:RESPONSIB
%-RESPONSIB

:	just feel . . awful, and you feel . .	188	ö	ö	-%	
:	more responsible, because I was	189	ö	ö	-%	
:	the most senior person there. And	190	ö	ö	-%	

Further more The Ethnograph can either show on the screen or print out, lists of codewords that have been applied to a file. The lists can either be given alpahbetically or as to the frequency of their appearance.

Figure 6 shows the lists of codewords used in Interview One:

Frequency list of codewords used in coding INT1 5/6/92

N	CODEWORD	N	CODEWORD	N	CODEWORD	N	CODEWORD
15	PROCED	12	OWNUP	12	ACT/PASS	11	HONESTY
10	SUPPORT	9	COVERUP	9	DRUGROUT	8	LEARN
8	DR	8	REACTRESP	8	REACTOTH	6	PATHARM
6	EX-DIA	5	RESPECT	5	CONSEQ	4	RESPONSIB
4	MISTAKE	4	ORGANI	4	STUDENT	4	DISCI
4	COUNSEL	3	CONFID	3	EX-ANTID	3	BLAME
3	METOO	3	EX-DROPTAB	3	CHECK	2	SELF-CARE
2	PAT	1	STANDARDS	1	EX-SYNTO	1	EX-CHILD
1	OUTSPOKEN	1	HUMOUR				

ALPHABETICAL List of codewords used in coding INT1 5/6/92

N	CODEWORD	N	CODEWORD	N	CODEWORD	N	CODEWORD
12	ACT/PASS	3	BLAME	3	CHECK	3	CONFID
5	CONSEQ	4	COUNSEL	9	COVERUP	4	DISCI
8	DR	9	DRUGROUT	3	EX-ANTID	1	EX-CHILD
6	EX-DIA	3	EX-DROPTAB	1	EX-SYNTO	11	HONESTY
1	HUMOUR	8	LEARN	3	METOO	4	MISTAKE
4	ORGANI	1	OUTSPOKEN	12	OWNUP	2	PAT
6	PATHARM	15	PROCED	8	REACTOTH	8	REACTRESP
5	RESPECT	4	RESPONSIB	2	SELF-CARE	1	STANDARDS
4	STUDENT	10	SUPPORT				

About 600 pages of text, leaving a wide right margin, were finally produced. The lines of each text were numbered by The Ethnograph. The wide margins offered enough space to "doodle" and to try out various codes that could be applied to the texts, thus "code mapping" it (Seidel et al 1988). Sometimes segments could be allocated to more than one code. Finally, the line numbers with their allocated code words were fed into the coding menu of The Ethnograph. Then the coded version of a text were produced as hard copies.

The Ethnograph appeared to be a helpful tool to get acquainted with the data and provided an easy means of organising them. The programme also proved helpful when searching for illustrative extracts from the data. These could easily be found by taking recourse again to the code words applied to the different texts. The Ethnograph has further features that may be used in the analysis of qualitative data. In this study, the programme was only used in the manner described above.

Group discussions and interviews

As soon as the formatted and numbered texts from The Ethnograph were at my disposal I consecutively read through them, noting thematic units which I marked on the margins of the transcripts accordingly. For instance when nurses talked about their own reactions or the reactions of others to the incident they related, I wrote a respective code word in the margins, noting the line numbers of these occurrences. In this fashion I coded throughout the texts. During this first level of analysis, I simply used my personal perception of the contents in order to find categories of thematic implication. Strauss suggests a coding paradigm which can be used as a frame of reference for given "categories" (Strauss 1987). The four aspects of this coding paradigm, namely: 1) conditions; 2) interaction among actors; 3) strategies and tactics; 4) consequences; appeared to be applicable to my first intuitive coding scheme. Still, some of the aspects Strauss names could be allocated to two or more of my thematic units.

About 65 code words of my coding scheme related to:

1) - the circumstances of the mistake
- the procedure of drug administration
- mistakes happen to everybody
- feeling responsible
- the self image of nurses
- harm/no harm done

2) - the involvement of patients
- the involvement of doctors
- the involvement of students
- the nursing hierarchy/trust and respect
- teaching and learning
- support of colleagues/friends/family

3) - the feeling of guilt and shame
- reporting mistakes/owning up/covering up

4) - reactions to the incident
- structural consequences
- the disciplinary procedure

With the help of The Ethnograph different data sets could easily be looked at together from the thematic coding point of view. I could now isolate the 'stories' about experiences with medication errors. The respondents generally referred several times during the interviews and group discussions to the various incidents they chose to address. This meant that the sequences had to be pieced together in order to make a coherent story. I then wrote short summaries on the incidents, thus working at a purely descriptive level of analysis.[1]

Oftentimes these texts had to be amended as to the actual occurrences of events when, at a later stage, I noted a detail in the transcripts that previously had escaped my attention. The objective of this first step was to capture the story-lines as the respondents told them.

---

[1] See Appendix Five

Hereafter I wrote two papers on the process described above, one referring to the German Group Discussion and one to the interviews. This helped me to get an overview of the data and their contents. I became familiar with my thematic codes and started to discern similarities as well as deviances across the various data sources.

I then proceeded to examine each interview in turn, writing accounts of what seemed to be most important in each participant's discourse, thus isolating the dominant themes in each set of data. I also tried to portray each participant as he or she appeared to me through the interview. These accounts were factual descriptive representations of my interpretive coding. They were an important source during subsequent analysis of the data.[2]

Five of the accounts were sent to the respective participant asking for feedback. The nurses gladly responded and found the accounts appropriate. Sometimes additions or elaborations were made on my interpretations. These I included in the appropriate files for later reference, thus adding to the data.

I decided not to send all accounts back to the sources as I had sufficient reassurance on the validity of my coding and interpretation from the first five respondents. I found that by not involving the participants any further at this stage, my writing became easier. I could be more straightforward in expressing myself, not having to guard against the censorship of the respondents.

At this stage, I asked three colleagues to appraise my accounts and to provide an assurance that I saw the respondents in the light they had presented themselves in the interviews. The colleagues felt that I had captured the main issues of the respective interviews correctly.

The analysis of data presented a certain difficulty. I had to distinguish between different types of narrative - which in the first place was narration of what happened to the participant, and secondly how people reacted to what happened. Thirdly I had to discern the

---

[2] Two such accounts are included in Appendix Six

narrator's talk about the perception of other nurses involved in an incident and how this perception was utilised in his or her own discourse.

Self reports and UKCC Documents

A further task lay in processing the self reports. They too were transcribed and fed into the Ethnograph. I treated them in a similar way as I did the group discussions and interviews. Coding proceeded accordingly and summaries of the stories were written. These data provided a back-up to the data of the group discussions and interviews. The language of the self reports was more concise and to the point. Still, coding could focus on the same codes as were used previously.

The UKCC documents provided a different quality of data. They consisted of detailed and repetitious questions by members of the Professional Conduct Committee and of explanations by witnesses and the nurses involved in the actual incidents, the aim of a disciplinary hearing being to reconstruct the occurrence of an incident and to understand the actions of the people involved in order to establish or to reject the allegation of professional misconduct.

Here, too, I extracted the stories and applied my coding scheme, although I restricted it somewhat to the circumstances of the incidents, the reactions of the people involved, and the consequences on personal, institutional, and disciplinary levels. Of the documents I only transcribed selected parts and fed them into respective files in The Ethnograph. Extracts from the documents were used later on to substantially verify discourses from the other data.

Arriving at themes

An organisation of the coding schemes was effected by the writing of the summaries of all incidents and by the factual descriptive representations of my interpretive coding (descriptive accounts). Seidel et al refer to "Conceptual categories which may or may not have obvious and explicit connections with the 'code mapping' scheme" (Seidel et al 1988). Such "conceptual categories" I called 'themes'. They could be subsumed under five headings. The themes thus isolated from my data were named:

1) **The procedure of dealing with medication errors**
2) **The role of the medical staff**
3) **The image of the nurse and of nursing**
4) **The situation of student nurses**
5) **Support in the situation of medication errors**

This first level of analysis had started with the first data I collected, it continued alongside with the data collection and included the writing of the summaries and of the descriptive accounts. It lasted for about 12 months and was finalised in Chapter Seven of this thesis, 'Themes emerging from the data'.

At a higher level 'key issues' could be isolated as is described subsequently. In this study, the analysis at the second and third levels proved to be independent of the coding. The coding however, was a necessary step to proceed to a more theoretical level of analysis.

THE SECOND LEVEL OF ANALYSIS

Diagrams and text on diagrams

As I worked on the texts during the first level of analysis, relationships between the various themes began to emerge. Here the second level of analysis had its starting point. I could, for example, see the connection between the drug routine as the nurses described it, their image of nurses and nursing, and the trust patients put into the actions of nurses. Or it became clear that an understanding of human fallibility was a driving force in the way students were taught to handle the administration of medication. Another example would be the relationship between the nurse's picture of her or himself and the feeling of devastation after a medication error had been made.

Van Manen uses the metaphor of knots in a web when he speaks about phenomenological themes:

> So phenomenological themes are more like knots in the webs of our experiences, around which certain lived experiences are spun and thus experienced as meaningful wholes. Themes are the stars that make up the universe of meaning we live through. It is by the light of these themes that we can navigate and explore such universe (Van Manen 1984 p. 59).

This very aptly describes what I practised during this stage of analysis. As the interrelationships of themes surfaced, I wrote short notes on my observations. I then compiled these notes in diagrammatic form using A4 sized sheets at first but finding it necessary to work on flip charts later. I differentiated the connections and relationships between themes as they became apparent.

Strauss (1987) advocates visual methods of data analysis. I found my own preference in constructing diagrams which linked up various themes forming an empirical model. This model can be equated to Berger's understanding of the dialectical formation of social reality (Berger 1969). My model has the form of an open circuit that homes in on the question 'What does it mean to a nurse, to be involved in a medication error?' It provides the structure for an overview over the data at the second level of analysis.

Below, the model in its most abstract version is displayed. In its absolute diversification it represents the data in an organised form. It takes note of all themes that were discernible during the first level of analysis.

Figure 7 Overview - An empirical model:

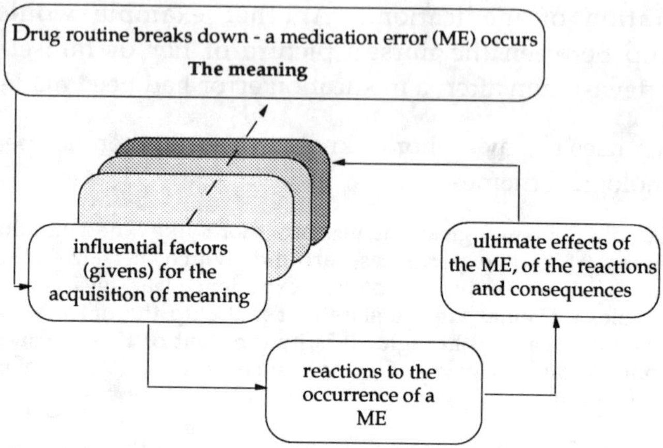

As a next step at this level I verbalised the diagrams. This made my thinking accessible on a verbal basis. One effect of constructing the model was the necessity of having to look more closely at the reasons why medication errors happen. The relation between the breakdown of the drug routine, an ensuing medication error, and the effects of the same became obvious. This was the origin of the diagram 'The drug routine' in Chapter One.

The second level of analysis arose from the first one. In the diagrams of the empirical model the discourse of my participants can be seen as represented in an abstract manner. The work at this second level of analysis lasted for about three months.

The Third Level of Analysis

Analysing key issues at a theoretical level

The formulation and description of the themes at the first level of analysis as well as the factual representation of their interrelationship at the second level of analysis were concrete and rested on procedures that did not much more than organise the empirical data. As mentioned above, the analysis of qualitative data "proceeds from a concrete to a more analytical or theoretical level" (Seidel et al 1988). The question is, how is the researcher led to this theoretical or analytical level?

Some elements which at first I had grouped among the themes proved to have qualities that were not simply accounted for by their relationship to other themes. These elements appeared across the themes and they promised access to a deeper level of analysis. For instance the elements of *power and identification* could be linked to the themes of 'The disciplinary procedure', and 'The image of the nurse and of nursing', as well as to the themes of 'Support', 'The situation of student nurses', and 'The role of the doctor'. Such a link would in each case change the perspective and open up entirely new dimensions for the understanding of phenomena connected with the experience of medication errors. Thus it would not have done these elements justice if they were treated as a theme among others.

Examining these elements of which at first there seemed to be many, it emerged that they could be grouped under three headings which appropriately I called 'key issues'. The key issues are:

1) **Subjection and power - Identification and change**
This key issue includes the nurses' identification with a professional role, and adherence to or avoidance of the disciplinary procedure.
2) **Guilt - and reconciliation**
This key issue refers to the experience of guilt and shame; to living with the knowledge of human imperfection; and also to the concepts of forgiveness and reconciliation.
3) **Learning from mistakes**
This key issue addresses the internalisation of affective learning objectives. It refers especially to the decision-making process; and explores the meaning of learning from personal experience or from the experience of others.

Referring back to van Manen's metaphor of "themes being the stars that make up the universe of meaning we live through" (van Manen 1984), the key issues can be compared to suns on whose position the others stars orient and whose light illuminates them, in fact renders them visible.

Each key issue is unfolded in a separate chapter in Part Four of this thesis. It appeared that my research question provided the common denominator that linked the three key issues together. By referring to power, to guilt and reconciliation as well as to the key issue of learning from mistakes, I have "identified" three of the "objects" (Parker 1990), which the discourse is about. The analysis of the three key issues as objects, illuminated the research question at a deeper theoretical level. The third level of analysis lasted for about nine months.

Parker (1990), suggests some criteria that refer to the researcher's framework of analysis. Parker's criteria were not used as a systematic guide-line, but they informed the access to analysis at this third level. On the basis of discourse analysis I used the three key issues to fit the discourse into a "coherent system of outside knowledge within the analysis". Also the "connections, allusions, and implications which the texts evoked" could be addressed in reference to the three key issues. Parker suggests that by reflecting on the terminology used and by treating the contents of the discourse "as an object" the researcher engages in "moral evaluation and political choices"). Furthermore, Parker states that "discourse analysis cannot take place without locating its object in time". The objects discourse refers to "are constituted in the past" (Parker 1990). The historical location comes into play in this study where I take heed of official policies and guide-lines and their development, which influenced nurses' understanding of specific experiences. It also features in the third chapter of Part Four in this thesis when the historical perspective of teaching and learning ethics in nursing is considered.

The relationship between the empirical model and the key issues

The three chapters of Part Four of this thesis (Chapters Nine, Ten, and Eleven) represent an elucidation of the empirical model. By discussing the key issue of 'subjection and power, identification and change' in Chapter Nine, the first cornerstone of the model *(influential factors (givens) for the acquisition of meaning'* in situations of medication errors) is being dealt with at a deeper level. In Chapter Ten, the second cornerstone of the model *(reactions to medication errors)* is explored by looking at feelings of guilt and shame as voiced by the nurses in the data. Chapters Nine and Ten provide the basis for Chapter Eleven, where the key issue of learning from mistakes is pursued. This chapter represents the third cornerstone of the model *(ultimate effects of the medication errors, of the reactions and consequences).*

Theory free observation and theory laden observation

In the three chapters of Part Four of this thesis I draw on theories that have been formulated in the social sciences. I wanted to arrive at a dialectical distinction between the "received view" of logical positivism that argues for theory free observation and the notion of observation that arrives at theory (Pittman Weekes 1986). Pittman Weekes addresses this notion by saying:

> It is theory that provides observation with a point of view (..) Consequently, theory performs dual function, it provides a statement about reality and a perspective from which to interpret reality (Pittman Weekes 1986 p. 15).

I try to maintain the "dynamic balance" between theory free observation and theory laden observation. The "continual awareness that all phenomena are interconnected, interrelated and interdependent, and as such cannot be observed as isolated entities, but only as integrated parts of a whole" (Pittman Weekes 1986) is discernible throughout these three chapters. Part of 'the whole' are the lived experiences of people as well as theories that have been postulated within the social sciences.

Nursing understood as a "practice science" (Bishop and Scudder 1990) needs this dialectical approach in order to enlighten the phenomena nurses encounter when engaged in practice. Nurses never act solely as nurses. Being encompassed in a social reality that is subject to the perceptions akin to all people, the application of social science theory can only further the interpretation and understanding of the nurses' world.

Thus, at the third level of analysis social theory is used to provide the interpretive perspective which helps to understand the social context within which medication errors sustained their meaning for the nurses who experienced them. Pittman Weekes delineates the subjectivity that is inherent in qualitative research in nursing which can be set against theoretical writing. She remarks:

> Because nursing is primarily a practice discipline, it seeks to know individuals in all their uniqueness and particularity. Nurses cannot accomplish this task by approaching scientific investigation as detached, naive examiners of observables; rather, they must approach it as informed scientists aided by theory. One also needs to remember that there are few, if any, absolute truths. In fact, truth may be somewhat like an onion, with many layers that need to be revealed. The only way to reveal succeeding layers is through the conjoint use of theory and observation (Pittman Weekes 1986 p. 19).

Such a manner of observing and interpreting the material at my disposal allowed for an analysis at a more theoretical level, distinct from the concrete method of analysis of the first and second levels. It finally added to a deeper understanding of nurses' experiences and thus, to a body of nursing knowledge.

PART III

DATA ANALYSIS - THEMES AND KEY ISSUES

If there were no "that"
There would be no "this."
If there were no "this"
There would be nothing for all
these winds to play on.
So far can we go.
But how shall we understand
What brings it about?

(Thomas Merton: The way of Chuang Tzu)

CHAPTER 7
THEMES EMERGING FROM THE DATA

INTRODUCTION TO THE CHAPTER

In this chapter the themes which were touched upon by the nurses participating in this study are addressed. A description of the main themes at this point of the thesis seems appropriate, as they represent an essence of what nurses talked about during the group discussions and the interviews; and what was conveyed in the self reports and documents. The themes are related to the points addressed in Chapter One regarding the administration of medicines. In this chapter however, they are seen from the perspective of the data. The themes emerged from the data as a result of the first level of analysis. They convey how nurses perceived their experiences of having been involved in medication errors. They are described, and illustrated with extracts from the data but no interpretation is attempted at this stage.

Most of the main themes interconnect and it is not always easy to differentiate between them. Therefore some peripheral themes are also touched upon in the exploration of the main ones. The chapter has five main sections. Each section relates to one of the main themes. At various points throughout the chapter I refer to policies and guide-lines and have included relevant excerpts.

A SHORT DESCRIPTION OF THE THEMES:

1) The procedure of dealing with medication errors

This theme is introduced first because it supplies the means of understanding some of the actions and reactions which frequently follow a situation of medication error as is addressed hereafter. It is closely connected with the theme of support but focuses on the medication error itself and how it is dealt with officially. It mentions policies and guide-lines regarding drug administration and deals with the relationship between staff and management, thus addressing trust and mistrust, owning up to a mistake and covering it up.

2) The role of the doctor in the situation of medication errors

As medical and nursing work are closely linked, doctors' involvement in medication errors is obvious. This theme examines the role doctors play in dealing with medication errors and it shows the difference of perceptions doctors are thought to have as to the occurrence of medication errors.

3) The image of the nurse and of nursing

This theme comprises the views of how 'others' see nurses and nursing and how this perception of others influences nurses' view of themselves. In addressing this theme, again I focus on one aspect of nursing work, namely the administration of medication. The picture the nurse has of herself/himself and the influence the experience of having made a medication error are expressed here.

4) The situation of student nurses

This theme focuses on the student nurse and her/his involvement in medication errors. It addresses the perspective of students when they were involved in medication errors.

5) Support in the situation of medication errors

This theme includes being supported through the experience of having made a medication error, as well as the lack of expected support. It also addresses the bearing support has for nurses in order to regain their professional confidence after having made a medication error.

The Procedure of Dealing with Medication Errors

Fear of the procedure

Whenever nurses talked about their experiences with medication errors the term 'the procedure' permeated their narratives. This term was used when nurses referred to the disciplinary measures taken at various levels in the nursing hierarchy, in order to deal with a medication error. The justification for the recourse to disciplinary measures was said to be that it protected the public from harm or possible harm.

This justification was employed by managers and generally accepted by nurses. Whether or not a medication error would become subject to any part of the disciplinary procedure, would depend on the nurses handling it, and not so much on actual harm done to a patient. Often however, nurses would report even a harmless mistake if detection was likely. The report would be made out of the fear of it being found out later, which might have more serious consequences for a nurse.

I asked nurses why they would report mistakes. Joan for instance said:

> *I don't believe in covering up anything because .. you might be found out .. and if you cover it up that's going to make it an awful lot worse, you know, what, what initially is perhaps .. a small problem, is going to grow into a very big problem if you're trying to cover it up, and it's then discovered in some other way ... (INT2 558-569).*

If a nurse judged a mistake to have no harmful consequences for the patient, and if it was not otherwise likely to be detected, it might well be covered up.

Some of my respondents said clearly that after having gone through the ordeal of 'the procedure' they would think twice before they again reported a mistake. Jane said:

> *I know from ... what other people said at the time ... the only result of treating me like that , ehm .. everybody seeing me to be treated like that, was that .. in future mistakes would be covered up, (INT11 EX1 1048- 1055).*

Nurses might not report mistakes for fear of a small incident having big disciplinary consequences. Pearl said:

> *...it's this big fear... fear of consequences that (...) but it prevents people from... maybe often from owning up to things .. ehm, and it makes it very difficult for someone to own up and it just puts up that immediate barrier, ... (INT3 1123-1131).*

The nature of these *'consequences'* is described in this section.

Dealing with a medication error at ward level - or reporting it further.

A senior nurse might well deal with a mistake at ward level and thus prevent a mistake from being taken further up the hierarchy. In Interview Nine, Chris's mistake, even though quite serious, was dealt with by the doctor and taken up by the unit manager. The unit manager did not take the incident further. I asked Chris as to the decision her unit manager had taken:

> *MA: ... did she think about, reporting it further?*
>
> *Chris: Well, normally .. in the past is has .. gone to (...) the senior nursing officer. And .. I really don't know, why she didn't take it to (her) (...) (...) So, she said to me, I don't think actually, this need to go to (her) (...) I'll put it (the report) into your file, and it will stay there .. for a year, and after which ... can forget about it. (...)*
>
> *MA: It might have even gone further ... (Chris: Yes) ... was it at (your unit manager's) discretion, to decide, not to pass it on? I mean, she took it on herself ..*
>
> *Chris: She did !*
>
> *MA: That's quite..*
>
> *Chris: And I don't think it was just because of who I am .. and what I am. I think she'd do that for anybody, depending on the severity of the thing, (...) and (...) the outside circumstances (...) ... she decided upon herself. But .. it didn't need to go any further (INT9 EX1 567-631).*

Mike, in Interview Seven, openly spoke about his preference to deal with medication errors in an unorthodox way. I asked him, how he felt about reporting mistakes that may be brought to his notice in his position as a charge nurse. He said:

> *...a medication error with a drug, that was potentially life threatening to the patient .. ehm .. you would maybe have to .. mention that to someone .. higher up the nursing hierarchy... (INT7 299-305).*

But Mike would prefer to deal with a situation himself:

...I personally wouldn't be in favour of that approach, if I felt, well I could deal with that, there and then, with the staff nurse .. (...) I would be quite happy not to mention it to, .. to my nurse managers (INT7 305-314).

He knew that he would in fact violate the given rules:

MA: And this decision is within your .. ehm, scope of decision-making?

Mike: No, I should .. if I make any drug error .. if drug errors are made, I should .. fill out an incident report form, and .. mention it to my nurse manager.

MA: Would you?

Mike: No, .. no, (...) if it was an error made by one of my staff nurses, .. ehm .. and it was the first time they had ever made an error, as far as I knew, then, no I would be quite happy to deal with it myself, if the doctor was happy, .. (INT7 316-337).

It appeared that the person to whom a mistake was first reported, had to decide, whether or not it was to be taken further up the hierarchy and followed up by disciplinary measures. This decision would depend on the circumstances prevailing in the area, and on the attitude of the nurses concerned. If medication errors were an issue of immediate sensitivity, the likelihood that a mistake would be followed up was great, as was the case in Jane's example in Interview Eleven.

In Interview Eleven, Jane told me how she had been doing the drug round with a student who mistakenly gave some tablets to the wrong patient. From the type of tablets given no harm would ensue to the patient. The doctor did not want to follow the incident up any further, but Jane reported it to her senior nurse for fear of being found out. She stated that at the time a *'witch-hunt'* had been on in the district about medication errors and even slight and harmless occurrences were taken up and dealt with in a severe and harsh manner.

Jane's immediate superiors would have liked to deal with her incident at ward level. Jane recalled:

I reported it to my ward sister, ..(...) she wanted to sort it out at her level, but she realised, she couldn't, and she took it up to the nurse manager (...) he wanted to sort it out at his level.. (MA: mmh), (...) but .. he felt, he couldn't and he had to take it higher, and it was because, ... this director had just put the fear of God into everybody, (INT11 EX1 1394-1411).

...created a feeling of resentment, because, we felt, that everything had been taken out of our hands. We weren't allowed to sort it out ourselves. I know the ward sister in particular ..., she thought that her position had also been undermined, because she wasn't allowed to deal with it (INT11 EX1 660-665).

However much the attitudes of managers varied with respect to dealing with medication errors, having to go through the various levels of 'the procedure' was perceived as threatening by the respondents of this study.

The following extracts from a self-report sum up the first steps of 'the procedure':

...and she (the student) suddenly realised she'd given the wrong patient the Insulin. She admitted she'd forgotten to check the name band.

I called the doctor straight away and he said just keep an eye on her BM stix.[1] I documented everything and informed the nurse manager on for the hospital (REP1 32-42).

Incident forms were filled in. I was then off for a couple of days, then on to night duty. A lot of crying took place. My ward sister was very supportive, and also my family - my mother is a nurse.

(...) I had a formal meeting with the surgical nursing managers. I had an RCN Representative with me, as I felt very threatened. He was very helpful. I had to explain what had happened - saying it was my fault, and then the manager told me what I should do in future if busy. This incident was on my record for one year (REP1 49-65).

Reporting another nurses' error also presented a problem. A nurse in the Scottish Group Discussion said to another participant who had actually been involved in the error that was being discussed:

I felt awful, because I had reported it to the nurse.. the nursing officer, and because of this, one of my colleagues was going to be ... pulled up! (GD-SC EX1 95-100).

I felt I was ehm .. betraying you. (addresses her colleague) I mean, it had, it had to be reported, because, there was obviously a discrepancy in the books (GD-SC EX1 192-195).

In example one, which Sean related in Interview Four, Sean had talked to the doctor who was quite happy to leave the incident without it being followed up any further, but Sean felt that it should be brought to the

---

[1] Instant test for blood sugar

attention of the nursing hierarchy. He reported it to his nursing officer and 'the procedure' took its course for the nurse involved. Sean's general opinion was:

> *...because of the fact that I actually knew of the drug error, I have to go and see my immediate superior about it and report that (INT4 EX1 216-220).*

> *Sean: Yeah, we are told, that, you know, as soon as there is a drug error, you have to be..*

> *MA: Yeah, but it's your decision!*

> *Sean: Well, I put it this way, I would hate to deal with a drug error like that... and then be found out by a nurse manager, that I have dealt with it on ward level, and not reported it to her (INT5 EX1 744-756).*

> *I think the reason why I would report, a drug error, is ... so that I was keeping in the right (laughs), maybe that's a terrible thing to say, but.. you know, I'd hate to get sort of dragged over the hot coals, because of someone else's mistake, (INT5 EX1 772-779).*

In example three, Sean only *'challenged'* the nurse, but said that he was very young then and that he might act differently now. He would not hesitate now to mention a similar situation to a senior nurse. Justifying this attitude he said:

> *...wasn't any harm done, other than the fact, that she might not meeting her ..eh.. drug technique, ehm, and then I thought, maybe its my fault, you know, she is maybe doing something wrong, I'm the only person that's supported it, you know, she's maybe caused someone great harm, ehm, in the past. You know, if I didn't bring this up, ehm (MA: mmm), I could be held to blame just as much as she is maybe, ... (INT5 EX3 2436-2449).*

Writing statements and the blot in the copy book!

After a mistake was taken up by the nursing hierarchy, generally statements had to be written by all personnel concerned. Thereafter the situation might be discussed with the nurses concerned and then forgotten about. Often however, a report would be included in the nurses' files.

Having a *'clean record'* was mentioned by Joan as of great importance:

> *...you don't want a blot on your copy-book, you know, 'cos obviously that goes into your record and, and it's ... about two years it's there, (INT2 416-421).*

The following extract shows how Jane saw and understood this part of the disciplinary procedure:

> *...it goes into your record, for a certain length of time. It's like a written warning. And .. which doesn't actually mean anything unless you're going to.. you wanted to change jobs, it's not a very good idea, because obviously it's in your record. If you keep your slate clean for six months, then it comes out, it's totally wiped out and there is no problem, and .. so that .. in terms of.. punishment or whatever ... nothing really happens, but it is the whole process of being dragged up in front .. various committees and panels, ... (INT11 EX1 84-101).*

According to the nurses I talked to, the length of time such a report would be kept in a nurse's file varied from three month to five years.

The disciplinary Policy Procedure of one Scottish region differentiates between:

1) oral warning - This 'shall be recorded and retained for three months';

2) first written warning - 'within the ensuing six months the warning will be removed';

3) final warning - 'within the ensuing twelve months the warning will be removed' (Lothian Health Board 1983, p. 4).

After such a time a past incident should have no bearing on a nurse's professional appraisal. In Document Three, reference was made to a previous medication error of the defendant and a *'single stage final warning'* was mentioned. Also in Document Two a previous medication error of the defendant was referred to. Her manager was asked by members of the Committee about the performance of Nurse B.. The legal assessor intervened:

> *Legal Assessor: (...) it would be my intention to advise the Committee, in those circumstances that this should be treated effectively like a spent conviction. It shouldn't be considered by them and no further answers should be given on that (DOC2 p. 63).*

It was made clear that *'a spent conviction'* should have no bearing on the judgement of the present case. On the one hand a nurse's performance had to be taken into account at a disciplinary hearing, on the other hand, a spent conviction must be valued as such.

The counselling threat!

One further measure following a hearing at hospital level would be the so called 'counselling'. In the same source as above it is stated that:

> Counselling is **not** a disciplinary action. Counselling is a positive means by which managers can advise, guide and correct members of staff with the aim of maintaining good standards of performance and conduct. (Lothian Health Board 1983 p. 1, emphasis in the original).

However, the perception of counselling my respondents presented was slightly different, as the following data extracts show:

...disciplining and counselling in our country is quite a funny thing, you, you're told you are going to be counselled, but in fact its not counselling, you get a damn good telling off (INT1 187-192);

...and of course she got a real telling off (laughs) she got disciplined and counselled and God knows what else (INT1 EX3 254-257).

...taking her through the, the counselling thing..(INT1 1319-1320).

MA: Who did the counselling?

Joan: The nursing officer...

MA: How did you feel about it?

Joan: ... Oh, I didn't mind, I didn't mind, because I think... it doesn't do us any harm, if .. you know, if, if we made a mistake, then we'll have to .. be accountable for it and you have to be able to stand up .. (INT2 EX1 249-267).

Joan: I didn't get severe counselling (INT2 EX1 322-323).

Pearl: ...they should have sat down, there should have been a counselling session, between the pair, and the senior, (...) and worked out why .. it happened (...)

MA: Well, was the senior.. in a position, to eh, to counsel,(...) Could she ..

Pearl: No, (...) she didn't communicate very well, (INT3 EX2 1194-1212).

Pearl: I think it is becoming a bit more acknowledged that counselling skills are very important (...) but even so .. ehm ...part of your role in that (...) capacity is to.. should be to counsel, I mean, if you're unable to deal with things, perhaps you shouldn't be in that particular role.. (INT3 EX2 1237-1255).

I had a counselling session, which really wasn't a formal counselling session. She was very supportive (INT9 EX1 209-212).

Some participants had experienced counselling as having a punitive character, even though all had an understanding that this need not be so.

Checking knowledge; supervision; in-service training; suspension from giving out drugs

In some instances the nurse responsible for a medication error would be examined on his or her knowledge of the drug administration procedure. Thus, Henry was asked by his manager to recite the hospital policy on drug administration:

> *...we went though the procedure manual. He told me that I hadn't read the procedure manual properly, and then focused mainly on procedural things (INT10 EX1 257-261).*

In this situation the nursing officer dealt with the medication error as if it had been due to a lack of Henry's knowledge of the drug administration procedure. No other factors were taken into account. A similar attitude could be distinguished in Interview Four, where Sean connected medication errors closely with the technique of giving out drugs:

> *...a drug error .. of any type ehm (...) its pointing to your drug-checking technique (INT4 37-41).*

This was exemplified in example three, when Sean talked to the student about routine drug-checks after the 'near error' had occurred. Three times he recounted how he went '*over the technique*' with the student. Also regarding example one, Sean mentioned several times how he went through the drug-routine with the staff nurse who had made the error while doing a drug round with a student. The student had not noticed the mistake. Sean said:

> *...we went through ehm ..(...) the control, storage and administration of medicines, with the staff nurse (INT4 EX1 323-335).*

In-service-training seemed to be a part of the normal procedure after a medication error had occurred. In the first example, related by Sean in Interview Four, he explained that after the error the staff nurse was supervised by a more senior nurse when giving out medicines According to Sean who was partly responsible for this measure, being controlled and observed was supposed to be helpful for the staff nurse.

She herself took this very hard as Sean indicated. It took her a long time to regain her professional confidence. Sean explained:

> *...and the upshot of it was, she had been .. counselled about it, got in-service training, and .. she was on like a probation for three months period, where she had to have all medicines checked by a night sister, (INT4 EX5 1607-1613).*

If a mistake was thus categorised as due to a lack of knowledge and skills it would be dealt with accordingly. The nurse would have in-service-training and be supervised in her drug administration technique.

If any other causes for making a mistake had been taken into consideration, such as stress through too great a workload, or any personal problem, it would have occurred to Sean or his manager-colleagues that examining the nurse who was responsible for the error as to her drug-technique, giving her in-service-training, and putting her under supervision while doing the drugs, could not have helped her. Also the fact that the student who had checked the drugs *'felt so choked up with the 'flu' (201-202)* would not be remedied by these measures.

Having to administer drugs under supervision, or even being banned from giving out drugs for a certain period of time seemed to be common practice after a medication error had occurred. Jane, in Interview Eleven, was allowed to carry on working in her capacity as a staff nurse, but could not give out medicines until her case had been heard at a regional level. She said:

> *... everything was taken very seriously. It involved me being .. suspended from being able to administer drugs .. until the whole situation was sorted out (INT11 EX1 50-55).*

Demotion and dismissal

A further possible measure taken at hospital management level could be the demotion or even the dismissal of a nurse. Gerald, in Interview Five, mentioned this threat by referring to the sister who had been responsible for the error in which he also was involved. Gerald said:

> *... she had been quite severely disciplined .. I think she'd been told that her job was on the line, if this happened again (...), .. there had been charge nurses who had been demoted to staff nurses' status (INT5 EX1 518-528).*

From Document Five it is discernible that Nurse T. was offered work as a staff nurse after first having been dismissed from her post as a ward sister when the incident had happened. This decision was made by the local health authority after Nurse T. had appealed against her dismissal which had been decided upon by the hospital management. This was discussed at the meeting of the Professional Conduct Committee:

Committee member: Okay. And that at that hearing you were reinstated by the Health Authority Panel?

Nurse T.: Yes.

Committee member: Can you tell the Committee the decision of that panel?

Nurse T.: Yes. They said I was to be reinstated as a Staff Nurse .. (...)

Committee member: And this was not acceptable to you?

Nurse T.: No, it wasn't (DOC5 p. 14/15).

Also Nurse C., according to Document Four, was dismissed from her position as a sister in charge after she had been involved in what was considered a drug error. At the meeting of the Professional Conduct Committee the disciplinary action of the local Health Authority was referred to several times. The following statements were made (the Senior Nurse Manager of the local hospital authority was called upon as a witness):

Manager: I appointed Nurse C. to the post that she had then (at the time of the incident) occupied as the Day Hospital Sister.

Committee member: And she was dismissed as a result of the matters we have heard about?

Manager: Yes.

Committee member: (addressing Nurse C.) We heard that you were sacked for that error of judgement. How do you feel about that?

Nurse C: I feel that it was a gross injustice. (...) considering it was a first offence ...

Committee member: On the evidence here today I must say I have some sympathy with you (DOC4 pp 3/4; 11).

Nurse C. was still found guilty of *'misconduct in the professional sense'*. However, her name was not removed from the register.

Hearings at regional level

In some cases, a medication error was reported to the regional health authorities. Again, this would depend on how sensitive the general feeling about medication errors was in the area at the time. It would also depend on the disposition of the managers responsible, and possibly on the personal relationships between management and staff. Often a representative of the RCN or the Trade Unions was involved to assure a fair deal for the nurse responsible and to provide some support. The outcome of such a hearing, according to my respondents would be an official caution, a report in the nurse's file, and a counselling session.

Document Three featured the hearing of a case before the Professional Conduct Committee, where an overdose of Digoxin caused a patient's death. Here a doctor wrote up the wrong dosage and the nurses additionally miscalculated from this erroneous prescription the amount needed for an intravenous infusion. The case was at first investigated in the hospital and then heard at the level of the local Health Authority. This brought about a written warning for one of the nurses who was involved in this occurrence, as well as having to work on day-duty for a period of time and take part in an introduction and re-training programme. The local Health Authority then referred the case to the Professional Conduct Committee of the UKCC.

Hearings before the UKCC Professional Conduct Committee

In some cases there will finally be official hearings before the Professional Conduct Committee. This however, will only be the case if a report has been made to the UKCC.

Reports may be made by patients or their relatives, by colleagues, by a hospital management, or by a health authority. The six cases at my disposal are said to be representative of medication errors reported to and dealt with by the Professional Conduct Committee. (Verbal communication by the Assistant Registrar, Standards and Ethics of the

UKCC). I have no knowledge as to how the six cases were reported to the UKCC. The cases vary as to severity of harm done to the patients. In three of these cases the death of a patient resulted from the incident.

The hearings by the Professional Conduct Committee would be conducted under juridical circumstances and aim at establishing or not establishing professional misconduct on the part of the nurses responsible. Furthermore, it would be decided by the committee whether or not a nurse's name is to be removed from the professional register.

The six cases involved eight nurses. In only one case was a nurse's name removed from the register. In four cases the nurses concerned were found guilty on the charges of professional misconduct but their names were not removed from the register. In one case the two nurses concerned were not found guilty of professional misconduct.

The Professional Conduct Committee and the fear of being removed from the register play an important role in the whole issue of medication errors. One of the first statements Pearl made during our interview was:

> *Pearl: And you feel very .. you feel very vulnerable, and you only have to mention .. drug errors, (...) I really think it's fear, it really is ..*
>
> *MA: Where do you think that fear comes from?*
>
> *Pearl: Its fear of .... the big thing I suppose that you think of .. error in medication! .. struck off the register (...) which is very dramatic, (...) that's the worse thing, that can happen apart from.. never mind the fear of what I have committed ..(INT3 74-96).*

An explanatory paper of the UKCC '...with a view to removal from the register...' enlarges on the system 'for considering complaints against registered nurses, midwives and health visitors'. Regarding the purpose of a Professional Conduct Committee hearing the paper states:

> - to hear evidence under oath and to decide whether matters alleged are proved;
>
> - to consider proven facts in context and decide whether, in professional terms, they constitute misconduct;

- to hear information about the respondent's previous history, and any submissions in mitigation of the proven misconduct;

- to decide whether the name of the practitioner should be removed from the register in the interest of patients or clients.

However, the purpose of these committee proceedings is not:

- to punish the practitioner appearing before the committee (though the person whose name is removed may so interpret a decision of removal from the register); (UKCC 1990 pp. 2-3).

Pyne states that the "basic premise of professional discipline is about the protection of the vulnerable public and not about punishment" (Pyne 1981 p. 64).

The immediate circumstances were generally taken into account during the official hearings of the UKCC. Here questions as to the staffing level and work load were asked to establish a clear picture of the circumstances that surrounded a medication error. This was important in order to assess individual nurses' responsibility. In Document Three a representative of the RCN summarises:

In order to reach a just and fair conclusion on the judgements that were made, they must be viewed in the context of the environment in which they occurred. We have shown that the unit was extremely busy on that particular night, and Nurse S. was acutely aware that amongst all other clinical interventions that you have heard about, this infusion for Mrs B. was extremely important and was long overdue. (...) In short events were happening so quickly that night that there was little time for objective assessment of the requirements. We submit that it was a combination of all these factors which resulted in an overdose of Digoxin being administered (DOC3 p. 14).

Positive functions of the disciplinary procedure

Even though 'the procedure' was perceived as a kind of punishment it was also accepted as a necessary step. It was sometimes perceived as helpful. Some of my respondents said clearly that they knew they had done something wrong and that they were quite willing to accept the consequences.

I expected to get ... warned .. for what I had done (INT10 EX1 227-228).

> *...it was something I'd done wrong, which I had to pay for, (...) will take whatever the punishment is, .. which .. for me was going through all this hassle, (INT11 EX1 277-283).*

Some nurses were surprised at *'getting off lightly'*. The respondent in Self Report Two commented thus:

> *There was no consequential action taken. I feel that I got off lightly (REP2 107-109).*

And Gemma who had gone through disciplinary measures at quite a high level said:

> *...it was difficult to believe that this was all that was going to happen, (INT6 EX1 899-901).*

It can be said that the disciplinary procedure also acted to re-establish the image of the nurse. The knowledge of the existence of this procedure and the actual execution of it, re-asserted the meaning of 'qualification' which would justify the trust patients have in nurses. In some situations, the fact of having undergone disciplinary measures, had a restorative function. Accepting 'punishment' and thus, being freed of guilt constituted an important element of coming to terms with one's imperfections. Henry, talking about his colleague in example four indicated this by saying:

> *...she felt that she had done something so bad, that she would have.. you know, it might have been better for her to go down and get a disciplinary (INT10 EX4 1392-1396).*

Reports, statements, hearings and counselling were accepted as deserved; as in Interview Ten, example four, where no error actually happened but the nurse felt the situation had to be dealt with on an official level. She could not overcome her feelings of guilt otherwise. Or in Gemma's situation, where no harm had come to the patient, the incident was taken through 'the procedure' and Gemma felt this to be justified.

It emerged that the disciplinary procedure itself with all its levels caused a lot of fear in most nurses, as there seemed to be no assurance that a situation would always be dealt with dispassionately and fairly. It very much depended on the relationships among nurses, whether or not an incident was reported. It also seemed to depend on the disposition of senior staff, whether or not an incident was taken further up the nursing hierarchy.

Nurses felt that owning up to a mistake should not in the first place expose nurses to disciplinary measures, but should be an opportunity to identify the causes that led to the incident and should allow for the elimination of the same.

It appeared that whether or not a nurse would report a mistake, largely depended on how an error he or she was involved in or witnessed, was being handled by the nursing hierarchy, and whether or not nurses had experienced fair dealings with medication errors. However, being disciplined (and in this context 'the procedure') was seen as an important step by some nurses, to come to terms with their medication errors.

THE ROLE OF THE MEDICAL STAFF

Doctors 'sorting things out'

According to the UKCC Advisory paper on the administration of medicines only doctors are to prescribe medicines. It falls within the duties of nurses to give out medicines according to the written prescriptions of doctors. Still, there may be exceptions when nurses will administer medicines without previous prescriptions of doctors. One exception can be the 'standing order' in certain circumstances. Generally the drugs to be given, and the situations to which this may apply are agreed upon beforehand in detail. This is common practice even though understood by the nurses as being illegal:

> *...but I mean, we all .. just illegally, we give Pethidine.. and Diamorphine, and then we get the doctors to sign for it later on .. (INT1 1031-1035).*

In most cases nurses first informed the medical staff of any mistake that occurred during drug administration. Mostly doctors did not see any need to take an incident further or have a nurse disciplined for a mistake.

A common practice seemed to be that nurses would ask a doctor to retrospectively write the patient up for the drug given. This would set the records straight and clear the nurse of having made a mistake.

In example one of the Scottish Group Discussion, this was mentioned after a nurse had given either Pethidine or Papaverine to a patient. (One of which had been prescribed, the respondent did not remember which). In order to *'clean up the books'* the patient was afterwards written up for what he had been given. General laughter of the group as this was related, indicated this to be common practice (GD-SC EX1 100-109).

Mike, in Interview Seven, related an incident where a colleague of his had found out that a nurse had mistaken Diamorphine for Morphine. He wanted the nurse to deal with the error herself. She found a solution by asking the doctor to write up a single dose of Diamorphine:

> *...she had gone and spoken to the doctor about it, and the doctor had written up a 'stat'* [2] *dose of Diamorphine, and she had signed it, retrospective .. (INT7 EX2 1377-1382).*

In Interview One, example two, a patient got an injection of Diamorphine twice. The first dose had not been recorded in the patient's notes. The incident was discussed at ward level. Doctor was informed by the ward sister and wrote up an extra dose of Diamorphine:

> *...don't worry about it, Thelma, I've got the doctor down and ... he's written it up. So its been prescribed now. We sorted it out (INT1 EX2 688-691).*

In Interview Two, example one, a nurse had forgotten to sign for the routine medication a patient had had (Valium and Co-Proxamol). A second dose was administered by Joan who took over the drug-round from this nurse. Joan became quite upset when this nurse simply wanted to sign for the first dose given, leaving Joan with the problem of the second dose. The doctor sorted the situation out, by prescribing the first dose as a 'stat' dose. In these incidents doctors were found to be

---

2 An abbreviation used in medical prescriptions, meaning 'immediately'

helpful in a practical way. Simple solutions were found when minor errors had been made that had no great consequences.

Pearl also mentioned how a medical doctor took the side of a nurse while her colleagues gave her little support:

> *... the one strong supporter she had, who helped her to get through the incident, was an obstetrician ... (INT3 EX2 492-494*

Nevertheless, some nurses did not seem to put too much trust in the way doctors would stand up for nurses. In the Scottish Group Discussion the following opinions were voiced:

> *Nurse: ... I found that .. med.. usually the medical staff are so .. ehm.. (GD-SC 1223-1225).*
>
> *Nurse: But they wouldn't be .. if it came to a court of law ...*
>
> *(General agreement of participants) Yeahh!! Yeah, they wouldn't be!, they wouldn't, that's right!*
>
> *Nurse: You'd be the one who would be ehm .. responsible (GD-SC 1235-1241).*

Doctor's fault?

As one reason for medication errors doctors' illegible handwriting was addressed:

> *...he had written .. 2 units, but the 'u' .. was such a scri.. you know, was such a scribble, it looked like 24 (...) so I had it checked, you know, (INT5 EX3 791-798);*
>
> *I ... never give them out, I just write 'prescription illegible' (INT5 EX3 826-828).*

Still if such a situation should lead to a medication error, the nurse might well be held responsible. He or she should be certain of what is to be given.

> *...the error was in the fact that .. the doctor had written up the chart and the chart hadn't been written up .. in.. in a legible way. (...) she (the nursing officer) said, you know, that's an understandable error. And did I realise .. the consequences of not checking .. thoroughly (INT10 EX5 681-695).*
>
> *...(assistant matron) gathered the facts, reprimanded me, even though the house officer agreed that his writing was unspecific enough to have been misread (REP5 11-16).*

It could also happen that a nurse questioned a doctor's prescription if she was uncertain about it. In fact nurses have a duty to do so.

Hilary, in Interview Twelve, demonstrated this with an example from her early nursing days:

> *I noticed that one had been written up.. the dosage ... it was not what it normally was, and I queried it (INT12 EX2 448-451).*

> *Hilary: ...she was... Indian, and... well I put it down to the fact that she probably had difficulty with the.. writing the drugs up in the Kardex..*

> *MA: I mean, how did she react, was she angry, .. or ..*

> *Hilary: No, no she was just glad that I had not given the drug. And wrote up the correct dosage (INT12 EX2 569-584).*

In two cases among my data which were brought before the Professional Conduct Committee, doctors' mistakes in writing up medication did not prevent the nurses from having to go through the disciplinary procedure at the highest level. Both nurses involved in the situation reported in Document Three, were found guilty of professional misconduct.

In Document Six, a serious mistake occurred through the intravenous administration of an overdose of Lignocaine. The doctors involved did not use the customary way of writing up the prescription which led the nurses to believe that they were to give the written amount of Lignocaine in each hour instead of throughout the stated time. Here the problem seemed to be rooted in the fact that nurses and doctors had difficulties in communicating. The nurses queried the prescription but were told to proceed with the administration which amounted to a lethal overdose for the patient. The nurses had to go through the ordeal of the disciplinary procedure at the highest level, but finally were not found guilty of misconduct. Still, they had to prove that they did act in good faith and that they could not have avoided the error:

> *Committee member: Could you identify to the Committee what your view is on the sort of climate which existed in the unit? I am thinking about the relationships between nursing and medical staff?*

> *Nurse M.: Usually if you queried something written it has got to the stage that they tell you they are the doctor and you are the nurse. On that night we queried the dosage with the doctor and he clarified it. We were told so often 'You are the nurse, I am the doctor' (DOC6 p. 44).*

Difficulties in communication between nursing and medical staff was most likely the cause of this mistake. Also in Documents Three and Four it was clearly a lack of communication which led to the drug incidents. The following comments were made:

> *Nurse S.: ... and the doctor found it very difficult to communicate with the nursing staff (DOC3 p. 10).*

A combination of factors led to this incident where a lethal dose of Digoxin was administered to a patient. The doctor wrote a wrong prescription, and the nurses made a mistake in calculating the amount to be given.

> *Committee member: Just one further question. What was your relationship with the medical staff normally, when you requested visits?*
>
> *Nurse C.: With most of the medical staff my relationship was fine. (...) I think they had respect for my clinical judgement. With this doctor there had been problems ...*
>
> *Committee member: So that there had been previous problems regarding requests for visits to patients?*
>
> *Nurse C.: From this doctor, yes (DOC4 p. 12).*

According to her clinical judgement Nurse C. had given a (therapeutic) dose of Valium Elixir to a patient who had convulsions. The doctor had verbally indicated that a much smaller dose was to be given. He had refused to attend the patient immediately. He also refused to write up the dose retrospectively. Nurse C. was found guilty of misconduct by the Professional Conduct Committee.

It also became apparent that nurses experienced the errors doctors might make or had made, as being dealt with more benignly by the medical hierarchy. In the German Group Discussion the nurses expressed the view that doctors can make mistakes without having to fear consequences:

> *...and the doctor only said it's nothing tragic. (...) Change it (the infusion that had been given at too high a speed) and the thing is done with. But I don't know what would have happened if I had connected it. That would have had consequences, really bad consequences (GD-D EX4 1168-1179);*
>
> *I don't know, everyone of us knows about things that happen, but a doctor will never be blamed. Or if (a doctor) did something, (...) nobody would say he should change his job..(GD-D EX8 1965-1973);*

...if I remember .. during all these long years I am nursing .. surely .. five patients who only suffered harm because some doctor (...) who acted carelessly, or simply made a mistake ..(...)...and doctors among each other seem to judge these things differently, yes, nobody would say he should quit his job.. (GD-D 1997-2008);

...like the medical staff...they seem to handle these things better (...) or maybe it is that each one says that can happen to you too, better to hold your tongue don't say anything .. (GD-D 2318-2326).

Sean, in Interview Four, talked about a situation where a doctor had given 40 mg of Frusimide to the wrong patient. This patient had a fresh myocardial infarction. Sean was quite upset about the incident. But his ward sister felt that the medical staff should deal with it among themselves. Sean finally did talk to a senior doctor about it, but the incident was not taken up.

In Interview Ten, Henry mentioned an incident he had heard about from a colleague, where a doctor had been given the drug-cupboard keys by a sister, in order to prepare intravenous injections himself. The doctor made a serious mistake, but the sister had to answer for it:

...the sister went through a severe disciplinary .. procedure for that. She got a written warning, for handing over the drugs and the keys. And I think the doctor get off light.. (10 EX5 2267-2273).

Doctors' attitudes to medication errors appeared to be far more relaxed than that of nurses. Doctors often helped nurses to sort out errors by using their prescribing authority. Where the relationship between doctors and nurses was one of trust and where good communication prevailed, a doctor would be happy to cover up a nurse's mistake, providing no serious harm had come to a patient. A doctor would primarily sort out the medical side of a mistake and not insist on reporting it to the nursing hierarchy. Nurses, on the contrary, seemed to be more obsessive about initiating 'the procedure'.

In situations where there was tension between the medical and the nursing staff, mistakes happened due to the lack of trustful communication. That is, nurses were not able to ask for clarification and doctors did not supply appropriate information. Mistakes made by doctors were said to be dealt with more lightly within the medical hierarchy than among nurses.

Generally doctors operated from a position of greater power which was assured by their deeper medical knowledge and their position of primary responsibility for a patient's medical treatment.

THE IMAGE OF THE NURSE AND OF NURSING

Nurses' reactions to patients' perception of nursing

The public image of nursing and of nurses is generally marked by high expectancy. Characteristics such as practical skills, compassion, patience and knowledge are attributed to nurses. The picture nurses have of themselves is influenced in its production and maintenance by public opinion of nursing and of nurses. It is also influenced by the training nurses receive and by the values which are transmitted during nurse education. Most strongly however, the image nurses have of themselves is influenced by the individual patients nurses have contact with in the context of their work. Nurses, like everybody else, respond to the expectations and the manner with which they are approached. But nurses also have to reconcile the reality of everyday life (which includes errors), with the image that they are expected to live up to.

Patients convey to nurses the idea that 'nurse knows best' and that her/his judgement can well be trusted. Nurses participating in this study commented on patient's views of nurses in the following manner:

> *...but I suppose, again, patients think, well, nurse knows best.. (INT9 EX1 414-417);*
>
> *...she didn't even question the fact that why she hadn't had (her Insulin) (...) because, well nurse surely knows best. And that's .. one of the attitudes a lot of people have, .. (INT9 EX1 1696-1703);*
>
> *... and a lot of that I think is 'cos we stand in a uniform. They see us as this person on a pedestal.. (INT9 EX1 2052-2055).*
>
> *I think the attitude is .. in nursing this thing, you know, a lot of it is that you .. don't make errors. That you, you know, tend to have a perfectionist viewpoint on things. Through your training . You know, you should never be in a situation where you make an error (INT10 EX1 988-998).*

The quotes above were taken from the discourse of nurses about patient's perceptions of nurses and nursing. These perceptions led to the nurses' image of themselves which is illustrated in the extracts below:

> *...if we made a mistake, then we'll have to .. be accountable for it and you have to be able to stand up, and ... say, well .. I did it, it was my fault .. (INT2 EX1 262-267).*

> *I take my responsibilities .. very seriously, I'm very serious about my work, and, and you know, I, I just .. people come in for a service, which .. and they trust you .. and they, they put all their trust in you, when they come into hospital, and I think that we have .. eh .. you know, its, its our responsibility, to make sure that we fulfil that trust.. (INT2 EX2 765-777).*

Being responsible for patients' welfare, and being accountable for their own actions was seen by the participants of this study in the context of the image described above.

To ascertain patients' welfare through professional standards

In order to ascertain patients' welfare, nurses are qualified to carry out the various tasks according to accepted standards. This qualification includes knowledge and skills in the administration of medicines. The UKCC Code of Professional Conduct makes statements about these matters:

> Each registered nurse, midwife and health visitor shall act, at all times, in such a manner as to justify public trust and confidence, to uphold and enhance the good standing of the profession, to serve the interest of society, and above all to safeguard the interest of individual patients and clients.
>
> Each registered nurse, midwife and health visitor is accountable for his or her practice and in the exercise of professional accountability shall:
>
> 1) Act always in such a way as to promote and safeguard the well being and interests of patients/clients.
>
> 2) Ensure that no action or omission on his/her part or within his/her sphere of influence is detrimental to the condition or safety of patients/clients.
>
> 3) Take every reasonable opportunity to maintain and improve professional knowledge and competence (UKCC 1984 p. 2).

As to the administration of medicines the UKCC has issued an advisory paper which addresses legislation and the doctors' and the pharmacists' roles as well as the role of nurses as regards the administration of medicines. It states:

> The exercise of professional judgement (which involves the application of his/her knowledge and experience to the situation faced) will lead the practitioner to satisfy himself/herself that he/she is competent to administer the medicine and prepared to be accountable for that action. Once that decision has been made, the practitioner follows a sequence of steps to ensure the safety and well being of the patient, and which must as a prerequisite be based on a sound knowledge of the patient's assessment and the environment in which care is given. (Various details as to checking and administration as well as recording follow here), (UKCC 1986 p. 7).

On several occasions respondents addressed pharmacological knowledge as well as knowledge of the drug administration procedures as being of great importance in order to live up to the expected standards.

> *I think we all know exactly what the procedures is, for giving medicines is, (INT7 EX1 410-412);*

> *I think I have a good knowledge of the drugs that are being given (INT7 EX1 440-442).*

Thus, the image nurses have about their own professional qualification is instilled by the initial nurse training and education; and it is further underpinned by updating their knowledge and their skills. The attendance at post-qualification courses appeared as a subject of investigation in some of the UKCC documents that were at my disposal:

In Document Six the manager of Nurse P. and Nurse M. is being questioned by a member of the Professional Conduct Committee:

> *Committee member: Would Nurse P. and Nurse M. to your knowledge have a CCU (Coronary Care Unit) course?*

> *Manager: No, they have not (DOC6 p. 34).*

In Document Three similar questions are posed regarding Nurse E. and Nurse S. Regarding Nurse E.:

> *Committee member: In terms of in-service training and lectures and seminars, what sort of programme has she undertaken?*
>
> *Manager: She has had annual lifting lectures, annual fire lectures, and she has attended various lectures and seminars; Nurses Role in Organ Donation; Care of the patient being nursed on a Ventilator; Pain Relief Seminar in 1988; and an updating on drugs in the continuing education department; (...)*
>
> *Committee member: In terms of the extended role,[3] does she have a variety of certificates in relation to that?*
>
> *Manager: Yes, she did (DOC3 p. 17).*

Regarding Nurse S.:

> *Committee member: Is it right that she also was in receipt of extended role certificates?*
>
> *Manager: She was (DOC3 p. 19).*

The possession of such certificates seemed to be of great importance in order to identify the lack of knowledge or skills as a possible cause of a mistake. These certificates represented an assurance that an individual nurse was in the position to uphold high standards while exercising her or his duty. In a way they provided an exoneration for managers and senior nurses: if a mistake happened, it should not have been due to a lack of skills or of knowledge. To ascertain this, rested with senior management staff.

The shattered image

Nurses are socialised into their roles during basic nurse education and training. The learning process that is initiated here and augmented in post qualification courses gives nurses a specific image of themselves. The knowledge and the skills that are taught and learned during training and during post qualification courses easily carry the notion of the need for perfectionism. Thus, nurses are taught to comply with the

---

3 The 'extended role' of nurses refers to certificates issued after appropriate theoretical and practical instruction regarding the administration of certain drugs by special techniques.

image of the professional who always copes and who never makes mistakes. This is reinforced in practice by patients and by colleagues. Socialisation, as Berger states, is more than learning:

> The individual not only learns the objectivated meanings but identifies with and is shaped by them. ... and makes them his meanings. He becomes not only one who possesses these meanings, but one who represents and expresses them (Berger 1969 p. 15).

Being socialised as nurses who carry this burden of expected perfectionism, it was not surprising when the participants of this study commenting on their experience of having made a medication error, said that they were devastated, that their confidence was shattered, or that they felt they had let themselves down. Some examples from the data are:

> *I felt sick. I lost a lot of my confidence and there is never a day but I think about it and I am very cautious when giving out medication now, although I was never aware of not being careful before the incident (REP2 91-97).*

> *The occurrence then was a nightmare. It fairly shook my confidence (REP2 114-115).*

> *Felt very angry about it. Reactions - anger, fear, ashamed, let people down (REP3 67-68).*

> *..she lost all confidence after that .. (INT3 EX2 592).*

> *I was actually .. quite annoyed with mysell ... (INT5 EX1 129-130).*

> *I felt I'd sort of let mysell down.. (INT5 EX1 141-145).*

> *I'd let my standards slip.. (INT5 EX1 494-496).*

> *I mean, I could have died, there and then, on the spot .. I thought the end of my world had arrived, I felt terribly sick, I felt horrified, (INT6 EX1 215-220).*

> *...it was the most devastating feeling.. (INT6 EX1 416).*

Some nurses felt that they should not carry on with nursing any longer. Gemma for example said:

> *...and feel.. internally that you were a failure.. 'cos I just kept saying, (...) I should pack this job in. (...) if I could make a (...) mistake like that (...) I had no business holding that position (...) I was almost convinced.. that I really should give up nursing, quite convinced .. (INT6 EX1 878-892).*

Having made a medication error affected the core of nurses' image of themselves. The reactions very often were independent of whether any harm had come to the patient or not. For instance in Gemma's situation the patient suffered no ill effects.

Going through the procedure of dealing with a medication error in some instances seemed to serve the reconstitution of the impeccable image of a nurse. The reported reactions to a medication error can well be understood if this image of the nurse is taken into account. It can also be understood that, many nurses felt they had to report an error they had made, even if it was an insignificant one. What a nurse was and represented had to be reconstituted by *'sorting things out'*. But it can also be understood that fearing the public destruction of their image, nurses hesitated to report a mistake, especially if this image was reinforced by patients' positive comments on nurses' skills or knowledge.

A realistic picture of self

In several interviews the respondents remarked that after their mistake had happened, colleagues sat together, sharing experiences and realising (sometimes for the first time) that nearly everybody had some stories to tell of personal involvement with medication errors:

> *I didn't know, any of my staff had ever had any of these problems until .. I sat there that morning and (...) and they all said, but sister, this has happened to me, and this is happened to me and blablabalblabla .. (MA: mmm), Ehm .. and I thought, "gosh, yes well, I'm not the only one.." (INT9 EX1 1578-1588).*

Living through the experience of having made a medication error contributed in many cases to the formation of a new, a different image of self. Chris said:

> *I don't think I'd ever questioned, ever before, whether I was a good nurse or not. I always thought, I was a good nurse. And .. I was good at me job and ..(INT9 EX1 1278-1277);*

> *MA: (referring to the effects of having made a medication error) What about your own image .. of yourself? As a nurse? ...*

> *Chris: It's probably pretty tattered at the moment, eh .. I always felt .. I was .. a good nurse. I set myself .. standards, high standards. Ehm ... I expected others around me too .. to meet them too. (MA: mmm), Eh .. and when this happened, that just crumbled. (...) I did feel, I wasn't fit to be a nurse, how could I do this to somebody. Why did I forget.. now, how did I miss that.. that was ridiculous, and .. the image of myself wasn't probably as great as I'd thought .. previously.. (INT9 EX1 1767-1787).*

By having experienced the involvement with a medication error and by having shared this experience, often a more realistic picture of self as a nurse emerged. Nurses would be more empathic with themselves as well as with colleagues. This was expressed by Chris, when she said:

> *I have more understanding now. (...) I would be able to say to somebody, listen, this has happened to me, I know how you feel, (...) because I have experienced it (INT9 EX1 1318-1328).*

THE SITUATION OF STUDENT NURSES

Learning to deal with mistakes

This theme focuses on the responsibilities of both student and trained staff when giving out medicines. Students are not supposed to give out medication unsupervised and they are supposed to ask the trained staff if they are not sure of any procedure or action in which they are to take part. However, of the 63 single incidents concerning drug errors brought to my notice in the data, 23 incidents involved students. In this section the situation of nursing students as it relates to the occurrence of medication errors is addressed.

To date, the greater part of a student nurses' time is still spent in practical situations on the ward. Here a student becomes inculcated with the idea of having to cope, of being responsible.

Chris talked about an experience she had as a student. She was made aware of nearly making a mistake while being assessed on drug administration. The senior nurse in this case drew her attention to the fact that she had forgotten to shake the bottle of Nystatin suspension before drawing up the amount needed.

... sister coughed and said, ohhh, I think, we better do that all again. And I thought .. what have I done wrong? (...) And she said to me, I would have failed you on your drugs-assessment, if .. you, again, hadn't shook that bottle, 'cos it says in red writing, you must shake the bottle, person's got to get the right dose of Nystatin. And it's an error. So I never forget to shake the bottle now (INT9 EX2 803-820).

Chris might well have learned that mistakes easily happen but can be prevented by vigilance. She might also have learned that mistakes must not immediately be punished but that there could be room for a learning experience.

Another respondent, Thelma, also recounted a situation from her student days:

... during my nurse training a friend ... I think she dropped a bottle of tablets on the floor (laughs) and picked them up and put them back in the bottle .. (INT1 EX3 249-254)

The student nurse was severely reprimanded by her seniors:

... she was taken to some senior nurse ... somewhere up in the turrets of the Royal Infirmary and she was really, really given a basting for that .. and she was an excellent nurse. (...) It really shattered her, INT1 EX3 1592-1505).

Thelma mentioned this occurrence twice in the context of our interview about medication errors. The situation had greatly influenced her:

I mean, I think that's stuck in my mind (INT1 EX3 258-259).

Both, Thelma and her friend might well have added to their personal picture of a nurse that mistakes must never happen and if they do, hopefully they are not found out.

Whose responsibility?

Several times respondents pointed out that qualified staff are responsible for any action taken of students. This also applies to mistakes students may make. The student nurses' situation during training in this country is quite an ambivalent one. They are asked to take part in the work-routine of the ward where they are placed, but in critical situations, for example when mistakes do occur, their student status grants them a certain immunity. This was conveyed by Gerald's discourse. He had experienced the protection a student enjoys when his own first error occurred:

I was seen by the clinical teacher, and that was that. The charge nurse, she was actually disciplined by the nursing officer (INT5 EX1 57-62);

I was protected as a student (INT5 EX1 394-395).

But for Gerald it was also clear, that now, being a staff nurse himself, he in turn had to accept his responsibility for students:

I always feel that ... even though I am doing drugs with a student .. you know, Its me .. I'm the trained, you know, I'm the registered nurse. So this... that's where I, .. you know, the buck stops (INT5 EX1 408-415);

MA: You would feel responsible, if a student made a mistake..

Gerald: Aha, if its me that is supervising, you know, I would feel responsible, because I am a trained member of staff, ...(INT5 EX1 590-596).

Other respondents too accepted this responsibility clearly:

I felt very numb and the student felt upset. I knew I had done a drug error as I had not gone to the patient with her (REP1 44-47).

Henry, regarding a student in his charge who had made a mistake said:

And I felt really sorry for her and I felt responsible for her as well (INT10 EX1 356-358).

However, it was Henry who had to answer for the situation. The following exchange took place when he talked about the consequences of the incident:

Henry: I discussed it with her, and I tried to tell her, that it wasn't her fault. I explained my responsibility for .. that situation (...).

MA: And it had no further consequences for her? Students are covered in a different way, aren't they?

Henry: Yeah..

MA: Yeah, they are allowed to ma.. make mistakes..

Henry: Yeah! That's true (INT10 EX1 462-471).

This was even applied to students who had undergone previous training and already had gained a nursing qualification. Pearl, in Interview Three, referred to example two, where a student-midwife gave too much Insulin to two pregnant women. The Insulin had been checked by the midwife in charge who was occupied with a life-threatening situation at the time. Pearl talked about the consequences the incident had for the midwife:

> *Pearl: But the sad thing out of (...) the whole situation, was that the girl had to go through the procedures, the midwife, because she was responsible. (...)*
>
> *MA: Not the student?*
>
> *Pearl: Not the student midwife. No, because she was protected under the fact that she was a student status. (...) although it seems so wrong, because she ..(...) would have been trained to give Insulin in her nursing training, 'cos she was you know, trained nurse already, but in, in the rules, its the midwife, the trained midwife, that's responsible. The student wasn't (INT3 EX2 456-483).*

Gerald emphasised that it is part of the trained staff's duty to teach; and that included taking a certain amount of responsibility for a student's action:

> *I mean there is me, I'm, you know, .. I'm their, I'm.. they are training. I'm there to .. teach (INT5 608-611).*

This was seen in a similar light by other respondents:

> *...its important to .. work with students as much as possible, 'cos I think you're more cautious, when you work with students (INT4 EX1 1354-1359).*
>
> *...we always checked (medications) with students, when we were on, because obviously they have to gain confidence in dealing with drugs, (INT4 1746-1749).*
>
> *...on this floor, from what I can see anyway, when the staff nurses do the drugs with the students, that is exactly what they do. And it is time consuming, it takes twice as long to do the drug round as it normally would, when you're only doing it yourself. But they do it. Ehm .. and I suppose that's all part of it, its the education right throughout (INT9 2068-2080).*

There also seemed to be a certain protectiveness from the side of the trained staff. Fearing that a student might be severely reprimanded, Anne said regarding a mistake a student had made under her supervision:

> *I was more concerned of it for the student, because the student's .. you know, would have got in trouble, I thought, well it was my fault, (INT8 EX2 161).*

Gerald however, saw the situation of a student quite realistically. Of course, a student could not just do what he or she liked, without being held responsible:

> *...if I (as a student) had went in, see, I went in actually, taken that drug by mysell, got the keys, got it, given it by myself, then I think, I, you know, I would have been.. open to, you know, sort of problems (INT5 EX1 395-401).*

The student in Henry's example was said to know of her own responsibilities. This was discussed among the trained staff:

> *...the student nurse should have known better, in the first place not to give medicines out, (INT10 EX1 594-597).*

The checking and giving out of drugs is the responsibility of qualified nurses. They have the legal responsibility for a medication error a student under their supervision might make. This was clearly demonstrated in Document One, where allegations were made against Nurse A., being the nurse in charge. Even though the student had administered the lethal dose of nebulizer-fluid into the patient's vein no charges were held against her by the UKCC as she was not yet registered. She only appeared at the UKCC hearing and gave evidence. In fact it was mentioned in the document that she was about to take her final examinations as a nurse in the near future. Obviously she had not been suspended from duty, nor was her training terminated.

The charges drawn up against Nurse A. by the Professional Conduct Committee of the UKCC in this case were:

> *1) That you (...) failed to give adequate instructions to a student nurse on the administration of a drug via nebulizer;*
>
> *2) That you (...) failed to ensure that a drug was correctly administered to a patient;*
>
> *3) That you (...) initialed a drug prescription sheet without ensuring that the drug had been administered by the correct route;*
>
> *4) That you (...) failed to notify the Doctor immediately on your discovery that a drug had been incorrectly administered to a patient; (DOC1 p. 1,2).*

All charges were supplemented with the charge of professional misconduct. Nurse A. admitted to the facts of the charges but not to the counts of misconduct. In the hearing Nurse A. was finally found guilty of misconduct, but her name was not removed from the register.

Doing the drug round with a student was understood as an added responsibility for qualified nurses. The participants in this study made it clear that they accepted the responsibility for the act of giving out the medicines as well as for the teaching process they were engaged in. They saw their duty in instructing and teaching students and in supervising their actions. Of students, it was expected that they would act under instruction and under supervision only. They should be aware of the fact of being engaged in a teaching/learning process and they should accept the responsibility for their own learning without overstepping their limits. When talking about mistakes that happened to students, the participants accepted that students were protected from disciplinary action.

Support in the Situation of Medication Errors

Regaining professional confidence

The theme of support was addressed in most interviews, self-reports and during both group-discussions. By support nurses seemed to mean helpful behaviour of colleagues and others toward the nurse responsible for the medication error. As has been mentioned above, nurses stated how the experience of having made a medication error caused them extreme distress and how their confidence was shattered even to the point where they felt unfit to be a nurse any longer.

The main objective for a nurse after having gone through such a stressful situation, would be to utilise the lessons learnt in the process, and to integrate the experience into her/his personal and professional life, in order to regain her/his professional confidence. Getting support from others helped this process. Getting no support was experienced as hindering, as making the whole situation worse. Both being supported or support being withheld, presupposed that the mistake was known about.

Possibly one of the reasons why nurses admitted even to negligible mistakes in drug administration (as some of my examples show), could have been the need to expose themselves to the supportive acts of colleagues and others, even at the risk of being subject to punitive measures. Unfortunately sometimes, going through 'the procedure' in an official way was the only outcome of reporting a mistake.

In the following section I first address situations where nurses experienced a disappointment in their hope of being supported. I then describe how support was given and experienced. I show what support consisted of and how and by whom it was given.

Disappointment in the need for support

Pearl, in Interview Two, example two, talked about a situation of a colleague, where this colleague was dropped *'like a hot potato'*:

> *...that was just horrifying how everybody else.. like dropping her like a hot potato, you know, .. (INT3 EX2 527-528).*

Apparently from the nursing side nobody, *'but a couple of midwives'* supported her through this difficult time. It was the obstetrician *'who helped her to get through the incident'*. This was perceived as almost *'bizarre'*. It should have been *'the other way round'*, meaning that support was expected by Pearl of the nursing colleagues, not of the doctor.

> *Pearl: (...) she had a couple of midwifes who were supporting her to a certain extent, but basically,.. nobody wanted to know.*
>
> *MA: How did the others act .. towards her?*
>
> *Pearl: Fairly cruel, ... (INT3 EX2 539-547).*

This nurse was suspended from duty for a time, and even after the incident was resolved she was not allowed to be in charge of the unit any more.

> *...her immediate superior .. just ..you know, she would ignore her more than anything else, and when she did come back after her suspended time of duty .. she refused to let her be in charge of the ward... (INT3 EX2 548-554).*

Gemma, in Interview Six, mentioned the lack of an official opportunity to be helped through the situation by a counsellor:

> *I think, not having anyone at home, really.. to go home and weep on somebody's shoulder (MA: yeah), is sometimes very .. the hardest part.. (MA: I was wondering ..), I got one son, ehm, but I mean, eh .. what does a young 20 year old interested, in what his mother gets up to, really, ehm .. so there isn't really anybody from that point.. (INT6 EX1 1052-1063);*

> *...in a situation like that, it would be nice to have had a counsellor (INT6 EX1 449-452);*

> *I think that's where we, we let down our colleagues, really (INT6 EX1 1064-1082).*

Chris, in Interview Ten, example one, felt that she could not even talk to her husband about her mistake:

> *I didn't even tell my husband this. 'cos I felt, I was admitting, I was a .. a rotten nurse.. (INT9 EX1 295-297).*

In some instances nurses felt that they were let down by their managers, that they did not get the help and understanding they had hoped for. For instance Henry, after he had informed his manager of the mistake, experienced that the matter was followed up according to 'the procedure', but no sympathy was offered to him.

The situation was dealt with in a punitive manner:

> *I felt heavy disciplined, I felt I had been let down.. (INT10 EX1 289-291).*

The nursing officer had called him to his office. Henry had to bring the Kardex along and both went through the situation. Henry described the attitude of the nursing officer as of little help:

> *I found his attitude very dictatorial, (INT10 EX1 179-180).*

> *...he took it through a sort of like, very disciplinary approach.. (INT10 EX1 182-184).*

This was substantiated by Chris in Interview Nine:

> *...a lot of them said .. they knew what their managers were like, and if .. they could have got away with not telling the manager, they wouldn't have, bec.. they wouldn't have told them, because they knew .. kind of, what the response is going to be. And it was going to be dreadful. They would wipe the floor with them, and take it as far as they could possibly take it, giving them no support at all, really just made them feel more wretched than they already did (INT9 1223-1238).*

A participant in the Scottish Group Discussion was very blunt about the perception she had of her nursing officer:

...one of the worse nursing officers that you would hope.. and you would.. you would die, (GD-SC EX1 474-477),

I got a phone call, he said 'Over in my office, now!' (GD-SC EX1 765-766).

Also Jane in Interview Twelve, talked about the lack of support from her manager. After her mistake (a relatively minor one) she was banned from giving out drugs. As to the manner her situation was dealt with, she felt that this was done in a very harsh way:

...our director of nursing services .. was .. a real dragon, she was absolutely hated by everybody, (INT11 EX1 994-997);

...and the nurse manager, eh, was also on the Committee, (...) obviously the nurse manager couldn't say anything overtly, but .. ehm .. he more or less .. said to me, that he felt that she had been extremely harsh. I mean, no .. nobody .. felt, .. that the situation was constructive .. in any way. (INT11 EX1 1011-1021).

I had asked my respondents to talk about what helped and what hindered in dealing with the situation of a medication error. The lack of support which resulted in the solely punitive character of the disciplinary measures was experienced as unhelpful and hindering in regaining professional confidence.

Support given by medical staff

One first important feature of support emerged as coming from the side of the medical staff. Generally nurses felt that it was most important to inform a doctor about a mistake. Example one, in Interview Seven showed how the medical reassurance was of paramount importance and was sufficient for Mike to deal with the mistake. Informing the doctor to safeguard the patient's well- being was all, Mike felt, that was needed in his situation. He did not think it necessary to report his error to the nursing hierarchy.

...but because it was a, (...) a cardiac drug, ehm .. I felt, that I had to .. find out from the doctor, I had to inform the doctor that I had given a patient who wasn't prescribed that drug, that drug (INT7 EX1 356-363).

...if the medical staff are aware that I have made a drug error, then any sort of .. danger, that I placed this patient in, at least the medical staff are aware.(...) So they would have known .. straight away, (INT7 EX1 616-624).

> *...the house officer who was on duty (...) told me that, .. now, I needn't worry about it eh, and we left it as .. at that.. (INT7 EX1 58-72).*
>
> *I found he was very sympathetic, Ehm, .. he was concerned about me, (INT7 EX1 204-206).*
>
> *I think .. the, the, the remark that he made, showed, that he was eh .., did help me. Because, he obviously didn't get annoyed, he, he eh .. he tried to calm my fears (INT7 EX1 227-232).*

The reassurance on medical grounds after a medication error had been realised, played an important role for most nurses:

> *After theatre the Surgeon came to the ward to 'slap my hand' and reassure me that the patient was alright, that the anaesthetist had been able to adjust the anaesthetic. The anaesthetist never mentioned the incident to me (REP2 64-70).*
>
> *But .. I really must say this specific doctor reacted well. There was no uproar.. (...) He talked sensibly with me (GD-D EX2 253-261).*
>
> *...but I must say, I really thought this doctor's reaction was very good.. (GD-D EX2 322-325).*
>
> *But as I said it is to be noted how everybody agreed on the positive reaction of the doctor. (GD-D EX4 1198-1201).*
>
> *...so immediately I phoned the medical staff, who were .. absolutely wonderful about it, (GD-SC EX3 930-932).*
>
> *...you being reassured by the medical staff, that there is no damage, and that makes you.. well, OK! (GD-SC 1560-1563).*
>
> *...when I told the doctor, the doctor said, well, I'm happy with this, ehm.. you told me, so .. don't take it any further, (INT11 EX1 258-262).*

In some situations the doctor talked to the patient and explained the medical implications of the mistake:

> *However he (the resident) came to see the patient and told him that the pharmacy had issued the drug in a different dose and not to worry but we would observe him! (REP4 24-32).*

The understanding attitude of most medical staff was remarked upon frequently. It emerged that nurses greatly relied on the support given by doctors. Doctors' reassurance helped them to overcome the distress caused by having made an error in the administration of medication.

Supportive managers

Reporting an incident and having it dealt with in an official manner, seemed to be a way of overcoming an otherwise insurmountable feeling of guilt. This was important to most nurses participating in this study in spite of a doctor being notified of a situation and being satisfied that it needed not to be taken any further. Some nurses felt that not bringing a mistake to the attention of the nursing hierarchy would add to the problem. Jane, in Interview Eleven explained:

> *I have to inform my manager, and I think I ... ehm, that was the right thing, becau.. to do, because we had had it drummed into us so much ... you must do this.. you will do this.. If.. to me if I hadn't have said anything at that stage .. and then, it had come out into the open, later .. I mean having made the mistake.. its hard to admit it, but, .. it was .. it was something I'd done wrong, which I had to pay for, and .. okay, to be honest and admit it at that stage, .. will take whatever the punishment is, .. which ..(...) to cover it up, and .. to me that's a far worse crime to cover it up (INT11 EX1 264-288).*

A report was generally made to the next senior person, be it the charge nurse, the unit manager, or a nursing administrator. Approachability was an important feature nurses included in the notion of support. Being approachable had two components. First it was embedded in the personality of the senior person. Secondly it depended on the way the hierarchical structure of a given institution was set up. Both components are addressed in turn. As to the first component, Chris said:

> *She (the nursing manager) was very good, she really was excellent. She said to me then, 'right, fine, go away and write a statement', (...) she said to me, (...) 'I can't make you feel any worse than you already do now' (INT9 EX1 531-540).*

In spite of the positive aspects mentioned above, fear and apprehension persisted when nurses talked about having to deal with managers and the nursing hierarchy. Possibly the negative experiences nurses had themselves or heard about, influenced them strongly. Jane said:

> *...its the whole process of being dragged up in front .. various committees and panels, (INT11 EX1 98-101).*

Nurses seemed to find it hard to overcome their fear of the managerial hierarchy. This was not surprising as to some managers it seemed to be important to make sure that their status was well known and recognised. Even though these managers too appeared to present a face of good will and approachability. The following extract from the interview with Sean demonstrates this:

I was very sort of sympathetic, and when I talk to people I like to be very sort of,... person to person like .. having said that, you know, I think she would obviously, be very aware of the fact that she was a staff nurse, and I was her charge nurse, remember, (...) I was really doing it .. ehm, as her immediate superior. You know, because I had to do it, you know, as part of the routine (INT4 EX1 2250-2260).

But then again, some nurses mentioned that the first reaction of their managers was really helpful and understanding. To the one respondent in the Scottish Group Discussion it came as a surprise, when her manager whom she had described as *'one of the worse nursing officers..'*, behaved in an unexpectedly civil manner:

...she knew (the staff nurse who had made the error), 'I'm in for a hard time here', and .. fortunately, he came in and he was very friendly. Which took us all by surprise! (GD-SC EX2 541-546).

Helpful and supportive reactions of managers can be demonstrated with further examples:

Nurse: I phoned my charge nurse at home, and would tell him, what's happened, and again, he was very supportive,

MA: What did he say?

Nurse: (...) "these things happen", (...) he didn't .. sort of shout at me (...) he said ehm .. "we all make mistakes, and .. we all learn from them", (GD-SC EX3 990-1005).

Joan, in Interview Two made some interesting comments on the aspect of approachability. Joan felt *'lucky'* about both, the way her *'management'* (meaning the hierarchical structure) was organised and how the responsible person dealt with problems in a *'humane'* way. Generally Joan felt that it was important to have a trusting relationship with the management, this would be helpful in dealing with medication errors:

...you have to have .. somebody that you feel that you can approach, and say ..look, I feel I've done .. I feel, I may have done something wrong, and not just with.. you know, bigger issues, like .. drug errors, with smaller things as well.. (INT2 1550-1558).

Approachability was not seen as contradictory to having respect for seniors. Joan said:

> *More approachable, again, more approachable, so .. that doesn't stop you having respect for them .. , you still have the respect, (INT2 1483-1486).*

In this interview the second component of approachability came to the fore. Here the hierarchical structure of the institution was addressed. Joan mentioned that their unit managers have their offices on the ward which ensured an easy access to them. This also made for a closer relationship between staff and management.

> *...they are just at the end of the corridor, and .. we see them every day, they know us on first name terms .. they ehm, .. they are human beings to us, you know, they are not,... the hierarchy, which I think, in some parts of nursing they are, (INT2 1462-1470).*

Support from the side of the managers was linked with the time they spend with the individual nurse and with the way they handled the situation. Chris, in Interview Nine said:

> *...and reported to my nursing officer that, it.. that happened. (...) I had a counselling session, which really wasn't a formal counselling session. She was very supportive. Ehm, asked how the lady was, kept an eye on the lady, ehm .. through phone calls that day to see how she recovered the day after. (INT9 EX1 205-217).*

It also seemed to be of importance for most nurses to be reassured about their professional qualities. This went with trust in their abilities from the side of the managers. If a nurse was suspended from giving out drugs alone, or from giving out drugs altogether, this made it very difficult for her to regain her confidence and to feel supported through the experience.

Jane, in Interview Eleven, felt this difficulty in her own situation too. She had been banned from giving out medicines, but she thought this measure to be justified:

> *I felt, yes, OK, its justified not to give out drugs. But what I .. ehm, .. felt bad about, was the position, that put me in, (...) it put me in a very awkward position. (...) I, I was a senior staff nurse at that stage, I .. when I was on duty, (...) we had to bring a nurse over from another ward .. to give out drugs ((INT11 EX1 612-636).*

Having to carry on with the normal duties seemed to be most helpful, even though this was hard to do. Gemma, in Interview Six, thought this to be the best way of getting over the experience:

> *I mean I had to get in there, and get on with the job of running the ward .. which was busy, (INT6 EX1 467-470).*

As for supportive measures from the side of superiors, the most important factor was to take time and make efforts to help to identify the cause of the error and to implement changes that could help to prevent further occurrences. This was emphasised by Henry:

> *I think the most helpful situation was the latter situation where, things were discussed, at ward level. Something constructive came out of it (INT10 EX4 1920-1925).*

Pearl, in Interview Three, said hypothetically:

> *...there should have been a counselling session (...) and worked out why .. it happened, and then look at the situation, did we not have enough staff on, if so, we need more staff, we can't let this happen again (INT3 1195-1203).*

Furthermore, it was experienced as helpful, if a senior nurse tried to keep an error within the unit and not make it her first objective to follow the disciplinary procedure up to the highest level. This was mentioned by Thelma in Interview One, when her ward sister decided to destroy the statements already written:

> *I instantly told sister that I had made a mistake (...) I accepted my fate, quite stoically, I mean I knew I was for the chop (INT1 EX1 229-246);*
>
> *Well, I just wrote down what actually happened, and I put it in an envelope and put it on our boss's desk. ...but the next morning the sister said, 'I have (...) torn it up, we don't need ..'(INT1 EX1 444-449);*
>
> *...said to me, 'I am not going to report this ... because .. I feel that you know exactly what you have done, why you have done it, I am actually responsible as well, and we've both learned from this and I am not going to take it any further'. She had taken advice from one of her peers, another sister, I think, and they decided that they wouldn't take it further, that I'd already crucified myself enough without going through ... Now whether or not she should have done that, I don't know, because there are procedures to be followed and ... but within that do we not have the ... eh ... can we ... can we be selective or can we ... I don't know, I don't know. But she didn't report it ...(INT1 EX1 264-284).*

If an error had to be followed up and the disciplinary procedure had to be engaged in, it was felt to be supportive when senior nurses exhibited sympathetic behaviour. This could be by contacting a Union representative who would explain the official procedures to be followed and accompany the nurse to the hearings at Board level. An example was given by Gemma:

> *I said 'What do I do next?' And she told me, (...) she said it would .. it would have to go to senior nursing level and .. that there would be an interview, and she suggested that I get my .. ehm, RCN representative .. .. to accompany me (INT6 EX1 300-317).*

Gemma, being subject to the investigation herself felt in her position as a ward sister, and as the person responsible for the error, that she should help the other nurses with the production of their statements:

> *...one of them was an enrolled nurse, (...) to pacify her, but to really .. back her up, (...) as she would have to write an incident (report) and I would check it for her, and you know, that she was, was laying out correctly, (...) but to reassure her, I was the one that was carrying the can, from the word 'go', (INT6 EX1 1398-1407).*

In most situations managers were said to be supportive, when nurses felt that they could approach them and talk about the occurrence. Respect for the position of authority did not increase for managers who appeared unapproachable. Where contacts were frequent between nursing staff and managers, mistakes seemed to be dealt with in a low key manner. A certain fear of the hierarchical structure however, could be discerned even though nurses did experience positive reactions to their medication errors.

Support by colleagues and 'others'

By far the greatest support most respondents talked about was given by colleagues. The support generally consisted in making time for talking about the incident among the team and by sharing experiences. Chris became quite animated when she talked about the reactions of her staff to the situation she had been responsible for:

> *The staff on the ward were fantastic. (...) they really were supportive .. because I'd.. I felt embarrassed, I was ashamed (INT9 EX1 327-335);*

> *...we discussed aaall .. those kinds of things (...) it was good to think, even it.. you weren't the only in the world to have done this (...) Ehm .. and listening to other people that was really .. supportive, 'cos you think.. well, (MA: mmm), they're fine, and they've picked themselves up from this (INT9 EX1 1252-1268);*

...we all.. we sat in the morning, when I first came on, (...) we chatted for a good half an hour then. And then when we do this handover in the afternoon , we have got a full hour, (...) And I think the whole hour was spent .. just .. going over, and over and over, and over. And then everybody at that point was saying, how .. 'this has happened to me'. And 'this was the circumstances', and 'this is how it was dealt with'. (...) I'm glad we spoke about it early, because .. that.. that was still fresh. It helped me right then, when I needed it (INT9 EX1 1531-1562).

I had asked Henry how the other staff in the ward reacted to his medication error:

Henry: Very supportive, yeah!

MA: In what way? What.. what was it..

Henry: Ehm .. supportive in .. the fact that, when I sat down and discussed it.. my feeling, my lack of confidence, in actually doing medicines (...) they tried to.. tried to make me look at it from the angle that that kind of thing does happen in an acute ward (...) and eh .. they also mentioned that they had made drug errors before. (...) just to sort of make.. make me not feel as if .. I was a major criminal (INT10 EX1 582-604).

Pearl, in Interview Three, mentioned the fact that it was most helpful for her to have a friend who also was a nurse in the same unit, with whom she could share many professional problems:

I talked ... (...) I'm sure yes, I mentioned it to .. ehm, ..one colleague, who .. we often chat about .. work. we're sort of friends like (...) we use each other as.. support .. mechanisms (INT3 EX1 374-383).

Henry related how a friend of his had confided to him his involvement with a medication error. His friend told Henry about the error a fortnight after it had occurred. Henry felt sympathetic towards him but thought it deplorable that there had been so little trust within his friend's working situation that he felt unable to admit to the mistake:

...he just panicked and .. he didn't tell anybody, he just watched the patient (INT10 EX3 835-838).

Talking to friends who were not nurses was not found to be helpful at first. The following dialogue with Gemma illustrates this:

MA: Have you sort of, had .. a possibility, or opportunity to talk to somebody since?

Gemma: Well, ehm.. only a, a friend of mine, I went through it all, and she was very sympathetic. I left it all till .. the whole thing was over and done with (...) I did pour it out to a .. couple of friends, but .. that's not what you want to talk about, when you are private ..(INT6 EX1 519-537).

Talking to a lay person did not eradicate the feeling of being devastated, as Gemma related. Her friend did not really understand the implications of what had happened.

> *...although as I say, eventually in time.. I, I said all to that .. close friend of mine, who sat and listened to it, and clucked, and sort of a 'hhaa' at the right time .. she didn't really understand the ins and outs of it. (...) she didn't take in the implication of it at all .. (INT6 EX1 1144-1158).*

To Joan in Interview Two, it provided an important source of support that she could share the situation with her family :

> *I'm sure I went home that day and said what had happened, you know, because you do have to get that sense of relief (INT2 EX1 480-486).*

Talking to a partner was helpful also for Henry, who stated that he found it easy to talk to his wife about anything. He said:

> *Henry: I talked to my wife about it. (...) .. she was supportive of me. (...) She worried quite a lot about it.*
>
> *MA: How did you feel about talking to her?*
>
> *Henry: Embarrassed! But no .. I felt easy, talking to her. I would talk to her more than anybody else. (...) But she is not a nurse. So she had .. quite an even balanced view of it. She didn't understand what medicines were given. But you know, she kind of talked ... supported me through this, what, if I am going to get the sack, what, if I can't do this job. (...) And she said, well, you are a very capable person. So she made me feel a lot better .. inside (INT10 EX1 1003-1061).*

Thelma's husband was a doctor thus, she found it good to talk to him. As already mentioned, Chris could not share her experience with her husband. She very strictly distinguished between professional problems and her private life.

As for Gemma, the situation she related, was experienced as one of the worse things in her life. The other one was divorce. What helped her through this most difficult time, where her professional identity was at stake, was her awareness of the value of her work.

> *...and trying to think that ... you were doing a job of value, in the long run, and in the meantime was to teach ... others, junior to you .. that eh .. mistakes can be made by even the most senior ... (INT6 EX 945-951).*

Thus, regaining and re-establishing her professional confidence made it possible for her to live with the knowledge of having made a medication error and to use her experience for the benefit of others.

Sharing the experience of having made a medication error with colleagues, was most important for my respondents in order to come to terms with their mistake. Being trusted by their superiors to carry on with their work as usual, helped to regain confidence in their professional abilities. Talking to friends or even close relatives who were not involved in nursing, was generally, but not always regarded as helpful and supportive.

Support given by patients

Involving patients actively in dealing with a medication error in some instances seemed to be helpful to nurses. Chris, in Interview Nine, talked to the patient whose Insulin she had forgotten and to the patient's husband. She found that both were very sympathetic:

> *Ehm, but I, I, I apologised to her, and she was saying, no, no, you know, these things can happen, (INT9 EX1 409-414);*

> *...thank goodness in many ways, they were the kind of people they were. Because he (the husband) had said, 'Ooch, you know, these things can happen, and .. (my wife) seems fine now and ..' (...) I mean he really could have .. gone to town with me. Yeah, ehm .. but they were .. very, very good.. (INT9 EX1 434-446).*

I specifically asked Chris how she felt, talking to the patient and her husband after the incident:

> *MA: So, I suppose talking to the relatives about .. having forgotten the Insulin, must have been very difficult as well!*

> *Chris: It was, because, then I was admitting to him.. and I was the sister of the ward. I have done this, and he was wonderful, he was, (...) he was a very, very nice gentleman, (...) And I did tell him .. all the story I told you, 'cos I felt, why shouldn't the man know .. all the circumstances. It wasn't I had just forgotten his wife's Insulin. Ehm .. and he.. his wife had been .. ehm, hospitalised for many years. In and out, and in and out, and in and out. Because of all her medical problems that she had, apart from her diabetes. And I think, because of that, he had some appreciation of .. what the ward situation was like. And it isn't always .. textbook fashion there's other things happen too. Ehm, and I do think, he probably appreciated .. (INT9 EX1 1722-1765).*

Also in the German Group Discussion one nurse felt that it was very important to talk to the patient about the mistake she had made:

> *...and after I had talked to the patient I told the doctor who felt that wouldn't have been necessary. (...) and I said it was important for me as regards to the trust ... (GD-D EX3 487-502).*

Patients and their relatives were said to be very understanding. Henry reported that the lady, who had been given too large a dose of Largactil by a student while Henry was attending to a patient who suddenly had a seizure, understood the situation well as she had witnessed it herself.

In some instances patients did not seem to take the situation very seriously, but still several nurses felt it was important to inform them. Gemma said:

> *I would expect her to be horrified, and yet.. you know, she didn't take in the implication of it all (INT6 EX1 1155-1158).*

Also in Interview Two, example two, where the breast milk of two mothers had been mixed up, Joan talked to the women concerned. They thought the incident rather funny as they did not really understand the possible implications of this mix-up.

Generally the respondents in this study felt that their respect for a patient compelled them to inform the patient about a mistake. This openness was rewarding as generally the patient's response was experienced as supportive.

Time-Talk-Trust

I have identified three components of support which played a role in what it meant to be supportive and to accept support.

First there was the time allocated to a situation where problems connected with the occurrence of a medication error were to be solved. Then there was the necessity to talk and be listened to; and lastly there was the trust in the personal and professional abilities of the nurse who made the error, expressed by colleagues, managers and patients.

This meant that colleagues, doctors, patients, managers and others made time to talk and that they would express their basic trust in the nurse who has made a medication error. On the other hand the nurses themselves would be prepared to invest time in order to discuss the situation which led to a medication error. They would be open to discussion and have trust in others, in order to utilise the mistake as a learning experience. As a result the nurses could see the value of their work, trust and like themselves, and regain professional confidence in order to carry on with life and work.

As for those giving support, they saw the positive results of their way of acting. For them too, a medication error could turn into a learning experience. In the end this would reinforce the relationships of all concerned.

CHAPTER 8
AN EMPIRICAL MODEL

INTRODUCTION TO THE CHAPTER

The phenomenon of medication errors is approached in this chapter from a structuring and descriptive viewpoint. A model is presented which portrays the structural context for the occurrence of medication errors. This empirical model gives an overview of most themes that were addressed by the participants of the study as described in the previous chapter.

This chapter represents the second level of analysis. It features two sections. In the first section the reality of medication errors is addressed and this reality is brought into context with Berger's perception of the construction of social reality (Berger 1969). The empirical model is outlined in this section. Figure 8 depicts as its main features three cornerstones. In the second and much longer section the three cornerstones are verbalised and described in detail. Figures 9-11 show the cornerstones in diagrammatic form.

With the empirical model the relationship is explored between the occurrence of a medication error, and (1) the factors or givens that were influential for nurses' acquisition of meaning after a medication error had occurred; (2) the reactions of nurses and other health care staff to this situation; (3) the ultimate effects, brought about by having lived through the experience of a medication error and the way with which it was dealt. I show how the givens or influential factors were changed by the experience and how they were turned into a new basis of givens which will be responsible for the way a medication error is reacted to and affects nurses and nursing.

The empirical model structures the large variety of themes which emerged from the data. One objective of this model is, to demonstrate the wide spectrum of subject matter that is related to the research question.

THE REALITY OF MEDICATION ERRORS - A FUNDAMENTAL DIALECTIC PROCESS

The leading question of this thesis was formulated as: "What does it mean to a nurse to be involved in a medication error?"

The occurrence of a medication error takes place within the social world of the health care services. In this study I concentrated specifically on the hospital setting. The action of nurses, as that of any other individual, is closely connected to the reality of their life world. Action generally is deployed as reaction to the experiences made in the context of this life world. At the same time any action within this reality has an effect on its structure, stabilising it or effecting change.

Berger describes the inherent dialectical character between the individual and society. He states:

> Society is a dialectical phenomenon in that it is a human product, and nothing but a human product, that yet continuously acts back upon its producer (Berger 1969 p. 3).

Berger addresses this fundamental "dialectical phenomenon" as consisting of three moments: externalisation; objectivation; internalisation (Berger 1969).

> Externalization is the on-going outpouring of human being into the world, both in the physical and the mental activity of men. Objectivation is the attainment by the products of this activity (again both physical and mental) of a reality that confronts its original producers as a facticity external to and other than themselves. Internalization is the reappropriation by men of this same reality, transforming it once again from structures of the objective world into structures of the subjective consciousness (Berger 1969 p 4, parentheses in the original).

The world is being perceived and acted upon within a specific reality. This reality influences human behaviour; but at the same time the actors influence the structures that constitute this reality.

This dialectical process can be traced in the health care setting when examining the phenomenon of medication errors. The meaning that is inherent in the experience of having been involved in a medication error is derived at on the basis of an existing reality, which is perceived and understood as external to the actors. In living through the experience of a medication error the individual nurse objectifies this reality in concrete acts. These acts are reactions which engender ultimate effects on the social reality of the life world. These effects are finally internalised as a new reality, which in turn acts as a new or a changed backdrop for subsequent experiences.

The diagram below shows the dialectical process of the construction of the social reality which supplies the context for the occurrence of medication errors. The diagram depicts an abstracted version of the empirical model. The three cornerstones of this model are:

- **Influential factors (givens) for the acquisition of meaning;**
- **Reactions to the occurrence of a medication error;**
- **Ultimate effects of the medication error, of the reactions to it and of the consequences that followed its occurrence.**

Figure 8 : Overview - of empirical model

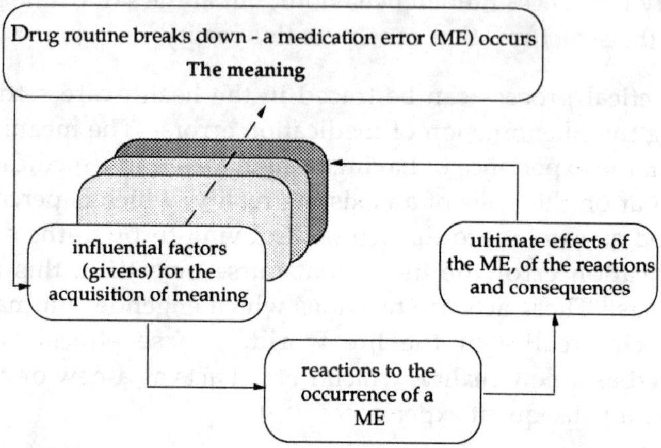

Each one of these cornerstones is addressed in turn in the next section, preceded by its diagrammatic representation. Hereby an overview is effected over the data of this study. This overview represents a structured picture of the nurses' reality regarding their experiences with medication errors.

THE THREE CORNERSTONES OF THE EMPIRICAL MODEL

Influential factors (givens) for the acquisition of meaning in the situation of medication errors

A medication error generally is an isolated and rare situation within the career of a nurse. The participants of this study spoke about their experience in terms of an exceptional occurrence. However, the meaning that was attributed to medication errors was not only acquired alone from the fact that they happened. The individual meaning of a medication error depended on a variety of givens.

These givens could be said to represent the social reality which in turn influenced reactions to a medication error as well as the ultimate effects of such an occurrence. Figure 9 gives a summary of this reality.

Figure 9: Influential Factors

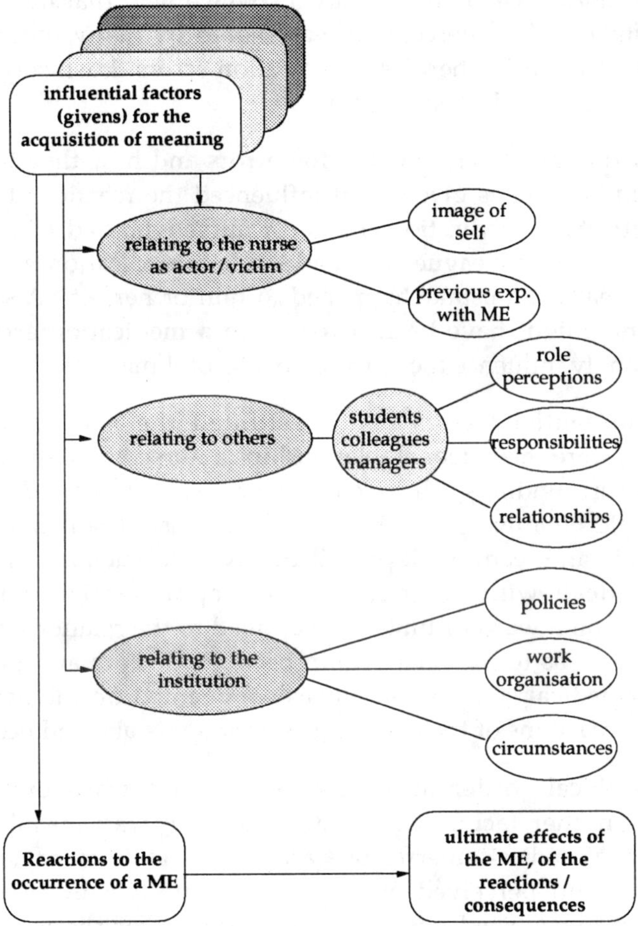

Medication errors happened in the context of personal relationships and against the backdrop of certain institutional work-settings; they involved people who had a personal understanding of nurses and of nursing. The categories of personal relationships and of a given institutional work setting comprised influential factors of how meaning was individually acquired.

The image a nurse had of her or himself as a nurse and as a person, as well as the perception a nurse had of nursing, were the bases on which meaning was arrived at. Several nurses mentioned the fact that an image of nurses existed among patients which held that nurses do not make mistakes. This perception was shared by many nurses until a mistake did happen. Therefore, medication errors drastically changed the image a nurse had of her/himself.

Previous experiences with medication errors and how they were dealt with, could be seen as givens that influenced the reactions to and the ultimate effects of medication errors. A nurse who had witnessed the victimisation of a colleague who had made a medication error would react with fear if a mistake happened to him or herself. Also the fact that a nurse might have been involved in a medication error before would strongly influence the reaction to a second mistake.

Further influential factors that constituted the backdrop for any experience, were the personal relationships a nurse had with the people in her/his surroundings. The micro climate on a ward would be good or bad. It could be impregnated by trust or mistrust. If an atmosphere of comradeship and team-work prevailed, any crisis such as a medication error was dealt with differently than if apprehension marked the relationship on a ward or unit. This applied to the relationship among nurses as well as to the relationship between doctors and nurses and other paramedical staff. Most nurses commented on the helpful and supportive reactions of their colleagues after a mistake had occurred.

The hierarchical order in an institution, on a ward or on a unit provided another factor which influenced the way meaning in the situation of a medication error was arrived at. How management was understood and perceived by the ward or unit team and the way management was acted out, was most decisive for the meaning that nurses assigned to their experiences. Approachability and availability was addressed as of great importance by the respondents in this study. It was important to the nurses of this study that they could trust their managers and their charge nurses and that they were easily approachable. Nurses felt that a good rapport with their managers made it easier to report mistakes. If managers showed their availability through their frequent presence within a ward setting nurses felt more at ease with them. If problems were discussed as they occurred on a day to day basis, medication errors would be dealt with in an atmosphere of trust.

Still, some nurses feared or even hated their managers because they had experienced them as rude or aggressive. Some situations were reported in the data where nursing managers hid behind rules and regulations and insisted on following their procedure books regardless of the circumstances that led up to a medication error.

Very often students were involved in the medication errors, as participants of this study mentioned. The trained staff's perception of the student's role played an important part here. The responsibilities involved in having students in a given clinical area were generally accepted by the trained staff. It influenced the way medication errors were dealt with. Generally the most senior person giving out medicines was held responsible if a mistake occurred. However, the participants distinguished between the personal accountability each nurse had for her or his own action, and the professional responsibility of the nurse in charge.

Finally the institutional work-setting was addressed as of importance. The organisation of work, and staff distribution were closely connected with the management structure of the work place. Being understaffed was a cause for stressful situations which predisposed staff to making errors.

The immediate circumstances surrounding the occurrence of a medication error were also taken into consideration in this context. Distracting incidents like the sudden collapse of a patient could add to the difficulty of an already precarious situation where a heavy work load and staff shortage caused a nurse to work under unusual stress.

Policies and their momentary importance also played a role in the way medication errors were perceived and dealt with. They too formed part of the influencing factors of how the experience of a medication error acquired meaning. The way policies were understood and acted upon very much depended on previous, especially recent, occurrences of medication errors. Several nurses felt that their situation would have been dealt with quite differently if the hospital management had not been alerted to the problem of medication errors by some recent incidents.

In some situations it appeared that the procedure for dealing with medication errors had been recently looked into because their occurrence was to be reduced. This influenced the way a specific occurrence would be dealt with. One nurse mentioned the *'witch-hunt in drug errors'* which was going on at the time when her mistake happened. Another nurse mentioned that after a new nursing officer had taken up his post medication errors were dealt with in a much tighter manner than before.

The influential factors for the acquisition of meaning proved to be related. The image of the nurse and of nursing was reflected in the relationships among staff and students. The perception of the managerial roles influenced these relationships by the way a given work setting was organised and run.

These factors constituted the externalised reality of nurses' social world which, via the objectivation in lived experience, would be internalised during the dialectical process of reconstructing or fashioning anew this reality with the added experience of having been involved with a medication error.

Reactions to the occurrence of medication errors

Taking into account the influential factors or givens that provide the context in which medication errors occur, I now proceed to describe the reactions to medication errors which my respondents talked or wrote about. Figure 10 summarises these reactions.

Fig. 10: Reactions to the occurrence of a medication error

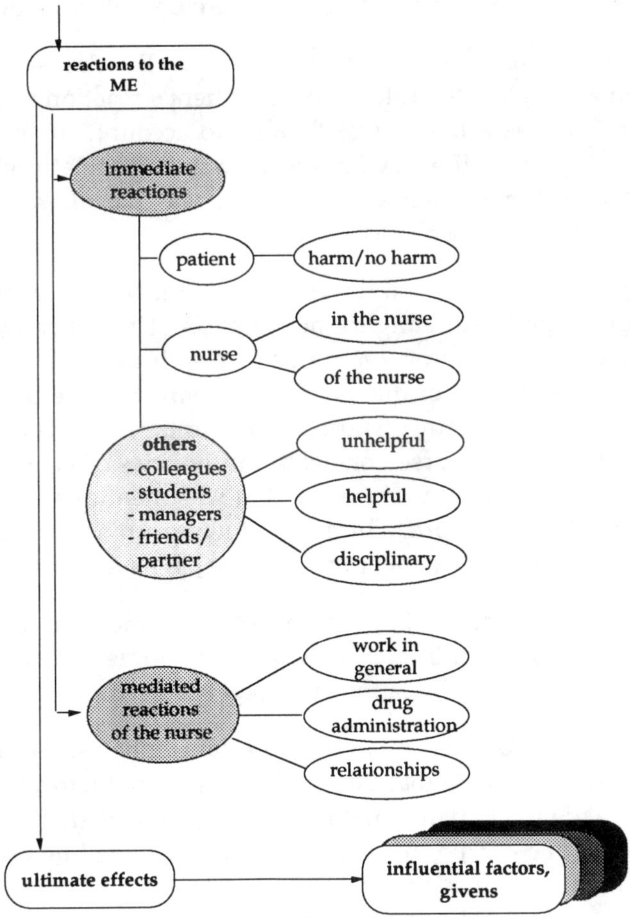

I have differentiated between immediate reactions and mediated reactions. The immediate reactions can be seen from the perspective of the patient, the perspective of the nurses concerned, and that of others such as colleagues, managers and friends or partners. Those reactions which did not directly concern the error itself but were caused or affected by it, I have called mediated reactions. I do not see them on the same level as the ultimate effects. The mediated reactions can be perceived from the nurses' point of view as a kind of reactivity which in turn would bring about the ultimate effects of the experienced medication errors. Both types of reactions are described below.

If the patient's perspective is taken, naturally the severity of a medication error played a role as to the patient's reaction to it. At first the physical or medical side was taken into account. If serious harm was done to a patient, the way he/she as well as the relatives reacted to the situation, differed from a mistake that was harmless and had no medical or physical consequences.

The scope of patients' and relatives' reactions varied from compassionate understanding to indifference. Theoretically a process of litigation against a nurse or against a health authority could have been the extremest form of the possible reactions to a medication error. In the data that were at my disposal no accounts were given of patients who actually did sue nurses or health authorities after a medication error. Only the possibility of such action was mentioned. The notion was conveyed that the procedure of following up an error would be followed more strictly if a patient was known to have a critical attitude.

The other end of the scale of possible reactions to medication errors was said to be that of total indifference by patients. Some patients were said not to worry at all if a medication error had occurred.

Generally patients or their relatives were said to be understanding. It was conveyed in the data that this could even be so if harm had actually come to a patient. Patients often took into account the image of the stressed and overworked nurse whose error may well be excused. At any rate the nurse must not be blamed. Blame, if any, must only be accorded to the health authorities who allowed a situation of understaffing to develop that would be open to unsafe practice. Cynically, more financial resources would possibly be made available to the health authorities if such situations were made public.

Patients' reactions to the fact that a medication error had occurred seemed to be independent of the harm done to him or her. Nevertheless, some patients were said to be easily upset if a medication error had occurred.

In this context the question was addressed by several respondents whether or not a patient should be told of a medication error. Generally the opinion was voiced that the patients had a right to know about any irregularities in their treatment. The nurses in this study agreed, that patients would not lose their trust in a nurse if they were informed of a medication error. Patients would on the contrary, generally be appreciative of the fact of being told. In the group discussion of the German senior nurses this question was thoroughly discussed. One nurse maintained that the patient's trust in the nurses' honesty was of greater importance than to uphold an image of infallibility.

In the Code of Professional Conduct of the UKCC it is explicitly stated that registered nurses; midwives; or health visitors must:

> ..report to an appropriate person or authority, having regard to the physical, psychological and social effects on patients and clients, any circumstances in the environment of care which could jeopardise standards of practice; (UKCC 1984)

The nurses in this study did not indiscriminately feel that all patients must be told if an error occurred. If the knowledge about a medication error would be detrimental to the state of health of a patient, nurses would discuss this with senior and medical staff and possibly decide to withhold such information from a patient. This could apply to seriously ill patients, to psychiatric patients, or to elderly confused patients.

The reactions of patients to a medication error influenced the reactions of nurses and in turn the reactions of others. But it was remarkable how most nurses reacted with concern and worry about the patient. The first question asked by nurses in situations related to a mistake in the administration of medication was 'How is the patient?' and 'What will be the medical consequences?'

Exposing a patient to harm or to potential harm by having made a medication error, caused in many nurses the damage or destruction of their self-image. The nurses talked about having lost their confidence, about being embarrassed and about the feeling of guilt and shame.

Sometimes anger was voiced at the organisational structure or at circumstances out of their own control that had caused the mistake. In the diagram pertaining to the reactions to medication errors these internal reactions of devastation or anger are termed 'reactions in the nurse'. In the diagram above these reactions are to be differentiated from the immediate action that was taken, following the mistake. This is termed 'reactions of the nurse'.

The first reaction of the nurse responsible was then to safeguard the patient from further harm. This often took the form of keeping the patient under close observation. In order to open a situation to medical scrutiny and action a doctor was in most cases informed.

Generally nurses would inform a third party. This could be a doctor, the patient, colleagues or managers. Most nurses found it important to talk to friends or partners about their mistake. Some, on the other hand did not impart their knowledge of an error at all. This was to be attributed to previous negative experiences with the disciplinary procedure. Some nurses had experienced the unfortunate situation of being blamed and ostracised. There was even talk of criminalisation.

The reactions of others greatly depended on how the mistake was made known. Naturally colleagues and seniors reacted angrily if a nurse had tried to cover up a mistake. In the examples my respondents talked about, the fact of owning up to a mistake and admitting to one's responsibility played a foremost role. Some nurses however, felt that minor mistakes need not to be made public, providing no harm was done to the patient. Often the situation was discussed in the team amongst colleagues.

Mostly the reaction of others, especially of colleagues was found to be helpful and supportive. This was often the case with manager's reactions too. Often the disciplinary procedure was followed with sensitivity to the nurses' feelings. But several nurses talked about the unhelpful reactions of seniors whose sole concern seemed to be to move correctly through the disciplinary procedure. This in turn caused sympathy and understanding among colleagues.

As to mediated reactions concerning work in general, my respondents mentioned that it cost a lot of additional energy to carry on with the routine work that had to be done. The feeling of insecurity caused by lost confidence in the professional abilities made it a hard task to function adequately. Still, for some nurses it proved to be helpful to overcome feelings of devastation and incompetence if they could turn to the work at hand. Subsequent further drug-administration was undertaken with great care. Some nurses talked about their reluctance to handle drugs after an error had happened to them. They would have avoided this task if possible. The situation demanded the need for reassurance and practical help from the side of the team. To be supervised in the administration of drugs or to be examined as to procedures was seldom appreciated; to be suspended from giving out drugs, or even from duty was felt to be most unhelpful.

Naturally the experience of having made a medication error often brought about a strain on the relationship with others. This could be within the family or among friends. One respondent mentioned the crisis he and his wife went through following a medication error which had been badly handled by a manager.

The 'influential factors' together with the immediate and mediated 'reactions following a medication error', were decisive in bringing about the meaning which the experience of a medication error had for a nurse. This is expressed in the 'ultimate effects' which medication errors had as is shown in the next section.

Ultimate effects of medication errors, of the reactions to them and of the consequences that followed their occurrence

Most medication errors my participants talked or wrote about, had profound effects for the nurses concerned and for all others involved, whether patients, students, or managers. Often a medication error had also effects for the institution in which it happened. Irrespective of the harm done to a patient, and irrespective of how the mistake was dealt with afterwards, these situations often left an indelible impression on the nurses who went through the experience.

Figure 11 provides a summary as to the effects the experiences with medication errors had on the respondents in this study. It also includes the effects medication errors may have had on the institutional setting in which they occurred.

Fig. 11: Ultimate effects of the medication errors, of the reactions and consequences.

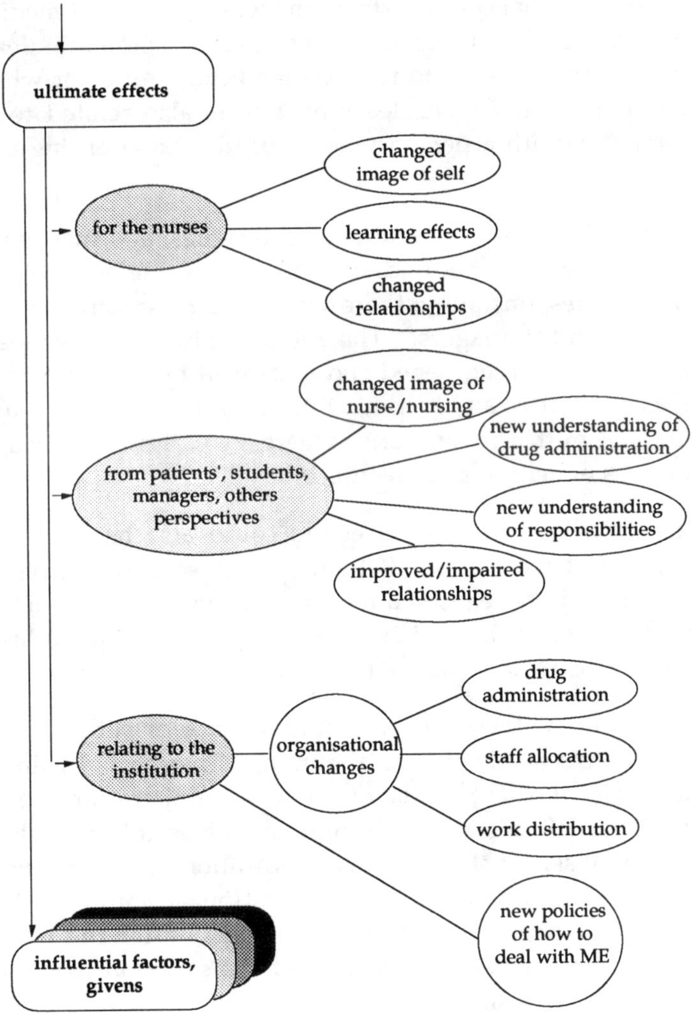

After having been involved in a medication error, nurses saw themselves in a different, possibly a more realistic light. They would see themselves as being subject to mistakes and human errors. Thus, their image of themselves and of nursing underwent changes. Most nurses talked about the learning effects of their experiences. These learning effects related to drug-administration generally; to being more solicitous, observing the drug routine more thoroughly, and not allowing any disturbances or distractions while giving out medications. They also related to a better discernment of how to deal with medication errors, whether to report a medication error or whether to deal with it internally. The learning effects also related to having greater empathy with a person who would be experiencing a similar situation.

Often the relationships with students, colleagues, and managers were affected. There was a better understanding of the student's role and the trained nurse's responsibility; there was more, or sometimes less trust in colleagues and managers. The relationship with a colleague or manager would be strengthened and improved by having experienced her/him as supportive and helpful. But the working relationship could also suffer and mistrust could arise where a colleague or manager was experienced as unhelpful and unsupportive.

Ultimate effects of medication errors could also be seen from the perspective of the patients. Patients' perception of nurses and of nursing became more realistic after a medication error had happened. Greater awareness of the patient's own responsibility as to his or her treatment was also said to be the result of a medication error.

Nursing students witnessing a medication error or being involved in one, saw a more realistic picture of nursing. They would gain a better understanding of the pitfalls of drug administration. Students experienced qualified staff and senior nurses as role models. They witnessed how senior staff handled medication errors and how they dealt with one another in such a situation. Similarly for other colleagues or managers not directly responsible for the medication error, but still concerned with the effects, the situation would acquire the character of an exemplar.

A medication error could also be the cause for restructuring policies in the institution where it had happened. Organisational changes as to drug-administration, as to staff allocation or work distribution could be effected. A ward sister would become more assertive in assuring a sufficient staffing level of her unit after she had gone through the ordeal that followed a medication error which happened while her unit was understaffed.

Furthermore, guide-lines of how to deal with medication errors came under scrutiny and were possibly amended.

Key Issues

Medication errors were perceived against the background of previous experiences. They caused distinctive reactions, and they had various ultimate effects. A new reality was thus constructed in which the daily life of a nurse will take place and which will provide a new context for subsequent experiences.

The sources for this chapter were the data of my study. The discussion of medication errors could well include further topics and themes. I restrict this discussion to the points mentioned in the group discussions, the interviews, the self reports, and the UKCC documents.

During analysis at this second level some factors or elements repeatedly appeared in the exploration of the material which could not be characterised as themes. Nor could they simply be subsumed under any of the five themes that were described in Chapter Seven. A relationship to each of the themes however, became obvious.

These factors I identified as:

1. **Subjection and power/identification and change**
2. **Guilt and reconciliation**
3. **Learning from mistakes**

I named them 'key issues'. They are also reflected in the cornerstones of the empirical model. In the fourth part of this thesis they are explored in depth. The experience with medication errors causes reactions which in their effects cause a change of the givens. The first key issue 'Subjection and power/identification and change' can be equated to the first cornerstone of the empirical model. The givens of a situation, whether they relate to self, to others, or to institutional givens, are taken as a point of departure. Various concepts of identification are discussed in Chapter Nine. The second key issue 'Guilt and reconciliation' addresses one specific reaction to the experience with medication errors. Even though guilt and shame are personal reactions they prove to bear on societal and communal aspects embedded in the second cornerstone of the empirical model. This is explored in Chapter Ten. The third key issue, 'Learning from mistakes', can be derived from the third cornerstone of the model. Elements connected with teaching and learning are innate to the ultimate effects described in the third cornerstone. Chapter Eleven is devoted to the key issue of learning from mistakes.

Part IV
Making a Medication Error - The Meaning of the Experience

What have we learned from living since we started, except to find in others what we are?

Rainer Maria Rilke (1875-1926)
from: Everthing beckons to us

CHAPTER 9

SUBJECTION AND POWER, IDENTIFICATION AND CHANGE

INTRODUCTION TO THE CHAPTER

In this chapter I address the key issues of subjection and power, link them to questions of moral decision-making, and discuss how changes take place in nurses' comprehension of situations where medication errors occurred. These are central aspects related to the first cornerstone of the empirical model. They are unfolded and investigated in the context of the data.

Caring for the sick, vulnerable 'other' can be understood as an answer to basic human needs. Nursing and its development into structured professional care-giving however, has been driven by various humanistic, religious, political and commercial interests. In order to protect professional standards from personal or political influences, moral baselines of practice are accepted by the members of the profession. Such baselines for nursing have been defined in concrete ethical codes during the first years of this century. They continue to be reformulated and restated according to changing perceptions and developing needs. Viens analysed the history of nursings' codes of ethics. She maintains:

> One essential characteristic of a profession is a code of ethics, an implicit contract, through which the profession informs society of the standards and values by which it functions (Viens 1989 p. 45).

Women and men who decide to undergo training or education in order to become professional nurses, commit themselves to the moral values expressed in relevant codes of ethics. The International Code of Ethics states:

> The fundamental responsibility of the nurse is fourfold: to promote health, to prevent illness, to restore health, and to alleviate suffering (ICN 1973).

Ethical codes represent an ideological force for the professional to which he or she is subjected.

The subjection of the individual to the ideological powers that are manifest in societies has been addressed by Althusser. I show how the paradigm of 'being hailed' by an ideological force can be traced in nursing and in nurses' submission to the authority of codes of ethics in nursing and to rules and guide-lines used in connection with the administration of medication. Althusser's notion of identification (which is part of his concept of 'interpellation', or of 'being hailed'), was developed further by Pêcheux. I take Pêcheux's understanding of 'identification' into the realm of nursing and illustrate it with examples from situations of nurses' experiences of medication errors. In the main line of my argument I show how various forms of identification justify modes of action that do not necessarily comply with stated rules.

This chapter has six sections, the first three of which contain the topics outlined above. In the fourth section I address the relevance an ethic of care and an ethic of justice have in the actions decided upon by nurses, after an error in the administration of medication has occurred. In section five the argument is extended further and embraces aspects of human relationships which are shown to be influential in situations of decision-making. In the last section professional competence, as it relates to decision-making in situations of medication errors is discussed. The connection between professional competence, personal identification and the concept of interpellation is shown.

Interpellation - Althusser's Theory on the Individual's Subjection to Power

Althusser, a French Neo-Marxist philosopher (1918-1990), centres his work on questions regarding the formation of social structures. Taking into consideration economic, political, ideological and theoretical paradigms, he denies the "simplistic Hegelian-Marxist" understanding "that the economic 'base' is the sole determinant of particular historical situations" (Mann 1983, inverted commas in the original). His comprehensive view of social structures can make a contribution to the understanding of the social reality of the nursing world as represented in nurses' discourse. Althusser's essay *'Ideology and Ideological State Apparatuses, Notes towards an Investigation'* (first published in 1969) provides a theoretical basis on how discourse can be analysed as to the ideological or political meaning of words (MacDonell 1986). I have chosen Althusser's theory on the individual's subjection to power which is unfolded in this essay because it offers a baseline for an interpretation of nurses' discourse in the present study.

Althusser examines the phenomenon of the "reproduction of the submission of the labour power to the rules of the established order". In his essay *'Ideology and Ideological State Apparatuses'*, he analyses the constitution of the individual as subject. In doing so, Althusser refers to the relation of the subject (small-s-) to the Subject (capital -S-). His main topic is the individual's subjection to power (Althusser 1971).

Althusser stipulates that the human subject is constituted by what he terms "interpellation". By identifying with the interpellator/the system, or what he calls the Subject, the individual subjects him/herself to its ideological power. Althusser manifests that "*all ideology hails or interpellates concrete individuals as concrete subjects,* by the functioning of the category of the subject". The "category of the subject" is to be seen and understood in the context of the notion of determinism. Althusser sees the ideological forces, that is the Ideological State Apparatuses, as inevitably subjecting individuals to their power (Althusser 1971, italics in the original).

An imperative hail, or an appeal is addressed to every individual, through the various institutional manifestations of power. The subjection, Althusser talks about, is "always already" manifest through the various controlling forces of the "Ideological State Apparatuses". Among these Althusser identifies: the churches; the educational systems; the trade unions; the family; the cultural systems (arts, sports etc.), (Althusser 1971). The health care systems can easily be placed among them. He says:

> You and I are ***always already*** subjects, and as such constantly practice the rituals of ideological recognition, which guarantee for us that we are indeed concrete, individual, distinguishable and (naturally) irreplaceable subjects (Althusser 1971 p. 161 f, emphasis and parenthesis in the original).

Althusser maintains that "all ideology is *centred,* that the Absolute Subject (for instance God) occupies the place of the Centre, and interpellates around it.." and thus "*subjects* the subjects to the Subject". This gives the subjects their identity and thus recognition of themselves. The Subject can take its form in any ideology, interpellating, hailing the individual with imperative power. The individual is constructed in his position as subject by answering this interpellation, identifying with its ideology. Ideology, Althusser defines according to the Marxist view as "the system of ideas and representations which dominate the mind of a man or social group". The "it's me" as an answer to the question "who is there?" subjects the 'me' to the one who calls (Althusser 1971).

In his essay, Althusser calls this a "duplicate mirror-structure" in which the following four aspects of subjection and identification are ensured:

1. the interpellation of 'individuals' as subjects;
2. their subjection to the Subject;
3. the mutual recognition of subjects and Subject, the subjects' recognition of each other, and finally the subject's recognition of himself;
4. the absolute guarantee that everything really is so, and that on condition that the subjects recognize what they are and behave accordingly, everything will be all right: Amen - 'So be it' (Althusser 1971 p. 168, inverted commas in the original).

Althusser states that

> The ideological representation of ideology (in the Ideological State Apparatuses) is itself forced to recognize that every 'subject' endowed with a 'consciousness' and believing in the 'ideas' that his 'consciousness' inspires in him and freely accepts, must '*act* according to his ideas', must therefore inscribe his own ideas as a free subject in the action of his material practice. If he does not do so, 'that is wicked' (Althusser 1970 p. 157, emphasis, inverted commas and parenthesis in the original).

He further asserts that anyone who does not "..do what he ought to do as a function of what he believes (...) is either 'inconsistent' or cynical, or perverse" (Althusser 1971 p. 158, inverted commas in the original).

Some of the examples, Althusser uses to demonstrate his thesis, refer to Judeo-Christian tradition. Althusser mentions the Moses of the Old Testament, but also refers to Christian initiation and the Dogma of the Catholic Church. Being called, or 'interpellated' by a Subject and subjected "as subjects presupposes the *existence* of a Unique and Central Other Subject, in whose Name (for instance) the religious ideology interpellates all individuals as subjects" (Althusser 1971, italics and inverted commas in the original).

This, however, is a figure found in all religious traditions. It can be understood as the basic paradigm for the human need to enter transcendental relationship. This can be substantiated further from the point of view of history of religion. The earliest documentation of religious texts tell the story of interpellation, subjection and recognition.

The Bhagavad-Gita describes how the god Vishnu in the form of Krishna reveals himself to Arjuna, a young man of the warrior class, and calls him into his service. The interpellation is made by the double imperative of listen! (give ear) and look! (behold):[1]

---

[1] All quotations from the Bhagavad-Gita are taken from The Bhagavad-Gita, with a commentary by R.C. Zaehner (1969), edited by R.C. Zaehner, Oxford: Clarendon Press (Parentheses in the original).

> The Blessed Lord said: Now once again, (my) strong-armed (friend) give ear to my all-highest word which I shall speak to you, for therein is your delight and your welfare is my wish... (Bhagavad-Gita 10/1).

> The Blessed Lord said: Son of Pritha, behold my forms in their hundreds and their thousands; how various they are, how divine... (11/5).

Krishna gives his hailing of Arjuna affirmative power by endowing him with a celestial eye that enables Arjuna to see what he is shown:

> But never will you be able to see Me with your (natural) eye.
> A celestial eye I'll give you, behold my power as Lord! (11/8).

> The Blessed Lord said: Because I desire to show you favour, Arjuna, by my Selfs (sic) own power I have shown you my highest form, (11/47).

After having experienced the vision of Vishnu, Arjuna is shown his destiny and is compelled to subject himself to the all powerful God.

> Do works for Me, make Me your highest goal, be loyal-in-love to Me (11/55).

The destiny of all humanity according to Hindu tradition is the perception of ultimate immortality which is attained by surrendering to one's personal destiny. Having understood this, Arjuna can obey his duty as a member of the warrior class and fight his cousins, which at first he had refused to do (Zaehner 1969).

> Better (to do) one's own (caste) duty, though devoid of merit,
> than (to do) another's, however well performed (18/47).

> Never should a man give up the work to which he is born,
> defective though it be (18/47).

Subjection in Hindu religion is the surrender of all attachment, the achievement of Yoga which "means sameness-and-indifference" (Zaehner 1969).

Another example of the paradigm of subjection can be seen in Islam. The word 'Islam' itself, stems from the Arabic word 'aslama' (to surrender to God). First and foremost it meant the submission of Mohammed to the will and power of God. Mohammed knew himself to be called to act as God's interpreter and the administrator of his laws. Later 'Islam' was understood as the submission by Mohammed's followers to his teaching and to the political and juridical order that was founded by him on the basis of Arabic, Judaic, Christian and Gnostic elements.[2]

I turn now to the example of the encounter between Jahwe and Moses, which Althusser mentions in his essay. It starts with God calling Moses by his Name (Exodus 3:4).[3] Moses replies "Here am I" (Exodus 3:4) and God gives Moses his assignment. The encounter ends with God revealing his name to Moses as "I am who I am" (Exodus 3:14). This example supplies a paradigm for the status of human beings as being created or being called into existence and in turn, answering this call. The name 'Moses' meaning 'the one that is born' or 'the one that was drawn from the waters'.[4] Being told and retold countless times, the story left its impact on human understanding of relationship.

Althusser also uses the doctrine of Christian salvation to illustrate his point. I shall shortly analyse the story of Mary, mother of Jesus Christ as an example of interpellation; demonstrating that here the basic figure of a human transcendental relationship has found its way into the tradition of the Christian religion.

> ... And the virgin's name was Mary. And he (the angel) came to her and said "Hail, o favoured one, the Lord is with you!" (Luke 1:27b, 28).
>
> ... you will conceive in your womb and bear a son, and you shall call his name Jesus. He will be great, and he will be called the Son of the Most High (Luke 1:31b, 32);

Again we have an interpellation, the hailing; a commission; and then clearly, an act of subjection:

---

2 See Lexikon für Theologie und Kirche, Band 5 (1962) "Islam."

3 All quotations from the bible are taken from The Old and New Testaments, Revised Standard Version (1952 and 1946) W M. Collins Sons + Co Ltd., New York, Glasgow

4 See Lexikon für Theologie und Kirche, Band 7 (1962) "Moses."

> And Mary said, "Behold I am the handmaid of the Lord; let it be to me according to your word" (Luke 1:38).

Countless other examples from different religions, from biblical tradition, and from church history, could be cited. Also fairy tales and myths of all ages and regions tell the story of subjection and identification.

The sequence is always the same. In fact it is the same in all spheres of social life: Interpellation and subjection to the power that hails, and the subject's identification with that power.

Religious manifestations illustrate the basic figure of subjection as well as the conflicts that arise from any such subjection for daily action, as was shown in the example of Arjuna.

The paradigmatic sense of this can be traced in all walks of every human's life. Any decision made in answer to an interpellative force will give rise to conflict as other imperatives demand their due, be it the decision to be a teacher, a mother, a friend, or a nurse.

The fact that all religious traditions address this paradigm in one form or aother, indicates the basic human condition of being free to make decisions, but not free not to make decisions. We cannot avoid conflict.

It is important to note the elements of mutuality and voluntarism between subject and Subject. It is also notable that by the act of submission the subject acknowledges his/her own identity. This includes the recognition of subjects in likewise positions. It is not only the 'here am I', but also the understanding of an individual's position in a group of subjects 'here are we!'. The social element gives value and stability to an act of subjection.

CONTINUATION AND MODIFICATION OF ALTHUSSER'S WORK - PÊCHEUX'S THEORY ON IDENTIFICATION

Continuation and modification of Althusser's work

"... an important modification to Althusser's argument" is claimed by Silverman (1985). He sees a variety of possibilities for the constitution of the subject. To him it is not only the institutional structure (of the Ideological State Apparatuses) which exercises power. He allows for individual choice that rests with personal concerns. However, he does admit to the "subject-relations that are certainly discoverable in the real world" (Silverman 1985). Thus, according to Althusser, individuals who are hailed or "interpellated as subjects with a personal identity" will respond: "It really is me, I am here, a worker, a boss, or a soldier!" (Althusser 1971).

Following Althusser's arguments, according to MacDonell, "an ideology, however dominant it may be in an Ideological State Apparatus, does not exist without opposing ideology" (MacDonell 1986). She draws attention to the fact, that, even though Althusser does not explicitly state this, the shaping of ideology takes place antagonistically.

Althusser admits that the occasional "'bad subject' may act provocatively in the state apparatus" (Althusser 1971, inverted commas in the original).

This is well demonstrated in another example from the Old Testament. In 1400 BC Amenophis II, King of Egypt imposed upon the Hebrews hard conditions and various rules regarding the civil life. We are informed of one sequence of events:

> And he said to his people, "Behold, the people of Israel are too many and too mighty for us. Come, let us deal shrewdly with them, lest they multiply, and if war befall us, they join our enemies and fight against us (...) So they made the people of Israel serve with rigour, and made their lives bitter with hard service, in mortar and brick, and in all kinds of work in the field; (...) But the more they were suppressed, the more they multiplied and the more they spread abroad.

> Then the king of Egypt said to the Hebrew midwives, one of whom was named Shiph'rah and the other Pu'ah, "When you serve as midwife to the Hebrew women, and see them upon the birthstool, if it is a son, you shall kill him; but if it is a daughter, she shall live." But the midwives feared God, and did not do as the king of Egypt commanded them, but let the male children live. So the king of Egypt called the midwives, and said to them, "Why have you done this (...)?"
>
> The midwives said to Pharaoh, "Because the Hebrew women are not like the Egyptian women; for they are vigorous and are delivered before the midwives come to them." So God dealt well with the midwives. (...) And because the midwives feared God he gave them families. (Exodus 1:9-21)

The Hebrew midwives practising in Egypt had to obey the orders of Pharaoh, but they were also bound to the law of their God. Here, two competitive forces hailed the individual. Obviously the interpellative force is connected to deontological reasoning. For Shiph'rah and Pu'ah it was a question of whose law to obey.

The Hebrew midwives did not act solely from intuition. It is stated that they "feared God", and therefore did not do as Pharaoh commanded them to do. 'To fear God' in biblical terms includes cognitive knowledge of God and an act of obedience according to this knowledge. So it follows, that they justified their action on well informed deontological grounds. Obedience to the divine law of God was shaped in disobedience to the civil law of the Egyptian king. In opposition to profane law, Pu'ah and Shiph'rah made their answer to God's call. Shiph'rah and Pu'ah shifted their allegiance from obedience to Pharaoh's law to obedience to the law of the Hebrew God. They disidentified by answering a stronger hail, using their professional expertise to move into a new position. Their motive to obey God more than Pharaoh however, was based on teleological argumentation.

Pêcheux, as MacDonell points out, has followed this notion in his description of three modalities of identification by which "subjects may be constructed" (MacDonell 1986).

Pêcheux, another French Neo-Marxist Philosopher, investigates further the aspect of identification within Althusser's concept of interpellation. In his book, <u>Language, Semantics and Ideology</u> (1975),

Pêcheux describes possible alternatives for the constitution of the subject.

Identification

In what Pêcheux describes as the 'first modality' the subject subjects himself as "the 'good subject' who spontaneously reflects the Subject" (Pêcheux 1975, inverted commas in the original). This represents Althusser's figure of interpellation. Pêcheux calls this modality 'identification'.

Counteridentification

The 'second modality', Pêcheux states, "characterises the discourse of the 'bad subject'". Here we have the "trouble maker" who struggles "against ideological evidentness on the terrain of that evidentness". This modality of 'counteridentification' uses the discourse of the identified with "a negative sign, reversed in its own terrain". The "counter-discourse" in the second modality appears as "the symmetrical inversion" of the discourse in the first modality (Pêcheux 1975).

Disidentification

In the 'third modality' Pêcheux identifies a "non-subjective position", which he calls 'disidentification'. In this modality, Pêcheux claims, lays the power of social and political change. Only by disidentification "a subjective process of appropriation of scientific concepts and identification with the political organisations 'of a new type'" is paradoxically realised. In the process of the third modality "ideological interpellation continues to operate, but as it were against itself " (Pêcheux 1975, inverted commas in the original).

Thus, it can be said that "disidentification" is an effect of working against "prevailing practices of ideological subjection" (MacDonell 1986). Disidentification, MacDonell states, in opposition to counteridentification, comes "from another position, one existing antagonistically, with the effect that the identity and identifications set up in dominant ideology, though never escaped entirely, are transformed and displaced" (MacDonell 1986).

The story of the Hebrew midwives could serve well as an example of the third modality. But we can go further and argue that they identified with the force that had the greater interpellative power and thus subjected themselves, to speak in Althusser's terms, to their chosen Subject. It follows that any form of disidentification is in turn an answer to a more powerful interpellative force; and any answer to a new hail or interpellation must needs contain an element of disidentification.

To return to the example of Moses: he too developed his loyalty to the Hebrew God's call against his primary socialisation at the court of the Egyptian king. Or Mary, on hearing the interpellation of God's angel, disregarded the conventional role of a young woman of her time and social surroundings. Heeding the ancient prophesy that any woman in Israel may become the mother of the Messiah, she accepted this as her calling instead.

Earlier, I described the act of submission as a 'basic paradigm for the human need to enter transcendental relationship'. I gave examples of men and women, becoming subject to a Subject by answering an ideological appeal. However, it was assigned to women by patriarchal societies, to identify with the basic paradigm of submission as appropriate to their nature. Men have yielded to the temptation to submit to the ideological understanding of being in positions of power in their relationships with women. This, for centuries has been the interpellative force of men's domination over women.

When entering the nursing profession, the basic human need for care is an imperative force that informs a person's decision. However, domination has forged nurses' relationships with doctors, clerics (especially in Germany), and with the authoritative powers of legislative bodies. Nursing, as it developed, became a subservient task, understood as an answer to the natural 'hail' of domination and power. This is felt sorely by many nurses who did not take into account the patriarchal structure of our health care services when choosing their profession. Benner and Wrubel indicate that the need for care has as it's centre human interdependence.

> Caring and needing care point up (sic) the centrality of interdependence and our essential reliance on others (Benner and Wrubel 1988 p. 368).

Nurses, as professionals are beginning to develop an ethical sense for the need to identify with the imperative force of interdependence rather than with the 'natural' hail made by domination and power. This is demonstrated in the following sections.

SUBJECTION AND POWER IN THE CONTEXT OF MEDICATION ERRORS

The three modes of identification as revealed by the data

Althusser, Pêcheux and later MacDonell in Britain, worked on the general structure of subjection and power. They understood the development of ideology within the greater context of the historic class struggle.

In this study the positions of Althusser, Pêcheux and MacDonell are not taken further. Instead an application is now made to nursing, specifically to the situation of drug administration. However, the concepts of 'Interpellation' (Althusser) and 'Identification' (Pêcheux), help towards an interpretation of nurses' experiences with medication errors. The data at my disposal are examined as to the evidence they yield for nurses' identification, counteridentification and disidentification. I supply a profile of how the concept of interpellation in the three modalities of identification, according to Pêcheux, is apparent in the settings of the health care systems and how they are lived by nurses in the way they handle medication errors.

The struggle that is part of the construction of the subject in various arenas of social life is mirrored in the discourse of the participants of this study. I show how nurses try to find their position by making decisions according to the understanding they have formed of the various imperative forces that govern their professional life.

Responsibility and accountability as an ideological component of nursing (Identification in the discourse of nurses)

Being socialised by nursing education and training, nurses are obviously subject to the codes of nursing practice. These codes include the notions of beneficence and of non- maleficence (UKCC 1984).

Generally, nurses will learn during their training to spell out the 'it is me, a nurse'; they will identify with the expectations that are laid upon them by society in answering the imperative force of the institution 'Health Care Service'. In the UK, Nurses are subject to the regulations of their professional body, the UKCC.

In the context of medication errors, nurses understood themselves as being subject to the rules of drug administration and to the procedures which followed the occurrence of mistakes. Responsibility and accountability were the key issues here.

In the first modality of identification a strong deontological line of argumentation governed the decisions made by nurses in the event of a medication error. Obedience to the rules, the duty to report mistakes, and the nurse's right to take an incident further up the hierarchy, to be dealt with in a disciplinary way, dominated the discourse here.

Accepting responsibility, and being accountable for their action, appeared to be an important aspect in nurses' discourse. In the terms of nurses dealing with the administration of medication an act of submission to the stated rules of conduct can be illustrated with the following extracts from the data:

> *... but I think (...) facing up to* ***your responsibility, being accountable*** *for what you do, that's what its all about, and I believe very strongly (...) and if one of those things is, making a mistake, you should account for it (INT1 EX2 888-897);*
>
> *... if we made a mistake, then* ***we'll have to be accountable*** *for it.. (INT2 EX1 262-264);*
>
> *... you are in a* ***responsible position****, and you are abusing that responsibility if you make it your decision, to hush something up (INT3 764-768);*
>
> *... as a registered nurse, if I made a mistake.. (MA: mmm), I mean, I feel having to own up to it, if it is my fault, (INT5 EX1 584-587).*

These and similar comments were made in nearly every data source. The next extracts show an understanding attitude toward the nursing officers who acted on their perception of accountability. The nurses whom I interviewed attributed the right and duty to their seniors of taking the matter further up the hierarchy.

Thelma, the midwife in Interview One, even though she was not the only one responsible for the error, made it obvious that she was quite prepared to accept the mistake as her responsibility. She used the expression *'of course'* twice. *'Of course'* this mistake had to be reported. Thelma said, that as soon as she understood that an error had been made she felt *'absolutely sick'* and that she told sister about the occurrence. She knew that this mistake was not harmful to the patient. Sister's first reaction was to follow the official procedure.

Thelma said:

> *The point is, giving the drug to the wrong person. And I was well aware of that (INT1 EX1 178-181)*
>
> *Thelma: ... and she (the sister) said, well you realise we'll have to tell ... the boss, and this will have to be reported and I said yes,* ***of course*** *...*
>
> *MA: Who was the boss?*
>
> *Thelma: Well, the boss was our midwifery manager from the maternity unit and I said, yes* ***of course****, I realise that.. accepted my fate, quite stoically, I mean I knew I was for the chop, (INT1 EX1 233-245),*

Other examples of clear submission to the rules can be illustrated with the following extracts:

> *I felt horrified, there was no way that I could deny that that was what we had done, (...) obviously,* ***it had to be reported*** *(INT7 EX1 220-235).*

In Jane's case the director of nursing services felt, that *'..procedure hadn't been followed, then* ***there would have to be*** *.. proper investigation')*, and Jane, hesitantly but clearly stated:

> *Jane: she's a ward sister, if the same thing happened again, if .. if a nurse reported to her a mistake ..*
>
> *MA: Knowing that the same .. procedure would be followed again?*
>
> *Jane: yeah (...) Well, she doesn't have any choice, (...) you have to .. very much* ***you have to follow the rules,*** *(INT11 EX1 672-686)*

In this context the 'slippery slope' argument was used in order to justify seemingly harsh decisions. Thelma said:

> *I mean she had every right to take it as far as she wanted to take it, really. (...) if you are prepared to hide things and not own up to your mistakes, what other things are you prepared to do? (INT1 EX1 1009-1017).*

Here Thelma used the words: *'she had every right'*, this again shows the submission to rules which ultimately safeguard patients:

> *I think it's best to have certain procedures, things like that, because, (...) it probably makes it quite clear what the consequences for you personally can be (...) and also (...) to protect the patients, (INT1 1296-1305).*

The 'slippery slope' argument was also used several times in this context to show concern for patients:

> *... if you've the tendency to try and do that (hush things up) with something small, you might do it with something bigger (INT3 768-774).*

The next example demonstrates how the modality of identification could cause disruption of the interpersonal relationships amongst a ward team rather than to solve a problem. Sean was presented to me by his nursing manager as an eager, compliant and helpful charge nurse who

> *... should be furthered in his career. And taking part in your study might stimulate him to think about taking a degree himself. Perhaps you could push him a bit (Comment of nursing manager before introducing me to Sean).*

In our interview Sean never talked about mistakes he had made himself, but dwelt on the disciplinary procedure he had been involved with, when another nurse, junior to him, had made a mistake. Sean said:

> *... I have to go and see my immediate superior about it and report that (INT4 EX1 218-220).*

Sean had exercised his duties as a charge nurse very correctly. No fault could be found officially with his conduct. A staff nurse had mistakenly given 25 mg of Melleril instead of 10 mg to an elderly confused patient. Sean had known that the ward had run out of 10 mg Melleril tablets. He had *'provisionally discussed'* with one of the doctors that the night medication for this patient could be omitted for that evening until the correct dosage was obtainable from pharmacy the next day. Of this he had not informed the staff nurse. The mistake could possibly have been prevented, had he done so. (Sean however, never actually referred to the incident in this light).

After the incident the staff nurse was not allowed to handle drugs without being supervised until the matter was dealt with by the director of nursing services. Even though Sean presented himself as a helpful and understanding manager, his strict adherence to the rules caused the staff nurse a lot of distress. During three weeks of uncertainty the ward atmosphere *'suffered badly'* as Sean said in our interview; and the staff nurse was ready to leave nursing. In the fourth week after the incident, Sean went to see the director of nursing services, in order to find out, how the situation was to be handled further. He was told that the decision to allow the staff nurse to do the medicine rounds unsupervised, had to be made by the second ward sister and by Sean himself. The ward sister and Sean discussed the situation and decided to ask the staff nurse if she was happy to go back to the old routine of checking drugs with a student or junior nurse. Sean and the other ward sister *'offered'* to now and again check the drugs with her as a kind of *'subtle minor supervision'* .

Sean did not take it upon himself to deal with the situation. He sought the reassurance of his superiors in each step he took. He had clearly demonstrated his identification with the system. By doing so he had sacrificed the well-being of a staff nurse, as well as the ward climate.

The above cited extracts from nurses' discourse illustrate the first modality of identification. Nurses identified with their role as being responsible for the welfare of patients and of being accountable for their actions. In the event of a medication error nurses demonstrated their willingness to own up to mistakes even at the cost of submitting themselves as well as colleagues to the disciplinary consequences.

Looking closely at what nurses actually said, it emerged that the concepts of 'responsibility' and 'accountability' were used to position themselves as subjects. The discourse reveals the identification of self but also the "recognition of each other" as Althusser had termed it, that enhances the recognition of self. The use of personal pronouns indicates this recognition: *'Your responsibility'; 'you should'; 'we'll have to be'; 'I feel'; 'she doesn't have' - 'you have to'.* Once even the generalising form of *'it had to be reported'* was used.

Furthermore, words like *'no choice'; 'rules'; 'right';* were being used in connection with *'telling';* and *'reporting'.* Here a deontological aspect of nurses' understanding was revealed. Nurses saw and understood themselves and their colleagues as being subjected to the rules that are dictated by ethical codes, and by policies and guide-lines. The explicit statements which had a stereotype character, established and re-established their own and their colleagues position within the order of responsibility and accountability.

Acting against the rules (Counteridentification in the discourse of nurses)

Having had negative experiences with harsh or even unjust application of the consequences, that is, with having to go through the procedures of disciplinary action in a hard-line manner, some nurses quickly learned to 'counteridentify'. This is shown in the examples of Henry and of Jane.

After his medication error, Henry was given quite a rough time by his nursing manager. Henry said that he immediately realised his mistake of not closing the drug trolley and making sure that the student did not continue with the distribution of drugs before he attended to a patient who had injured himself. He knew where he had acted wrongly.

I asked him what he felt after he had realised that a medication error had occurred:

> *MA: (...) what did you feel?*
>
> *Henry: Panic! (laughs) Complete panic! I felt very guilty. I felt .. you know, that I was responsible (INT10 EX1 337-340).*

Henry reported the incident. As to the way it was handled, he said:

> *I felt heavy disciplined, I felt I had been let down.. and I .. and I wanted to leave nursing at that point in time. Because I was.. like going in .. I'm just being so .. scared to something else happening.. (INT10 EX1 289-297).*

He described the attitude of his nursing officer as *'not conducive'*. Henry said that he knew the nursing officer:

> *... to be a quite a ruthless character (...) he was a very.. very stickler for procedures and stuff like that.. (INT10 EX1 514-517);*

He was questioned by the nursing officer about the procedures of giving out medicines, and three days later the situation was further discussed with two nursing officers of the hospital and he got a written warning that was to stay in his file for six months. He was seriously cautioned. It must be left open whether Henry's immediate reaction of *'panic'* was caused solely by the realisation of having made an error or whether it was influenced by the anticipation of the expected 'disciplinary procedure'.

Henry said to me at a later stage during our interview that he had learned from this situation that it would be better not to report a mistake. He had then been newly qualified and this had been his first experience of a medication error.

He said further:

> *I expected to get .. warned .. for what I had done. But I expected to get some support.. (INT10 EX1 227-229).*

I asked Henry why he had reported the incident in the first place:

> *MA: Yeah .. what made you report it?*
>
> *Henry: I felt I had the responsibility.*
>
> *MA: Doctor said it was alright..*
>
> *Henry: I was following procedure ..*
>
> *MA: (laughs) How would you act today?*
>
> *Henry: Ehm ... ... if it was in a similar situation, **I would feel very reluctant, to inform the nursing officer**. Unless I knew the nursing officer and I knew that they were going to support me ... (INT10 EX1 490-507).*

But I think, because I'd just started out .. in my nursing .. I'd never been involved in a.. ehm .. kind of testing the ground. But I felt that I was.. that that was the fairest way to do things. Because it.. you know, that.. the way I see it .. if a procedure is there and I think it's a .. you know, it covers everybody and that way it would be unfair on the nursing officer if .. that incident had .. taken place and .. I hadn't informed him about it. And if something had happened in between time, I would have (been) in more trouble.. (INT10 EX1 521-540).

As a newly qualified staff nurse, Henry tried to do things as he was supposed to do them. But he knew, he was *'testing the grounds'* and quickly learned that owning up and reporting a mistake would not always be the best way to handle a medication error.

MA: Yeah, what do you think, you learned from the mistakes you made?

Henry: Ehm .. first lesson I learned from the first incident .. was .. ***don't tell the nursing officer****! (INT10 EX1 912-914).*

From Jane's discourse a similar development can be demonstrated. She and a student had been involved in a minor medication error. The doctor who was informed of the incident felt that it did not have to be taken further. But Jane thought that she did not have a choice as far as reporting the incident to ward sister was concerned, because of the emphasis that was laid at the time on 'the procedure' that had to be followed after medication errors. No harm had come to the patient, but the consequences were bitter for Jane.

... for me there .. it really wasn't any decision to make. I didn't .. there wasn't anything else, I could do, other than ... (INT11 EX1 202-206);

... so I knew exactly what had to be done... (INT11 EX1 250-251);

I have to inform my manager, (MA: mmh), and I think I ... ehm, that was the right thing, (INT11 EX1 264-267).

After the error Jane was suspended from giving out medications and then had to attend hearings at various levels. Finally she was given a written warning.

A certain disparity could be sensed from Jane's talk. If she had known the consequences her honesty would have, she *'probably'* , or *'perhaps'* would not have said anything:

> *... **perhaps**, if there hadn't been such ... ... ehm, ... an emphasis eh .. a **witch-hunt** at that particular time about drug-giving, maybe .. **I wouldn't have said anything**. But we've been told, now, this is the procedure, this is what we must do .. (INT11 EX1 378-383);*

> *... providing that, I mean .. no harm had come to the patient, and if I knew, what was going to happen to me, in terms of having to admit it, and knowing that I had learned by the mistake, and that for me to know, and to learn by it, was sufficient .. then I think I would have **probably kept it to myself** (INT11 EX1 1107-1117).*

Still, being asked, how she would act in future, Jane said:

> *... yet even now .. having been through something like that, I wouldn't .. **I don't think I could just cover it up** (INT11 EX1 784-788).*

Referring to this statement in a written communication later on she pointed out:

> *... although I think it is important to be honest own up to mistakes, if I were in that particular situation with that particular nurse manager **I don't think I would have owned up if I had been aware of the consequences** .. (Written communication Sept. 1991).*

Jane had apparently changed her mind as to what was important to her. In the interview she seemed to identify with what was officially expected of her by the nursing hierarchy. Reading my account of our interview, where I remarked on the fact that in spite of being hurt, she would own up again, Jane felt the need to rectify this and indicate her true feelings. Here the force of having to be honest to and about herself was also an imperative to her. She had to own up to her true feelings.

This goes well with Althusser's statement that a person cannot act easily (or talk) against his or her conviction. Jane could not be inconsistent with herself. This meant to her, amending in writing, what she had actually said in the interview.

The modality of counteridentification is well illustrated by the next extracts from Jane's discourse. Asked how the other nurses on the ward would feel about owning up, Jane said:

> *If a similar mistake, had been made, .. **I think they would have covered it up** (INT11 497-499);*
>
> *I think they felt that .. well, if that is what I'm going to have to go through, for owning up to making a genuine mistake,.. ehm .. I don't think, **I don't think they would have owned up to it** (INT11 521-528);*
>
> *I know from .., what other people said at the time, but .. the only result of treating me like that, ehm, .. everybody seeing me to be treated like that, was that .. **in future mistakes would .. would be covered up**, and I think, possibly more serious .. mistakes .. (INT11 1048-1057).*

Henry too supported this, when he referred to a colleague who had made quite a severe error:

> *I don't think he is bad, I can understand his situation. And I think a lot of people go through that (...) And it's through experiences where they feel that .. it's not really conducive for them to actually inform anybody. **In fact they are better off not informing people**. I think that varies depending on what support is given (INT10 EX3 854-869).*

Similar opinions were expressed by several other participants:

> *... if it's somebody, who terrifies you, and .. you know.. you just can't approach .. then they are going and try cover it up, because they are so frightened, of what might happen, you know, what this person might say or do .. then you know, **they are going to .. try and cover up more** .. (INT2 1360-1369).*
>
> *... because of this severe dealings with minor errors, **they .. try and cover up major errors too,** (INT7 1251-1254).*

Joan also expressed a sense of understanding for covering up a mistake in order to protect self from possibly unjust consequences. Regarding example one from our interview she ascertained:

> *I felt that she (another staff nurse) was **covering up for herself** (...) that .. sort of inner.. **self-protectiveness**, that you have you know, you don't want a blot on your copy-book, (INT2 EX1 380-417).*

Joan said this even though she did not agree with the way that nurse wanted to handle the situation.

In the extracts above a certain sympathy was voiced for situations where other nurses would not follow the rules. Clear statements were made: Mistakes *'would be covered up'*; nurses *'were better off, not informing anybody'*; and they *'are going to try and cover up'*. Concerning self, the statements were more cautious, including inhibitive expressions like *'perhaps'* or *'probably'*. I suggest that by stating what other nurses might do, the participants conveyed their agreement as to covering up a mistake under certain circumstances. Thus, we find situations, were nurses expressed the possibility of acting against the rules.

An interesting turn can be found in Sean's discourse when he mentioned that many nurses do not own up to their error. Here he used his knowledge of other nurses counteridentification in order to convey the merit of his own total identification with the disciplinary system:

> *I said, there is (...) **plenty of them** that make drug errors, time and time again and **don't report it**, you know, (INT4 EX1 706-709).*

Sean contrasted his own inflexible attitude against the attitude of those nurses, who did not act as they should.

However, the nurses I had talked to would only keep quiet about minor mistakes. A differentiation was made where serious harm to patients would be involved:

> *... it would depend on the sort of medication error. Ehm .. I think, eh .. a medication error with a drug, that was potentially life threatening to the patient .. ehm .. you would maybe have to .. mention that to someone .. higher up the nursing hierarchy (INT7 299-305).*

Covering up a mistake, dealing with it in an unconventional manner would furthermore only be possible, if this error seemed to be a 'one off' situation. Mike, for example, said:

> *... if it was an error made by one of my staff nurses, .. ehm .. and it was the first time they had ever made an error, as far as I knew, then, no I would be quite happy to deal with it myself, (INT7 327-334).*

Looking at the details of nurses discourse, it can be said that Henry and Jane, but also the participants in Interviews Two and Seven, would divert into the modality of counteridentification. In doing so however, they generally attached certain conditions to this modality, or they gave an explanation why they would act as they said. This is highlighted here:

> *... **if I was in a similar situation** ... I would be very reluctant to inform the nursing officer... (INT10);*

> *... I don't think I would have owned up **if I had been aware of the consequences...** (written communication of Jane);*

... ***if somebody who terrifies you*** *... then they are going to cover it up... (INT2);*

... ***because of this severe dealings with errors*** *... they are going to ... try and cover up (INT7).*

The experience of *'severe dealings with errors'*; or *'to be treated like that'* would be a justification to act against the rules. Here indeed the concept of accountability is being turned against itself. Providing, no harm comes to a patient; and providing it is not an on-going thing, nurses would feel justified not to subject themselves or their colleagues to the procedure normally to be followed when a medication error occurs. The stronger appeal however, would be to cover up for self or colleagues, so that hurt through inflexible application of the disciplinary procedure would be avoided.

In summary: Nurses would counteridentify with the rules and not report mistakes in selected situations. In the examples provided, however, they still felt bound to the concepts of responsibility and accountability.

Bringing about change (Disidentification in the discourse of nurses)

I now turn to the modality of disidentification. To differentiate between counteridentification and disidentification, can at times be rather difficult. But if the portrayal of disidentification as being a means for social change is followed, some instances from the data will point to this modality. In the fashion of counteridentification, acting against the rules was tied to resentment against the *'witch-hunt'*, or *'the ruthless character'* of a manager. Here, the attitude 'against' power, that was sometimes wielded unjustly, characterised nurses' decision not to comply with the imperative force of rules and regulations.

In the modality of disidentification, acting against rules has a further objective: To find out why an error has happened; examine the causes; and if possible, bring about changes in order to prevent further errors; as well as, giving support to the nurses involved. By trying to deal with a situation of medication error at ward level, nurses were prepared to take a great deal of responsibility upon themselves. Here, an inspired innovative force of a caring attitude went further than 'acting against', or 'counteridentifying'. Here, a search for development and positive change marked the decisions in situations of medication errors. 'Disidentification', is thus characterised by a teleological stance.

In Mike's discourse the elements of disidentification emerged, even though at first it seemed, that he, by not reporting his own error would counteridentify:

> *I knew .. that I was not following the correct procedure that's laid down by the (local health board). Ehm, I knew I wasn't .. I knew I was breaking the rules, (INT7 648-653);*

We talked about how he would handle errors made by his staff:

> *I would be quite happy not to mention it to, .. to my nurse managers (INT7 312-314).*
>
> *I also think that I have ... enough respect amongst my staff, .. to deal with any error, that they would make .. with equally, if not more .. eh .. result, than .. dragging somebody up in front of a board of nurse managers ..(...) and make sure that the nurse was .. an awful lot more careful in the future, .. (INT7 1214-1232).*

Mike did not think the present system where each and every error was supposed to be reported was *'flexible enough'*. To him an error could be used constructively, the result would be important. The right way to go about it is indicated in the next extract:

> *I would be quite happy to sit down with her, or him .. **discuss the error, trying to find out how it happened**, again, and find areas, that had led to the error happening .. (INT7 1608-1614).*

Looking at Henry, we had at first seen a strong tendency to counteridentify. However, having also experienced a different manner of dealing with a medication error than the first one described, Henry had chosen his preference. Regarding example four he said:

> *... the person (ward sister) said, well that's alright, and **looked through the situation** and said, here's where you went wrong, and .. **it was discussed** (INT10 EX4 1329-1333);*
>
> *And I (...) believe that .. (...) anybody can make an error, and it depends on whether people .. use the.. the procedures to make it a disciplinary event, or a supportive event. (...) **and learn something at the end of it** (INT10 889-901);*
>
> *... on the second .. situation, having seen, how this staff nurse was supported, ehm .. I think I learned that it is OK to actually **inform somebody who might understand** .. the situation and.. and help you actually get through it (INT10 915-923);*

> *... and **it's discussed** at ward level, and **a decision** has been made at ward level, then I think that's fine (INT10 EX4 1814-1817);*
>
> *And then I think that a staff nurse should, or the nurse in charge on .. on a management meeting, **should be able to discuss the situation without naming names**, however, and discuss ... (INT10 EX4 1817-1823).*

The ultimate outcome of this situation was: The drug routine was changed in such a way that the possibility of making errors was diminished.

Three modalities of identification

It may seem, that the modality of disidentification appears as the better motivation for action in events where medication errors had to be dealt with. I want to resist the temptation of equating the modalities of identification with certain levels of moral development that are either reached or are not attained. All three modalities have their own values, and are justifiable. They were adopted depending on what interpellative force was felt strongest. This depended on a given situation, on circumstances, and on the relationships that existed between actors. Any one position, thus, can be equally valuable.

Going beyond Althusser, not to act according to one's supposedly recognised identity does not simply indicate 'inconsistency, or cynicism, or perversion'. Moving away from a certain position of identification is not 'wicked', but a necessity according to circumstances. Moving to a new position provided consistency as to answering to the needs of self and of others. It indeed presupposes different modalities of identification as Pêcheux suggests. However, none of the three modalities can simply be attached to nurses or nurses' discourse as labels. In the same interview sometimes all three modalities may be found. Nurses might move back and forth through all modalities. They may well comply with the modality of identification at first; then utter expressions which might demonstrate a certain degree of counteridentification; and they might then move on to the modality of disidentification.

AN ETHIC OF JUSTICE AND AN ETHIC OF CARE

In the next two sections the meaning of personal relationships is examined. At first, the three modalities of identification are positioned in context with an ethic of care and an ethic of justice. It is shown how the various elements of interpellation and ethical argumentation can be understood. Then, positive or negative relationships amongst staff, and the effect of these on the decisions made in the situation of medication errors is addressed.

It seemed that the modality of identification fell in with the notion of an ethic of justice. The right action was being decided on according to deontological argumentation. The responsibility for the proper care of the patient stood in the foreground and thus justified that 'the procedure' was followed. However, this care was oriented on rules and policy. It disregarded consideration for other nurses involved in a medication error, as well as it possibly disregarded care for self.

The maxim in this modality was, to own up to a mistake regardless of the negative consequences this may have for self or for other nurses involved.

In the second modality regard for personal hurt or the possibility of colleagues to be hurt gave rise to counteridentification. Here caring for self and seemingly caring for colleagues' well-being was used to justify aberration from rules. A counter-position to the institutional hierarchy was taken up. An ethic of care was the driving force for action here. In this position the ethic of justice and the ethic of care could not be reconciled. They must needs oppose each other.

In the third modality however, an integration of both positions seemed to be paramount for the decisions made by nurses. The responsibility to care for patients, to assure that no harm will come to them was not the only central force in this modality. Good and safe care for patients was seen in close relationship with nurses' well-being. Action was taken that regarded both, the deontological element of a decision to be made as well as the ultimate outcome of a situation. Here also a teleological basis was included for decisions made in the event of medication errors.

In the modality of disidentification the ultimate goal seemed to be to investigate the circumstances that led to an error; to take into consideration the situation as it presented itself; and to change practices that favoured the occurrence of medication errors.

Benner and Wrubel address this aspect in the context of deliberations on nurses learning to cope with care giving under adverse circumstances. They write:

> Shifting one's perspective from that of a deficit view of the situation (i.e., assessing how deficient the real is compared to the ideal standard) to one of discovering the possibilities inherent in the situation opens up new coping options. Seeing only the deficits can block perceptions of the possible, but the deficit view may also paralyze action if the emotional response is one of moral outrage or disappointment. If one reacts with moral outrage, one may not see alternative lines of action that would help the situation. Disappointment may breed disillusionment, and the person may cope by giving up the ideals altogether (Benner and Wrubel 1988 pp. 396/397).

Where only the deficits in a situation were seen (the *'ruthless character'* of a manager; or the situation of a *'witch-hunt'*), disillusionment may indeed be the only way to cope with the experienced disappointment; and the notion of counteridentification may govern a nurse's reactions. Where on the other hand, in the modality of disidentification the outlook was shifted away from a deficit view, room could be made for positive changes.

In the modality of disidentification, an ethic of care did not negate the value of an ethic of justice, but by integrating the elements of both justice and care, a freedom of choice become possible that did not shun a certain disregard of rules in situations where strict adherence to them could cause more harm than good.

This freedom took into account the ultimate effects of a decision. It did not do so by being afraid of the slippery slope argument (if minor mistakes are not followed up according to procedure, big ones may be concealed). It was the regard for the well-being of the nurse as well as the interest of the patient, one enhancing the other, that provided a wider scope of decision-making faculties.

A State of Transition and Indecisiveness (Loggerheads and Bosom-Buddies)

So far the reality of human relationships has only lightly been touched upon. Likes and dislikes; sympathy or antipathy influenced the decisions several participants in this study talked about. This is addressed next and appreciated in connection with an integration of justice and care. The focus is on reporting mistakes other nurses have made.

It was notable that some participants exhibited an element of doubt as to the decisions to be made, where reporting other nurses' mistakes was concerned, or where more than one nurse was involved in an incident.

Thelma, in Interview One example one, mentioned that her charge nurse had not been so sure about the way she was going to handle the situation of Thelma's error. Thelma had written a report and had left it for the ward sister to deal with:

> *Well, I just wrote down what actually happened, and I put it in an envelope and put it on our boss's desk, (INT1 EX1 444-447).*

> *But the next day she actually said to me, '**I am not going to report this ... because** .. I feel that you know exactly what you have done, why you have done it', (...) She had taken advice from one of her peers, another sister, I think, and they decided that they wouldn't take it further, (...) Now whether or not she should have done that, I don't know, because **there are procedures to be followed** and ... but within that do we not have the... eh ... can we... **can we be selective** or can we ... I don't know, I don't know. But she didn't report it ...(INT1 EX1 263-284).*

Another similar situation was experienced by Thelma in example two. Thelma felt she ought to report an incident where she had, together with a student midwife, administered a second dose of Diamorphine to a patient. A fellow-midwife had given the first dose of Diamorphine and had not signed for it correctly in the patient's Kardex. The midwife told Thelma, not to take the occurrence any further, not to bother, just to forget about it. This caused Thelma a problem.

Thelma realised that she had not seen the entry about the first dose, which her colleague had made on the prescription sheet rather than in the Kardex, and she had given the patient a second dose. Thelma immediately owned up to it to that midwife:

> *... immediately I owned up to it and said, 'well.. she's had another dose of Diamorphine,... oh, dear, you know, I've made a big boob here',... (INT1 EX2 649-653).*

A discussion ensued as obviously only Thelma and the other midwife knew about the mistake:

> *... now the other midwife ... said (...)'she's only had 10 mg and we often just give 10 mg 3 hourly anyway (MA: sure), stop worrying about it', I said 'yes, but wasn't prescribed', and she says ... 'oh, just give it a break, leave it alone, stop getting upset about it'. I .. a couple of times said, '..yeah I really should do something about it', she says, 'forget it, leave it, don't worry about it'. And .. she's actually ... was in charge of post natal at that point. So... I left it, and I went home, ... (INT1 EX2 654-674).*

Thelma informed the student midwife. She too, thought the occurrence not worthy of reporting. She suggested that possibly a doctor could retrospectively prescribe the extra dose given. Thelma's conscience did not let her rest:

> *... this is just not right, it's just not right, I can't do this. (INT1 EX2 677-679).*

After she got home, Thelma phoned the senior midwife who had taken over the shift, and spoke to her about having given another dose of Diamorphine to a patient. This was difficult for her, as she did not want to compromise the other midwife. On the other hand she felt guilty as she herself had not immediately told sister about the occurrence:

> *... I didn't really want to say, well its all her fault, but I didn't own up to my mistake, you can't do that... (INT1 EX2 1137-1140).*

Sister's reaction to the phone-call was a great relief to Thelma. Sister had realised the situation and got a doctor to prescribe the second dose of Diamorphine retrospectively. She indicated that she was glad that Thelma had phoned her and admitted the mistake:

> *I said, 'do you realise, that I made a drug error this morning and gave a second dose of Diamorphine'. And .. she (sister) said, 'yes, I do realise that, and don't worry about it, Thelma, I've got the doctor down and ... he's written it up. So its been prescribed now. We sorted it out. ... I'm glad you phoned me' (INT1 EX2 683-692).*

Here altogether four nurses were involved in a minor incident. The midwife responsible and the student did not think the incident worthy of reporting. Thelma did, and sister felt that her honesty was praiseworthy even though she herself had settled the incident already with the doctor.

Covering up for each other, sorting things out on ward level as far as minor incidents were concerned seemed to be common practice. In both examples Thelma had mentioned, the bureaucratic machinery of the disciplinary procedure had not been involved. Thelma said:

> *Thelma: ... **possibly we do,.. cover up for each other** when we ..shouldn't have, (...) .. you know **we all want to save our own skin,** no harm is done.*
>
> *MA: What d' you think, should have been done? (...)*
>
> *Thelma: Well, the proper procedure, the proper thing was to have reported it, as I did, and then .. for the sister to, to take that further (INT1 EX2 1536-1552).*

Thelma saw and described the dichotomy between the duty to adhere to policy and the need of loyalty towards colleagues. Especially as she herself had been treated leniently in the first example, it was difficult for her to decide what to do in the second one.

The personal relationship among staff was a factor to be taken into account here. Thelma expressed her perception of the dilemma in the following way:

> ***It's probably not ethical**, but then you've got to look at the relationship that you have with people you are working with, is it going to affect that (INT1 1578-1582).*

For Thelma the main issue was that generally midwives would report an error, but on the other hand to her it was feasible to have a doctor to *'sort out the records'* and, for the sake of a good working climate among staff, deal with a minor medication error on ward level. This she would term *'covering up for each other'*.

However, she was undecided about this approach as she had also stated emphatically that the procedure must be followed.

Joan, the midwife in Interview Two, regarding a mix-up of breast-milk talked about similar occurrences:

> *I thought, what do I do? Do I go and tell the nursing officer? Do I go and speak to the person that did it? Do I .. forget about it and .. (INT2 EX2 636-644).*

The midwife responsible for the mix-up had tried to cover the incident up and told the nursery nurse who knew about it, not to mention it to anyone. Joan recounted:

> *... because she (the nursery nurse) had said: Oh, I shouldn't have told you, I knew I shouldn't have told you. She says.. eh ... 'cos (the midwife) is my friend .. (...) and (I) said (...)* ***you can't always cover up for your friends,*** *you've got to do what you believe to be right .. (INT2 EX2 1095-1103).*

Personal, friendly relationship amongst staff would have been no reason for Joan to cover up a mistake:

> *... you know, I felt, she should have .. gone and said herself what she had done, and not just ignored the fact, that she had done it .. (INT2 EX2 632-635);*

> *Ehm.. but* ***you feel really bad about reporting somebody for doing something wrong,*** *And it's not the fact that they have done something wrong, it's the fact that they've not owned up to it .. (INT2 EX2 745-751);*

> *I don't want to appear to be telling tales on other people, but on the other hand, my .. ehm .. responsibility.. (INT2 EX2 675-678).*

It would possibly have been easier to talk to the midwife, had Joan known her better:

> *...* ***had it been somebody that I was .. much more .. close to (...) I may have gone about it in a different way ..*** *because If I had felt that I'd known the person well enough to go up and speak to her, take them aside, if you like, say, look ... (INT2 EX2 1110-1119).*

So what happened was:

> *So in fact I did go, and see that midwife and I said to her and .. I'm sorry, but I find out that this is happened, and I really feel that you should have come and, and .. said .. yourself what had happened, I said, but* ***I just can't ignore it,*** *I said, and I told the nursing officer about it, and eh ... She said: Oh!!, that's alright, that's alright.. I knew, somebody would find out..!! (INT2 EX2 659-670).*

In the end Joan was quite sure of her action and attitudes. She expressed this by saying:

> *... to go back and find out the same thing again, I would probably do exactly the same thing (INT2 EX2 1157-1160).*

In the first example which Joan related during our interview, she had given a second dose of Valium to a patient because the first dose had not been signed for. The nurse who had made the initial mistake wanted to sign retrospectively which would have left Joan with the sole responsibility for it:

> *I was really angry with her ..you know, I shouted at her: No, you can't do that! (INT2 EX1 376-379).*

But her initial anger soon gave way to serious reflection what to do and why:

> *... and that was just **your** initial anger, and you know, ..annoyance, (INT2 EX1 383-384).*

Here, Joan used the more distancing version of the second person **'your** initial anger', as she sometimes did during the interview, implying that even now, in recounting the incident, her own anger was not the main feature of her reaction.[5]

Joan reflected on her colleague's possible reaction to her outburst and acknowledged that the staff nurse most probably had realised shortly afterwards that 'the procedure' had to be followed:

> *... when she stood back from the situation and realised. Well I think she then knew, well, yes, you've got to go about this in the proper manner .. (INT2 EX1 397-402).*

Furthermore, she bore no ill feelings towards her colleague after the situation was settled:

> *... once that was done, that was that, **there were no ill feelings between us**, eh, or anything like that (MA: you worked ..as before) oh, yes.. (INT2 EX1 434-438).*

This example shows how the personal relationship among staff affected the way an error was dealt with and how in turn an error might affect this relationship. To Joan it was important '*to go about it in the right manner*'. The midwife responsible might have wished for another outcome, (that is keep the incident concealed) but she seemed to accept it, when the procedure took its course.

---

[5] The use of various grammatical forms and an interpretation of this use is enlarged on in the next chapter 'Guilt and reconciliation'

Gerald, in Interview Five, example one, also mentioned the effect, which reporting a medication error had on a personal relationship. The situation Gerald referred to happened when he was a student nurse on a psychiatric ward. Under the supervision of his ward sister he gave a monthly depot injection of Depexol, a Phenothiazine, to a patient with schizophrenia. It was forgotten to record the injection on the patient's medication sheet. Both, Gerald and sister, were off duty the next day when the injection was given again, even though the patient had said that he had had his dose. As this had not been recorded, the patient's protest was not heeded. The next day, Gerald heard by chance how some nurses discussed this situation. He *'checked'* into the discussion and verified that the injection had been given. The sister who had supervised Gerald was present too and acknowledged the fact. The nursing officer was informed about the incident. Sister, Gerald, and the nurses who had given the second injection, had to write statements. Sister had to see her unit manager, a senior nursing officer. Gerald actually felt that the mistake had not been his fault and that the disciplinary action taken against the sister supervising him was justified:

> *... she was disciplined basically (...) it was her fault, she was a trained nurse, she was supervising and that and it had been her error (...) And it was noted in her ehm .. file I think that she was basically told that .. it better not happen again (INT5 EX1 335-343).*

Gerald thought that the sister might blame him for the mistake and for the onset and outcome of the disciplinary procedure. Their basically good relationship suffered after the incident:

> *... and .. **prior to the mistake, I'd had a good relationship with her**, ehm, **after that** ... Ehm .. **really we didn't get on** she was really... I think she, I think she blamed me in the ... you know, we didn't really get on after that... (INT5 EX1 1 98-205);*

> *... I mean the atmosphere between me and the sister was a bit sort of .. frosty, you know, (INT5 EX1 510-513).*

Sean provided a further example of how personal relationships might influence decisions. He suspected a senior nurse of having given an injection of Heparin too early. He did not get on well with this nurse:

> *Her and I just didn't hit it, hit it off, and maybe if we had got on better (MA: mmh), I could have spoken to her about it, (INT4 EX3 2427-2431);*

> ***I might have mentioned it, if .. that staff nurse and myself hadn't been at loggerheads,*** *(INT4 EX3 2409-2412);*
>
> *.. I didn't accuse, but I challenged.* ***Her and I didn't get on very well,*** *and there was a great deal of friction between us..(INT4 EX3 1089-1092).*

Apparently that staff nurse had handled the situation in a way that did not satisfy Sean. He suspected that she had given Heparin at 6 p.m. instead of 10 p.m., and had then asked the night nurse not to give the 10 p.m. dose but to sign for it. The night nurse and Sean's colleague were friends. Sean mentioned this incident several times:

> *I saw her talking to the night staff, in private, and I think she was saying to the night staff, by mistake I gave him his Heparin at six o'clock, don't give him at 10 o'clock tonight, ... (INT4 EX3 1056-1062);*
>
> *... I saw her talking to the .. the night staff, ehm* ***the two of them were sort of bosom buddies,*** *(INT4 EX3 2391-2394).*

It appeared that here, because of a good personal relationship between two nurses, a minor medication error was dealt with in an un-bureaucratic manner.

If the discourse of nurses is examined who found themselves between Scylla and Charybdis as far as their loyalties were concerned, the following details can be discerned:

Nurses felt themselves bound to the rules of drug administration and to the guide-lines that are to be followed after a medication error has occurred. This applied also to minor errors. *(There are procedures to be followed..; I just can't ignore it..)*

However, where a minor error was concerned the situation was not always clear: *(..can we be selective .. I don't know).* As a general rule, Thelma, felt that it is uncommon to cover up a situation entirely (even if it is a minor error), but understanding was voiced when nurses were reluctant to own up to a mistake. Thelma did not say 'she wanted to save her skin'; she said *'we all want to save our skin'.* She may have said this, knowing that in a similar situation another nurse might cover up for her *(..possibly we cover up for each other..).*

Where nurses knew each other well, situations of medication errors could be dealt with privately *(I saw her talking to the staff nurse - the two of them were bosom buddies..).* Thelma on the other hand felt that *'You can't always cover up for your friends.. '.*

But where personal relationship was not strained, or where nurses knew each other well enough it would be easier to deal with a minor error *(..had it been somebody I was more close to .. I may have gone about it in a different way..; I might have mentioned it .. ; if that staff nurse and myself hadn't been at loggerheads).*

Thus, personal knowledge of each other and a good working relationship can be said to be helpful in finding ways of dealing with medication errors. On the other hand, if relationships were strained or indifferent this presented a hindrance in sorting out a situation un-bureaucratically.

The reactions of a nurse to being reported could be indifferent *(... there were no ill feelings ..);* or a nurse could develop a feeling of animosity towards a colleague. In Gerald's situation, in Interview Five, example one, the relationship between sister and himself was positive at first. This may have lead him to talk about the facts of the error. The relationship changed after sister had been disciplined *(... prior to the mistake I'd had a good relationship with her, ... after that we didn't get on).*

At the cost of covering up a mistake, nurses would possibly strive to preserve a friendship or a good working relationship. They would be willing to break rules. Thelma described this dilemma, saying that she felt it was *'probably not ethical'* to cover up for each other, but that the working relationship had to be taken into consideration.

At this point it is interesting to use an example from the Scottish Group Discussion (example one). Two nurses who had been involved in such a dilemma were taking part in the discussion. Their interaction here showed how much both were still affected by the situation which must have taken place about a year prior to my data collection.

The nurse who had made the mistake was obviously still distressed by the incident. She was the first participant to start off with a personal experience of a medication error. She talked very fast and incoherently and it was difficult to follow what she was about to say. One of the other participants interrupted and offered to tell the story which the nurse gladly accepted.

This colleague had been involved in the incident insofar as she had found a discrepancy in the DDA-Book.[6] She reported the discrepancy to her senior nurse and then traced the mistake to the nurse responsible. Several times throughout the group discussion she mentioned how difficult a task she found it, to report this error.

Here some extracts from the group discussion are reproduced. (Nurse A.: is the nurse responsible for the error; Nurse B.: is the nurse reporting it; MA: is the researcher):

Nurse A.: ... it's ... difficult ... the realisation that .. you can actually make an error. It's happened to me! ....

MA: You want to .. tell us the story?

Nurse A.: ... (...) it's diff.. (..?..) I just had ... (..?..) (..?..)

MA: So.. what happened?

Nurse B.: Maybe I should start!

Nurse A.: Oh yeah!..

Nurse B.: (...) on a daily basis we checked the (...) DDAs, (...) And .. I couldn't work it out. I went through the books, (...) it was either Pethidine or Papaverine .. either or .. ehm .. the numbers didn't count up, (...) 'cos I couldn't understand it I.. I reported it to .. the nursing officer in charge, and then I went through it again, and realised what the mistake had been. (...) and I felt .. terrible, because I felt ... well .. really, no harm had come to the patient, they got some sedation, OK! Wasn't what was prescribed for them, (...) but then I felt awful, because I had reported it to the nurse.. the nursing officer, and because of this, one of my colleagues was going to be ... pulled up! (...) there had been a definite drug error made, but it wasn't in.. in my opinion a very dangerous one.

Nurse A.: (...) its not an excuse (..?..)

Nurse B.: (...) I just felt awful then, (...) the patient was comfortable and we had spoken to the doctors... (The drugs were prescribed retrospectively as they were given) (21-146)

(...)

---

6 The book where drugs listed under the Dangerous Drugs Act are recorded.

Nurse B.: (...) and I felt, I felt terrible, having to.. having to confronting you (addresses Nurse A.)

Nurse A.: (...) ... because it was a DDA, couldn't ... (..?..) it was really traumatic ..

Nurse B.: It was traumatic for everybody, because I remember this, I felt I was ehm .. betraying you (addresses Nurse A.) I mean, it had, it had to be reported, because, there was obviously a discrepancy in the books and .. (...) I felt like was betraying one of my colleagues, although a mistake had been made, (...) it was a harmless mistake, but at the same time, .. it couldn't be covered up.

Nurse A.: I could understand ...

Nurse B.: ..just felt .. terrible, I think it had an effect on all of us, you know, it just.. (163-211)

(...)

MA: (addressing Nurse A.) How did you .. react to ehm Nurse B.'s.. you know, sort of worry about, having to report it?

Nurse A.: I don't think she had any option ...

Nurse B.: I knew I didn't have any options, and .. but I felt bad, I had to do it!

Nurse B.: And if it had been an ordinary drug, it may never have been found (328-341).

(...)

Nurse B.: I felt embarrassed as well, (...) I felt awful, I felt that I was wishing it was me, that made the drug error, (...) I having to .. report it, (...) but its difficult, I just felt so awful at finding it, and having to report it (...) knowing that has to be done, I have to go through the procedures (...) that's what you have to do, but still .. difficult! (1584-1602).

This dialogue exemplifies paradigmatically the meaning which a nurse might attribute to reporting a mistake of a colleague. Both nurses identified with the rules to be followed after a medication error had occurred. The dialogue shows the dilemma Nurse B. had been in, when having to decide on her action. It also shows that the nurse responsible for the mistake comprehended this dilemma.

A medication error can affect the whole ward team no matter how the mistake is handled. In this example the friendly relationship of Nurse A. and Nurse B. had not suffered, but apparently a positive professional working basis was established. Acting according to rules does not have to destroy friendship in such a case.

Showing compassion as well as adhering to rules are not mutually exclusive. Thus, an element of the ethic of justice as well as an element of the ethic of care can be integral aspects of the decision-making process after a medication error has occurred.

KNOWLEDGE AND SKILL - A DECISIVE FACTOR

In decisions to be made in a situation after a medication error has occurred, varying aspects were taken into consideration. In this section the value of professional competence in the context of decision-making in the situation of medication errors is examined. This is closely related to changing personal identification and answering different interpellative forces.

Looking at circumstances as well as at the specific nurses who made 'lenient' decisions, it may be said that these nurses possibly had a high degree of professional competence at their disposal. Being sure of possible harmful or unharmful consequences for patients, allowed some nurses by using their expert judgement, to deal with an error themselves rather than having to refer it to a higher authority.

This was demonstrated by Mike. His own mistake, as he said, was due to '*complete and utter stupidity*'. Mike stressed the fact that he was well versed in the skills of drug administration, as well as that he had a good theoretical knowledge of everything that was involved with the administration of drugs.

Part of a nurse's duty while giving out medicines to patients is to know the drugs, their effects and side effects. An interesting misunderstanding occurred during our talk when I asked Mike about his '*knowledge of what the patients are actually getting*'. I had wanted to address his estimation of possible medication errors on his ward, but he answered:

> *I think I have a good knowledge of the drugs that are, are being given. (INT7 440-442).*

Here, he may well have referred to his pharmacological knowledge. Later during our interview this became clear:

> *I think I'm, I have sufficient knowledge of, of drugs .. to realise, when (...) a drug error is likely to cause a patient any harm..* (INT7 1202-1213).

This knowledge allowed Mike to disidentify with the procedure to be followed according to current policy. He knew his knowledge would allow for deviation from policy without causing harm to anyone. He could act with appropriateness because of his theoretical and practical expertise. The fact that he had called on the doctor's judgement regarding his own medication error, established this insofar, as he acknowledged another expert opinion in the situation.

I argue that the same could be applied to the sister in Thelma's situation (Interview One, examples one and two), who did not report the incident further but felt it was sufficient if she knew about it. Also the ward sister in Henry's positive learning experience could, because of her professional competence say '.. *well that's all right'*. She looked into the matter, found out where the problems lay, and dealt with it at ward level.

It could well be that in situations where this competence was lacking or still in the process of being developed, nurses did not allow themselves to deviate from the stated regulations of dealing with medication errors. They had to look to higher authority to supplement a certain professional insecurity.

This could also apply to nurses in higher management positions who did not have the clinical up to date expertise in the administration of medication any more, but only their knowledge of legislative procedures to fall back upon. The harsh treatment of Jane in Interview Eleven could thus be accounted for.

A constant dialectical move between the maxims of justice and care, between the deontological and teleological groundings of decisions has to be made in order to differentiate between what ought to be done and what is best to be done in a given situation. The example of the Hebrew midwives, Shiph'rah and Pu'ah illustrated this dialectical move. Shiph'rah and Pu'ah used their professional expertise to argue against Pharaoh. He could not gainsay their statement that the Hebrew women had already delivered when they arrived to assist with the birth. Not being present during delivery they naturally could not prevent the live birth of a Hebrew boy child. In this way they avoided harm to their own people.

In order to make decisions in the situations described, nurses will oscillate between regarding official policy and regarding the good for self and for others. This is not a question of decisions made according to prevalent moods, but a deep identification with what an actor believes to be most beneficial in a given situation. Nurses will always find themselves in situations of dilemma. Adopting an ideal (e.g. strict adherence to rules in order to benefit patients) will not prevent a nurse from possibly causing harm to a colleague, or even to an entire team. Professional competence however, will allow for some leeway in the decisions to be made and can give appropriateness to new positions of disidentification.

CHAPTER 10
GUILT AND SHAME - RECONCILIATION WITH HUMAN PRECARIOUSNESS

INTRODUCTION TO THE CHAPTER

The nurses in the study talked in strong terms about the reactions they had when they realised that they had made an error in the administration of medicines. They referred to their feelings of guilt, of being humiliated, embarrassed or ashamed and used expressions like *'I felt sick'; 'I could have died'; 'I was devastated'*. In this chapter I give an interpretative representation of nurses' discourse about guilt and shame. I describe how nurses experienced being and feeling guilty and ashamed, and how they dealt with forgiving self and with reconciling self with the experience of their own precariousness.

The key issues of guilt and reconciliation link this chapter to the second cornerstone of the empirical model. Guilt was one of the reactions 'in the nurse' following a medication error. This key issue binds together the themes of 'The procedure of dealing with medication errors', 'The image of the nurse and of nursing', and 'Support'. I make implicit and explicit reference to these themes throughout this chapter.

The chapter consists of five sections. Using theological, psychological, and sociological paradigms the key issue of guilt and its connection to the phenomenon of shame, is outlined in the first section. Remembering, as being part of the experience of having made an error in the administration of medications is highlighted in the second section as is the perception of medication errors as a taboo-subject. The third and fourth sections deal with coping strategies used in discourse. Here some, but by no means all, functional uses of specific grammatical forms of speech as employed by the nurses are explored. In a last short section a summary is given of how reconciliation was addressed by the nurses in this study. The subject of reconciliation could merit more space. It is however, not dealt with seperately at great length as it is implicitely addressed throughout this chapter. Coming to terms with ones own precariousness begins where personal failure is verbalised. The talk about medication errors in itself is a starting point for becoming reconciled with such an experience.

GUILT AND SHAME - OUTLINE OF THE SUBJECT

In the preface of his book Guilt: man and society (1971), R. W. Smith named guilt as a "basic category, like power, identity, death, or love". Smith further mentions that the focus of guilt "is on the creation, maintenance, and repair of boundaries within society and within ourselves". This indicates the diversity with which the concept of guilt has to be dealt with if an attempt is made at addressing the issue.

In order to understand what guilt may mean in a certain context it serves well to look at perceptions of human nature and at the role guilt is said to play within a specific perception. It is theology that first and foremost deals with human nature. Therefore, the subject is first delineated using a theological perspective.

Theology has understood guilt as a central problem of humankind. Religious teachings includes answers to the basic question of how the ever recurrent experience of failure in our acts toward self, towards others, and towards society can be reconciled with a happy and content existence in this world or in another world.

The core of most answers given by Christian and other religious authorities lay either in the acceptance or in the defiance of human nature.[1] One view sees human nature as basically good but deviant. This view understands people as being able to accept and tolerate each

---

1 See Lexikon für Theologie und Kirche (1962) Band 7, "Natur,"; "Naturrecht,"; Band 9, "Sola-fide-Prinzip."

others' failures. Human nature, in this view, is gifted with an imagination that can see a better tomorrow. This perspective implies an inner-worldly promise or presumption that we can live each day anew in the hope that less hurt will prevail or that hurt, and thus, guilt can be overcome.

Another view would have it that human nature is basically corrupt and tainted and is in need of redemption that is only attainable and finalised in another world. This leaves us with a similar hope as described above, which however, has less promise for the daily task of living. This view puts reconciliation further out of reach, but it explains the reality of persistent wrongdoing and failures.

A third perspective may be obtained by the assurance that on the one hand, creation, including human nature, is good, and on the other hand, the understanding that in view of the presence of evil in this world, a different and new existence that overcomes the brokenness of the present one can be expected. The tension that is created by this perspective allows for the perseverance to strive for 'a good life' here and now, but at the same time it allows for the transcendence of the here and now. This tension has the inherent power to provide a significance to human life that lies not solely beyond this world.

Guilt can be understood firstly within the framework of the individual make up and development of a person. Secondly the social or communal aspects of guilt can be highlighted by referring to the shared values of a community which may be violated by an individual's or by a group of individuals' behaviour.

Theology has greatly profited by the psychological endeavours to describe the dynamics of guilt. Freud referred to normal existential guilt, and pathological guilt. Normal guilt he called "remorse" (Freud in v. Stein 1990), which literally means 'eating again' - a word which captures the "gnawing quality of guilt". A difference has to be acknowledged between the reality of guilt and guilt feelings. In extreme pathological situations guilt feelings can even turn into "neurotic guilt" that has no grounding in real guilt But furthermore, people can be encountered who appear guilt-less. This may be accorded to "sociopathic development" (v. Stein 1969).

A twofold differentiation of guilt can be made, by taking behaviourist theory, theory of the human sciences, as well as theological and philosophical elements into account. First, there is pathological guilt, which may be divided into "too intense guilt", as seen in classical neurotic and psychotic symptoms; and conversely, an "absence or confusion of guilt" which is often termed "character disorder", or "antisocial and dysocial personality disorder" (v. Stein 1990). Second, there is "existential guilt", which is also referred to as "real guilt", "normal guilt", or "authentic guilt". This is the guilt which theology also addresses as "human reality", reflecting a "cosmic order" (v. Stein 1990).

For Buber existential guilt

> ...occurs when someone injures an order of the human world whose foundations he knows and recognizes as those of his own existence and of all common human existence (Buber 1971 p. 92).

Where psychology has sought to deal with guilt feelings, Buber in his essay on existential guilt, addressed the "ontic character" of guilt. Just as important as treating feelings of guilt, Buber claims, is the confrontation with its existential reality (Buber 1971). Buber very crisply delineates his understanding of existential guilt. He states:

> Personal guilt, whose reality some schools of psychology contest and others ignore, does not permit itself to be reduced to the trespass against a powerful taboo (Buber 1971 p. 97).

Buber sees the knowledge of guilt and the human ability to reflect on it as the source for the emergence of taboos. He contends "that guilt does not exist because a taboo exists to which one fails to give obedience". Taboos can only come into existence because of the "primal fact" that humans as humans "can become guilty and know it". Buber refers to the ability of human beings "to remember" as a factor that constitutes existential guilt. Thus, the knowledge of guilt is linked to the "insight (...) into the impossibility of recovering the original point of departure", that is "the real insight into the irreversibility of lived time" (Buber 1971).

Guilt is not a cognitive application of a certain feeling. Kolakowski says:

> We do not accept our moral convictions by admitting "this is true", but by feeling guilty, when we act perfidiously toward them (Kolakowski 1992 p. 178, my translation).

Kolakowski draws attention to the fact that the "ability to perceive ourselves as being guilty" it is not so much the aspect of trespassing a stated law, a rule or moral code, but rather the "existential act" of questioning our "position within a cosmic order". It is not the knowledge and "acceptance of a certain value judgement" and "the fear of punishment", but "a feeling of deferential awe" in view of our own actions which has disturbed the "world harmony". (Kolakowski 1992, my translations).

This is a fear, Kolakowski says, after transgressing not a law, but a taboo. Kolakowski argues further that the taboo is an "immovable pylon in every viable moral system" as well as an "integral contingency of religious life". The ability to feel guilt constitutes our moral systems. A system of punishment will cause fear of vengeance. A cosmic order has taboos the transgression of which are the cause of guilt, as much as the ability to feel guilty is the source of taboos. Kolakowski describes the taboo as "a necessary link between the veneration of eternal reality and the knowledge of good and bad". Law and cosmic order and fear of punishment and the "consciousness of guilt" are not to be confused. Fear of punishment and the knowledge of guilt are two distinct entities (Kolakowski 1992, my translations).

To enlighten the concept of "consciousness of guilt", Schneider's psychological perspective of guilt and shame is helpful. Schneider (1990), defines shame as a "response to failure and the shortcomings of the self in relation to the ego ideal". A distinction between guilt and shame can be made by referring to guilt as representing "the psychology of conscience and thus, the threat of punishment; while shame exhibits the psychology of narcissm and thus, the threat of less love" (Schneider 1990). Shame is, Schneider says:

> ..the emotional price we pay for our encounter with the discrepancy between our ideals and our reality (Schneider 1990 p. 1162).

This does not take the above mentioned aspects of guilt as a constituting factor of a cosmic or of a human order into account. But it sets shame into relation with guilt and defines it on an affective level. Schneider refers to the difference between guilt and shame by asserting that shame is more closely connected to the affective perceptions of a person. Shame seems to be generally related to embarrassment and humiliation, whereas guilt refers to debt or injury, to responsibility, duty and obligation. However, shame is closely connected with guilt and the feelings of guilt. Schneider states that the "sense of felt inadequacy is often more salient for people than any feeling of wrongdoing". (This was certainly expressed in the data with which the participants had supplied me).

The etymological roots of the word 'shame' lie in the Indo-European meaning 'to cover'. Therefore, shame is "a painful feeling of being exposed, uncovered, unprotected, vulnerable" (Schneider 1990).

In the context of shame, Schneider, refers to the need of the self for "some time off-stage, a private space, before it (the self) is ready to go public". It is important "to have a space to oneself within which to develop before one can maintain one's balance in front of others" (Schneider 1990). This accounts well for the *'state of shock'* after a medication error has been realised, during which the self may recover, or for *'being absolutely sick'* and thus, having time to recuperate.

Having made a medication error left the nurse in most cases with the knowledge that a certain order has been broken. For some nurses this would bring about an acute awareness of being guilty. Guilt or feelings of guilt in the situation of medication errors were connected to factual occurrences or to imagined facts. Shame, on the other hand concerns personal inadequacy. It can be seen as a feeling projected forward, and as being caused by the fear that patients, colleagues, or friends may think a nurse less capable of doing her/his job. Capps asserts that the "traditional language of guilt ... no longer has much relevance" (1993). He argues that societal changes within the last 20 years have produced what he calls "the narcisstic self" which revolves around shame rather than guilt. Capps differentiates:

> Whereas guilt arises in experience from failing to meet the expectations, real or perceived, of others, shame is felt when the self has failed to attain its own goals, when the realization occurs that the self is incapable of achieving its ambitions (Capps 1993 p. 34).

This was expressed by some nurses when they referred to '*letting oneself down*'. Indeed, from this perspective it is the self that is "damaged by this assessment" (Capps 1993). Capps states that "Shame has replaced guilt as the experience that causes individuals to feel bad about themselves". Even though Capps found that people still "used the language of guilt", he maintains that in most cases shame is the emotional driving force, as the feelings involved are related to a "depleted" or a "diminished" self.

The nurses in the study, however, referring to medication error indicated both, an experience of guilt and of guilt feelings as well as shame. Most nurses were acutely aware of having caused harm to another person. This, they clearly expressed in their concern about the well being of the patient who was possibly affected by the mistake. The shame then, that nurses felt was grounded in concrete guilt or at least in its possibility. In the next section details of nurses' discourse are examined which reveal how they experienced guilt and shame and how they came to terms with their experiences.

Discourse about Guilt and Shame

I'll never, ever forget

Guilt and shame are said to be associated with feelings that linger in the memory and are evoked anew when thinking about the situation that caused them. A past event brings about present feelings.

When trying to discern the meaning which nurses designated to their experiences of medication errors, written accounts are of a special value. By writing about their experiences, the participants were compelled to reflect on the past more than they would do during an interview. In three of the self reports the lasting effects of the experiences were mentioned. In these self reports a considerable time had elapsed since the occurrence of the error. This is what the writers expressed:

> ***...there is never a day but I think about it.. (REP2 93-94);***

The incident happened about 11 years ago when the writer, an experienced nurse, returned to day duty after working for 13 years on night duty. The next statement was made by a senior manager. The incident happened about 20 years ago when she was a ward sister.

> *The patient suffered no ill effects - I did -* ***I will never forget*** *the incident (REP4 36-38);*

The writer of the next sentence is now a senior community nurse. The incident she referred to took place about 19 years ago.

> ***Never wholly recovered the mental anguish*** *of those hours (REP5 71-72).*

Buber's reference to "the impossibility of recovering the original point of departure" (Buber 1971) could not be underpinned more accurately. Buber says:

> I, who have become another, am the same
> (Buber 1971 p 90).

But also during the group discussions some participants stressed how, even now they were still affected by the medication errors. For instance the nurse who during the Scottish Group Discussion gave the first example, said:

> *It was really traumatic (...) I just felt raw there (...) every time I do the drug trolley.* ***And even now..*** *(GD-SC EX1 186-217);*

In the German Group Discussion no direct mention was made as to too long lasting feelings of guilt or shame. Two extracts addressed the emotional effects a medication error had 'for a while':

> *Of course, it stays with me* ***for quite a while.*** *(GD-D EX3 918-919);*

> *On the whole she has managed to digest it fairly well (...) about a fortnight she avoided to look after intensive care patients.. (GD-D EX4 1269-1276).*

In the interviews lasting effects of the experiences were affirmed by several participants:

*She had said that, you know, as long as she lives, **she'll never, ever forget..** (INT4 EX1 2181-2183);*

*And **I don't think I'll ever forget it as long as I live**. It really was bad (INT9 EX1 171-173);*

*I mean, I have got over it to a degree now, but **I never forget** (INT9 EX1 308-311).*

However, going through the texts it became obvious that not all nurses mentioned the lasting emotional affects of their experiences. Mike for instance, said that he didn't lose any sleep over the incident:

I went off home after that, (...) I can't say, it disturbed my days sleep at all (INT7 EX1 95-98);

The patient was not harmed, by mistakenly being given another patient's medication. Mike related how the situation happened; he then said:

...but I was keen to find out, how the gentleman was, when I came back on for my night-shift, that night, and he was fine. And .. that was it, I didn't give it another thought, at all after that. (INT7 EX1 118-124),

At the beginning of our interview he had said:

*...as to my feelings about it, .. I was **extremely .. eh, upset** (INT7 EX1 81-82);*

Mike had never before talked about his mistake. While talking about it in our interview, the following dialogue ensued:

MA: Did you, did you ever talk to anybody .. friends, relatives, colleagues, about the situation?

Mike: No!

MA: This is the first time?

Mike: Yes!

MA: Hhmm, how do you feel about it?

*Mike: Ha, ha, ha, its strange, I suppose yeah, Ahh .. I find it .. its really **embarrassing**, making a drug error, (INT7 EX1 800-815).*

During our interview he pointed out several times how embarrassing the situation had been for him. Towards the end he admitted:

> ***I was distressed by the embarrassment****, I had caused myself, and I was distressed by the potential damage that I could have caused the patient, it was certainly a, ehm .. something that I would, I wouldn't want to happen again ... (INT7 EX1 1649-1657).*

Mike used the words *'I was extremely upset'* and *'I was distressed by the embarrassment'*. Mike generally talked in the past tense, indicating how upset he had been at the time and how the embarrassment of having made a medication error had distressed him. Still, he did use the present tense when he answered my question *'How do you feel about it?'* saying *'It's really embarrassing, making a drug error'*. This indicated the lasting effects of Mike's experience, even though at first he had tried to convey that he was not too deeply affected.

Mike did not use the word 'shame' or 'being ashamed'. Nor did he talk about being or feeling guilty. But his use of the word *'embarrassed'* in connection with *'being upset'* and *'distressed'* may well point to a deeper emotional involvement than the general use of the phrase 'being embarrassed' indicates. By naming his feelings as *'distress'* and connecting them to *'the embarrassment (he) had caused himself'* as well as to *'the potential damage that (he) could have caused the patient'*, Mike showed that he had to deal with an affective element that was not eliminated by the fact that no harm had come to the patient. Not following the drug routine was a shameful experience for Mike. And potentially causing danger to a patient included an element of feeling guilty.

Using the present tense in connection with the second person singular was a means of conveying the lasting and generalisable impression a medication error had left. It was employed by several participants. Joan for instance said:

> *...To go back to how you feel about it: (...)* ***I was devastated*** *.. I thought* ***what have I done****? (INT2 EX1 209-213.*

And Pearl said:

> *And you* ***feel very vulnerable*** *.. (INT3 EX1 74-75).*

Here both, Joan and Pearl, switched to the present tense indicating that their reactions were not simply a thing of the past.

Thelma, on the other hand, generally used the past tense throughout our interview. She had talked about how strongly she felt as to dealing with her mistakes *'in the right manner'* and she frequently referred to how upset she had been at the time. She presumably had worked though her experiences.

She stated that:

> *I think **at the time I was worried** and .. probably upset, that would have affected my home life, (INT1 EX1 1711-1714).*

To Thelma, the incidents she had been involved in, as well as the feelings connected with them, obviously were now a matter of the past. Joan and Pearl, by switching to the present tense located them in the here and now.

A taboo subject

The German writer of a self report mentioned that by writing the report she addressed the subject for the first time in 20 years. She still remembered the feeling of shame which she could not verbalise at the time :

> *And shame, even **great shame** I felt for myself and in front of the colleague, about the fact that such a thing ... (REP6 59-63).*

Pearl talked in the beginning of our interview about the fear that prevailed with nurses when the issue of medication errors is brought up. The fact, that the issue is a very sensitive one was touched upon throughout our conversation.

> *...this kind of thing, that **its such a taboo.. subject...** (INT3 1180-1182).*

Pearl made it clear that there existed a great deal of fear in some nurses where medication errors were concerned. This fear partly pertained to the vulnerability of nurses in their position of responsibility. An error caused nurses to be afraid of the so called 'procedure' that would follow any medication error if it was reported and taken further up the nursing hierarchy.

Some quotes from Pearl's discourse illustrate this.

> *And you feel very .. you feel very vulnerable, and you only have to mention .. drug errors, or medication errors, and immediate .. you probably find barriers .. I really think* ***its fear,*** *(INT3 74-80);*
>
> *It's* ***fear of*** *..hahh .. the big thing I suppose that you think of .. error in medication! ..* ***struck off the register*** *you know, (INT3 85-88);*

But Pearl also alluded to more than the fear of punishment:

> *I think its the fear of what .. eh is going to happen to you, that's the worse thing, that can happen, apart from.. never mind* ***the fear of what I have committed ...*** *(INT3 90-96);*

The second part of this extract fits in with what Kolakowski terms "a feeling of deferential awe" which constitutes the "existential act" of questioning the personal position in a cosmic order. By making a medication error a certain order has been injured. Doing no harm is a basic concept of nursing as it is a basic moral principle of human interaction.

Jane expressed this in view of the fact that her case was dealt with simply from a punitive perspective. She obviously felt that there is more to the act of making a medication error than giving rise to punishment. She said:

> *I also thought that .. in a way* ***the emphasis .. was wrong,*** *because I felt* ***I was being punished .. for having done a wrong action,*** *which to me is wrong.* ***It should have been .. because of the potential harm you could have done*** *to .. a patient (INT11 915-920).*

The principle of doing no harm provides the foundation of mutual trust between patients and carers. Even though no actual harm may have come to a patient by the occurrence of an error, the fact that the 'order' has been injured (the drug routine has broken down) brought about the feeling of guilt in the nurse responsible.

The feeling of guilt is closely connected to the responsibility that has been accepted by a nurse. This was expressed by some nurses in the interviews when the reactions to medication errors were discussed. For instance Pearl, in Interview Three, said:

> *...****it's the guilt feeling,*** *that you .. the fact that you have given .. to a baby as well, I suppose that is so helpless, (INT3 EX1 128-131).*

Here, Pearl connected her guilt-feeling with her position of being responsible for a baby. She emphasised the baby's helplessness. It was not giving an extra dose of Iron that made her feel guilty, but rather the fact that she had violated the trusting relationship between herself and the baby's parents.

In Joan's situation the incident could not be ascribed to her responsibility alone, Still, she said:

> *...that initial feeling is still the same, that you feel .. dreadful .. that you have actually done .. a drug error, something that .. you know .. it's .. **a major thing in your line of work** ...(INT2 EX1 240-246).*
>
> *I thought: what have I done?!! (INT2 EX1 212-213).*
>
> *...and really, you think well, should I been practising ... (INT2 EX1 511-522).*

By accepting responsibility a nurse places her/himself within a certain order. Gemma, in interview six, knew herself to be the one who was to be blamed for the occurrence of the incident she related. She accepted this position emphatically by saying, that it would be easy to *'blame the hospital management'* as being responsible for the pressure at work that put her under stress when the incident occurred. Further along the line one could *'blame the Health Board'* and *'even the Minister of Health'* for not providing sufficient resources for the health services. Gemma said, blaming a higher authority could go on indefinitely and:

> *...if you wanted to, end up with **(blaming) God for putting you on earth**... (...) Where do you go, where do you stop? You have to say, no, it stops here, **it is my fault** (INT6 EX1 1537-1542).*

With this statement she accepted her existence as a precarious one, an existence that ultimately has to deal with personal guilt as a consequence of a wrong action.

Buber's and Kolakowski's understanding of existential guilt found a clear expression in what Gemma said. She made a connection with the acceptance of being on earth and thus, responsible for a certain order of things. In her discourse she affirmed an understanding of existential guilt. Seeing her mistake in the context of an institutional set-up but also in the light of personal failure, confronted Gemma with her own precariousness. She made sense of this reality by accepting her part within it.

Henry, in Interview Ten, also made a clear connection between his feelings of guilt and his responsibility:

> *I felt very **guilty**. I felt that I was **responsible** (INT10 EX1 338-340).*

But he too indicated the close connection between guilt and shame. Having failed in his responsibility affected the image he had of himself. The following dialogue highlights this:

> *MA: Yeah, now, you spoke about a feeling of guilt .. where does it come from, what is.. what is it?*
>
> *Henry: Ehm ... (...) from the feeling that you have let yourself down. That you have not been .. as perfect as you would like to be. And that (...) **you're eh, capable of making errors**. (INT10 963-976).*

Thelma, in Interview One expressed this by saying:

> *...you can think we are invulnerable ... yeah, I'm careful, I'm clever, I don't make mistakes, but then you do make mistakes and I think **it makes you very humble** for some time .. (INT1 1657-1662).*

The fact of having done wrong, of harming or potentially harming another person was expressed with language that indicated an awareness of guilt. But it also included the shameful awareness of personal imperfection. Being thus uncovered before oneself and before others, caused feelings of embarrassment and shame, and made *'you very humble'* as Thelma put it.

Having harmed another person, having broken patients' trust, and having let oneself down, is not something easily talked about. Talking about the cause of one's guilt and shame may increase the embarrassment. Thus, having broken a taboo, the means by which the taboo was broken understandingly becomes a taboo subject not to be talked about. By ascribing a taboo status to medication errors they are assigned a central but forbidden space in nurses' reality. However, as has been mentioned before, and as is addressed later, talking about the cause of one's own imperfections resulted in the acceptance of personal precariousness and fallibility.

COPING STRATEGIES AS FOUND IN THE DISCOURSE OF NURSES

General remarks

Looking closely at what nurses said in connection with guilt, the feeling of guilt, and of shame, revealed several strategies as to how nurses managed to cope with the experience of having made a medication error. In this section four aspects are highlighted. These are: first, physical reactions which nurses mentioned in the context of their mistakes; second, coping by covering up the possible shame of exposure or by delaying reactions to the incident; third, knowledge about the fact that all human beings are subject to mistakes; and fourth, the need to carry on with the work immediately at hand.

A state of shock: delayed reactions, covering up or owning up

It is generally accepted that being ill excuses a person from actions otherwise expected. In a state of shock people do or omit things and are not held responsible. Most participants in this study alluded to physical reactions after their realisation that they have made a medication error. Some examples are examined here, as to the use of guilt and shame language.

Thelma mentioned the physical feeling of being *'absolutely sick'*; of feeling *'ill about the whole thing'*; generally feeling *'dreadful'*; and *'devastated'* in relation to the first example she related. In relation to the second example she used the following expressions:

> *I felt pretty sick with myself,* ***I felt very worried about it,...*** *(INT1 EX2 414-416),*

She talked about being *'emotionally upset'* and about *'being worried'*. In both instances she made it clear that she reproached herself:

> *I felt* ***devastated****, how I could possibly have made such a stupid error! (INT1 EX1 168-171);*

The emotional upset in the second episode caused her inability to think straight:

> *I think I was too emotionally upset, that I'd done it, that* ***I wasn't thinking,*** *well, actually what should we do at this point,... (INT1 EX1 1520-1524).*

This inability may have been the reason for her to have heeded the suggestion of a second staff nurse who also was involved in the error, *'not to worry '*, and *'to forget about it'*:

> *So... I left it, and I went home, and driving home I was thinking about it the whole time, and thinking, I just... this is just not right,* ***it's just not right, I can't do this****. So I got home, immediately phoned work, and I spoke to one of my other colleagues, .. (INT1 EX2 673-681).*

This passage shows how Thelma used the drive home after work as the 'offstage or private space' I have alluded to earlier, in order to come to a decision as to her conduct.

In Interview Nine, it became apparent that shame prevented Chris from contacting any of her friends or family, she too needed that private space to come to terms with *'being a rotten nurse'*, as she put it. She said:

> *I didn't even want to phone anybody (...) 'cos I felt I was admitting,* ***I was a .. a rotten nurse****. (INT9 EX1 293-298).*

In Interview Two, Joan differentiated between a first reaction and a later reflection and action. Joan said as to the second midwife who was responsible for an error:

> *...but she obviously just wanted to .. her initial reaction was to ..* ***cover up for herself*** *... (INT2 EX1 171-174);*

> *...but then when she* ***stood back from the situation*** *and realised .. Well I think she then knew, well, yes, you've got to go about this in the proper manner .. and eh and that was fine after that ... (INT2 EX1 397-404).*

Joan displayed understanding for the fact that the second midwife at first wanted to cover up the mistake.

A further example was given by Henry, when he related an incident that had happened to a friend. Henry said:

> *Henry: ...****he just panicked*** *and .. he didn't tell anybody, he just watched the patient. basically .. really worried about it for a couple of days.*
>
> *MA: So, when did he tell you?*
>
> *Henry: I think it was* ***a while after it****, was about* ***a fortnight after****.. (INT10 EX3 836-845).*

It is evident that the immediate reactions of emotional upset have to be taken into consideration when regarding the decision-making process after a medication error has occurred. The language used conveyed the experience of being guilty and of feeling guilty and ashamed. Being in a *'state of shock'*, or *'panicking'* accounted for not being able to think, for *'covering up'*. *'Standing back'* first, allowed for reflected decision-making. Not losing the respect of peers and seniors as well as self-respect were motivating agents either for owning up or for covering up *(I was admitting, I was a rotten nurse)*. Some nurses would own up to a mistake in order to appear honest in spite of possibly being looked upon as negligent *(Its just not right, I can't do this)*. Nurses, however, might cover up a mistake and possibly only talk privately to friends about it. Whatever the decision, in the examples given above, the nurses mentioned great concern about the situation *(..felt very worried..; ..really worried about it, watched the patient basically)*. Having covered up an error, might then be an additional source of guilt and shame causing further worry and emotional upset.

Covering up

So far I have given examples of nurses who had owned up to their mistakes either officially or privately. The context of guilt however, as addressed in this chapter, calls for mentioning a further perspective. A person may actually be guilty but not feel guilty, and thus, act accordingly. It has to be differentiated from the delayed reaction that may terminate in not owning up to a mistake.

This was alluded to by some participants. Joan mentioned the nurses who had mixed up the breast milk of two mothers:

> *...she was very flippant about it.. (INT2 EX2 785-786)*

Pearl also gave examples of a certain lack of guilt-feelings she had perceived in colleagues:

> *...they didn't exhibit .. great 'angst' about it or anything and .. **they weren't ehm, upset** by it. They just seemed to **take it in a stride** (INT3 EX1 1839-1843);*
>
> *Pearl: ...you are in a responsible position .. and you are abusing that responsibility if you make it your decision to hush something up. (...)*
>
> *MA: Do you feel, do you think, everyone feels like that?*

*Pearl: No, I'm sure I don't, I'm sure, people feel differently about that. I'd hope most, I'd hope **most people in this sort of a profession** would, feel like that, I hope, **I feel we should** .. otherwise they would abusing their ...(INT3 764-786).*

Pearl included herself in this view *(..we should)*, but she did not take honesty for granted:

Its all to do with honesty as well hasn't it, if you can't admit your failures.. to a certain extent .. makes life a lot more difficult.. (INT3 881-885).

The following exchange took place in the interview with Pearl, when we were discussing morals generally and addressed honesty specifically:

MA: .. you said .. ehm .. it takes a lot of humility ... (Pearl: aha) .. to admit things.. and ..

*Pearl: I think it does, and **I think** that's what makes it hard for people (...) because **we all** like to think that we don't do things .. we don't make mistakes, (...) **You take it very personally**, some.. (...) **some people** .. och .. its water off a duck's back, (...) **but other people** it's .. you know, ehm ..they take it very personally... (INT3 1619-1638);*

Pearl talked from a personal perspective *(I think ..)* and she included herself *(we all ..)*. She used the words *'you take it very personally'* at first and then switched to a more distancing form of speech, saying *'some people (...) it's water off a duck's back!'*. What Pearl said, may be seen as evidence for the view that some people don't seem to be affected personally when they have made a mistake. Most probably Pearl had experienced colleagues who felt not guilty for having made a mistake as no harm had come to a patient.

Referring back to Gemma's statements, quoted in the previous section, it might be reasonable if a higher authority were blamed for being responsible for too great a work-load and understaffing, or for other circumstances that precipitated a mistake. Gemma had at first used the second person singular *(**you could** blame management; **you could** ... blame the Health Board; and **you could** ... blame the Minister of Health;* and finally, *so **if you wanted to**, end up with God for putting you on earth*), she then switched to the first person singular saying *'you have to say, **no**, it stops here, **it is my fault**'*. By using the second person singular first, Gemma indicated that other nurses may be inclined to protect themselves from this feeling of guilt while she herself could not argue in this way but had to see the fault in her own action.

Pearl also conveyed this message. But she at first, used the third person plural *(it's hard for **people**)*, then, she used the first person plural (***we like to think, we** don't make mistakes..)*. Here she included herself. Then again, she used the third person plural *(..a lot of **people**..; ..for **some people**.. it's water off a ducks back)*. Finally, she contrasted this statement, still using the third person plural, by saying *'..**but other people** (..) take it personally'*. Pearl, at first, had talked about other nurses, then she included herself in the statement, but later again she mentioned how *'some people'* are not very much affected by making a mistake, while *'others'* take it personally. I presume that Pearl included herself in the last group in the same way as she had talked about the humility it took to admit to a mistake:

> ***You** should be (...) **humble enough to admit that you can make** a mistake (INT3 756-758).*

When talking about the humility that is needed to own up to a mistake, she used the second person singular. This distanced her from the issue but included her at the same time.

Still, Pearl made excuses for situations where this humility might be lacking, saying:

> ***Unfortunately** in a lot of situations **you feel very open** to .. you know, the attack that might come (INT3 760-763).*

Both, Gemma, and Pearl, had talked about mistakes they had made and had admitted to. Both included themselves in this discourse, using the first person singular or the first person plural, but at the same time both also generalised by using either the second person singular or the third person plural.

A similar way of talking was employed by Anne, but here it seemed to have another objective. Anne complained about the harsh way students were dealt with if mistakes happened to them. She said:

> *They seem to make too much of it.. (INT8 EX3 658-659),*

referring to teachers and administrators. Anne then said *'..perhaps **some people** need it'*, because *'**they don't have** so much of a **conscience**'*, and *'..**it seems to bother some people more than others**'*.

A little earlier during our interview she had stated:

> *I suppose, (...) **if you could live** with it **on your conscience**, giving out the wrong medicine well, that's OK, but **I couldn't**. .. (INT8 532-536).*

Anne, too, had used the distancing second person singular when she mentioned that not all errors are owned up to by the nurses who are responsible for them. She contrasted her own sensitive conscience against other people who, she claimed, lacked this conscience. In her speech, Anne, used the third person plural when referring to *'people'* who *'did not have much of a conscience'*. In contrast to this she used the first person singular, pointing out that she could not live with a bad conscience. Thus, Anne implied that other people probably experienced guilt less than she would.

During our interview, Anne, did not talk about errors she had made herself. She only mentioned errors others had made while she herself was indirectly involved. She took pains to show that the one mistake where she might have given the wrong tablets to a patient, most probably was no mistake at all (example one).

Pearl and Gemma showed their understanding for the difficult situation a nurse might be in, after a medication error has occurred. Both, in a way felt a certain solidarity with such a situation; both had admitted to their own errors. They had gone through the experience of personal guilt. They had felt the humiliation or shame connected with it. Both showed a congruency between being guilty and feeling guilty.

It seemed, that most nurses who had consented to participate in the study had a clear, and in a way, similar perception of what constituted an error that has to be dealt with *'in the appropriate manner'*. Most nurses talked about their own mistakes and conveyed that they suffered from being guilty and from feelings of guilt and shame. Owning up may be delayed, but generally mistakes were talked about. However, this does not represent the complete reality. The nurses in this study also talked about others, who would prefer to hide mistakes, and who for various reasons would cover them up.

It happens to all of us!

One element that recurred in all data sources was the reference made by my respondents to the fact that making an error in the administration of medication is an experience common to all nurses. In fact one of the participants I talked to when recruiting interviewees said that, whoever claims to never having made a medication error, lies.

The knowledge of this shared experience was commented on frequently as a solace. Being human and therefore likely to be in a situation of precariousness helped to understand and accept self as well as it helped to understand others. It seemed to be a condition of forgiving self and also forgiving others for the act of transgression. I present some examples of what nurses said in this respect.

The first set of extracts shows a progressive acceptance of the fact that human beings are liable to make mistakes. Four times during our interview Jane came back to this thought and each time she verbalised a different aspect of it:

> *... quite a few of the nurses said to me, oh you know, we've made mistakes in the past .. ehm,* ***its surprising how common it is,*** *(INT11 530-533);*

Here, Jane expressed surprise at the fact that her experience was shared by other nurses. In the next extract she mentioned the healing effect this knowledge had on her:

> *People sharing their experiences. So* ***I didn't feel*** *.. gosh,* ***you are the worse nurse ever, that's ever made a mistake*** *.. 'cos people ..* ***it was nice that people that people admitted that they'd ...*** *(INT11 584-590);*

When she talked about the understanding she would have in future for other nurses who might be in a similar situation as she had been, Jane made the following statement:

> *...everybody makes mistakes (INT11 872-873);*

This fact did not count as an excuse for herself:

> *I felt oh, .. yes it does happen. Not that ..* ***not that that's an excuse****, but, ehm .. made me realise, well, you know, other people are .. fallible .. (INT11 978-983).*

Jane made this statement in the context of talking about the disciplinary hearing in which her director of nursing services told her that she should think about leaving nursing. She was in fact put to shame publicly which aggravated the shame she felt already. Knowing that making mistakes is part of human nature, helped her, to carry on working as a nurse in spite of her experience.

The following examples underpin the shared knowledge of human fallibility and demonstrate how this knowledge can be of help for reconciling self with this fact in the face of having made an error:

> *But then* ***we're all fallible****, mistakes do happen, (INT1 1057-1058);*

> *...everybody realised, that* ***it could have been me!*** *And .. nobody condemned, you know, nobody sort of pointed a finger and .. she's made a mistake (INT2 EX1 490-496);*

> *...she has made a mistake, but* ***we all make mistakes sometimes*** *(...) you know, a drug error (...) we are all capable of doing that.. (INT3 EX2 585-590);*

Chris pointed out how the knowledge of not being the only one to make mistakes helped her to cope with her own situation. This is shown in the next set of extracts :

> *...we're only human (INT9 EX1 244);*

> *...it was me, but* ***it could have been anybody else*** *(INT9 EX1 495-496);*

> *I didn't know, any of my staff had ever had any of these problems until .. (...) and they all said, but sister, this is happened to me, (...)* ***and I thought, gosh, yes well, I'm not the only one*** *(INT9 EX1 1578-1587);*

> ***...it was good to to think****, (...)* ***you weren't the only one in the world*** *to have done this (INT9 1257-1258);*

'It was good to think...' and *'...we are only human'* were two key expressions nurses used. This knowledge or awareness could be seen as a basis for forgiving self and therefore providing the basis for dealing with others in a fair and gentle manner that makes room for the development of honest decisions.

You just have to keep on...

A further coping strategy can be mentioned in this context. Even though it had been difficult, Gemma, for example felt that the challenge of work helped her to come to terms with her mistake. She said:

> *I mean I had to get in there, and get on with the job of running the ward (INT6 EX1 467-470).*

Seeing that life went on, and being confronted by the demands of her work, Gemma knew that the ill effects the incident had on her, could be overcome. She said, referring to the tears she was fighting with during our interview:

> *I can't run round like this all the time on duty (INT6 1042-1044),*

Asked, how she actually overcame the *'self-doubt'*, that is still raising its *'ugly head now and again'*, she referred to the value she put on her work as a nurse:

> *MA: I was wondering, how do you overcome it, or .. how did you overcome it?*
>
> *Gemma: Eh ... ... I don't, I don't really know.. just .. work and, and trying to think that .. that* ***you were doing a job of value****, in the long run, and in the meantime was to teach ... others, junior to you .. that eh .. mistakes can be made by even the most senior and... (INT6 EX1 939-951)*

But still sobbing she admitted:

> *It is a bit difficult, when you.. I think you just have to keep on... (INT6 EX1 975-977).*

The difficulty of carrying on with the work in the context of which an error had occurred was referred to by several respondents. Chris talked about *'picking herself up again'*. The positive side of this was expressed most clearly by Gemma. By carrying on with the tasks duty demanded, the professional identity of being a nurse would be re-confirmed and re-established. Being trusted and trusting self in this respect was more than a supportive element. Expressions of trust took on the function of helping nurses to cope with the situation. To regain professional confidence was a key to alleviating the feelings of guilt and shame.

I HAVE DONE IT! -OR- IT HAPPENED TO ME!

General remarks

In this section some discursive means are explored, whereby nurses distanced self from the occurrence of a medication error they had been involved in or whereby they identified with it. The participants would use either a passive or an active form of speech. In this section close attention is paid to the use of both forms. Looking at the contexts in which the active or passive form was employed reveals the meaning extended by this use.

The German Group Discussion helped me to become aware of these two forms. In the German language the word 'passieren' is commonly used in narrative. This word stems from the Latin word 'pati' and means 'to undergo', or from the form 'passivus' meaning 'susceptible of suffering'. By using this word an indication is given that the nurse is the suffering one, even a victim of 'it' that 'happened' to her or him. Once my awareness was drawn to this passive element, I also noted the active form, when nurses talked about what they had 'done'.

The use of a passive form of speech denoted that *'something has happened'* to them they or their colleagues were not responsible for. Nurses would say for instance: *'I do not know why it happened..'* or *'...something happened to me'*. This is shown as a further coping strategy which can be read as a concealed way of distancing self from the incident in order to protect self. But it was also used to protect patients, colleagues, or students. The passive element was generally not used with a clear description of what happened. Nurses referred to *'it', 'that', 'things', 'something'* when relating general feelings in relation to the situation. Of all occasions where nurses spoke about a mistake in the passive form only once the word mistake occurred, once the word error was used, and once the situation was referred to as hitch/mishap.

The active form of speech occurred when errors were described in detail, or in the contexts of self-accusation, or when talking about or to someone else. Nurses would say: *'I have given by mistake...'* ; *'I did not check properly'*; *'I did not pay attention'*; *'What have you done?!'*; .

In the introduction to the German Group Discussion, I myself, had used both forms:

> *MA: We all know the situation when I suddenly realise 'for God's sake, that was wrong!' - perhaps it was the wrong dose which* ***I have given*** *or the wrong patient... (GD-D 16-21).*

Here I had used the active form. A little later I said:

> *MA: I can imagine, that - well '****this happened to me...****' (64-65).*[2]

In this second instance I had used the passive form.

The use of passive and active elements of speech in the Group discussions

In the first example a story was told about an error that nearly occurred. Here, the active form was used to describe the situation:

> *It's so easy to do, ... I mean,* ***I almost made*** *a drug error (GD-SC EX5 252-254).*

The error was prevented in time and the nurse saw no need to distance herself from something that did not happen. She accepted responsibility for the possibility of making an error.

By using the passive form and calling the mistake 'that', or 'it', nurses distanced themselves from the occurrence. This can be illustrated with the situation recounted in example three, where one nurse talked about giving too much Insulin to a patient. The nurse said:

> ***I too have*** *on an occasion* ***injected*** *someone too much Insulin (GD-D EX3 415-416);*
>
> *... and thought, o God,* ***what have you done now!*** *(...) said to my colleague, my God,* ***I have given him too much*** *Insulin (GD-D EX3 434-438).*

On giving the account she used the active form. When she talked about going to the patient and telling him about it she said:

> *...to go to him and tell him myself - because it was me - and to tell him,* ***this and that has now happened*** *..(GD-D EX3 467-471).*

---

2 I had said: *'Ich kann mir vorstellen, daß .. also,* ***mir ist es passiert..****'*

Telling the group how she talked to the patient, she used the passive form. Indeed, this seems far more appropriate, than saying bluntly to the patient *'I have given you too much Insulin'*. Having owned up to her mistake, accepting her responsibility, she could now afford to soften her speech, and present the situation in the more distancing, passive form to the patient.

The protective mechanism can also be traced in the next example. A ward sister recounted the situation when a student came to her in order to confess the mistake he had made:

> *...and then he came to me and said,* ***something happened*** *to me, something something dreadful. I said "Did you kill someone?, (...)" "No, not as bad as that,* ***I have****, by mistake, because I did not know,* ***given*** *Markumar to the patient again." (GD-D EX1 150-158).*

At first in the ward sister's account the student's reaction was represented in the passive form, later, giving details, she referred to the situation in the active form. Picking up on this example on a later occasion during the discussion, this ward sister told us how she first heard about the situation:

> *... and then my colleague Anita came to me and said, listen, this and that* ***has happened to Manfred*** *(...) then he came to me and said, Anita has most probably spoken to you already, but this and that* ***has happened*** *(GD-D EX1 817-826).*

It is noticeable that only once during the account of example one the active form was used by the ward sister. This was when she recounted what Manfred, the student had said himself when he described the incident. Talking retrospectively, the passive form provided some means of distancing. By talking about the occurrence in the passive form, the ward sister, in a way, used a protective shield for the student.

An almost identical pattern can be discerned in the Scottish Group Discussion. The next extracts exemplify this and show how the Scottish nurses used language in a protective way. In the first example one nurse tells the story of a second nurse who was also taking part in the discussion. The nurse who told the story had been involved in reporting the mistake. (This story has also been drawn upon in Chapter Nine). The first nurse started off to give her account:

> ***It's happened to me!*** *GD-SC EX1 26;*

The second nurse continued to explain the situation:

> *... and in fact the patient* ***had been given*** *the wrong prescribed drug (GD-SC EX1 71-73);*
>
> *...* ***there had been*** *a definite drug error made (GD-SC EX1 101-102);*
>
> *I thought,* ***that's what's happened*** *(GD-SC EX1 135-136);*
>
> *...OK,* ***we maybe made an error****, but it's not a bad one (GD-SC EX1 147-148).*

At first the nurse who made the error started off with using the passive form. Her colleague continued and used the pluperfect *'the patient had been given'* and *'there had been made'* to construct a passive representation. Even though she helped her colleague to relate the story she did not use the second nor the third person, which would have been easier. In the third extract she used the clear passive form, saying *'that's what's happened'*. The nurse had been upset by the fact that she could not but report the incident. This had caused her to feel guilty about the whole situation too. Her discourse showed solidarity with her colleague and, including herself in the situation *(OK, we maybe made an error)*, revealed that she accepted human fallibility for herself too.

A further situation showed the protective use of language, where a vulnerable colleague was concerned, but at the same time it also showed a clear sense of reality. A ward sister told the story of a staff nurse which involved her dealings with a rather unsympathetic nursing officer:

> *... and the staff nurse came running up to me, in tears! "I made..* ***I gave ..*** *so and so ..* ***the wrong medication****" (GD-SC EX2 406-409);*
>
> *OK, right,* ***let's see what you have done!*** *(...)* ***What did you give?*** *(GD-SC EX2 420-424);*

The staff nurse was represented by the participant as using the active form. In clarifying the situation the ward sister also used the active form, but relating to the group what she had said to the nursing officer, she used the passive form again:

> *...went to phone the nursing officer ... right,* ***this is what happened!*** *(GD-SC EX2 455-457).*

It seems that by selecting specific forms of speech a protective mechanism was employed. The next example from the Scottish Group Discussion gives an interesting mix of the active as well as the passive forms of speech. The nurse had turned away from the drug trolley in order to answer a ringing telephone. In this instant a patient took a bottle of Haloperidol tablets off the trolley.

> *MA: Mhh, what happened?*
>
> *Nurse: Well, what happened was ...(GD-SC EX5 852-854).*
>
> *The phone was ringing (...) I was doing the drugs and did turn away to the phone ... (GD-SC EX5 863-867).*

The nurse told the story clearly and used the active form in describing her movements. She reported the incident to her nursing officer:

> *I told the duty nursing officer **what had happened** ... (GD-SC EX5 935-936).*

The nursing officer was very sympathetic. The nurse then talked about phoning her charge nurse at home:

> *I phoned my charge nurse at home, and would tell him, **what's happened** (GD-SC EX5 990-992);*
>
> ***He just said**, "you learned from it", and "**these things happen**" (...) he wasn't angry, (...) he said, "**we all make mistakes**" (GD-SC EX5 997-1004).*

Having reported the matter to her nursing officer, this nurse, then, sought the support of a her charge nurse. Telling the story, she had used the active form *(and did turn...)*. Talking about reporting it, she had used the passive form. Hereby she distanced herself from the incident. She represented her charge nurse as using both forms *(These things happen; we all make mistakes)*. This indicated that the charge nurse also helped the participant to distance herself from the incident. It furthermore indicated that the nurse needed the active immediacy of the supportive effect that is conveyed by the mentioning of shared human fallibility.

Active and passive forms in the self reports

Some further examples from the self reports show similar patterns. In the first report the nurse used the active form throughout while describing the incident. This nurse made her own involvement very clear and did not deviate from her first chosen style. Towards the end she stated:

> *When I discovered that **I had given** the wrong dosage I felt absolutely awful (REP2 88-90).*

Also the writers of third, fourth, and fifth reports employed the active form only:

> ***Gave** the drug to the wrong patient (REP3 46);*
>
> ***I gave Thyroxin** to a patient (...) My heart sank, **what had I done..?** (REP4 13-19);*
>
> *.. **gave** Pethidine .. (REP5 8).*

From these examples it can be seen that the respondents had a clear understanding of their personal involvement with the medication errors they related. They probably had thought well about the way they would put their experiences in writing.

In the German Self Report the nurse used the active form first to relate the incident. There was no doubt that she had been about to make a serious mistake. She wrote:

> *...I mistakenly **moved my hand** towards an ampoule of Natrium Citricum... (REP6 26-29)*

Reflecting on it as to her feelings towards the whole situation, especially as to the reaction of a male colleague who apparently behaved in a rather domineering way she used the passive form:

> *And shame (...) that something like this, **such a blunder could have happened to me** (REP6 60-64).*

She could distance herself from it and used the passive form when she related the absolutely negative reactions of a colleague. The colleague seemed to gloat over the fact that this nurse who was about to undergo her training as a tutor and who had trained and worked in Great Britain could be caught out, nearly making this mistake.

In the next example from Self Report One, the nurse at first used the passive form twice:

> *I had been qualified for six months when the drug incident **took place** (REP1 3-5);*

*The day **the incident took place...** (REP1 11).*

Then referring to the nurse who under her supervision gave Insulin to a wrong patient she wrote:

*...she suddenly realised **she'd given** the wrong patient the Insulin (REP1 33-34).*

She then mentioned her personal responsibility and still used the active form:

*I knew **I had done a drug error** as **I had not gone to the patient with her** (REP1 45-47).*

She further described how the incident was followed up and how this caused her to feel threatened. Here she used the passive form again:

*I had to explain **what had happened** - saying it was my fault (REP1 60-62).*

Towards the end of her report she mentioned in a sympathetic way:

*I also now have empathy towards other nurses **when it happens** to them (REP1 73-75).*

Here, the act of making the error had been carried out by one person, but the responsibility lay with another. The writer of this report, a charge nurse, had expressed her active involvement *(I had done a drug error, as I had not gone to the patient with her)*.

The incidents where the passive form was used were restricted to the German report, where the nurse had good reasons to distance herself from an unjust situation; and to the first report when the nurse related the difficult situation of reporting the error; and again when she expressed her sympathy with nurses who find themselves in similar situations.

Active and passive employment of speech in the interviews

When looking at the discourse of the participants in the interviews, it can be noted that the active form was used when the participants stressed the fact that they acknowledged their responsibility. In addition the respondents used the first person plural and thus, denoted their involvement in an incident.

Anne, in Interview Eight, in respect to example two said:

> *I stood there and watched* ***her do it'*** *(INT8 EX2 40-41);*

When relating how she reported the incident to the nursing officer she used the active form as well as the first person plural:

> *So we just explained* ***what we'd done'*** *(INT8 EX2 279-280).*

Henry, in Interview Ten, tells part of his first example in the student's own words:

> *And she said "Oh,* ***I have just given*** *her medicine to somebody else" (INT10 EX1 157-158).*

He used the active form again, when talking about his part of the story:

> *...what I felt was wrong was, that* ***I hadn't closed the trolley*** *before going out..(INT10 EX1 196-199).*

In both situations, Anne and Henry, had not actively given out the medication, but they both acknowledged their responsibility. Anne did so implicitly, by saying, *'... what we'd done';* Henry, by describing his neglecting to *'close the trolley'*.

When talking about the discussion of the incident among staff, Henry first used the passive form and then switched to the active form:

> *...they knew the situation ..* ***that had happened****, they tried to make me look at it from the angle that* ***that kind of thing does happen*** *in an acute ward (...) and discussed with me the fact that* ***the student nurse should have known better****, in the first place* ***not to give*** *medicines out.. .. They also mentioned that* ***they had made drug errors before*** *(INT10 EX1 587-599).*

By talking in the passive form in the first part of this extract, the distancing element is used *(that kind of thing does happen).* The second part contains an accusation against the student. This, Henry, puts in the mouth of his colleagues *(she should have known better ... not to give medicines out).* The statement exonerated Henry. In his second example Henry again acknowledged his part of the responsibility, when another nurse thought that she had made a mistake:

> *...and I said "****It's my fault*** *for .. having written out the Kardex, and .. not given the drug out.* ***Having done it in the wrong procedure****.." But nothing really has happened (INT10 EX4 774-780);*

> *"...look .. we haven't done anything wrong.., but .. if anybody did anything wrong,* ***it's me .. because I didn't follow procedure there****, (INT10 EX4 1319-1323).*

Here, Henry used the active form first in connection with the first person singular. In the second extract he used the fist person plural together with the active form.

Pearl, when relating her experiences in Interview Three, described how due to the negligence of a nurse on the previous shift who had not signed for a drug, this drug was given again. She said:

> *.. no matter whether the other dose hadn't been signed for, they were at fault, but* ***I was still .. involved****, and I'm the one, you know, who would be held (...) responsible. (INT3 EX1 64-74).*

Pearl did feel responsible but she used the passive form in saying *'I was involved'*, thus, distancing herself slightly from the incident.

Finally a few more observations follow as to the usage of the active or the passive forms of speech in the interviews. The illustrations are by no means exhaustive. At the beginning of an interview frequent use had been made of the passive form in order to introduce an incident. This allows the conclusion that during the 'warming up period' of the interview the respondents were inclined to distance themselves from the occurrence to be related.

> *I just go sort of through ... exactly* ***what happened*** *(INT1 EX1 74-75);*
>
> *...****I have been involved with*** *.. some instances (INT3 EX1 46-47);*
>
> *...it was* ***an incident that occurred*** *without me realising it. And* ***what happened*** *was ...(INT6 EX1 67-70);*
>
> *...that's the only example, I think .. actual drug error,* ***I've ever been involved in*** *(INT5 EX1 35-38);*
>
> *Ehm, .. well, the incident I was going to tell you about was one* ***that happened*** *.. to me ..* ***an error that I made*** *(INT7 EX1 17-20).*

In the last example above, a deviation from the stated rule may be noted. Still, Mike relaxed quickly at the beginning of our interview. Thus, he was able to talk about his experience in the active form.

Some nurses indeed, started their narratives right away in the active form without many preliminary turns of speech. But also the nurses who had started off with some remarks in the passive form changed to the active form later on in the interview.

Gemma's talk in Interview Six, at first did not seem to fit into the pattern described above. She used the passive form throughout, even when describing *'what happened'*. She employed the pluperfect and thus, arrived at a passive representation of her talk.

> *One patient **had been given** a blood transfusion, and it **had been put up** by .. a staff nurse, and **had been countersigned by me**, and .. it turned out that the wrong patient did have...(INT6 EX1 82-87).*

Gemma, as had been mentioned before stressed the fact that she was responsible for the incident. Gemma however, showed a strong emotional involvement while we talked and probably needed the more distancing form of speech. Several times she mentioned her feelings of being guilty, her being ashamed and doubting her own abilities:

> *I think self-doubt (...) certainly lasted for a long time, and they do raise their ugly head now and again.. (INT6 932-937).*

Chris would use the passive form, talking about herself, still wondering how this could have happened to her:

> *...**you** of all people, .. because **you are the ward sister** you think, it should never be you, **it should never happen to you** (INT9 EX1 234-237);*

> *It's that how you feel **when it first happens**, you think **it's only you**, and **you are** hopeless (INT9 1259-1262).*

Here, the distancing effect of her talk was still enhanced by the use of the second person singular. However, Chris also once used the active form, saying:

> *I do feel (...) **I was hopeless** (...) not fit to be a nurse, **if you do** things like that (INT9 EX1 303-307).*

Furthermore, the passive form was employed when talk centred around the theme of support. In this context Chris said:

> *...they all said, but sister, **this has happened to me**.. (INT9 EX1 1583-1585).*

Pearl indicated her compassion for a badly treated colleague by using the first person plural in connection with the active form:

> *...**she has made a mistake**, but we all make mistakes sometimes. (...) But **we are all capable of doing that**.. (INT3 EX2 585-590);*

She included herself in a situation that she had not been involved in, but the way in which it was handled had effected her emotionally *(...she has made ... we are all capable of doing that).* Using the active form in this context emphasised her personal concern. She had no wish here to distance herself from the situation of a nurse who had been treated unjustly.

One last glance at the use of the active or passive forms of speech is to reveal its function in the context of 'prospective talk'. When nurses mentioned their fear of again making a medication error they did so as a rule in passive terms:

> *Who is to say **it** could never **happen again**? (INT9 1397-1398);*

> *I'm just being so .. scared to .. **something else happening again** (INT10 EX1 295-297).*

The extract above is a good example of how meaningful the employment of certain grammatical forms can be. Henry had started off the sentence in a manner that would only allow its continuation in the active form (*'..scared to ..'* do it again). He stopped himself and finished it off in the passive form. *(..something else happening again).* This conveys Henry's perception about future acts which may not altogether be within his control. He may well want to be careful and concientious when giving out medicine. He may want to adhere to the prescribed policies of drug administration. But he also realised that he may be 'subject' to mistakes. Thus he acknowledged his precariousness which caused him to be *'scared'*.

Reconciliation

I have so far described perceptions of guilt in connection with medication errors. I have also addressed the experience of shame and have explored how the feelings of guilt and shame were expressed. Nurses made it clear that they were aware of their own imperfections and of the imperfections of the structures within which they worked. Having 'made' an error or having experienced that an error 'happened' to them confronted them with personal failure in an area where the essence of nursing comes to the fore.

Some means of coping with personal failure have been demonstrated from the discourse of the participants in this study. These coping mechanisms were used in order to come to terms with one's personal failures. 'Coming to terms with' means to become reconciled. Reconciliation can be seen as a counterpoint to the concepts of guilt and shame.

The realisation *'I was not the only one to do such a thing'* greatly helped in this respect to place self within the sphere of human fallibility. Remarks like *'we are all human, we all make mistakes'* revealed themselves as crucial in this context. To see self in respect to others, presupposes that a nurse in the situation of having made a medication error takes the gaze off self and looks around: *'not that that's an excuse'*, as one nurse said, but it helped her in coming to terms with her mistake.

To regain an appropriate confidence in the abilities to function as a nurse appeared to be one central aspect when medication errors were discussed. This too may be understood as a part of the process of reconciliation. The trust that was expressed by others, immensely furthered a nurse's ability to *'pick herself up again'*, to regain confidence and to carry on with her or his duties.

The trust of others however, represents only one side of the process of reconciliation. The nurse's trust in herself and her/his ability to forgive self in spite of *'having let oneself down'* seemed the crucial aspect in the process. This ability of course can be greatly aided by the trust voiced by others, but it also needed the personal response of the nurse concerned.

Here the core of the notion of forgiveness is touched. Forgiving means extending trust into future acts. Giving credence in advance as to the conviction of a person's abilities and value. However much this may be done by friends, colleagues, or others, if it is not met from within by the person by 'fore-giving' self, self reproaches will continue. Forgiving therefore depends ultimately on the sense that is individually made of life, and on how a person sees her/his place in this world. It depends on how human nature is appreciated and understood. It also depends on what significance is ascribed to existence. Doing *'a job of value'* helped to give significance to a nurse's existence in spite of having once failed in this 'job'.

A further perspective can be identified as helpful for the process of reconciliation. A medication error has to be evaluated within the institutional and organisational context in which it occurred. The nurse who has made the error can derive help from this evaluation, be it by addressing circumstances that exonerate a nurse who felt responsible for a mistake, or be it by going through the process of the disciplinary procedure. Covering an error up, is *'just not right' (We have to be accountable; ... you've got to go about this in the proper manner).*

The disciplinary procedure provides a ritual of forgiveness. Even though it leaves scope for misuse in itself, it nevertheless has a reconstituting power. If regarded from this perspective 'the procedure' of disciplinary action can be seen as an important constituent of the moral order between the carers and the cared for. It is not simply a question of atonement for a certain wrongdoing that lies behind nurses' owning up to their mistakes and thus, accepting the disciplinary procedure. It is not exoneration or disciplining of individuals that is to be attained by 'the procedure'. It is the reconstitution of an order that rests upon accepted responsibility and mutual trust.

Decisions taken in the course of disciplinary action provide borders which delineate the scope of tolerance for the afore mentioned human fallibility. In the last extreme, by removing a nurse's name from the professional register, this nurse is firmly placed outwith the institutional set-up. As traumatic as such a decision may be for the nurse concerned, it is made in order to protect a vulnerable public as well as the profession. However, those nurses who after a disciplinary hearing are found guilty of misconduct, but whose names are not removed from the professional register, experience a positive act towards being reinstituted or reconfirmed in their professional role as nurses.

I have used the extreme example of removal from the register, to illustrate the meaning any disciplinary measure taken or not taken, has for the process of reconciliation. A sentence like *'I'll not report this further'* said by a charge nurse after a colleague has admitted to a mistake, also readmits the nurse back into the community of professionals and gives her or him a further chance to prove professional competence. It does so just as much as does the official restoration to the register of persons previously removed for proven misconduct.

Guilt, and the feelings of guilt can only be overcome by accepting an irrevocable past and by addressing the future. The movement from past failure to future possibilities of proving oneself may be hindered by the phenomenon of shame. This, as has been shown from the discourse of the participants arises from the experience of '*letting oneself down*' or '*not living up to one's expectations*'. In an "inadequate" or "depleted self" (Capps 1993) '*self doubt will raise their ugly heads now and again*' as Gemma had said. In the beginning of this chapter the understanding of human nature has been outlined from various theological perspectives. The direction for an answer of how to deal with both guilt and shame may be found here. A basic trust in the goodness of human nature would allow for failure and faillibility as well as for improvement and success. Such a trust accepts human precariousness as well as human achievements in the light of a final reconciliation which lies beyond the possibilities of human imagination.

It is only possible to deal with personal guilt, with feelings of guilt, and with feelings of shame, if their cause is talked about. Mike had mentioned the '*cathartic function*', talking about his medication error had for him. Even though talking about personal failure is uncovering and may enhance feelings of shame, it is nevertheless helpful as it induces the process of reconciliation with human precariousness.

CHAPTER 11
LEARNING FROM MISTAKES, TEACHING ETHICS IN NURSING EDUCATION

INTRODUCTION TO THE CHAPTER

In the previous two chapters an exposition was made of two major aspects related to the experience of medication errors. 'Identification and change' and 'Guilt and reconciliation' represented the first two cornerstones of the empirical model that was outlined in Chapter Eight. The present chapter links up with the third cornerstone of the empirical model: Ultimate effects of a medication error, and of the reactions and consequences that follow it.

In the model, I have named three areas as regards to the ultimate effects of medication errors. They relate to 'the nurse', to 'others', and to 'the institution'. Berger's concept of the 'dialectical phenomenon' of social change was used to delineate the relationship between experience and the constitution of social reality. In the context of the present chapter its applicability becomes obvious. By finally 'internalising' aspects of reality in a learning process "structures of the objective world" are transformed into "structures of the subjective consciousness". These structures then, as "a human product" (learning) act "back upon (their) producer" (Berger 1969).

In this chapter the experience of medication errors is looked at from the perspective of *learning outcomes* as they are *ultimately manifested* and represented in nurses' discourse. 'We learn from our mistakes' is a platitude often used in conversation. Learning is said to be manifested in behavioural changes. How is learning effected by mistakes? Nurses participating in the study often talked about the learning value their experiences with medication errors had for them. This alleged value is examined here in greater detail. Remarks such as *'you always learn from your mistakes'*, or *'I learned from this experience'* are looked at in the context of their occurrence in the texts of the data.

In respect to the key issue of 'Learning from mistakes', the themes of 'The disciplinary procedure', 'The role of the medical staff', 'Support in the situation of medication errors', and especially 'The situation of nursing students' resurface in this chapter.

Learning effects, as addressed by the participants, concerned various areas. Learning occurred at a personal level or collectively within nurses' work settings. Learning also occurred as part of a process of change in the organisational structure of nursing education and nursing practice in general, and thus it would effect changes in the understanding of hierarchy and the execution of power which ultimately has implications for the development of nursing as a profession.

In the three sections of this chapter various aspects of learning in practice are addressed. In the first section a humanistic approach to learning is discussed and brought into context with the risk of students making mistakes. In the second section nurses' discourse as to learning from mistakes is looked at and in the third section the impact mistakes may have at institutional and professional levels is examined. In all three sections I use some concepts as described in the teaching literature and I illustrate the points I make with examples from the data.

LEARNING IN PRACTICE

Learning in practice - a dilemma

Much has been said about learning in and through practice pertaining to nurse training and nurse education (Benner 1984; Alexander 1982; Heath 1979 and many others). Alexander addresses the three domains of learning and applies them to nursing.

She says:

> Learning to nurse is concerned with the gaining of knowledge and the development of intellectual skills and abilities (the cognitive domain); it is concerned with the developments of attitudes, values, the ability to adjust adequately in order to cope with different situations (the affective domain), and it is concerned with the development of skilled and dextrous manual techniques (the psychomotor domain), (Alexander 1982 p. 59, parentheses in the original).

Alexander examined the advantages of guided experiences. Two main points she addressed in her study were: Student "supervision by trained teachers - those who also participated in the theoretical input to the nursing course"; and also: "...the approach to teaching which followed the principle of active experiential learning" (Alexander 1982). This approach built on Carl Rogers's principles of experiential learning on which Alexander's study rested. Alexander assumed that:

> ... the introduction to the wards of supernumerary, teacher-supervised students whose nursing work is primarily dictated by their needs as students and not primarily by the needs of the ward is not detrimental to the needs of the patients (Alexander 1983 p. 9).

> ... the experimental method of teaching/learning would result in a more relevant and more realistic preparation for the daily work of nursing than is achieved by the present predominantly college-based methods (Alexander 1983 p. 9).

One main asset of this type of learning was the theoretical evaluation of practice in small groups which enabled students and teachers to discuss problems immediately after they were experienced. This type of learning not only contributed to practical skills in planning nursing activities, in carrying out a plan and in evaluating nursing action, it also gave opportunities to address ethical issues. Alexander mentions this aspect by referring to one of Rogers's principle of experiential learning which is:

> To place a student in direct experiential confrontation with practical problems, with ethical problems and with personal issues... (Alexander 1983 p. 41).

The value of acquiring practical skills in a reality setting is undisputed, even though it presents a dilemma as to patient safety. This dilemma is a basic one and applies to most areas of practical teaching in nursing. It is addressed in the present study as regards to medication administration.

On the one hand students should be able to learn their roles in surroundings where they are allowed to make mistakes and where they could learn from these mistakes. On the other hand patients must not be endangered. Holmes, examining alternatives to natural science foundations for nursing states:

> Certainly, the importation of phenomenology through humanistic principles into British nurse education has been fraught with problems. They stress autonomy and choice but it is difficult to reconcile these with the formal requirements imposed on statutory training programmes, (...) They are also difficult to sustain in the face of the hierarchical system in which clinical experience is gained; all too often, mistakes are seen as totally negative events rather than as opportunities for learning or as indicators of innovation; (Holmes 1990 p. 194).

One participant in the present study mentioned the fact that is questionable whether nursing was an area where students should be learning through their mistakes:

> *... in nursing - should we be learning by our mistakes? But we do! (INT1 1675-1679).*

However, being exposed to the practical arena of nursing will always include the possibility of making mistakes. The knowledge of human fallibility and the acceptance of the possibility of making mistakes means that nurses have to accept the inevitability of patients possibly suffering harm in the course of their being subject to nursing action.

It will be difficult to find a solution for this dilemma. Possibly only in the way mistakes are dealt with, the dilemma may be resolved, or at least it may be addressed in such a way that it will be possible to live with it. Compassionate understanding as well as following the disciplinary procedure and instituting punitive action will have their places accordingly.

Students, apart from being introduced to the routine of drug-administration will have to learn to understand this dilemma. They will have to learn that leniency as well as disciplining have their appropriate places, that each situation has to be dealt with on its own merits. Attitudes, values and opinions have to be taught and formed carefully. They are influenced by model situations in practice and by the modelled behaviour of teachers, seniors and peers. Alexander refers to the teaching of students by qualified staff. She states that student nurses' teachers

> ...are not only those who hold a formal qualification to teach, but also, and this to a considerable extent, ward sisters, staff nurses and their fellow students (Alexander 1982 p. 58).

Hilary, the participant in Interview Twelve, recalled from her own student days how she learned to be conscientious with drugs. I had asked her how she had been taught in respect to drug administration. She said that in one of the wards the ward sister was extremely diligent about doing drug rounds with students. She had asked questions about the drugs used and ascertained that the students adhered to the correct drug administration procedure. In another ward, Hilary felt that the qualified staff *'was very casual in working with drugs'*. Comparing the two wards, she said:

> *I felt a lot better, being tested on it, because I was learning more about the drugs. (...) well you know, what you would expect the average dose to be... (INT12 910-918).*

Hilary would adopt this method of doing medicine rounds with her own students. Here she would combine obvious cognitive learning with covert affective teaching In fact Hilary's ward sister role-modelled the teaching role for her effectively.

Chris, in Interview Nine, expressed that doing drug rounds with students had a definite teaching character as it not only includes diligent checking, but also explanations from the side of the nurse who works with the student. This made a difference to a drug round, being more time consuming in its function as a means of teaching. It will be slower, questions will be asked and answered on both sides. The drug-administration becomes a subject of discussion.

In the situation Sean related (example one), a student was supposed to check the drugs with a senior nurse. The student did not pick up on the mistake the staff nurse had made. This could well have been due to the fact that the staff nurse, set in her routine and fast in her actions did not heed the slower perception of the student. This occurrence gave rise to changes in the drug-routine in such a way as to let the most inexperienced nurse, generally the student, read out the labels and the particulars of medications to be given and the senior person would confirm what was read:

> *...all the trained staff had said they felt that that was the singular most important thing that they had learned, was the fact that we'd checked drugs much faster, the students aren't really seeing the labels, and it should be the slowest person, that asks, checks, .. (INT4 1843-1851).*

Thus, the learning situation of the student was taken into account. The student would be aware of the dangers and pitfalls of drug-administration and of her personal responsibility, but at the same time would have the chance to practice a nursing task safely under supervision.

The rule, that two nurses are to do medicine rounds in British hospitals has a problematic implication when it comes to using students as the second nurse to check the drugs. A change of drug round routine such as Sean described would make sense in the face of the fact that this would ensure that students learned the safe handling of medicines while being supervised.

In a situation that was related in the German Group Discussion, the dilemma of students making mistakes in the practice setting was solved differently. The ward sister changed the rules as to the administration of anticoagulants on her ward after a student had made a mistake. She said:

> *For myself I have drawn the consequences and have said that Markumar[1] tablets are only to be given out by qualified staff, and regardless whether a student is first, second, or third year, as a principle all tablets must be checked (GD-D 179-188).*

---

[1] Markumar is an anticoagulant

The mistake in this example was used to justify that potentially dangerous medications like anticoagulants were not to be given out by students, and furthermore that all tablets were to be checked. It is questionable, whether by limiting students' task scopes in the area of medication administration to certain drugs, that the learning-in-practice-dilemma can be solved. Learning-in-practice can only be safe and fruitful if the learner's role is given consideration. Students may be confronted with the challenge of the reality setting, but at the same time the safety of patients is to be assured by appropriate supervision.

Learning from other people's mistakes

In some incidents that were related by the participants of the study, mistakes made by other nurses appeared to serve a teaching purpose. Some nurses referred to the experience of other nurses that caused their own vigilance to be enhanced. Joan said regarding a mistake another nurse was responsible for:

> *...and it definitely makes you more careful (INT2 449-450).*

In Interview Three, where another nurse had forgotten to sign for a dose of Iron she had given to a baby, the dose was consequently given again by my respondent. About this situation Pearl said:

> *...it's a reminder to ourselves, to be a lot more careful, you know, to when .. to make sure you sign for things (properly?) (INT3 275-279).*

One nurse in the German Group Discussion, talking about the mistake of a colleague said:

> *But for me personally, the success was, that afterwards I really looked at each perfusion pump three times after I reset it GD-D 261-265).*

Gemma, in Interview Six, saw the possibility of learning from other peoples' mistakes differently. She felt generally that she had learned from her own mistake:

> *You learn from your own, I can't guarantee, that you learn from other people's, because eh, nothing hits you quite, in the gut, quite so much as .. your own error (INT6 1012-1016).*

Still, as to utilising her mistake in teaching others, Gemma said:

... and in the meantime was to teach ... others, junior to you .. that eh .. mistakes can be made by even the most senior and ... to make sure, that we are aware of how easy a mistake can occur (INT6 947-954).

Gemma hoped that the openness about her own mistake would help students to learn that mistakes can happen to anybody and that it would be all right to own up to mistakes.

Chris would also use the experience she had talked about in Interview Nine as an example for students:

MA: Would you tell.. let's say a student or a staff nurse about this incident?

Chris: Yes!

MA: Or would you just say it happened to me, and .. that's..

Chris: I would tell them!

MA: Yeah, as an example?

Chris: Yeah, I would.. no doubt, I would (INT9 1334-1348).

Jane, however, in Interview Eleven, said hesitatingly, that she was reluctant about talking to students about her experience. She said:

MA: Do you think you can influence students in any way .. so that they .. own up to their mistakes?

Jane: (...) I don't feel I could do that with students ... I don't think I would like to ... own up fully to the mistake I made.

MA: Well, yeah, you wouldn't use this example with students, telling them about it?

Jane: Not personally. I would say to them ... you realise this is what may happen ...

MA: So, what if students say, well, you are a nurse, did a mistake ever happen to you? Would you use it as an example?

Jane: I don't think so, no ...(INT11 837-865)

Even though I pursued the subject, Jane felt that she could not talk to students about her rather traumatic personal experience.

The role model function of senior nurses was addressed several times. Gerald, referring to a charge nurse he had worked with as a student, said:

> *I mean, he had a lot of influence on me... (INT5 1224-1235).*

Also Chris talked about a ward sister who was a positive role model for her:

> *...she taught you by example, she showed you how to do things, and they were always done right. She very rarely cut any corners on anything, she was thorough (INT9 2138-2143).*

Most respondents who touched on the subject, mentioned that they had been influenced by positive role models during their time as student nurses. They in turn felt that they could teach students best by working correctly and by setting positive examples. Pearl said:

> *Yes, you learn from example (INT3 853-854).*

The fear of making mistakes

Experiences with medication errors were frequently referred to in connection with the fear of making a mistake again. Mike, in Interview Seven, said:

> *I wouldn't want to happen again .. so .. eh .. it was a learning situation from that point of view, (INT7 1655-1667);*

> *...but certainly I learned, that, .. drug errors make you feel really bad, and it's something that that you want to (avoid ?), because you feel really bad (INT7 1703-1708).*

The next example refers to Anne, who, while doing drugs with a student was distracted and did not notice that the student gave a medication to a wrong patient. Anne talked about the student being frightened by the experience. About herself she said:

> *... and it frightened me sufficiently to make .. extra sure in future, (INT8 763-765).*

Fear, or *'angst'*, as one nurse termed it, was clearly connected with the experience of having made a medication error. Some nurses gave this fear a name by calling their mistake 'a learning experience' which brought about greater vigilance. If by fear, is implied that greater care will be taken in future while giving out medications, this can then be understood as a healthy form of fear. In the two examples quoted above, fear is explicitly mentioned. This indicates that the fear of being involved in a medication error again could be 'learned' by having made a mistake. Possibly other remarks that mention a commitment to greater vigilance in future are also driven by an element of fear even though not explicitly stated. Some nurses in the self reports used the word *'cautious'*, other nurses spoke about being more *'careful'*. In the written self reports several times almost identical wording as to the same effect appeared. The nurses wrote:

> *I found the whole thing very upsetting and certainly learnt the hard way (REP1 77-79);*
>
> *I was then very (cautious ?) about doing further drug rounds and even now 3 years on, I am still **careful** and especially never give injections on my own (REP1 67-71);*
>
> *I am very **cautious** when giving out medication now, although I was never aware of not being **careful** before the incident (REP2 94-97);*
>
> *I was told how careless I had been and that I must read labels properly. I have ever since (REP4 44-47).*
>
> *...it was a lesson I learned and I will never forget it. (REP2 125-126);*

Learning in practice by reflection

In the context of personal involvement and detachment in nursing, Benner says:

> Although we may decrease our errors through reflection and rehearsal, we cannot avoid them. We must have the moral courage to learn from our mistakes .. (Benner 1992 p. 111).

This also applies to the situation of medication errors. The risk of exposing self to the possibility of making a mistake is inherent in all human activity. The moral courage Benner refers to may well be seen in the willingness and in the ability to reflect on incidents. I would put forward that neither in the mistake itself lays the learning value, nor in the fear that may be produced by it, but in the way it is dealt with and reasoned about. In Alexander's study a positive learning climate enabled the students to develop skills and attitudes conducive to acquiring their role as nurses. Heath, referring to the concept of experiential learning, addresses a positive learning climate as "one of trust, mutual support, acceptance of the individual, warmth and respect" (Boydell 1976 in Heath 1979). Heath states:

> In such a climate, the learner can take risks (in the sense of trying out new behaviours), admit to difficulties and problems, give and receive feedback and cope with the allied stress, (Heath 1979 p. 22).

As mentioned earlier, Alexander advocates a theoretical evaluation of practice. If problems are discussed immediately after they are experienced, the student will be confronted with practical, ethical and personal issues (Alexander 1983). Nursing education according to Project 2000 is hoped to provide the practical aspects of the programme by students going "into the hospital setting, observing and practising nursing skills under the supervision of a qualified nurse" (Project 2000 p. 5). It is hoped that this guided experience provides room for such a confrontation as Alexander proposes.

Van Hooft mentions the possibility of learning from mistakes. This, presupposes reflection. He states:

> We can acquire a form of practical knowledge even when we disapprove of what we have done, although our confidence may be lessened in such a case. In these ways, moral empowering enters into one's motivation stance by way of reflection on previous action rather than merely by way of preparation for future action. As well, student nurses can gain courage to act from the example of their peers and seniors (van Hooft 1990 p. 214).

A reflective element that evaluates experience can well be used in situations of medication errors in a structured and objective oriented manner. In his book The reflective practitioner, (Schön 1983), Schön discusses aspects of coping with "unique uncertain, and conflicted situations of practice". He analyses "the distinctive structure of reflection-in-action" (Schön 1983).

Schön uses examples from architectural design and from psychotherapy which both provided situations where "a problem in finding the problem" marked his explications. In order to disentangle a problematic situation and finding a solution "a reflective conversation with a unique and uncertain situation is begun". The situation is reshaped in accordance with the expert's or supervisor's "initial appreciation of it, the situation 'talks back', and he responds to the situation's 'back talk' " (Schön 1983, inverted commas in the original).

Related to his examples of an architectural design-problem and the situation between client and psychotherapist, Schön talks about a "web of moves, discovered consequences, implications, appreciations, and further moves". Such a web also exists in the situation of medication errors. In exploring either situation "individual moves yield phenomena to be understood, problems to be solved, or opportunities to be exploited", within the context of this web. This, Schön says, represents the process of "reframing" the situation (Schön 1983).

By using this approach when reflecting on medication errors, various affective and cognitive learning elements can be identified in the way of understanding, solving problems, and exploiting opportunities. Learning in practice through incidents of medication errors can be greatly enhanced with the help of reflection using an approach that enters into conversation with the situation as was described by Schön. "Reframing" a situation of medication error according to its context makes it possible to focus on aspects of moral decision-making that are of immediate importance. The conversation with the situation shifts attention from the persons involved onto the problems to be investigated.

Learning from Mistakes at a Personal Level

The affective domain of learning

When nurses talked about personally learning from their experiences they referred to future actions regarding the distribution of medicines as well as to decisions to be made after a medication error has occurred. These decisions were moral decisions as they pertained to making resolutions for further conduct, to owning up to a mistake or to covering it up. Further moral aspects lay in the decisions made by other nurses involved in an error, albeit not responsible for it. These pertained to reporting an error and to disciplining as well as to supporting the nurse who has made the error and to helping her/him through the experience. The various moral decisions made in a situation of medication error related to attitudes and to opinions and fell within the affective domain of learning, but they did not exclude cognitive aspects of learning.

Making decisions in everyday situations is a moral skill based on knowledge, attitudes and on opinions as well as on personal and professional values. Thus, decisions made in the situation of medication errors are based on cognitive learning in respect to the administration of medicines and to rules, regulations and policies. The decisions made after a medication error occurred were clearly influenced by that knowledge base. They were also influenced by psychomotor skills in respect to handling medicines and they were associated with practical experience. However, only a balance between the three domains can bring about 'good' decisions.

Bloom et al have investigated thoroughly the domains of cognitive and affective learning (Bloom et al 1956; 1964). Their categories of cognitive and affective objectives have acquired a classical position in the field of curriculum construction and curricular research. Bloom et al also point to the relationship of the two domains and they understand them as linked closely to the learning of psychomotor skills.

The term 'psychomotor skills' is used in this context to denote practical, technical or physical activities. Coming from the area of child development psychology, the term is used by educationalists in the context of curriculum development. Greaves makes a six fold distinction of skills to be developed during nurse education. They can be enumerated as follows: 1) physical or psychomotor skills; 2) affective skills or skills of feeling; 3) cognitive skills or skills of thought and language; 4) behavioural skills or interpersonal and communication skills; 5) social skills; and 6) technical skills distinctive to nursing (Greaves 1987). In order to "produce a curriculum that is a complete and unified whole and fully representative of the world of nursing" Greaves contents that "the different skills, knowledge, attitudes, beliefs and values are ... interrelated and integrated" (Greaves 1987).

Nurse education, according to the comprehensive definition of Hockey (1980) includes:

> ... (the) education for care, the inculcation of empathy ... education for the respect of the individual, education for a spirit of inquiry, education for political awareness, education in the advancement of science and its use, education in the application of theoretical propositions, education in decision-making as well as in manual skills, education for change" (Hockey 1980 p. 910).

In this enumeration the cognitive, affective and psychomotor domains of learning are addressed. A good balance in the achievements of these goals will contribute to the possibility of learning to make careful and right decisions in a situation of medication error.

Discussing the relationship between the cognitive and the affective domain Bloom et al refer to the fact that a differentiation must needs be an artificial one. Most cognitive, and for that matter psychomotor objectives have an affective component. They state:

> ...although one could place an objective very readily in one of the three major domains or classes, no objective in one class was entirely devoid of some components of the other two classes (Bloom et al 1964 p. 8).

> In spite of the lack of explicit formulation, however, nearly all cognitive objectives have an affective component if we search for it (Bloom et al 1964 p. 48).

Bloom et al attend further to the relationship between affective and cognitive learning objectives. They maintain that cognitive objectives are used to attain affective ones:

> ...teachers use cognitive behaviour and cognitive goals as means to multiple affective ends. This occurs especially in areas where the problem of indoctrination arises. Cognitive behaviour may be used to indoctrinate points of view and to build attitudes and values (Bloom et al 1964 p. 56).

We seem to have developed a preference for approaching affective achievement by conveying theoretical content. By teaching ethical content it is certainly hoped that this teaching will influence a student's value system and result in discernible moral behaviour. As to nursing this has been studied by Ketefian (1981b); Swider, McElmurray and Yarling (1985); Cassidi and Oddi (1988); and Cragg (1988).

Bloom et al sustain that "we tend to focus attention on these cognitive goals as ends in themselves without (our) determining whether they are actually serving as means to an affective end" (Bloom et al 1964). Conversely of affective goals are used in order to achieve cognitive ones. This applies to "the development of interest or motivation" (Bloom et al 1964). But also the negative affect of fear of punishment is used in order to produce certain cognitive or psychomotor behaviours. This applies to the situation of drug administration, where the fear of harming a patient, the fear of the disciplinary procedure at all levels, and, ultimately the fear of being struck off the register, seems to be a frequently referred to factor that makes nurses abide by the stated rules and policies of drug administration. The fear of punishment may induce nurses to cover mistakes up so they cannot be dealt with (Campbell 1984; Johnson 1987; Heywood Jones 1988; Turner 1988; Carlisle 1991).

Bloom et al use the process of "internalization" as described for instance by Kelman (1958); English and English (1958); and Good (1959) to define the continuum on which affective learning takes place. They refer to this process as "not a product of any one theory or point of view ... not a new concept but a useful combination of old ones" (Bloom et al 1964).

Berger understands internalisation from a sociological perspective. In the present context it is seen in connection with personal development and learning. Both perspectives supplement each other. Internalisation of affective educational objectives is understood as internal continuous growth of values, opinions and attitudes that govern behaviour. The continuum of growth, so Bloom et al claim, "has different aspects" which are "multidimensional". Bloom et al manifest:

> Certainly it (the continuum of growth) has a simple-to-complex aspect as well as a concrete-to-abstract one. There is the external-to internal control transition. There is an emotional component that increases up to a point on the continuum. Finally there are the conscious-to unconscious aspects and the cognitive aspects of organization of attitudinal components (Bloom et al 1964 p. 31).

Bloom et al offer a taxonomy of affective educational objectives which encompass the process of internalisation. This process

> ...represents a continuous modification of behaviour from the individual's being aware of a phenomenon to a pervasive outlook on life that influences all his actions (Bloom et al 1964 p. 33).

The taxonomy proceeds from the simple to the complex in an incremental learning pattern. The first category is described as "*receiving*". It includes the subcategories of "being aware, the willingness to receive, and controlled or selected attention". The second category, "*responding*", includes "acquiescence in responding, willingness to respond, and satisfaction in response". The third category in the process of internalisation is called "*valuing*" and it includes the subcategories of "acceptance of a value, preference for a value, and commitment". As a learner is displaying a commitment to certain values the fourth category of "*organization*" may be attained. This includes the "conceptualisation of a value, and the organisation of a value system". The final stage of the internalisation process is represented by the fifth category, "*characterization by a value or value complex*", which includes the subcategories of "generalized set" (this means a "readiness to revise judgements and to change behaviour in the light of evidence"), and "characterization", which is defined as "a consistent philosophy of life". "Behaviour at the top level of the taxonomy", so Bloom et al maintain, "is perceived to be so deeply internalized that it is a habit" (Bloom et al 1964).

They summarise this internalisation process by saying:

> As internalization progresses, the learner comes to attend the phenomena, to respond to them, and to conceptualize them. He organizes his values in a value complex which comes to characterize his way of life. Internalization is seen as related to socialization but is not a synonym for it. The stages of the affective domain are seen consistent with an empirically and theoretically based point of view on conscience or superego development (Bloom et al 1964 p. 44).

A continuum of internalisation in nurses' talk about medication errors

In this section the positive and negative learning effects as well as the internal feelings and emotions that may influence affective learning in connection with medication errors are traced in the discourse of nurses and aligned to Bloom et al's categories of affective educational objectives. This illumines what nurses claimed to have learned by their experiences and it discloses some of the underlying reasons for their claims. Bloom et al, however, define the five steps on the continuum of internalisation as learning objectives. In the discourse of my participants such clear definitions cannot be discerned. I therefore do not strictly follow the five steps as described by Bloom et al, but confine myself to the concept of internalisation as a continuum, highlighting some of the marked differences of the learning outcome that are discernible.

The first group of extracts point to both, a high degree of internalisation, and at the same time express certain elements of doubt as to the learning effects of the experiences. I then move on to examples where doubt as to future action is expressed and conclude this part with extracts that exhibit a high level on the growth continuum. The data extracts refer to what nurses have said to or about other nurses as well as what they have said about themselves.

One nurse in the German Group Discussion talked about checking perfusion pumps after she had reset them. This, she claimed had become a habit to her. At first she said that her actions are influenced by her experience. She is committed to controlling and checking which is more than a general willingness to pay attention. The value of controlling her own action has become part of the way she organises her work now. She has got it *'in her blood'* as she said. The German sentence is not translatable in its literal sense.

She said:

> *... Das ist mir danach so in Fleisch und Blut übergegangen (...)* ***wahrscheinlich*** *... (GD-D 265-274).*

She added the word *'wahrscheinlich'*, (probably), which in its literal translation means 'seemingly true' or 'the truth shines through'. This wording does not convey a conviction as to future actions. Thus, what was first claimed to be a habit was renounced in the second part of the statement.

Chris had related how she overlooked the prescription of an Insulin injection for a new patient and consequently missed out giving it to her.

This resulted in a deterioration of the patient's condition, which could however, be rectified. Chris was very upset about her mistake and said that she had become:

> *...Superduper efficient when I do the drugs now (INT9 1415-1417).*

As to Chris' manager, Chris reported her as having said concerning the forgotten Insulin:

> *I **almost likely** would **never** ever do it again. Because once it happens to you, you never forget it (INT9 223-226).*

By using words like *'never'* and *'always'* a high degree of internalisation was indicated, but this was qualified by the words *'almost likely'*. Talking to a student, a ward sister in the German Group Discussion indicated a tentatively expected learning outcome:

> *...will **most probably** be a lesson for you, for the future (GD-D 163-165).*

This again indicated hope, but it also made concessions for the reality of life, where mistakes may happen.

In spite of being sure of the learning effect that his experience had for him, Mike would not commit himself. He said:

> *I **certainly** did take, (...) more care, when I was giving drugs out. Whether I still take that same level of care, (I may ?) have lapsed again (INT7 1659-1664);*
>
> *I feel, I did learn from it, eh .. maybe not ... **may be not in a long lasting strengthening** .. of my adherence to procedure and policy (INT7 1698-1702).*

In Interview One, Thelma talked about an experience that *'stuck in her mind'*. This may be taken as a learning reaction on a lower level of internalisation. Relating to example one in our interview she had her manager say *'... **you know** exactly what you have done'* and *'we have both learned from it'*. Here cognitive aspects of learning are being addressed. The knowledge of what has been done is hoped to bring about a learning effect in the affective domain. Thelma touched on what Bloom et al would classify as a first step on the affective learning continuum. Referring to a car accident when driving too fast round a corner she said:

> *...it makes you realise that **maybe** it makes you see the warning, **makes you aware**, when you look back on things, that you were stressed at the time, you're busy .. this is the time when easily more mistakes are made, (INT1 1687-1693).*

Thelma used words that relate to awareness and to a certain consciousness that is hopefully triggered off in times of stress. Her car accident taught her to apply this awareness in professional situations too. However, saying *'...maybe ... it makes you...'* indicates a careful and not absolutely certain hope that the learning arrived at through her car accident has not lost its effectiveness.

Also Pearl talked about mistakes being reminders to be more careful. That this would be so she assured me, after my question whether she had acted differently after her experiences, by saying:

> *Oh yes, I think you do, you, **you certainly**, you're more aware .. you are just, you are just that more aware when you are actually checking ..drugs, and checking things really, extra carefully, **I suppose**, (INT3 350-356).*

However, using the more distancing form of the second person this does not point to a high degree of internalisation. It remains at an abstract level even though she mentioned the concrete act of checking. She used the word *'certainly'* but also said *'I suppose'*. Pearl frequently used words like *'I think you are more aware..'* or *'..hope that she (hypothetical student) would be able to improve her practice from that..* . Here too, inconsistency makes it difficult to fix the experience as a learning outcome on a certain place along the growth continuum.

Utterances such as *'she's become more aware'*, and *'I think (she) will benefit from the experience'* (Sean in Interview Four), or *'something that almost likely'* a nurse would never do again, (Chris in Interview Nine), indicate a fairly low level within the process of internalisation.

Joan's remark in Interview Two regarding learning can be placed within a higher stage along the continuum of growth:

> *...and it **definitely** makes you more careful in future ..you know, I think, you have to learn from your mistakes, you do have to learn from your mistakes, (INT2 449-454).*

Saying that *'definitely'* a mistake makes people more careful, she also asserts that an obligation to greater care in future must needs be a learning outcome from experiences with medication errors. She linked this obligation to the memos that invariably appear to be seen and heeded by the nurses:

> *...every time these things happen in a hospital, there is usually some form of memo comes round just generally to say .. you know, (MA: yeah), be a little bit more careful, (INT2 1171-1176).*

This reaction from the side of management points to the expected need for deeper internalisation of the affective objective to take more care when handling medicines. By placing a memo to be read however, cognitive means are being used to affect this end. The often expressed anger or even contempt at such memos, and the disregard with which they are graced may indicate that they do have an affective force which defies their intention. Perhaps a cognitive approach, where nurses have already been touched at an affective level is resented. This in itself may be worth a study.

Another manager who was mentioned in the Scottish Group Discussion expressed himself in such a way that his conviction of the incident having a learning effect on the nurse appeared great. The following remark of his was reported by the participant in the Group Discussion:

> *...we make mistakes, and .. we all learn from them, but ehm .. **you will never** answer the telephone while doing a drug round again (GD-SC 1003-1007).*

The expression *'you will never'* indicates that a clear commitment is expected not to let herself be distracted again by telephone calls while doing the drugs. Whether this expectation can be met was left open by the nurse who gave the example.

Albeit, nurses claimed that past mistakes would induce a learning process, it cannot be discerned clearly who learned, or even what was learned. Only one nurse was sure that her experience had made such an impact on her future diligence in connection with the administration of drugs, that she is *'superduper efficient now'*.

However, where nurses talked about their learning experiences in connection with the decisions to be made after a medication error had occurred, a high level of internalisation can be demonstrated. In this area nurses' statements were unequivocal. With great certainty, several participants talked of how they do now and will behave when it comes to showing compassion and understanding when other nurses are involved in a medication error. The writer of Self Report One felt:

> *I also now have empathy towards other nurses when it happens to them (REP1 68-71).*

Pearl said as to learning to own up or to hide a mistake, that the way a nurse was treated, provided *'quite an element of learning'*. As for herself she had learned *'never to treat people like that'*. Her own negative experiences as a student had influenced her:

> *...it's given me a very strong .. will .. **never to treat people** .. **like that** (INT3 1476-1478).*

This was ascertained by Jane, who said:

> *...**there is no way** I would handle it like that, ... I mean to completely undermine somebody' confidence (INT11 1358-1361).*

It can be taken from what nurses disclosed to me, that seeing other nurses being treated harshly after a mistake had happened, they learned to cover their own mistakes up. Henry indicated as much when he said:

> *...first lesson I learned from the first incident .. was .. don't tell the nursing officer! (INT10 912-914).*

This would be a negative learning effect as far as honesty is concerned. On the other hand Henry also indicated that he had learned that it may be alright to own up to a mistake.

Regarding a second experience he said:

> *Something constructive came out of it,, and I felt .. OK .. I learned something from.. from that, because I can now .. deal with a situation like that better, because I can see that I can actually deal with it constructively (INT10 1924-1932).*

Also in the German Group Discussion this was addressed. One nurse said:

> *Yes, and most importantly (...) when I make mistakes, even minor ones, I don't have to be afraid to stand up for them. That too I have learned (GD-D 325-331).*

In one of the self reports a nurse wrote:

> *However, it also proved that I was/am capable of owning up to my error without knowing what the outcome was going to be. It was said to me at the time by the Charge Nurse that had he been me he would have kept his mouth shut (REP1 116-122).*

A nurse may hide mistakes in order to avoid being dealt with harshly or unjustly or simply to avoid the unpleasant disciplinary procedure which would expose her or his failure. Whether or not this is entirely due to a learning process connected with previous experience is hard to say. Some nurses felt that it was part of a person's character. Gerald, for instance, said:

> *...if you been, you know, brought up to admit to things, when you (made mistakes) I then I think you will do it. I think it varies with individual,* ***I don't think, it's something that you're taught*** *during, say your training and that. I think it's something you have prior to training, you know, I mean it's just .. I mean I think .. you either, ..****people will own up to their mistakes, or people won't, or people will blame other people,*** *you know,* ***maybe it's just partly your character,*** *(INT5 1036-1053).*

It was clearly felt however, that through negative experiences or through positive examples, reactions were influenced. Chris, after having experienced very lenient treatment said:

> ***I have more understanding*** *now (INT9 1318-1319);*

> *...and I..* ***hopefully*** *I'll be more of a help to them.* ***I'll be more supportive*** *to them than before, because I have experienced it (INT9 1325-1328).*

Remembering her own experience as a student and talking hypothetically how she would deal with students' errors, Pearl said:

> *...and half the time you were too frightened to query (INT3 1448-1449);*

> *...but yes* ***it's given me a very strong .. will .. never to treat people .. like that*** *(INT3 1476-1477).*

Pearl also felt that it was important to see the cognitive aspect of learning from a mistake. As to this she said:

> *...you'll take her aside and see, she obviously realised she's made a mistake, and go through it with her (INT3 1009-1012).*

She would however, make sure that correct disciplinary procedures were followed and would support the student through them:

> *...****and then hope*** *that she would .. be able to improve her practice from that (INT3 1041-1043).*

These extracts point to a strong commitment as to valuing fair treatment of nurses who have made a mistake. Still, it could only be *'hoped'*, that treating other nurses fairly would ultimately have a positive learning effect on them.

Hilary expressed her understanding of learning in situations of medication errors very clearly, when she aired her views on how students should be taught in the praxis areas:

> *Oh, I think, encourage them, and especially when they are learning, if they are working along with somebody, to be able,* ***to feel, you could make mistakes, and that it's OK everybody makes mistakes,*** *I think it's important to be honest and to say that mistakes do happen, and .. it's part of life and... to be able to ...take the mistake and to use it, that would be the important part as well,* ***for me it meant ... being more obsessive about drugs,*** *but I mean... (...?...) whatever the mistake was, if they could use it to..* ***improve their practice, then it's a benefit*** *(INT12 1471-1488).*

Hilary felt that two things could be learned by going though the experience of being involved in a medication error: Because *'everybody could make mistakes'*, students need not to be frightened to own up when they happen; and secondly, be more careful or *'obsessive'* as she put it, and use the mistake to improve practice.

In summary, it can be said that these two points represent the essence of what may be gained in the way of learning from mistakes. Bloom et al have described "a pervasive outlook on life, that influences all actions" as the highest level of internalisation in the affective domain of learning. This was generally not claimed by the participants of this study where the possibility of future errors came into play. How learning will affect behaviour very much depends on the circumstances of future situations. This can be understood from the sometimes hesitatingly alluded to reference to prospective behaviour as far as taking care in the administration of medication was concerned. It is not surprising therefore, that unspecified as well as contradictory statements have been made in the data of this study. It was stated by some nurses that they had learned from the mistakes others had made. This however, was doubted by others.

As to making decisions after a medication error has occurred, the learning effects were referred to with greater certainty. Some nurses had learned to own up to their mistakes because they had experienced understanding behaviour from the side of superiors. The courage that is needed to own up to mistakes, can certainly be enhanced and its application be improved by learning experiences. Most participants mentioned that they had learned to exhibit a greater degree of understanding in situations where another nurse made a mistake.

Learning from mistakes - An excuse?

Frequently it could be noted that the aspect of 'learning from mistakes' was not an assertion a participant in this study made about her or his own person. Often such a phrase would be put in the mouth of a colleague, a manager or charge nurse, when their reaction to the occurrence was mentioned.

From one incident related in the Scottish Group Discussion it emerged that the manager acknowledged the learning effect of the experience when he said that the nurse would *'never answer the telephone while doing a drug round again'*. Also in Interview Two it was the manager whom Joan reported to have said to her:

> *I think it was just one of these things that happened, **you learned** from, ehm .. and **it definitely makes you more careful in future** ..you know, I think, you have to learn from your mistakes, you do have to learn from your mistakes, (INT2 447-454);*

The same phenomenon was found in Interview Nine, where Chris related the mistake for which she herself had been responsible. In an indirect way she conveyed that her manager had felt that she had learned from her mistake:

> *...it was something that .. **I almost likely would never ever do again.** Because once it happens to you, you never forget it (Int9 223-226).*

This allows the conclusion that the assertion of 'learning from mistakes' was possibly not only used to allude to the learning aspect itself. Rather it functioned as an excuse. It may have been used by respondents in order to display the sense of extenuation that is hoped to pervade the judgement of a manager or charge nurse who dealt with the mistake.

In Documents Three and Five the fact of learning from mistakes was forwarded in mitigation at disciplinary hearings. The RCN Representative, speaking in mitigation for his defendant said, that

Nurse M. had been extremely upset about the incident and that she acknowledged the fact of having made a serious misjudgement. He asked the Professional Conduct Committee that *'those judgements are viewed in the context of all the circumstances'*:

> *She (Nurse M.) wishes the Committee to be aware* ***that she has learned some very important lessons*** *from that incident and she now wishes to try and put the matter behind her and continue with what appears to be a most promising career (DOC3 p. 5).*

In a similar context in UKCC Document Five, the nurse against whom allegations of misconduct were made, talked about the learning effect of her experience. The following dialogue took place when the RCN Representative questioned the defendant in mitigation:

> *RCN Representative: Have your previous errors, which you admit, made a difference?*
>
> *Nurse T.: Yes, they have. I think about it virtually every time I give the tablets out. I am extremely careful. I mean, everything is done by the book now, there are no short cuts, and* ***I think I have learned from it.***
>
> *RCN Representative: (...) Okay. And finally, Nurse T. I think the Committee would like to know from you how you feel about the series of events on that morning back in November 1986.*
>
> *Nurse T.: I think looking back and taking it in isolation, it looks absolutely horrendous.* ***I have learned by my mistake****. I certainly wouldn't do things the same way again. I did some stupid, stupid things, I know I did, and looking back it just looks dreadful (DOC5 p. 21).*

From the information on the cases which the documents yielded this sounds appropriate and honest. The statements were used to throw a positive light on Nurse M. and Nurse T. To have learned from their experience meant a reinstitution of their professional honour and would justify the Committee's decision not to remove the nurses' names from the register.

A further function of the common place of 'learning from mistakes' can be discerned from the discourse of some participants. The fact that another nurse or a student has learned from a mistakes may have been emphasised in order to cover up a certain personal insecurity of the respondents regarding the manner the situation had been dealt with. Perhaps, it was also used to cover up an aspect of a specific situation which a nurse felt uncomfortable with, without openly admitting this.

In the incident Sean had talked about in Interview Four, he had known that the 10 mg tablets of Melleril had run out. He had not mentioned this to the nurse who did the drug round that day. She inadvertently picked up the bottle with 25 mg Melleril tablets and gave too high a dose of this tranquillising drug to a patient. Sean assured me repeatedly, that the nurse involved in this medication error had certainly learned from her mistake. Possibly, some doubt arose in his mind as to how the situation had been managed. He said:

> *...and* ***she's become, more aware*** *of .. potential drug errors, as a result of it, and, I think,* ***will benefit*** *from the experience .. (Int4 1434-1438);*

> *...she'd definitely said, that you know, she'd learned an awful lot from ehm.. the incident, and I said well, you know, ... then you have to think that it's been* ***a positive side****, you know, I always like to think that we sort of make any mistakes, I said, but .. the main thing is that you learn from your mistake (INT4 1524-1534).*

Sean assumed also that the other staff on his ward had learned from this incident:

> *...and all nurses.. they were certainly more aware ..how careful they have to be, (INT4 2132-2135).*

His way of dealing with the situation had caused the nurse a great deal of anguish. It also caused the ward atmosphere to suffer. Sean, however, never mentioned that he himself had learned from the situation.

Furthermore, policy changes which were sometimes made regarding the drug administration routine, indicate that something was amiss in the first place. Sometimes the nurses responsible for such changes had admitted, that *'everybody had learned something'* thus, including themselves. In some cases however, this was only said of the culprit. For instance the ward sister in the German Group Discussion, who made it a rule that Markumar was not to be given out by students any more, and that in future all drugs given out by students were to be checked by qualified staff, might have made sure that students were supervised better in the first place. She, however, addressed the student who had made the mistake, saying to him:

> ***You are a student****, this will most probably be* ***a lesson for you****, for the future, when you give out medicines, that* ***you take more care*** *(GD-D 164-168).*

She said further:

> *And I also said to him, that in the end the fault was not his, but lay with the qualified nurse, who was on duty at the time. She should have checked, especially with Markumar (GD-D 169-175).*

From these examples it may be deduced, that an allusion to the learning aspect inherent in mistakes, may have had the function of a justification, excusing or diverting attention from a state of affairs that was responsible for an error in the first place.

RESULTS OF MISTAKES AT INSTITUTIONAL AND PROFESSIONAL LEVELS

A changing perspective of nurses' professionalism

The development of medicine and technology has confronted doctors and nurses with new and different tasks. Some of the duties, beforehand considered to lie in the charge of physicians, have been delegated to nursing staff. This included for example, venepunctures or the supervision of sophisticated technological equipment. Nurses undertook these charges gladly as this conveyed the perception of the highly qualified professional. In the wake of these developments special training was required which then came to be acknowledged with post registration certificates for specific extended roles. This led to the necessity for nurses having a deeper and more profound knowledge of patients' conditions in order to make appropriate judgements in connection with the execution of their new duties.

A new picture of the nurse evolved which was not simply that of the caring woman who tended the physical needs of the sick. This change in turn resulted in competitive role perceptions between doctors and nurses. An inquiry into the deeper implications of this development is not the object of this study. The decision-making processes in connection with the administration of medicines and subsequently in connection with medication errors as they reflect these changes, are being dealt with here. The changes in this respect reflect a process of learning at an institutional as well as at a professional level. Nevertheless, due to an advancement of medical science and of technology, more complicated medical prescriptions and more sophisticated modes of administering drugs, enhance the risks of making mistakes.

Stapleton, studying the learning needs of ward sisters in order to identify problems in connection with continuing education made the following comment:

> ...and nursing skills included an awareness of patient states that required immediate medical intervention or, perhaps more importantly, did not require such intervention. Acquiring enough knowledge to make decisions about the need for medical care as separate from nursing care developed in the vacuum which resulted from the way in which medicine was practised. To fill in this vacuum, nurses needed not only knowledge, but also professional confidence robust enough to withstand this type of decision-making. ... Medical care and nursing care are clearly complementary and not competitive... (Stapleton 1987 p. 92)

Nurses are supposed to act in accordance with the patient's best interest. But this ostensibly applies only as long as nurses' actions fall within their scope of prescribed duty. In 1980 Dorothy Hall, then Regional Officer for Nursing of the WHO said:

> ... in most countries of the European Region, the nurse who should be the major provider of organized, comprehensive nursing services, has come to be thought of as a hospital-based worker concerned mainly with servicing the various departments of that institution and creating an atmosphere in which the physician and his patient can meet and interact (Hall 1980 p. 152).

This indicates the need for developing nursing in a context of accountable professionalism as well as in relation to moral decision-making that is based on ethical principles. The case dealt with in UKCC Document Four exemplifies the dilemma a nurse may find herself in. The mistake dealt with in this document was not so much a mistake that harmed a patient. Here the problem lay with the relationship between a physician and a charge nurse.

The nurse in charge of a psychiatric day centre gave 20 mg of Valium Elixir to a patient who was distressed and hyperventilating. The nurse knew the patient to suffer from occasional epileptic fits and was aware of the fact that there was a threat of the patient's condition deteriorating if no medical intervention was effected. The doctor would not come to see the patient until after he had had his lunch. He told an enrolled nurse that the patient was to be given 5 mg of Valium. This order was conveyed to the nurse in charge who felt that this would have no effect in the given situation. The nurse had learned from past experiences that the doctor would certainly not come if she tried to summon him again. She did try to contact the consultant but was unsuccessful. After talking to the patient she decided to give her 20 mg of Valium Elixir from the patient's own supply, which the patient carried in her handbag. The patient settled within half an hour and slept for a while during which the nurse kept a check on her. The patient recovered well and could go home in the afternoon. The doctor however, when being told that the patient had been given 20 mg of Valium refused to write this up retrospectively. He reported the nurse who was dismissed from her position and duly charged with professional misconduct.

According to her experienced judgement as a nurse she had administered what most probably would have been prescribed by any doctor. At the hearing before the Professional Conduct Committee, the Union Representative said in mitigation:

> *Union Representative: The particular instruction that was actually given to the SEN was actually a breach of procedure. So even if Nurse C. had carried out that instruction she would have actually been in breach with the Authority's own drug procedure. She was in a Catch 22 situation, because if she had given it there could have been recourse to disciplinary action, in any event. (...)*
>
> *Nurse C. realises quite clearly that that isn't something that she should have done. She realises the fact that that was not her responsibility to take that sort of decision. (...) She was quite truthful in fact that she told the doctor what she had actually done (...)* ***and hoped (...) that there would have actually been some support from the doctor in that particular situation*** *(DOC4 p. 13).*

Nurse C. admitted the charge of professional misconduct The charge against her was upheld during the hearing but her name was not removed from the register. This situation undoubtedly presented a special kind of mistake. This nurse failed to adhere to the rules that medicines may only be prescribed by a medical practitioner. During the hearing she indicated that she had learned from the situation and that she would not again act in the same fashion. Being questioned by members of the Committee, the following exchange took place:

> *Member of Committee: You made a judgement, which obviously now you see was an error. How do you feel about that, looking back on it?*
>
> *Nurse C.:* ***It's not something that I would do again.*** *It's something I did at the time because I thought there was no other option available to me. But it isn't' something I would do again (DOC4 p. 11).*

It must be supposed that the Committee dealing with this case had not only the nurse's situation to assess, but also had to keep in mind general aspects of professional conduct. In a final statement the Chairperson of the Committee said:

> *Being found guilty, Nurse C., of misconduct is a serious matter and Council does in no way condone your actions in this matter. This Committee is not here to punish, but to protect the vulnerable public. However, after considering your case we have decided that although your actions are misconduct in the professional sense your name should not be removed from the Professional Register.*
>
> *On behalf of the Committee I ask you that you have a copy of the Council's Code of Professional Conduct, Administration of Medicines and other documents which indicate the standards of conduct expected from registered practitioners. We urge you to read it and think about it and recommend that you let them be your guide to your future professional practice.*
>
> *I would like to say on behalf of the Committee that we feel that this was an error of judgement, but that you must in future ensure that you follow policies and procedures laid down in any Authority with which you are working. (...) (DOC4 p. 14).*

It may be argued that overstepping the borders of their scope of duty amounts to professional misconduct. In the case of Nurse C., the decision she made to benefit the patient, damaged her career, as she did not adhere to the policies and procedures laid down.

Mike, in Interview Seven, while talking about the way nurses' mistakes are handled had said, that the lesson he had learned from his own mistake would not have been reinforced, had he gone through the official procedure. He had not reported his mistake to the nursing hierarchy, but dealt with it by discussing it with the medical officer and ascertaining the patient's well-being. Mike felt in the given circumstances this to be the right way of handling the incident. He was sure of his knowledge concerning the drugs that were in use on his ward, and he was certain of the drug administration procedure that should have been followed.

In this context Mike made a remark that can only makes sense in the light of the aforementioned case and if a wider view of learning is taken into consideration. Mike said, concerning senior managers who handle minor medication errors in a seemingly exaggerated way:

> *...maybe when you climb further up the ladder, you feel that, there is more to protect ... ... than just the nurse's feelings ... (INT7 1238-1242)*

Certainly, a dilemma exists for nurses when they want to act in the interest of patients where doctors seem to be un-co-operative or where doctors do not respect the professional expertise of nurses, or help them to gain it in a respectful and co-operative manner.

(It must, however, be mentioned that many situations have been related in the data of this study where doctors and nurses worked in good co-operation and where doctors respected the judgement of nurses. In some instances, the participants had also mentioned doctors' practice to rectify nurses' errors by writing up a prescription retrospectively, providing no harm had come to the patient).

A further example can be cited from UKCC Document Three, where two nurses gave a wrong dose of Digoxin to a patient who consequently died. They calculated the doctor's prescription wrongly. Had they not made this mistake in calculation, they would have noted that the prescription itself had been grossly wrong. And had the level of communication been more positive, any queries would possibly have been discussed, and an error prevented.

During the UKCC hearing of this case the following dialogue between the RCN Representative and Nurse S. ensued:

> *RCN Representative: Did you question that dosage any further with anybody else?*
>
> *Nurse S.: No.*
>
> *RCN Representative: Why was that?*

> *Nurse S.:* ***It was very difficult to communicate with the doctor****, who was actually present. I had some problems with him the previous night when a patient's condition had deteriorated quite rapidly and he had been actually present on the unit. I had asked him to seek further assistance and he had said that this wasn't necessary. The patient's condition deteriorated and indeed I went above his head to call the anaesthetist, and the doctor found it very difficult to communicate with the nursing staff. The patient subsequently arrested and died. It wasn't just myself that felt this.* ***It was very difficult to ask him questions about treatment which he had prescribed*** *(DOC3 p. 10).*

This extract shows that an element of negative learning had taken place (don't ask this doctor) which precipitated the fatal mistake the nurses made. As there was no communication between this doctor and the nurses, they simply tried to follow the prescription to master the task of administering intravenous Digoxin which basically was new to them. The incident involved the nurses in charge of the unit as well as the nursing officer in charge of night duty. The nurses were rightly found to be guilty of professional misconduct, but no mention was made of the fact that this could have possibly be prevented, had there been a better working climate between nursing and medical staff.

In another case heard by the Professional Conduct Committee (Document Six), the fact that the doctors did not write up a prescription in the usual way had the result, that the nurses concerned administered intravenous Lignocaine too fast in too short a period of time which caused the patient's death. On this occasion both nurses were not found guilty of professional misconduct. Nevertheless, the hospital management implemented the rule that infusions to be given via an infusion pump were to be set and controlled by doctors only.

The nurses involved in these cases will certainly have learned from their mistakes. At least they will have learned to improve and update their knowledge. But will they have learned to act independently as well as in co-operation? A perception of the subservient role of nurses was upheld by the nursing authorities in that they solely referred to regulations in the situation of decision-making in everyday practice.

Mike had said *'there is more to protect'*. This is not only done by adhering to a deontological mode of ethical argument. In the cases presented in Documents Three and Six the Committee took great pains to ascertain whether or not the nurses concerned were in possession of 'extended role certificates'. These certificates were proof that nurses are able to carry out certain techniques mainly used in intensive care therapy, for instance those that were formerly on the task list of medical practitioners. The nurses involved in the said cases had been issued with these certificates. The possession of such certificates however, is no guarantee that nurses do not make mistakes harmful to patients.

This dilemma seems to be addressed in the new formulation of the UKCC Code of Professional Conduct. In an advisory paper complementing these new rules the terms 'extended' or 'extending' roles, are regarded as "no longer suitable since they limit rather than extend, the parameters of practice" (UKCC 1992). The following statement is emphasised:

> In order to bring into proper focus the professional responsibility and consequent accountability of individual practitioners, it is the council's principles for practice rather than certificates for tasks which should form the basis for adjustments to the scope of practice (UKCC 1992 p. 8).

As to the scope of practice six principles are laid down, the third of which reads:

> The registered nurse, midwife or health visitor: (...) must honestly acknowledge any limits of personal knowledge and skill and take steps to remedy any relevant deficits in order effectively and appropriately to meet the needs of patient and clients (UKCC 1992 p. 6).

A changed perception as to the nurses role in practice can be seen in the new UKCC Code of Professional Conduct. Greater emphasis is placed on the personal responsibility of the nurse rather than on an assurance for safe practice that rests on the certificates formerly issued to objectify the extended role of the nurse.

Learning by mistakes - Ultimate effects

We speak against the backdrop of our environments and our social realities. Our discourse manifests and perpetuates this social reality, but it also forms and constructs it anew. Experiences of mistakes are ultimately reflected in changes within certain ward settings and also in changes within the profession itself.

Taking into consideration Hockey's vision of changes in the nursing profession, which include, as stated earlier, "an education for political awareness", and "education in decision-making" (Hockey 1980), it appears to be of importance, to comprehend the effects which personal experiences have at a general professional level. Some changes effected at an institutional level were induced by personal experiences in the first place. These changes make for more professional awareness and autonomy in decision-making. Hockey states:

> A nurse should be free to make her own decisions regarding her activities; she ought to know when, why and how she takes certain decisions and to be able to defend these in the interest of patient care (Hockey 1980 p. 909).

The following remarks epitomise a profound change at a personal level which finally effected staff management. Chris, the respondent in Interview Nine, mentioned how for a long time she had been willing to work under great pressure, not having enough staff on her ward, and how she was easily pacified by her managers to make do with the resources she had at her disposal. Chris said:

> *... constantly, constantly saying .. we're working on a shoe-string here, and something is going to happen. And nursing management very rarely take that on board, until something does happen. And I do get quite angry, 'cos I think, there again, you were just left in it (INT9 EX1 1795-1801).*

The experience of having made a medication error caused Chris to be more assertive in asking for more staff in order to cover difficult situations on her ward. She did not feel compelled any more to cope under all circumstances. And it also caused her managers to heed her requests. The following dialogue ensued:

> *MA: I have a feeling that your professional awareness is .. sharpened.. (Chris: Aha!) from this. (Chris: Yeah!)*
>
> *Chris: I do, yeah, because I would never be fobbed off now .. (...)*
>
> *MA: Do you feel that this kind of .. mm.. stronger assertiveness, gets you the staff?*
>
> *Chris: Yes! (INT9 EX1 1864-1881).*

A greater work load due to cuts in the resources of the health care services and at the same time more complicated medical treatment for more complicated and diverse diagnoses, brings about the necessity for change. But indispensable changes unfortunately are often only made after patients were put at risk and mistakes have occurred. However, a greater awareness of their professional position seems to influence nurses' decisions which have influence on policy making and on institutional work structures.

Changes in the perception of ethics

Lamb, in her essay on nursing ethics and nursing education summarises a clearly perceptible change in the apprehension of ethics in nursing. She examines the focus of literature concerned with ethics in nursing over the last hundred years. She comes to the conclusion that:

> Over time, major themes in nursing ethics seemed to have changed from a focus on moral character to professional obligation to ethical decision-making (Lamb 1982 p. 18/19).

This too can be seen as a reflection of social development. Lamb describes how "moral character" in nursing a hundred years ago was understood as "honesty, cheerfulness, discretion, kindness and obedience". It also included an emphasis on discipline, which was said to have been "a necessary component of nursing ethics teaching" (Lamb 1982). The following quote epitomises the prevailing conception of what the teaching of ethics in nursing meant:

> According to Nightingale (1882), a good nursing school provided training in 'moral qualities, customs and habits, and manners, without which no woman can be a nurse' (Lamb 1982 p. 6, inverted commas in the original).

A change to what Lamb termed 'professional obligation' characterised the perception of ethics in nursing some twenty to fifty years later, when much energy was spent on the formulation of ethical codes for nursing. Lamb explains:

> There seemed to be a gradual shift in attention from the nurse as a person to a focus on the person as a nurse. The theme of professional obligation seemed to become preeminent in nursing ethics (Lamb 1982 p. 6)

In this middle period, according to Lamb, the teaching of ethics in nursing was based on "an understanding of the social role of nursing". For Canada and the United States this meant that "the teaching of ethics was incorporated into courses designed to socialize students into their role as a nurse". But also "an integrated approach was suggested whereby educators took opportunities in all courses to relate ethical principles to practice" (Lamb 1982).

From the nineteen seventies onwards, the Anglo-American literature suggests that the teaching of ethics has become more deeply based on ethical theory. In the face of the changes outlined above this had to be a necessity well in line with the described extended role of the nurse. Lamb summarises this last period saying:

> Increasingly nurses affirm the importance of justifying positions on the basis of a coherent set of ethical principles rather than on the basis of codes of conduct or traditional practice (Lamb 1982 p. 15).

It is to be hoped that moral decisions made by nurses will indeed be increasingly influenced by ethical principles rather than by professional obligation only. The data of this study suggest that nurses are aware of their responsibilities towards their patients and towards each other. Many decisions that nurses made in situations of medication errors pointed to concern about their patients' as well as to concern about each others' well being. Yet, it is of importance, especially when mistakes have happened, to discuss and address the processes of decision-making openly and to point out underlying motivations which will inadvertently influence such decisions. This is not only in the personal interest of those involved with medication errors. Talking about experiences means to bring change and development into existence. Codes of conduct, policies and guide-lines may be read about and forgotten. The power of ethical principles to influence professional reality is released when they become part of spoken discourse.

Concluding Interpretive Remarks

Looking Through a Magnifying Glass

An increased awareness of ethical principles is responsible for a new sensitivity in this area. But it is not the theoretical teaching of ethics that finally changes attitudes, opinions and consequently conduct. It is the personal experience, reflected in an informed manner, discussed and taken seriously, be it with students during basic training or in post qualification courses, that makes for learning the skills of moral decision making. However, Van Hooft maintains that it is not the discourse on ethics that is "motivational in itself". Talking about ethics "cannot induce us to act in one way or another" (van Hooft 1990). It is indeed the life scene of practice, where ethics are applied, that they unfold their guiding and helpful function. We can all learn from experiences; from our own and from that of others. Seeing others act, makes us understand and internalise ethical theory. Even as onlookers we are part of the world we live in. Positive role models are remembered positively; and helpful attitudes, positive opinions and values may be gained by experiencing emphatic dealings with situations of conflict. Still, we do not learn from positive examples only. Situations that have been handled badly, causing hurt and confusion, influence us to no small extent.

However, it is in personal involvement that we are effecting the changes which are taking place within society, within the health care services, within institutions and within ourselves. Medication errors served as a magnifying glass in this study in order to discern some of these changes.

In the first place it is the factual occurrence of such a mistake itself that has to be assimilated and lived with. Accepting or resisting the reality of its occurrence is crucial for personal development. Secondly, medication errors instigate situations of conflict that ask for decisions to be made. These decisions affect patients, nursing staff and other health care workers alike. It is not only the disciplinary procedures by which medication errors are dealt with, that is of consequential importance. Of fundamental concern is the situation that led to such occurrences. By shifting the attention from the person involved to the situation itself, it can be transformed into improvement of work conditions and in the long term enhance the effectiveness of the treatment offered to patients.

THE VALUE OF ANALYSING DISCOURSE

Medication errors are invariably talked about. It was not difficult to obtain data for this study. Nurses readily offered to discuss their experiences. The collection of data in this study was a discourse about discourses. The nurses, as participants in this study, made their experiences public by reflecting on the medication errors they had been involved in; thus, addressing the profession as an entirety. It was my commission to reflect and interpret this discourse in turn. Hence analysis and interpretive writing provided a further discourse.

Analysing specific discourses "should bring about an understanding of the way things *were,* not the way things *are* (Parker 1990). This statement of Parker's commits discourse analysis to being an instrument of change. Not just analysis for analysis' sake, but with the knowledge that the way we talk makes us understand the object we talk about. Discourse objectifies experience, and by doing so opens it up for the evaluation of the experience itself. The analysis of discourse presupposes the personal involvement of all participants at a subjective level. And here is the focal point of all changes. By looking at what was meant by nurses when they talked about their experiences, the functional objective of their talk could be revealed.

Parker claims that "an attention to language can also facilitate a process of progressively politicising everyday life" (Parker 1990). This is exactly what the attentive listening to nurses' discourse about medication errors made possible. It showed the political implications that lay in personal thinking and acting. Berger (1969) talks about the "dialectical phenomenon" of society, which "acts back upon its producer" in that the social reality we live in is being changed by us as we concede to it and live within it.

The discourse which is created in this study attends to three key issues connected with the experience of having been involved in a medication error:

- Identification and change
- Guilt and reconciliation
- Learning from mistakes

These three key issues have been unfolded in Part Four of this thesis.

NURSES' MEDICATION ERRORS - AN INTERPRETIVE STUDY OF EXPERIENCES

Unwieldy, full of knots and possibly crooked, like a big tree. Such may be the appearance of an interpretive study using discourse analysis. What does it teach us, what is its use? Potter and Wetherell answer suchlike questions in the following way:

> One of the possible fruits of discourse analysis is to promote an informed critical attitude to discourse of this kind; to be more aware of its constructive nature and the close connection between the way textual versions of the world are put together and specific policies and evaluations are pushed (Potter/Wetherell 1987 p. 174/175).

There is no presentation of concise and exciting research findings with which to conclude. There is the offer thoughtfully to consider what nurses have said about medication errors, and what such experiences may mean.

Several courses were followed in the attempt to interpret what nurses said. Phenomenology as a basis for qualitative research may provide the thrust of the research question, but the empirical design of this study aimed at attaining "knowledge of reality of the sort we call probable truths" (Simmons 1992).

From the many-faceted reality that made up the participants discourse, some themes were isolated and looked at as they promised access to what nurses wanted to convey as meaningful. They could be illuminated by structuring them within the concept of an empirical model, which in turn provided the framework for the three chapters of Part Four of this thesis.

The identification with an imperative force that calls for subjection to its rules has been traced using the exemplar of medication errors. It is the constructive dialogue however, between the actors and the situation which makes for development and change. On a personal level it is "acceptance" which gives "meaning to actions which allows agents to say that they have acted well so as to empower those agents to perform difficult and caring actions again on future occasions" (van Hooft 1990). The people involved in such situations of conflict as medication errors represent, go through a process of learning. This learning is furthermore reflected at institutional as well as at professional levels. It makes for the changes which construct and reconstruct society.

FURTHER RESEARCH

This study covered ground hitherto not much traversed in nursing research. By using discourse analysis within the framework of this interpretive study it was possible to uncover and address various aspects of ' the procedure of dealing with medication errors'; 'the role of the medical staff'; ' the image of the nurse and of nursing'; 'the situation of student nurses'; and 'support in the situation of medication errors. This is but a limited selection of themes which could be addressed as of importance in the given context. These were the themes which emerged from the data of the present study as of foremost importance. The research question in this study was focused on the personal experience of the nurses involved in situations of medication errors; the decision-making processes; and the outcome of the experience for personal and professional development (Part One pp. 70/71). These aspects were addressed by examining them through the perspectives of the three key issues.

It is impossible to cover all aspects concerning the situation of medication errors in one thesis. But this study opens up the area for further research. Some of these areas are indicated in the empirical model.

First, it would be feasible to undertake studies which look more deeply at the 'influential factors or givens for the acquisition of meaning'. Especially the influence of unusual circumstances or the influence of workload and staffing levels on the occurrence of medication errors could provide material for further studies. It may also be of great interest to elicit the concrete meaning that local drug administration policies have for the nurses whose daily work is supposed to be guided by them.

Furthermore, the 'reactions to medication errors' leave wide scope for investigations. This applies to the reactions of patients and their concrete roles in such situations as well as to the reactions of the nurses involved. The question of how a nurse's work may be influenced by the experience of having made an error in the administration of medication may yield interesting answers for the area of practice professional performance.

Thirdly, the 'ultimate effects of the medication error, of the reactions to it and of the consequences that follow its occurrence' could prove to be a rich field for nursing research. Here the organisational perspectives could lead to studies in the area of quality assurance.

The area of feminism is touched upon only lightly in the present study. Questions of domination and power; of the nurses role as a woman; as well as the position of male nurses within the profession will certainly bear more research, as does the relationship between doctors and nurses. Ethical questions related to gender issues could yield interesting material for further studies if brought into context with the implications of having made a medication error.

As for the data sources, these have not to be confined to interviews, group discussions, self reports and official documents. For the analysis of discourse the examination of other written materials about medication errors could prove fruitful. It would be of interest to investigate the reports written on such occasions. Here, nurses verbalised in the first instance what has occurred. Further reports are written by senior staff and managers. These reflect the meaning of medication errors from a different perspective. The comparison between the initially written reports and later statements may reveal important details. The documents produced by the Professional Conduct Committees have also more to offer than becomes apparent in this study. Interviewing nurses who have been involved in disciplinary hearings at various levels and comparing personal views with the corresponding official documents could also be worthy of further study. Some medication errors are written about in local newspapers. By using the techniques of discourse analysis some interesting aspects relating to the public side of medication errors may be revealed from newspaper-stories. Moreover, notes, which appear in staff rooms after incidents of medication errors may supply material to be investigated. These are but a few examples. An abundance of discourse is available asking for detailed research using qualitative as well as quantitative approaches. Much scope remains to illumine the reality of what is being experienced in connection with medication errors and how these experiences "act back upon (their) producer" and restructure society as "a human Product" (Berger 1969).

Here, an attempt was made to understand what medication errors meant to nurses by listening to what they had to say about their experience with personal failure. '*Going over*' the situation with colleagues, talking about it, one respondent had said '*helped me right then, when I needed it*'. Being better equipped to deal with similar situations in future could be the positive outcome of a personal experience with a medication error. Understanding how another nurse may feel in such a traumatic situation and being able to sustain a colleague in regaining lost professional confidence may well be a further effect.

Nurses, as members of a health care profession are committed "to those people who require nursing care" (International Council of Nurses, Code for Nurses 1974). This, and similar statements found in ethical codes for nurses leave nurses vulnerable. Human fallibility does not stop short of high sounding ethical imperatives. Nurses remain exposed to the possibility of making mistakes. Their precarious situation deserves attention. To the participants of this study medication errors were traumatic occurrences. The most valuable support through such situations was given and received when the experience was shared with other nurses who had lived through similar situations themselves.

References

Alexander, M.F. (1982) Integrating theory and practice: An experiment evaluated. In: Nursing education. Recent advances in nursing, pp. 56-80. Edited by: M.S. Henderson, Edinburgh: Churchill Livingstone.

Alexander, M.F. (1983) Learning to nurse: Integrating theory and practice. Edinburgh, London: Churchill Livingstone.

Althusser, L. (1971) Ideology and Ideological State Apparatuses. In: Lenin and philosophy and other essays, pp. 121-173. (Translated by B. Brewster), London: New Left Book.

Arndt, M. (1988) Der Pflegeprozeß. Freiburg: Caritasgemeinschaft für Pflege- und Sozialberufe.

Aroskar, M.A. (1987) The interface of ethics and politics. *Nursing Outlook,* 35(6) pp. 268-272.

Austin, J.L. (1961) A plea for excuses. In: Philosophical papers, pp. 123-152. Edited by: J. Urmson and G. Warnock, Oxford: Claredon Press.

Austin, J.L. (1962) How to do things with words. London: Oxford University Press.

Baker, P.D. (1987) Moral competency: An essential element in the socialisation of professional nurses. *Family and Community Health,* 10(1) pp. 8-14.

Beauchamp, T. and Childress, J. (1983) Principles of biomedical ethics. (2nd ed.) New York: Oxford University Press.

Benhabib, S. (1987) The generalized and the concrete other: The Kohlberg-Gilligan controversy and moral theory. In: Women and moral theory, pp. 154-177. Edited by: E.F. Kittay and D.T. Meyers, Totowa, New Jersey: Roman & Littlefield.

Benjamin, M. and Curtis, J. (1981) Ethics in nursing. New York: Oxford University Press.

Benner, P. (1984) From novice to expert: Excellence and power in clinical nursing practice. Menlo Park, California: Addison-Wesley.

Benner, P. (1985) Quality of life: A phenomenological perspective on explanation, prediction, and understanding in nursing science. *Advances in Nursing Science,* 8(1) pp. 1-32.

Benner, P. (1992) Editorial. *Journal of Clinical Nursing,* 1(3) pp. 111-112.

Benner, P. and Wrubel, J. (1988) The primacy of caring. Menlo Park, California: Addison-Wesley.

Berger, P.L. (1969) The social reality of religion. London: Faber & Faber Ltd.

Bergum, V. (1989) Being a phenomenological researcher. In: Qualitative nursing research: A contemporary dialogue, pp. 55-71. Edited by: J.M. Morse, Rockville, Maryland: Aspen Publishers.

Betz, R.P. and Levy, H.B. (1985) An interdisciplinary method of classifying and monitoring medication errors. *American Journal of Hospital Pharmacy,* 42(8) pp. 1724-1734.

Bishop, A.H. and Scudder, J.R. (1987) Nursing ethics in an age of controversy. *Advances in Nursing Science,* 9(3) pp. 34-43.

Bishop, A.H. and Scudder, J.R. (1990) The practical, moral and personal sense of nursing. Albany, New York: Suny Press.

Bloom, B.S., et al (1956) Taxonomy of educational objectives: The classification of educational goals. Handbook I, Cognitive domain. London: Longman Group Ltd.

Bloom, B.S., et al (1964) Taxonomy of educational objectives: The classification of educational goals. Handbook II, Affective domain. London: Longmann Group Ltd.

Boydell, T. (1976) Experiential learning. Quoted in: J. Heath (1979) Tomorrow's approach to learning. *Nursing Mirror, 149(6) pp. 80 I-P.*

Brandt, M., et al (1988) A severity index for medication errors. *Nursing Management,* 19(8) pp. 80 I-p, Critical Care Management Edition.

Buber, M. (1971) Guilt and guilt feelings. In: Guilt: Man and society, pp. 85-116. Edited by: R.W. Smith, Garden City, New York: Doubleday & Co., Inc.

Bulmer, M. (1977) Problems, theories and methods in sociology - (How) Do they interrelate? In: Sociological research methods, pp. 2-33. Edited by: M. Bulmer, London: The Macmillan Press Ltd.

Burch, R. (1989) On phenomenology and its practices. *Phenomenology and Pedagogy,* No.7 pp. 187-216.

Callaghan, S. (1990) Breaking the chain reaction. *Nursing Times,* 86(44) pp. 36-38.

Campbell, A.V. (1975) Moral dilemmas in medicine. (2nd ed.) Edinburgh: Churchill Livingstone.

Campbell, A.V. (1979) Ethical issues in nursing. In: Readings in nursing, pp. 101-115. Edited by: M. Colledge and D. Jones, Edinburgh: Churchill Livingstone.

Campbell, A.V. (1988) Profession and vocation. In: Ethical issues in caring, pp. 2-9. Edited by: G. Fairbairn and S. Fairbairn, Aldershot: Avebury.

Campbell, D. (1984) Who carries the drug can? *Nursing Mirror,* 169(7) pp. 31.

Capps, D. (1993) The depleted self: Sin in a narcissistic age. Minneapolis: Fortress Press.

Capra, F. (1982) The turning point. Science, society and the rising culture. London: Wildwood House.

Carlisle, D. (1991) Just one slip. *Nursing Times,* 87(14) pp. 30-31.

Carr, D.S. (1989) New strategies for avoiding medication errors. *Nursing,* 19(8) pp. 38-46.

Cassidy, V.R. and Oddi, L.F. (1988) Professional autonomy and ethical decision making among graduate and undergraduate nursing majors. *Journal of Nursing Education,* 27(9) pp. 405-410.

Chiarella, E.M. (1988) Ethical dilemmas in curriculum planning. *Nurse Education Today,* No.8 pp. 96-98.

Clamp, C. (1980) Learning through incidents. *Nursing Times,* Oct. 2nd, pp. 1755-1758.

Cobb, M.D. (1986) Evaluating medication errors. *Journal of Nursing Administration,* 16(4) pp. 41-44.

Cohen, M.R. (1987) Medication errors. *Nursing,* 17(9) p. 8.

Cohen, M.R. (1988) Are errors waiting to happen? *Nursing,* 18(9) p. 18.

Cohen, M.R. (1989a) Medication errors. *Nursing,* 19(2) p. 18.

Cohen, M.R. (1989b) Why two professional should interpret orders. *Nursing,* 19(9) p. 11.

Cook, L. (1989) Nurses in crisis: A support group based on Travelbee's nursing theory. *Nursing and Health Care,* 10(4) pp. 203-205.

Cormack, D.F.S. (Ed.), (1991) The research process in nursing. (2nd. ed.), London: Blackwell Scientific.

Cragg, C.E. (1988) Nursing Ethics: Essential component of education. *Journal of Continuous Education in Nursing,* 19(6) pp. 266-269.

Crisham, P. (1981) Measuring moral judgement in nursing dilemmas. *Nursing Research,* 30(2) pp. 104-110.

Crowley, M.A. (1989) Feminist pedagogy: Nurturing the ethical ideal. *Advances in Nursing Science,* 11(3) pp. 53-61.

Curtin, L. and Flaherty, M.J. (1982) Nursing ethics: Theories and pragmatics. Quoted in: A. MacKenzie (1985) Learning to make decisions. *Nursing Mirror,* 160(8) *District Association Journal,* pp. vii-viii.

Cushing, M. (1986) Drug errors can be bitter pills. *American Journal of Nursing,* 86(8) pp. 895-899.

Davies, B. (1992) Women's subjectivity and feminist stories. In: Investigating subjectivity, pp. 53-76. Edited by: C. Ellis and M.G. Flaherty, London: Sage Publications.

Davis, A.J. (1973) The phenomenological approach in nursing research. In: Doctoral preparation for nurses, pp. 221-228. Edited by: E.A. Garrison, San Francisco, California: University of California.

Davis, A.J. (1989) Clinical nurses' ethical decisionmaking in situations of informed consent. *Advances in Nursing Science,* 11(3) pp. 63-69.

Davis, A.J. (no year) How nurses define ethical dilemmas. Quoted in: M. Johnstone (1989) Law, professional ethics and the conflict with personal values. *International Nursing Review,* 36(3) pp. 83-89.

Davis, A.J. and Aroskar, M.A. (Ed.), (1978) Ethical dilemmas in nursing. New York: Appelton-Century-Crofts.

Davis, A.J. and Slater, P. (1988) Ethics in nursing, implications for education and practice. *Australian Journal of Nursing,* 19(1) pp. 49-51.

Davis, N.M. and Cohen, M.R. (1989) Today's poison - How to keep them from killing your patients. *Nursing,* 19(1) pp. 49-51.

Dean, J.P. and Whyte, W.F. (1969) How do you know if the informant is telling the truth? In: Issues in participant information, Edited by: G. McCall and J.L. Simmons, Menlo Park, California: Addison-Wesley Publishing Co.

Dictionary of pastoral care and counselling. (1990) R. Hunter (Ed.), Nashville: Abingdon Press.

Donnelly, G.F.; Mengel, A. and Sutterley, D.C. (1980) The nursing system: Issues, ethics, politics. New York: John Wiley & Sons.

Downie, G.; MacKenzie, J. and Williams, A. (1987) Drug management for nurses. Edinburgh: Churchill Livingstone.

Downie, R.S. (1971) Roles and values: An introduction to social ethics. London: Methuen.

Doyle, A.C. (1891) Sherlock Holmes: The complete illustrated Short Stories. Reprinted Edition (1991), London: Chancellor Press.

Duncan, A.S.; Dunstan, G.R. and Welbourne, R.B. (1981) Dictionary of medical ethics. (2nd. ed.) London: Longmann & Todd.

EEC Directive 77/453 Official Journal of the European Communities. 20(L176). Luxembourg: Office for Official Publications of the European Communities.

Encyclopaedia Britannica. (1974 ed.) s.v. "Phenomenology".

English, H. and English, A.C. (1958) A comprehensive dictionary of psychological and psychoanalytical terms. New York: David McKay. Quoted in: B.S. Bloom et al (1964) Taxonomy of educational objectives: The classification of educational goals. Handbook II, Affective Domain. London: Longmann Group Ltd.

Ericksen, J. (1989) Steps to ethical reasoning. *Canadian Nurse/Infirmiere Canadienne*, 85(7) pp. 22-23.

Faddis, M.O. (1939) Eliminating errors in medication. Quoted in: R.A. Fuqua and K.R. Stevens (1988) *What we know about medication errors: Literature review.* Journal of Nursing Quality Assurance, 3(1) pp. 1-17.

Fairbairn, G.A. (1987) Moral decisions. *Senior Nurse*, 7(2) pp. 18-19.

Felton, G.M. and Parsons, M. (1987) The impact of nursing education on ethical/moral decision making. *Journal of Nursing Education*, 26(1) pp. 7-11.

Fetterman, D.M. (1989) Ethnography, step by step. London: Sage Publications.

Firth, H. and Britton, P. (1989) 'Burnout': Absence and turnover amongst British nursing staff. *Journal of Occupational Psychology*, 62(1) pp. 55-59.

Flanagan, J.C. (1954) The critical incident technique. Quoted in: C. Clamp (1980) Learning through incidents. *Nursing Times*, Oct. 2nd, pp. 1755-1758.

Francis, G. (1980) Nurses' medication errors - A new perspective. *Supervisor Nurse*, 8(11) pp. 11-13.

Frankena, W.K. (1982) Moral-point-of-view theories. In: Ethical theories in the last quarter of the twentieth century, pp. 39-79. Edited by: N.E. Bowie, Indiapolis, IN: Hackett Publishers Co.

Freud, S. (1930) Civilisation and its discontent. Quoted in: E. v. Stein (1990) s.v. "Guilt", Dictionary of Pastoral Care and Counselling. Edited by R. Hunter, Nashville: Abingdon Press.

Fry, S.T. (1986) Moral values and ethical decisions in a constrained economic environment. *Nursing Economics*, 4(4) pp. 160-163.

Fry, S.T. (1988) The ethic of caring. Can it survive in nursing? *Nursing Outlook*, 36(1) p. 48.

Fry, S.T. (1989) Ethical decision making - Part 1: Selecting a framework. *Nursing Outlook*, 37(5) p. 248.

Fuqua, R.A. and Stevens, K.R. (1988) What we know about medication errors: Literature review. *Journal of Nursing Quality Assurance*, 3(1) pp. 1-17.

Galtung, J. (1967) Quoted in: Bulmer, M. (1977) Problems, theories and methods in sociology - (How) Do they interrelate? In: Sociological research methods. pp. 2-33. Edited by: M. Bulmer, London: The Macmillan Press Ltd.

Garfinkel, H. (1967) Studies in ethnomethodology. Englewood Cliffs: Prentice-Hall.

Garritson, H. (1988) Ethical decision making patterns. *Journal of Pschological Nursing and Mental Health Services*, 26(4) pp. 22-29.

Gaze, H. (1987) A question of morality: Problems of the Royal College of Nursing's Ethics Committee. *Nursing Times/Nursing Mirror*, No 83, pp. 18-19.

General Nursing Council for Scotland (1978) Schemes of Training for the Register of Nurses. Section 1/19.

Gilligan, C. (1982) In a different voice. Boston: Harvard University Press.

Gilligan, C. (1987) Gender difference and morality: The empirical base. In: Women and moral theory, pp. 19-33. Edited by: E.F. Kittay and D.T. Meyers, Totowa, New Jersey: Rowman and Littlefield.

Giorgi, A. (1979) The relationship among level, type, and structure and their importance for social science theorizing: A dialogue with Schütz. In: Duquesne Studies in Phenomenological Psychology, Vol III, pp. 81-92. Edited by: A. Giorgi et al, Pittsburgh: Duquesne University Press.

Giorgi, A. (1985) Sketch of a psychological phenomenological method. In: Phenomenological and psychological research, pp. 8-22. Edited by: A. Giorgi, Pittsburgh: Duquesne University Press.

Glaser, B.G. and Strauss, A.L. (1967) The discovery of grounded theory: Strategies for qualitative research. Chicago: Aldine.

Good, C.V. (1958) Dictionary of Education (2nd Ed.). New York: McGraw Hill. Quoted in: B.S. Bloom et al (1964) Taxonomy of educational objectives: The classification of educational goals. Handbook II, Affective domain. London: Longmann Group Ltd.

Gray-Snelgrove, R.H. (1982) The experience of giving care to a patient dying of cancer: Meanings identified through the process of shared reflection. *Unpublished Ph.D.Thesis,* University of Toronto.

Greaves, F. (1987) The nursing curriculum: Theory and practice. London: Chapman and Hall.

Hall, D.C. (1980) The nature of nursing and the education of the nurse. *Journal of Advanced Nursing,* 5(2) pp. 149-159.

Hammersly, M. (1990) Reading ethnographic research: A critical guide. London: Longman Group Ltd.

Hammersly, M. and Atkinson, P. (1983) Ethnography, principles in practice. London: Tavistock Publications.

Hand, D. (1992) A change for the better. *Nursing Standard,* 6(26) pp. 22-23.

Haralambos, M. (1985) Sociology: Themes and perspectives. London: Bell & Hyman.

Heath, J. (1979) Tomorrow's approach to learning. *Nursing Mirror,* 149(6) pp. 22-23.

Hedin, B.A. (1989) Nursing education and sterile ethical fields. *Advances in Nursing Science,* 11(3) pp. 43-51.

Henderson, M.S. (Ed.), (1982) Nursing education: Recent advances in nursing. Edinburgh: Churchill Livingstone.

Hockey, L. (1980) Challenges for nursing. *Nursing Times,* 76(21) pp. 909-911.

Hodgin, L. (1984) Sarnia General develops medication error report. *Dimens Health Service,* 61(3) p. 25.

Holmes, C.A. (1990) Alternatives to natural science foundations for nursing. *International Journal for Nursing Studies,* 27(3) pp. 187-198.

Huggins, E.A. and Scalzi, C.C. (1988) Limitations and alternatives, ethical practice theory in nursing. *Advances in Nursing Science,* 10(4) pp. 43-47.

Husserl, E. (1931) Ideas: General introduction to pure phenomenology. (Translated by W.R. Boyce Gibson), London: George Allen & Unwin Ltd.

Illich, I. (1977) The limits of medicine. Medical nemesis: The expropriation of health. Harmondsworth: Penguin Books.

International Council of Nursing (1973) International Code of Nursing Ethics. Quoted from V. Tschudin (1986) Ethics in nursing, p. 52. Oxford: Heinemann Nursing.

Johnson, M. (1987) Drugs and discipline ... the use of formal disciplinary procedures for drug errors. *Senior Nurse,* 6(2) pp. 14-16.

Johnstone, M. (1989) Law, professional ethics and the conflict with personal values. *International Nursing Review,* 36(3) pp. 83-89.

Jones, I.H. (1988) Desperate measures. *Nursing Times,* 84(47) pp. 59-61.

Jones, I.H. (1989) When the crunch comes. *Nursing Times,* 85(30) pp. 53-54.

Kay, W. (1975) Moral education. London: Unwin Education Books, George Allen & Unwin Ltd.

Kelman, H.C. (1958) Compliance, identification, and internalization: Three processes of attitude change. *Journal of Conflict Resolution*, (2) pp. 51-60. Quoted in: B.S. Bloom et al (1964) Taxonomy of educational objectives: The classification of educational goals. Handbook II, Affective domain. London: Longman Group Ltd.

Ketefian, S. (1981a) Critical thinking, educational preparation and development of moral judgement among selected groups of practicing nurses. *Nursing Research*, 30(2) pp. 98-103.

Ketefian, S. (1981b) Moral reasoning and moral behaviour. *Nursing Research*, 30(3) pp. 171-176.

Ketefian, S. (1985) Professional and bureacratic role perceptions and moral behaviour among nurses. *Nursing Research*, 34(4) pp. 248-253.

Ketefian, S. (1987) A case study of theory development: Moral behaviour in nursing. *Advances in Nursing Science*, 9(2) pp. 10-19.

Kikuchi, J.F. (1992) Nursing questions that science cannot answer. In: Philosophic inquiry in nursing, Edited by: J.F. Kikuchi and H. Simmons, London: Sage Publications.

Kikuchi, J.F. and Simmons, H. (Eds.), (1992) Philosophic inquiry in nursing. London: Sage Publications.

King, I.M. (1976) The health care system: Nursing intervention subsystem. In: Health research. Edited by: W.H. Werley et al, New York: Springer.

King, I.M. (1981) A theory for nursing: Systems, concepts, process. New York: John Wiley & Sons.

King, I.M. (1983) King's theory of nursing. In: Family health: A theoretical approach to nursing, pp. 177-188. Edited by: I.W. Clement and F.B. Roberts, New York: John Wiley & Sons.

Knaack, K. (1984) Phenomenological research. *Western Journal of Nursing Research*, 6(1) pp. 107-114.

Kohlberg, L. (1958) The development of modes of moral thinking and choice in the years 10-16. *Doctoral Dissertation*, University of Chicago.

Kohlberg, L. (1972) The cognitive - developmental approach to moral education. *The Humanist*, 11/12 pp. 13-16.

Kohlberg, L. (1978) The cognitive developmental approach to moral education. In: Readings in moral education, Edited by: P. Scharf, Minneapolis: Winston Press Inc.

Kohlberg, L. (1984) The psychology of moral development. Essays on moral development. Vol II, San Francisco: Harper & Row.

Kolakowski, L. (1992) Falls es keinen Gott gibt. Freiburg: Herder.

Kramer, M. and Baker, C. (1971) Exodus: Can nursing afford it? Quoted in: S. Ketefian (1985) Professional and bureaucratic role conceptions and moral behaviour among nurses. *Nursing Research,* 34(4) pp. 248-253.

Kratz, C.R. (1984) The nursing process. London: Baillière Tindall.

Kurtenbach, H.; Golombeck, G. and Siebers, H. (1986) Krankenpflegegesetz mit Ausbildungs- und Prüfungsverordnung für die Berufe in der Krankenpflege, Kommentar. Köln: Verlag W. Kohlhammer.

Lamb, M. (1982) Nursing ethics and nursing education: Past perspectives and recent developments. In: Nursing education: Recent advances in nursing, pp. 3-19. Edited by: M.S. Henderson, Edinburgh: Churchill Livingstone.

Langeveld, M.J. (1983) The stillness of the secret place. *Phenomenology and Pedagogy,* 1(1) pp. 11-17.

Langeveld, M.J. (1984) How does the child experience the world of things? *Phenomenology and Pedagogy,* 2(3) pp. 215-223.

Leininger, M.J. (Ed.), (1984) Qualitative research methods in nursing. New York: Grune & Stratton.

Lexikon für Theologie und Kirche. (1962) Band 9, Freiburg: Verlag Herder. s.v. "Sola-fide-Prinzip", by K. Haendler.

Lexikon für Theologie und Kirche. (1962) Band 7, Freiburg: Verlag Herder. s.v. "Moses", by E.Sauser.

Lexikon für Theologie und Kirche. (1962) Band 7, Freiburg: Verlag Herder. s.v. "Natura pura", by J. Alfaro.

Lexikon für Theologie und Kirche. (1962) Band 7, Freiburg: Verlag Herder. s.v. "Natur", by J.B. Metz.

Lexikon für Theologie und Kirche. (1962) Band 5, Freiburg: Verlag Herder. s.v. "Islam", by W. Göbell.

Ley, P.; Jain, K. and Skilbeck, E. (1976) A method for decreasing patient' medication errors. *Psychogical Medicine*, No 6, pp. 599-601.

Liffrig, L.E. (1989) Decision making and conscience: Protecting values in a clinical area. *Nursing Management*, 20(2) p. 84.

Linschoten, H. (1979) The inevitability of phenomenology. In: Duquesne studies in phenomenological psychology, Vol III, pp. 49-59. Edited by: A. Giorgi et al, Pittsburgh: Duquesne University Press.

Long, G. (1982) The effect of medication distributionsystems on medication errors. *Nursing Research*, 31(3) pp. 182-184, 191.

Long, G. and Johnson, C. (1981) A pilotstudy for reducing medication errors. *Qality Review Bulletin*, 7(4) pp. 6-9.

Lothian Health Board (1981) Standard Procedures for Safe Handling, Administration, Storage and Custody of Medicinal Products in the Health Service. Edinburgh: Lothian Health Board.

Lothian Health Board (1983) Disciplinary Policy and Procedure. Edinburgh: Lothian Health Board.

Lunn, J.A. (1991) Concerning Carers: Occupational health for health care workers. London: Butterworth-Heinemann.

Lyneham, J. (1988) The ethics of teaching ethics. *Australian Journal of Advanced Nursing*, 5(4) pp. 10-11.

MacDonell, D. (1986) Theories of discourse: An introduction. Oxford: Blackwell.

MacKenzie, A. (1985) Learning to make decisions. *Nursing Mirror*, 160(8) pp. vii-viii, *District Nursing Association Journal*.

Mann, M. (Ed.), (1983) Macmillan Student Encyclopedia of Sociology. s.v. "Hermeneutics". London: The Macmillan Press Ltd.

Mann, M. (Ed.), (1983) Macmillan Student Encyclopedia of Sociology. s.v. "Phenomenology". London: The Macmillan Press Ltd.

Mann, M. (Ed.), (1983) Macmillan Student Encyclopedia of Sociology. s.v. "Althusser". London: The Macmillan Press Ltd.

Manthey, M. (1989) Vulnerable no more. (How nurses should develop techniques to reduce the feeling of vulnerability). *Nursing Management*, 20(4) p.26.

Mayberry, E. (1980) The nurses' experience of problem patients. *Doctoral Dissertation*, San Diego: Calif. School of Professional Psychology.

McFarlane, J. (1982) Nursing values and nursing action. *Nursing Times*, 78(28) pp. 109-112.

McFarlane, J. (1988) A paradigm of caring. In: Ethical issues in caring, pp. 10-20. Edited by: G. Fairbairn and S. Fairbairn, Aldershot: Avebury.

McGovern, K. (1988) 10 Golden rules for administering drugs safely. *Nursing*, 18(8) pp. 34-41.

Meleis, A.I. (1985) Theoretical nursing: Development and progress. London, Philadelphia: J.B. Lippincott Co.

Melia, K.M. (1989) Everyday nursing ethics. London: McMillan Education Book.

Merton, T. (1969) The way of Chuang Tzu. New York: New Directions Pubublishing Corporation.

Meyers, D.T. and Kittay, E.F. (1987) Introduction to: Women and moral theory. In: Women and moral theory, pp. 3-16. Edited by: D.T. Meyers and E.F. Kittay, Totowa, New Jersey: Rowman & Littlefield.

Morse, J.M. (1991) Strategies for sampling. In: Qualitative nursing research: A contemporary dialogue, pp. 127-145. Edited by: J.M. Morse, London: Sage Publications.

Murphy, C.P. and Hunter, H. (1983) Ethical problems in the nurse-patient relationship. London: Allyn & Bacon Inc.

Mustapha, S.L. and Seybert, J.A. (1989) Oral reasoning in college students: Implication for nursing education. *Journal of Nursing Education*, 28(3) pp. 107-111.

Nightingale, F. (1887) Nurses, training of, and nursing the sick. Quoted in: Lamb, M. (1982) Nursing ethics and nursing education: Past perspectives and recent developments. In: Nursing education: Recent advances in nursing. pp. 3-19. Edited by: M.S. Henderson, Edinburgh: Churchill Livingstone.

Nursing Times (1989) Is a mistake misconduct? *Nursing Times*, 85(43) p. 41.

Nursing Times (1992) Professional priorities. *Nursing Times*, 88(13) pp. 20-21.

Oiler, C.J. (1982) The phenomenological approach in nursing research. *Nursing Research*, 31(3) pp. 178-181.

Oiler, C.J. (1986) Phenomenology: The method. In: Nursing research: A qualitative perspective, pp. 69-84. Edited by: P.L. Munhall and C.J. Oiler, Connecticut: Appelton-Century-Crofts.

Omery, A. (1983) Phenomenology: A method for research. *Advances in Nursing Science*, No.1 pp. 49-63.

Packard, J.S. and Ferrara, M. (1988) In search of the moral foundations of nursing. *Advances in Nursing Science*, 10(4) pp. 60-71.

Packer, M.J. (1985) Hermeneutic inquiry in the study of human conduct. *American Psychologist*, 40(10) pp. 1081-1093.

Paige, S.D. (1980) Alone in the alone. A phenomenological study of the experience of dying. *Unpublished Dissertation, D.N.Sc.*, Boston School of Nursing.

Paine, W.S. (Ed.), (1982) Job stress and burnout. Beverly Hills: Sage Publications.

Parker, I. (1990) Dicourse: Definitions and contradictions. *Philosophical Psychology*, 3(2) pp. 189-204.

Pearlson, J.G. (1988) Development and implementation of systematic monitoring of medication errors. *Journal of Nursing Quality Assurance*, 2(2) pp. 77-81.

Pêcheux, M. (1982) Language, semantics and ideology: Stating the obvious. (Translated by H. Nagpal), London: Macmillan.

Pittman Weekes, D.L. (1986) Theory-free observation: Fact or fantasy? In: Nursing research methodology: Issues and implementations, pp. 11-21. Edited by: P.L. Chinn, Rockville, Md: Aspen Publications.

Pollock, L. (1991) Qualitative analysis. In: The research process in nursing, pp. 293-302. Edited by: D.F.S. Cormack, London: Blackwell Scientific Publications.

Poster, E.C. and Pelletier, L. (1988) Primary versus functional medication administration: Monitoring and evaluating medication error rates. *Journal of Nursing Quality Assurance*, 2(2) pp. 68-76.

Potter, J. and Wetherell, M. (1987) Discourse and social psychology. London: Sage Publications.

Potter, J.; Wetherell, M. and Chitty, A. (1991) Quantification rhetoric - Cancer on television. *Discourse and Society*, 2(3) pp. 333-365.

Powel, V.C. (1989) Caring for colleagues. *Canadien Nurse/Infimiere Canadienne*, 85(2) pp. 14-17.

Project 2000 (1991) 'Your questions answered'. Dept. of Health and the Central Office for Information, HMSO 5/91. O/N 13820 I 1313RP 50M.

Project 2000 (1992) Nursing, it makes you think. Dept. of Health and Central Office for Information, HMSO 10/92. O/N 12339/A/HAAH/J1670NJ 50M.

Pyne, R.H. (1981) Professional discipline in nursing. London: Blackwell Scientific Publications.

RCN (1987) Drug administration - A nursing responsibility. London: Royal College of Nursing, Dept. of Policy and Practice.

RCN (1990) Accountability in nursing. London: Royal College of Nursing.

Reilly, D.E. (1989) Ethics and values in nursing. *Nursing and Health Care*, 10(2) pp. 91-95.

Richardson, A. (1989) A new deal for carers. London: Kings Fund Informal Caring Support Unit.

Riemen, D.J. (1986) The essential structure of a caring interaction: Doing phenomenology. In: Nursing research: A qualitative perspective, pp. 85-108. Edited by: P.J. Munhall and C.J. Oiler, Connecticut: Appelton-Century-Crofts.

Rilke, R.M. (1977) Possibility of being: A selection of poems. (Translated by J.B. Leishman), New York: New Directions Publishing Corporation.

Roach, M.S. (1987) The human act of caring. Ottawa: The Canadian Hospital Association.

Rogers, C. (1969) Freedom to learn. Columbus, Ohio: C.N. Merril.

Rogers, M.E. (1970) An introduction to the theoretical basis of nursing. Philadelphia: F.A. Davis.

Roper, N.; Logan, W.W. and Tierney, A.J. (1985) The elements of nursing: A model for nursing based on a model for living. Edinburgh: Churchill Livingstone.

Roy, C. (1970) Adaptation: A conceptual framework for nursing. *Nursing Outlook*, 18(3) pp. 42-45.

Roy, C. (1981) Introduction to nursing: An adaptation model. Englewood Cliffs, New Jersey: Prentice Hall.

Ryden, M.B., et al (1989a) Multicourse sequential learning as a model for content integration: Ethics as a prototype. *Journal of Nursing Education*, 28(3) pp. 102-106.

Ryden, M.B., et al (1989b) Wrestling with the larger picture, placing ethical behaviour in clinical situations in context, (use of model building process to teach nursing ethics). *Journal of Nursing Education*, 28(6) pp. 271-275.

Scanlon, C.D. and Fleming, C.M. (1987) Nurses come together to face ethical issues. *Health Progress*, (Dec.),pp. 46-48, 52.

Schneider, C.D. (1990) s.v. "Shame". In: Dictionary of Pastoral Care and Counselling. R. Hunter, Nashville: Abingdon Press.

Schön, D.A. (1983) The reflective practitioner. How professionals think in action. London: Temple Smith.

Schröck, R.A. (1980) A question of honesty in practice. *Journal of Advanced Nursing*, 5(80) pp. 135-149.

Schutz, A. (1970) On phenomenology and social relations. Edited and introduced by H.R. Wagner. Chicago: University of Chicago Press.

Seidel, J.V., et al (1988) The Ethnograph: A user's guide. Littleton, Colorado: Qualis Research Associates.

Self, D.J. (1987) A study of the foundations of ethical decision-making of nurses. *Theoretical medicine*, No.8, pp. 85-95.

Sheahan, J. (1980) Educating teachers of nursing. *Journal of Advanced Nursing*, 5(1) pp. 71-81.

Sietsema, M.R. and Spradley, B.W. (1987) Ethics and administrative decision making. *Journal of Nursing Administration*, 17(4) pp. 28-32.

Silverman, D. (1985) Qualitative methodology and sociology. Aldershot: Gower.

Simmons, H. (1992) Philosophic and scientific inquiry: The interface. In: Philosophic inquiry in nursing, pp. 9-25. Edited by: J.F. Kikuchi and H. Simmons, London: Sage Publications.

Smith, R.W. (1971) Guilt: Man and society. Garden City, New York: Doubleday & Co. Inc.

Spiegelberg, H. (1982) The phenomenological movement. (3rd ed.) The Hague: M. Nijhoff.

Stanley, T. (1980) Ethics as a component of the curriculum. *Nursing and Health Care,* Sept., pp. 63-72.

Stapleton, M.F. (1987) The ward sister. A continuing learner. In: Nursing education: Research and developments, pp. 91-105. Edited by: B. Davis, New York: Croom Helm.

Steele, S.M. (1983) Values clarification in nursing. (2nd ed.) London: Appleton Century Crofts.

Stein, E. (1956) Problems of women's education. In: Writings of Edith Stein, pp. 126-160. Selected, translated and introduced by H. Graef. London: Peter Owen.

Sternberg, M. (1979) Ethics as a component of nursing education. *Advances in Nursing Science,* April, pp. 53-61.

Strauss, A. (1987) Qualitative analysis for social scientists. New York: Cambridge University Press.

Swider, S.A.; McElmurry, B.J. and Yarling, R.R. (1985) Ethical decision making in a bureaucratical context by senior nursing students. *Nursing Research,* 34(2) pp. 108-112.

Swider, S.A.; Yarling, R.R. and McElmurry, B.J. (1986) The moral foundation of nursing. *Advances in Nursing Science,* 8(2) pp. 63-75.

Taylor, S. and Bogdan, R. (1984) Introduction to qualitative research methods. (2nd ed.) New York: John Wiley & Son.

The Bhagavag-Gita. With a commentary by R.C. Zaehner. (1969) Oxford: Clarendon Press.

The Old an New Testaments. Revised Standard Version. (1952) Glasgow: W.M. Collins Sons.

Thompson, I.E.; Melia, K.M. and Boyd, K.M. (1988) Nursing ethics. (2nd ed.) Edinburgh: Churchill Livingstone.

Thompson, J.E. and Thompson, H.O. (1989) Teaching ethics to nursing students. *Nursing Outlook,* 37(2) pp. 84-88.

Travelbee, J. (1971) Interpersonal Aspects of nursing. (2nd ed.) Philadelphia: F.A. Davis.

Tschudin, V. (1986) Ethics in nursing. Oxford: Heinemann Nursing.

Turner, T. (1988) Rough justice? ... case of a school nurse. *Nursing Times*, 84(20) p. 19.

Turton, P. (1984) The drug round - is it working? *Nursing Times*, 80(11) pp. 18-19.

UKCC (1984) Code of professional Conduct. London: United Kingdom Central Council for Nursing, Midwifery and Health Visiting.

UKCC (1986a) Administration of medicines. A UKCC advisory paper: A framework to assist individual professional judgement and the development of local policies and guide-lines. London: United Kingdom Central Council for Nursing, Midwifery and Health Visiting.

UKCC (1986b) Project 2000: A new preparation for practice. London: United Kingdom Central Council for Nursing, Midwifery and Health Visiting.

UKCC (1990) '...with a view to removal from the register ...? London: United Kingdom Central Council for Nursing, Midwifery and Health Visiting.

UKCC (1992a) Code of Professional Conduct. London: United Kingdom Central Council for Nursing, Midwifery and Health Visiting.

UKCC (1992b) The Scope of professional practice. London: United Kingdom Central Council for Nursing, Midwifery and Health Visiting.

UKCC (1992c) Standards for the administration of medicines. London: United Kingdom Central Council for Nursing, Midwifery and Health Visiting.

UKCC (1992d) Prescribing by nurses. *UKCC Register*, No. 11, p. 7.

Uys, L. (1988) But she's just a student nurse. *Nursing RSA, Verpleging*, (11/12) p. 50.

v. Stein, E. (1969) Guilt, theory and therapy. London: Allen & Unwin.

v. Stein, E. (1990) s.v. "Guilt". In: Dictionary of Pastoral Care and Counselling. Edited by R. Hunter. Nashville: Abingdon Press.

Van Hooft, S. (1990) Moral education for nursing decision. *Journal of Advanced Nursing*, 15(2) pp. 210-215.

Van Kaam, A.L. (1959) Phenomenal Analysis: Exemplified by a study of "Really feeling understood". *Journal of Individual Psychology*, Vol 15, pp. 66-72.

Van Maanen, J. (1983) Epilogue: Qualitative methods reclaimed. In: Qualitative methodology, pp. 247-266. Edited by: J.V. Maanen, Beverly Hills: Sage Publications.

Van Manen, M. (1978) Objective inquiry into structures of subjectivity. *Journal of Curriculum Theorizing*, Vol 1, pp. 44-64.

Van Manen, M. (1983) Invitation to phenomenology and pedagogy. *Phenomenology and Pedagogy*, 1(1) pp. i-ii.

Van Manen, M. (1984) Practicing phenomenological writing. *Phenomenology and Pedagogy*, 2(1) pp. 36-69.

Van Manen, M. (1986) The tone of teaching. Richmond Hill, Ontario: Scholastic-TAB.

Van Manen, M. (1989) By the light of anecdote. *Phenomenology and Pedagogy*, Vol 7, pp. 232-253.

Van Manen, M. (1990) Researching lived experience: Human science research for an action sensitive pedagogy. London ON: Althouse Press, University of Western Ontario.

Vaux, K. (1974) Biomedical ethics. New York: Harper & Row.

Viens, D.C. (1989) A history of nursing's code of ethics. *Nursing Outlook*, 37(1) pp. 45-49.

Vincent, C.A. (1989) .Research into medical accidents: A case of negligence? *British Medical Journal*, Vol 299, pp. 1150-1153.

Waithe, M.E., et al (1989) Developing Case situations for ethics education in nursing. *Journal of Nursing Education*, 28(4) pp. 175-180.

Wessex Health Authority (1984) Drugs - Policies and Practices in Wessex. Bath: The Group.

Wieser, M.A. and Dann, M.H. (1987) Tracking quality assurance activities: Development of an administrative model. *Journal of Nursing Quality Assurance*, 1(3) pp. 14-22.

Wilkinson, J.M. (1988) Moral distress in nursing practice. *Nursing Forum,* XXIII(1) pp. 16-29.

Williams, A. (1990) Breaking the chain reaction. *Nursing Times,* 86(44) pp. 39-41.

Wilson, H.S. (1990) Research in nursing. Menlo Park, California: Addison-Wesley.

Wolf, Z.R. (1988) Nurses' work: The sacred and the profane. Philadelphia: University of Pennsylvania Press.

Wolf, Z.R. (1989) Medication errors and nursing responsibility. *Holistic Nursing Practice,* 4(1) pp. 8-17.

Woodruff, A.M. (1985) Becoming a nurse: The ethical perspective. *International Journal of Nursing Science,* 22(4) pp. 295-302.

Yarling, R.R. and McElmurray, B.J. (1986) The moral foundation of nursing. *Advances in Nursing Science,* 8(2) pp. 63-75.

APPENDICES

APPENDIX 1

Appendices regarding Group Discussions

1.1 Information for participants (German)

Marianne Arndt
Department of Nursing Studies
University of Edinburgh
September 1990

Kurzbeschreibung
Forschungsprojekt: "Aus Fehlern lernen"

In diesem Projekt soll der Prozeß untersucht werden, der die Entscheidungen bestimmt, die notwendig werden, wenn ein Fehler bei der Medikamentengabe aufgetreten ist. Aus den Erfahrungen von Krankenschwestern und -pflegern, die nicht weniger als drei Jahre nach dem Examen in stationäiren Bereichen tätig waren, sollen Aspekte der Entwicklung von moralischer Entscheidungsfindung gewonnen und für die Krankenpflegeausbildung nutzbar gemacht werden.
Die Ethik des Füreinander-Sorge-Tragens muß auch in der Sorge der Krankenpflegepersonen umeinander in schwierigen Situationen deutlich werden. So sollen im Endergebnis des geplanten Projektes Inhalte und Grundlagen einer Krankenpfleethik zum Ausdruck kommen, gleichwie Möglichkeiten entsprechender Vermittlung im Rahmen der Krankenpflegeausbildung angesprochen werden.
Fehler bei der Medikamentengabe stellen eine nicht gänzlich ungewöhnliche Erfahrung im Krankenhausalltag dar. In diesem Projekt geht es in erster Linie darum, den Erfahrungen von Krankenschwestern und -pflegern nachzuspüren, die durch die Reaktionen von Kollegen und Mitarbeitern im beruflichen Umfeld in diesen Situationen ausgelöst wurden. Einzelinterviews und Gesprächsrunden mit Krankenschwestern und-pflegern sowie schriftliche Berichte bilden den Materialhintergrund, dessen Analyse zum Verstehen einer Ethik des Pflegealltags beitragen soll.
In diesem Zusammenhang bitte ich Sie höflich, sofern Sie Interesse an einer Mitarbeit an diesem Projekt haben und an einer Gesprächsrunde zum Thema "Fehler bei der Medikamentengabe - Aus Fehlern lernen" teilnehmen möchten, den beigelegten Vordruck auszufüllen und mir sobald wie möglich wieder zukommen zu lassen. Weitere Fragen zum Projekt bespreche ich gern mit Interessenten. Selbstverstandlich werden die mit Kassettenrekorder festgehqltenen Gespräche vertraulich und gemäß den geltenden Richtlinien des Datenschutzes behandelt.
Ich danke Ihnen für Ihre Aufmerksamkeit und freue mich auf Ihre Teilnahme
Marianne Arndt, Unterrichtsschwester, Dipl.Rel.Päd.

1.2 Information for participants (Scotland)

Department of Nursing Studies
May 1991

LEARNING FROM MISTAKES

This research project is concerned with ethics in nursing and nursing education. It focuses on the situation where a medication error has occurred or was about to happen.
Mistakes do happen in our everyday practice of nursing. This raises several questions: How are these mistakes utilised for learning, for personal and professional development? What does it mean to be confronted with mistakes? What helps, what hinders in dealing with mistakes in everyday practice? What and how do we learn from mistakes?
In this group discussion senior nurses exchange their experience and personal views on how medication errors are dealt with.

- Please recall incidences you have been personally involved with!
- Briefly describe the circumstances (type of ward, patients, staff involved, medication given or omitted)
- How did patients and relatives react? - What was your own reaction? - How did colleagues react?
- How was the incident dealt with by superiors?
- What did you feel about it at the time? - How do you feel about it now?

It is **not necessary** that each participant gives account of an incident. It is more important, that the group shared views and feelings about a few situations.

1.3 Questionnaire regarding biographical data of the Scottish participants (group discussion, interviews, self reports)

Form 1

Sex:	Age:

Nursing qualifications:
1. General training completed in (year):
2. Further qualifications/specialisations (please state):

Practical experience:
Fields of practice /position held/number of months/years:

APPENDIX 2
Appendices concerning the Interviews

2.1 Information for display in the hospital where interviews were to take place

LEARNING FROM MISTAKES

This research project is concerned with ethics in nursing and nursing education. It focuses on the situation where a medication error has occurred or was about to happen.

What helps, what hinders in dealing with mistakes in everyday practice? What and how do we learn from mistakes?

I would like to talk to nurses of at least three years post basic experience about medication errors they have witnessed or have been involved in. All information is treated confidentially.

If you would like to participate in the study, please contact me before Feb. 28th 1991.

Marianne Arndt RGN, Ph.D.Student
Department of Nursing Studies
University of Edinburgh
12 Buccleuch Place
Edinburgh EH8 9JT
Tel. 031 650 8442 or private 031 665 3098

An appointment for an interview will then be set up.

Thank you for your cooperation.

2.2 Interview Schedule

February 1991

A) Introduction

The Study, Content, Objectives

B) Key-Questions and topics

What happens when we make mistakes? Do we learn from them?

1) Maybe you could talk about an example which you recall, where a medication error happened?
- the situation setting,
- the people involved,
- the incident itself?

2) What was it like for you?
- What did you feel at the time,
- What did you think,
- What did you say,
- Whom did you talk to,
- What did you feel about telling the truth?

3) How did others react?
- What was said,
- What was done,
- What was helpful, what hindered,
- Who was helpful, hindered?

4) What decisions were made?
- What did you do,
- What did others do,
- Whom did you talk to,
- What did you hear others say?

5) What effect did the situation have on you in the long run?
- professionally,
- personal,
- What do think about the incident now?

C) General perception of 'morality'

1) How do you feel about truth, honesty?
2) What do 'ethics' or 'morality' mean to you?
3) How do you decide how to act?

4) Where did you get your ideas?
- your family
- in school
- during nursing training
- who made an impression on you, how?

What has not been covered?

Is there anything you like to add?

APPENDIX 3
Appendices regarding the Self Reports

3.1 Advertisement in NURSING TIMES

INFORMATION WANTED

I am undertaking a research project on learning from mistakes involving the study of situations in which nurses have made mistakes in the administration of medicines and, consequently, how they learnt from them.

In order to gather a sufficient body of data, volunteer participants are needed. RGNs with at least three years' postbasic practice in general ward settings who wish to participate in the study with written accounts of their experience, should contact me for further information about the project.

Confidentiality is assured.

Marianne Arndt
Project 'Learning from mistakes'
Department of Nursing Studies
University of Edinburgh
12 Buccleuch Place
Edinburgh EH8 9JT
Nursing Times April 3, Vol. 87, No. 14, 1991

3.2 Reply to potential participants responding to the advertisement

Dear...

Thank you for your response to my advertisement in the Nursing Times of April, 3. 1991, indicating an interest in the research project *'Learning from mistakes'*.

I am working towards my Ph.D. at the University of Edinburgh in the Department of Nursing Studies and conduct this project during 1990/1992.

Mistakes do happen in our everyday practice of nursing. This raises several questions: How are these mistakes utilised for learning, for personal and professional development? What does it mean to be confronted with mistakes? How are nurses taught to deal with these situations while they are students?

We are all familiar with drug administration practices, yet this is an area where mistakes commonly occur. This is a very sensitive issue for individual nurses and for nursing practice. The ways in which situations of medication errors are dealt with vary enormously. I would like to collect some anonymous written accounts of nurses' experiences of true situations where medication errors occurred or nearly occurred.

These accounts will be analysed in terms of the decisions nurses made in reaction to the situation, and the reasoning that lays behind these decisions. I would also like to find out about the reactions shown by colleagues, superiors, patients, friends and family in response to the situations.

The nature of my study demands anonymity but at the same time it would be helpful to have some general information about the participants. If you are prepared to write a self report about an experience in connection with a medication error, please fill in the enclosed short questionnaire (Form 1) and write your account of a personal experience concerning a situation where a mistake in the administration of medicines has been made or was about to be made. In order to structure your self report you may find it helpful if you used the guide-lines printed on Form 2.

All information received will be handled confidentially but do not mention your own or anybody elses name or address.

Please send the questionnaire and your self report back to me by Mai 15.1991.

Thank you again for your willingness to participate. It is hoped that the findings will make a useful contribution to the debates that prevail in nursing education and in nursing ethics. In due course reports on the project will be made available in the relevant professional literature.

If you have further questions or comments please do not hesitate to contact me.

Sincerely, yours

Marianne Arndt RGN, Dipl. Rel Päd.
Ph.D.Student

(encl.: Form 1 - Questionnaire; Form 2 - Guide-lines)

3.3 Guide-lines for the writing of a self report

Form 2 - Guide-lines for the writing of a self report:
These 'Guide-lines' are designed to facilitate your self report. They may be used as a structure. If they hinder you in your writing please feel free to ignore them.

1. Give an account of the features of the situation you are going to recall.

   (eg. you were a student nurse on your first ward... Or you were in your second year as a staff nurse... Recall any details that you think are important to you.)

2. Describe the immediate circumstances surrounding the event you are going to recall.

   (eg. type of duty, number and kind of staff on duty with you..., workload, type of patients you looked after...)

3. Write about the situation you are going to recall as it presented itself.

   (eg.: What happened? Who was involved? What was the ultimate outcome?)

4. Reactions:

   What reactions did you meet with?

   (eg.: patients, colleagues, superiors, doctors, other non-nursing staff?),

   How did you react?, What did you think?, What where your feelings?

   What/who helped; what/who hindered in coping with the situation.

   Was any consequential action taken?

   (eg.: restructuring of the medication delivery system, new rules or regulations?)

5. Meaning:

   What did the occurrence mean to you then? Do you think that it had any effect on your development as a nurse? How did it effect your personal development? How do you see it today? What where the positive results, what where the negative results?

3.4 Information to recruit further participants to write self reports, displayed in a College of Nursing, Dept. Continuous Education

Department of Nursing Studies
May 1991

LEARNING FROM MISTAKES

This research project is concerned with ethics in nursing and nursing education. It focuses on the situation where a medication error has occurred or was about to happen.
Mistakes do happen in our everyday practice of nursing. This raises several questions: How are these mistakes utilised for learning, for personal and professional development? What does it mean to be confronted with mistakes? What helps, what hinders in dealing with mistakes in everyday practice? What and how do we learn from mistakes?
If you are prepared to write a self report about an experience in connection with a medication error, please fill in the short questionnaire (Form 1) and write your account of a personal experience concerning a situation where a mistake in the administration of medicines has been made or was about to be made. In order to structure your self report you may find it helpful if you used the guide-lines printed on Form 2.
All information received will be handled confidentially but do not mention your own or anybody elses name or address.

Please send the questionnaire and your self report back to me by Mai 30. 1991

Marianne Arndt
Dept. of Nursing Studies
University of Edinburgh
12 Buccleuch Place
Edinburgh EH8 9JT
Tel. 031 650 8442

APPENDIX 4

Appendices regarding UKCC Documents

4.1 Correspondence with Secretary of Disciplinary Committee

Marianne Arndt
Dept. of Nursing Studies
University of Edinburgh
12 Buccleuch Place
Edinburgh EH8 9JT
06.12.90

Mr. Reginald H. Pyne
UKCC
23 Portland Place
London W1N 3AF

Dear Mr Pyne

I am a Ph.D. Student in the Department of Nursing Studies at the University of Edinburgh. My research topic focuses on the decision-making process in nursing and on aspects of moral development in nursing education.

My questions are: Do we learn from mistakes? What helps, what hinders in dealing with mistakes in everyday settings of nursing practice?

I want to examine the situation of medication errors. The experience of having made a mistake has to be lived with and the way it is dealt with by self and by others will have a bearing on personal and professional life and development.

An interpretative approach to this study calls for a variety of data sources as this will contribute to the possibility of seeing the phenomenon from different perspectives. The data will consist of:

1.) 5 Written self reports of senior nurses, describing experiences in connection with medication errors.

2.) Taped and transcribed group discussion of 6-8 Senior Nurses, discussing the situation of medication errors.

3.) Taped and transcribed unstructured single interviews with 10 senior nurses on their experience with medication errors.

4.) The documentation and proceedings of 5 cases where the disciplinary bodies of the profession dealt with medication errors.

I am writing to you in order to gain access to case proceedings which dealt with the situation of medication errors. I very much hope that you will be able to assist me with the project.

I look forward to hearing from you. Yours sincerely Marianne Arndt,

Marianne Arndt
Dept. of Nursing Studies
University of Edinburgh
12 Buccleuch Place
Edinburgh EH8 9JT
23.10.1992

Ms. Jane Macdonald
Assistant Registrar
UKCC
23 Portland Place
London W1N 3AF

Dear Ms Macdonald

Mr. Pyne has last week sent me two sets of photocopied transcripts on cases where disciplinary action was taken by the UKCC after medication errors had occurred.

Having received the first two sets of transcripts, I am delighted to see how well they fit into my body of data for the study 'Learning from mistakes'. I understand that you will now take it in hand to prepare the remaining three cases for me and post them on in due course.

Thank you for kindly complying to the needs of my data collection in spite of your manifold responsibilities and pressure of work.

Sincerely

Marianne Arndt, RGN
Unterrichtsschwester, Dipl.Rel.Päd.
Doctoral Student

UKCC
United Kingdom Central Council
for Nursing, Midwifery and Health
Visiting
From the Office of the Registrar
28 November 1991

Ms M Arndt
Department of Nursing Studies
University of Edinburgh
12 Buccleuch Place
Edinburgh

Dear Miss Arndt

Thank you for your recent letter regarding transcripts sent to you by Reg Pyne and me. I am pleased that they fit into your body of data for your study. I am enclosing one further transcript because I think it is particularly interesting. We do not normally have transcripts made up where misconduct is not established, but I have done so as I think that this case is a particularly interesting one and believe that it can be used for teaching purposes. You will note from the transcript, that the Committee took the unusual course of finding that a serious medication error, where the facts of the allegations were admitted, did not constitute misconduct. This is likely to have been because the nurses concerned made no attempt to conceal the error and were fully open and frank about what had happened. Very often, it is not the error itself but the attempted concealment of the error which constitutes misconduct.

I hope you will find this transcript interesting and useful.

Yours sincerely

Ms Jane Macdonald
Assistant Registrar, Professional Conduct

APPENDIX 5

Summaries of medication errors

General Remarks

In this appendix all medication errors that have been mentioned in the data of this study are summarised. These summaries contain the facts of the various incidents as I reconstructed them from the transcripts. They represent an overview of the reality of medication errors that have come to my notice in the process of data collection.

TABLE OF CONTENTS

5 SUMMARIES OF MEDICATION ERRORS

5.1 GROUP DISCUSSION

Group Discussion Germany

Example One

The mistake involved a student, other nursing staff and a doctor. Markumar is an anticoagulant, one dose of which had nearly been given twice to a patient. The patient questioned the doctor about the second dose which had been handed to him by a student who did not know that Markumar was always given separately on that ward. The medicines he had prepared were not checked by anyone before he distributed them. The doctor reacted in a very angry and exited manner. A new policy was introduced by the ward sister according to which no student was to give out drugs without having them checked by a qualified nurse.

Example Two

This situation was remembered of some years ago, when the participant was a staff nurse on an Intensive Care Unit. The mistake had happened to a colleague. Two reanimations at the same time had caused a lot of tension. A third patient's infusion containing a vasodilator had to be changed. The infusion was aided by an automatic perfusion pump. Mistakenly the infusion pump was set at too high a speed by the nurse. The patient collapsed but could be stabilised. Doctors and nurses co-operated well.

Example Three

This incident was recounted by a nurse who some years ago had given too high a dose of Insulin to a patient who was in hospital for stabilisation of his diabetes. The ward was busy at the time and the nurse had mixed up the Insulin order. Main features: The nurse spoke to colleagues about it, then discussed it with the patient and afterwards with the doctor who felt that the patient needed not to be informed. This, however, was of great importance to the nurse. The blood sugar was checked hourly. No harm came to the patient. During the group discussion the question was addressed, whether patients would lose their trust in the staff if they were told about mistakes.

Example Four

Here, a nurse discovered that a doctor had set a perfusion pump with Dopamine (a hypotensive drug), at too high a speed. The blood pressure of the patient sank, but no further action had to be taken. No one was blamed.

Example Five

This situation happened in 1978 when the participant talking about the incident, was on night duty and had to give Antibiotics via intravenous infusion. The patient had an anaphylactic reaction but could be treated successfully in the Intensive Care Unit. Consequently in that hospital all intravenous medication was to be given by doctors.

Example Six

The incident happened 'some time back'. The ward sister of the participant had neglected to have the infusion pumps checked. Isoptin, a cardiac drug, was given to a patient too fast because the pump was faulty. Nothing was mentioned in the discussion about the effects this had on the patient. As a result this hospital has employed a technician who regularly checks all technical equipment used on the wards. The question of responsibility was discussed.

Example Seven

The example happened to the participant 'a short while ago'. A diabetic patient was ordered to have Aktrafel which was a new Insulin preparation unknown on that ward. It had to be given by a special syringe. A conventional syringe was used mistakenly and the patient got too much Insulin. The participants discussed the question of responsibility when new preparations and equipment is introduced and the flow of information is hampered. Information and co-operation between nurses and doctors featured in this example.

Example Eight

This incident happened 'some time ago' to one of the participants. An elderly woman being restless at night, had been given several doses of different tranquillisers without effect. The doctor decided to give intravenous Dormicum, which is a potent narcotic. This was a new preparation unknown to the nurses involved. The preparation was supplied by pharmacy in a concentrated form. The contents of the ampoule had to be diluted before administration. The nurse drew up the concentrated drug from the ampoule. The doctor did not notice the mistake and injected it. The patient collapsed but was resuscitated. Again the question of responsibility was discussed, also the need for nurses to update their knowledge when unknown preparations are being used for treatment.

Example Nine

Here a fatal mistake was recalled by a participant who was a staff nurse at the time of its occurrence. She was not personally involved with the incident.

An alcoholic patient on intravenous Distraneurin was restless at night. (Distraneurin is a rapidly acting hypnotic, frequently used in Germany for the treatment of delirium tremens). The night nurse opened the infusion fully to increase the dose as was usual practice in such a situation. Because of his restlessness the patient had been disconnected from his ECG-monitor. The nurse was called away to a neighbouring ward in order to help with an emergency. She was however, not supposed to leave the ward. Very much later during the night she was found that the patient was dead. She was questioned by the hospital matron but the situation had no further consequences. The nurse was allowed to continue to work on night duty. Several other incidents of negligence on her part were discussed by the nursing staff of the ward. They resented the fact that a situation like that was not followed up further and could pass without consequences for this nurse. This example gave rise to a discussion about responsibility and guilt and about professional accountability.

Example Ten

In this example a medical doctor's misfortune during a series of drug trials with an antithrombotic drug used in ophthalmology, was discussed. He had employed the drug on two patients with deep vein thrombosis and pulmonary embolism respectively. Both patients died of diffuse brain haemorrhage. During the group discussion guilt feelings were discussed, and the fact was mentioned that a doctor's position allows him to risk patient's well-being for the sake of research without having to account for possible negative results.

Example Eleven

This situation was recalled by the same nurse who mentioned example three. During her nursing training she had forgotten to clean a patient's umbilicus before an operation. The ward sister had taken the patient to theatre, where she was reprimanded by theatre staff. She cleaned the umbilicus without referring to the student. Later on she discussed with the student the procedure of preparing a patient for theatre. The non-threatening way in which sister dealt with the student taught this participant to own up to her own mistakes.

Group Discussion Scotland

Example One

This story was told by two nurses, both taking part in the discussion group, and both having been involved in the incident.
One participant of the group discussion and another staff nurse were taking stock of the dangerous drugs (drugs classified by the Dangerous Drugs Act). They found a discrepancy between the accounted for and the actually present ampoules of Papaverin and Pethidine. The discrepancy was traced back to another staff nurse who took part in the group discussion. She had given the wrong drug post-operatively to a patient. She had however, recorded it in the drug-stock book according to the prescription. Thus, there was one ampoule too many of this drug, and of the other there was one ampoule missing. (The two participants could not remember which drug was given and which had been prescribed). The nurse who had given the drug had just returned to nursing, it was her first day on duty.
The nurse who found out the mistake was very unhappy, having to report the incident to the nursing officer and to the doctor. The doctor retrospectively wrote up the drug that was actually given to the patient as it was similar in action to the one originally prescribed. Subsequently the case was dealt with at hospital level.
Reporting a colleague's mistake was addressed during the group discussion as the main problem regarding this example.

Example Two

One participant related an incident were a staff nurse on an acute psychiatric ward had given 600 mg. of an anticonvulsant instead of the prescribed 400 mg.. 600 mg. had been prescribed for another patient.
That morning 'mayhem' was going on in the ward. Ward sister (the participant) informed the nursing officer on duty. He was not her own nursing officer and known to be 'a ruthless character'. She tried to protect the staff nurse from the nursing officer. A quarrel ensued between herself and the nursing officer. He was then involved in sorting out the mayhem on the ward and eventually brought some more staff to help. When he attended to the nurse who had made the mistake he was said to be reasonable and pleasant.
Doctor was informed and adjusted the dosage of the anticonvulsant for the patient so it was levelled out during the day according to the prescribed total.
Still, the ward sister was held responsible by the nursing officer as she had been in charge of the ward. The relationship between the nursing

officer and the ward sister continued to be bad for some time but improved later.
One main point of discussion was the communication between nursing staff and nursing managers. Also the question of accountability was raised and discussed at length. General consent was expressed by all participants of the group discussion that the nurse who gave out drugs was responsible for her own actions.

Example Three

One participant related an experience where she had turned away from the drug trolley in the ward in order to answer a persistent phonecall. As the staff nurse in charge of a psychiatric ward that day, she was also responsible for giving out drugs. A very disturbed young woman took a bottle of tablets from the trolley and ate them. The bottle had contained seven tablets of Haloperidol. The nurse did not notice this and gave her an additional dose of 20 mg. of Haloperidol to calm her down. When the bottle was missing and searched for later on, another patient pointed out that this patient had taken the bottle from the trolley.
The staff nurse informed the nursing officer on duty and a doctor. A statement was written and the nurse was seen by her own nursing officer the next day. He was supportive and no further disciplinary action was taken.

Example Four

This example was recounted by one participant who was not personally involved in it. A doctor had prescribed three or four times the therapeutic dose of Gentamycin for a child. A nurse gave the medication without having it checked by another colleague; the child died. The nurse was severely disciplined. The different ways were discussed in which disciplinary measures were applied for doctors and for nurses.

Example Five

One participant talked about an error which she nearly made while working on a very busy post-natal ward.
Together with another midwife she was checking out a Diamorphine injection. Just in time she realised, that both of them had gone through the procedure of checking without realising that they had picked up 10 mg. ampoules while the patient was to have 5 mg. only. This near error was mentioned to illustrate how easily mistakes are made even if two people do the drugs.

5.2 INTERVIEWS

General Remarks

Each interview is introduced by a short description of the interviewee. The names are fictitious; the facts of the description correspond with reality but have been slightly altered to preserve anonymity.

Interview One (Thelma)

Thelma is a Scottish woman of about 35 years of age. She finished her nursing and midwifery education in 1987. She has worked for three and half years in various areas of midwifery. She is married and has a son and a daughter. She has been in her present post of staff midwife for two years.

Example One

The incident occurred when Thelma was a midwifery-student. Two women had been delivered on the same day and were to have injections of Anti-D within 72 hours of delivery. The drug for the first woman had arrived from pharmacy but was given by Thelma to the second woman. Normally the drug would be checked and given by two nurses. Thelma omitted to verify the identity of the woman and gave it to the second one. Later on the first woman got the second women's dose. No harm was done as both women had exactly the same prescription, and both doses were given within the required time limit. Patients and doctor were not informed. The incident was dealt with at ward level.

Example Two

Thelma gave, together with a student-midwife, a second injection of Diamorphine 5 mg. to a patient who had been given her prescribed analgesic by another nurse 1/2 hour earlier than usual. The patient had complained of pain and said to Thelma, that she had not have any analgesia. The fact that she had been given her dose was recorded by the other nurse on the prescription sheet only and not in the temperature chart, which Thelma had referred to. Doctor was informed later by the ward sister. He retrospectively authorised the medication.

No harm was done as normally Diamorphine is given up to 10 mg. post-operatively three hourly. The incident was dealt with at ward level.

Example Three

During their student days a fellow student of Thelma dropped a bottle of tablets on the floor. She picked them up and put them back into the bottle. The student was severely disciplined by the senior nursing officers.

Interview Two (Joan)

Joan is a 35 years old English married woman. She completed her general nursing training in 1979 and has been a staff nurse in various disciplines for more than six years. She has further qualifications as a nurse for the mentally handicapped and as a midwife. She works as a staff midwife in the delivery room and has been in this post for three years.

Example One

Joan gave a second dose of 2 mg. Valium tablets and Co-Proxamol tablets to a patient within two hours of her having received such a dose. The first dose had been given earlier because the patient had asked for her analgesic before she went to have a bath. The midwife who gave the first dose had not signed for the drugs. When Joan noticed the error and mentioned it to this midwife, she wanted to sign for the first dose retrospectively.
The patient was 'difficult' as she had previously experienced mistakes in her care. Joan informed the nursing officer, statements had to be written and both nurses were counselled. To avoid further complications the consultant was called. He prescribed the first dose as a 'stat' dose.

Example Two

Joan found that one twin baby has not had its scheduled feed of expressed breast-milk, whereas another baby has had two feeds. On being questioned by Joan the nursery nurse admitted that another midwife had mixed up the bottles of expressed breast-milk which were stored in the fridge.
Joan went to discuss the situation with the nursing officer who felt that the matter could not be left. Joan then informed the midwife who was responsible for the mix-up about the fact that she had consulted the nursing officer about the matter. The midwife was not much perturbed. Joan then made an official report to her nursing officer; statements had to be written and the midwife was presumably counselled. The parents of the baby who received the milk were told about the incident but were not very concerned

Interview Three (Pearl)

Pearl comes from the south of England and at the time of our interview she was 29 year old. She qualified as a general nurse in 1982 and as a midwife in 1983. She has worked in midwifery ever since being qualified and has been in her present post for five years.

Example One

Only a short while ago Pearl, working as a midwife in a neonatal unit gave a second dose of an oral iron preparation to a baby. The first dose had not been signed for. The mistake was discovered the following day when the nurse who gave the first dose mentioned that she still had to sign for the iron she had administered. Doctor and parents were informed, and as no harm would come to the baby the incident was not taken further but discussed among the staff only.

Example Two

A colleague of Pearl's and a midwifery-student gave too much Insulin to two pregnant women. The respondent only heard about the incident and witnessed the consequences for the midwife. The mistake occurred because the midwife in charge was very busy with another woman who was in a life threatening situation. The student midwife had asked her to check the Insulin for two other patients. Too high doses were given to the two patients by the student-midwife. Both women had to be treated medically to counteract severe harm that would have resulted from such an overdose.
The midwife had to answer for the mistake. She was backed only by the doctor but not by her colleagues. The case was dealt with by the hospital nursing manager and heard at local Health Board level. Sister in charge of the ward did not allow this midwife to be in charge of the ward after the incident.

Interview Four (Sean)

At the time of our interview Sean was 31 years old. He comes from the North of England. He has been a qualified nurse since 1982 and has worked as a staff nurse on surgical and medical wards for five years. He has held his present post as a charge nurse for the last three years.

Example One

While Sean was in charge of a medical ward in a cottage hospital, a senior staff nurse mistakenly gave 25 mg. of Melleril to an elderly, confused patient, instead of the prescribed 10 mg. The respondent discovered this as he knew that the ward had run out of Melleril 10 mg. tablets. He had discussed with one of the doctors that the night medication for this patient could be omitted for that evening until the correct dosage was obtainable from pharmacy the next day. He had not informed the staff nurse about this.

Sean reported the incident to the nursing officer and the medical staff. The doctor did not want to pursue it, as no harm would come to the patient. The staff nurse was not allowed to give out drugs with junior staff or student nurses, but only with another senior nurse until the situation had been dealt with by the director of nursing services. After about six weeks Sean wanted the situation sorted out as the staff nurse was very unhappy. She wanted to leave nursing altogether. The ward climate was badly affected too. Sean was told by the nursing officers that it was up to him and another charge nurse who worked on that ward, to go back to the normal routine. He proposed a 'subtle supervision' for the staff nurse from time to time.

Example Two

A young doctor gave 40 mg. of intravenous Frusimide to the wrong patient. Sean had checked the medication with the doctor and was to go with him to assist with the administration. While he answered a telephone call, the doctor went away and administered the drug. He gave it to a patient who had just suffered a myocardial infarction. This patient was in the next bed to the one who should have had the Frusimide.

The doctor felt that no harm would come to the patient, Sean offered to mark the medication given down in the Kardex, but the ward sister felt that it should be dealt with by the medical staff. Sean then reported the incident to his nursing officer who also felt that there was nothing further to be done, as this error would have to be dealt with by the medical staff. The medical registrar, whom Sean informed then, only wanted an eye kept on the patient. The patient himself was not told of the mistake.

Example Three

Sean, when a newly qualified staff nurse, thought that an older colleague had possibly given a Heparin injection to a patient at the wrong time. He was not sure of it. Sean tried to find out the time from the patient. He did not openly discuss the situation with the staff nurse. He only mentioned the possibility of a mistake as the drug times had been changed previously. The staff nurse denied the fact. Sean suspected her and another colleague, whom she was friendly with, of having signed the books so that they corresponded with the official prescription times.

Example Four

A student and Sean nearly gave too little/or too high a dose of Ampicillin capsules to a patient. The facts of the incident were not made

clear in the Interview. While he was doing the drug-round with a student, Sean's attention had been diverted by another patient who had asked a question of him.
Sean took this near-incident as an example how important it is that two people check the drugs.

Interview Five (Gerald)

Gerald was 39 years old at the time of our interview. He had been an English teacher and entered nursing as a mature student. He was registered as a psychiatric nurse in 1986 and as a general nurse in 1990. He has worked in psychiatric nursing for two years. He has held his present post as a staff nurse for one and half years.

Example One

Gerald was just about to finish his psychiatric placement while doing his general training. Gerald and the ward sister did the injections together. They forgot to chart the monthly Phenothiazine injection of a schizophrenic patient. It was given again the next day when Gerald was off duty, even though the patient said that he had already had it. Some days later, when Gerald heard the staff on the ward talk about this patient the situation was clarified. The ward sister was disciplined, whereas Gerald was protected by his student status. He was only cautioned by his tutor.

Example Two

This incident, a near-error, happened when Gerald was on night duty. Being very tired when doing the morning drug-round, he began to check out the 10 pm. drugs instead of the 7 am. ones. He realised this and waited until some other member of the team was available to check the drugs with him. He gave no further details.

Example Three

The third incident was a near-error, and happened while Gerald, in his role as a staff nurse was supervising a student nurse. Doctor's handwriting was illegible. 24 units of Insulin were checked out instead of 2 units. The dose was not given because Gerald realised it must be too much.

Interview Six (Gemma)

Gemma was 58 years old at the time of our interview. She qualified as a general nurse in 1975 and has worked in an accident and emergency department for five years and as a ward sister for nine years. She has held her present post as a ward sister of a gynaecological ward for the last three years. She had been married and has an adult son.

Example One

About two years ago Gemma checked a blood transfusion with agency nurses who helped out on her ward to overcome acute staff shortage. Two pints of blood were given to the wrong patient.
It was not noticed that another patient with the same condition and the same surname was supposed to have the blood. No reactions occurred as this patient had the same blood group. The patient was informed, also the medical staff; precautions were taken with the patient to be alert against possible later reactions.
The incident was dealt with at regional level and noted in the Gemma's files. An RCN Representative was involved with giving advice before the hearing and accompanied her to it. The whole situation caused Gemma a lot of distress.

Example Two

Gemma was a patient herself 20 years ago and was given some tablets unknown to her hitherto. Gemma questioned the staff nurse about the tablets, but was rebuked by her. The staff nurse had made a mistake but did not acknowledge it.

Interview Seven (Mike)

Mike was a civil servant before he entered nursing. At the time of our interview he was 40 years old. He is married and has three sons. In 1983 he qualified as a registered general nurse and in 1985 as a psychiatric nurse. He worked for about four years as a staff nurse on a geriatric ward and for the last four years he has been in charge of an orthopaedic ward

Example One

While on night duty as a staff nurse Mike mistakenly gave 100 mg. of Atenolol, a cardiac drug and beta-blocker to the wrong patient. Mike immediately informed the junior doctor who was on duty about the incident. The doctor was not unduly concerned but asked Mike to check the patient's blood pressure twice at half-hourly intervals. The patient was not told and no mention of the error was made either in the nursing report in writing, nor in the oral report. Mike was not sure whether the doctor noted the incident in the medical notes.

Example Two

A colleague of Mike told him about a staff nurse who had given Diamorphine to a patient instead of Morphine. Mike's friend had left it to the nurse to deal with the situation, hoping that she would sort it out appropriately. The nurse got a doctor to prescribe retrospectively a 'stat' dose of Diamorphine, which was then signed for by the nurse in the patient's notes and in the DDA book.

Interview Eight (Anne)

Anne is a Scottish woman of about 35 years of age. She qualified as a general nurse in 1976. She is married and has two children. Before her marriage she had worked as a staff nurse in theatre. For the last ten years she has worked as an agency nurse mainly on medical or surgical wards.

Example One

Anne worked on a regular basis at the same hospital. The incidents she talked about happened during that time. She was unsure whether or not she gave Tyridizine instead of Thyroxine to a patient. The patient was unusually sleepy after the drug-round. No harm was done. Anne discussed the incident was with a colleague/friend who reassured her that most probably she had not made a mistake.

Example Two

While giving out drugs, Anne and a student nurse were distracted by a patient choking and his visiting wife fainting at the same time. The student gave Vitamin tablets to a wrong patient while Anne's attention was focused on the distraction. She reported the incident to the nursing officer and the charge nurse. It was subsequently dealt with at ward level.

Example Three

A fellow student of Anne gave the wrong eyedrops to a patient. The student was frightened to tell anyone because of possible consequences. She discussed it with her peers only.

Example Four

Checking a Heparin injection with another agency nurse, Anne found that the dose was too high. An error was prevented.

Example Five

On night-duty Anne did not use Milton on an open bedsore as was usual practice on this ward, because she had no access to the lotion cupboard during the night. The patient was better served with a Calamine dressing according to Anne anyway. She reported the situation to the ward sister the next morning. The ward sister had no objections.

Interview Nine (Chris)

Chris is an Irish woman, about 36 years old. She qualified as a general nurse in 1975 and has worked as a staff nurse in various areas until 1985 when she was made a ward sister on a female medical ward, a post she still holds. She is married and has a two year old son.

Example One

Chris overlooked an Insulin prescription for a new patient. It was a very busy day with extreme staff shortage. A report about the patient had not been given comprehensively neither in writing nor orally. During the afternoon the patient was very ill for not having had her Insulin. By then Chris was off duty. Doctor was informed and could stabilise the patient. Both, the patient and her husband were informed. The incident was dealt with by the nursing officer. Statements were written, a counselling was given and it was recorded in the respondent's files. Chris was very upset but found it helpful to discuss the situation at length with her staff.

Example Two

When a student, Chris forgot during her drugs-assessment to shake a bottle of Nystatin-suspension. The examining sister drew Chris' attention to the fact. Chris repeated the procedure correctly and shook the bottle to assure that the right dose was to be given. An error was not made and Chris passed her assessment. She experienced a positive way of teaching.

Interview Ten (Henry)

Henry is a Scottish man of about 27 years of age. He worked as a postman until he took up nursing. He is married but has no children. His psychiatric training he completed in 1985 and his general training in 1988. He had worked in the care of the elderly for two years as a staff nurse and has held his present post on chronic psychiatric ward since 1988.

Example One

When Henry was just qualified he gave out the drugs in a psychiatric ward together with a student nurse. A patient had a fit and cut his scalp. While Henry was attending to the patient the student carried on with the drug round and gave 100 mg. of Largactil to the wrong patient.

Doctor was informed and felt it would suffice to explain the situation to the patient. He let her lie down, and asked for her to be observed for a while.
Henry informed his nursing officer, who reported the mistake to the nursing management. He was generally unsupportive. Henry had to recite the drug-administration procedure. Statements were to be written; Henry got a written warning and the incident was noted in his files.

Example Two

When a conversion student, Henry and a staff nurse misread the Insulin regimen of a patient, they gave the next day's dose. The prescription was badly written up by the doctor. Report was made to the nursing officer and the incident was discussed at ward level.

Example Three

A colleague of Henry told him about an error he had made. Instead of 100 mg. of Largactil tablets he had given 400 mg. to a patient. A 400 mg. container had been added to the drug-trolley and the nurse was unaware of it. At the time he did not tell anyone but watched the patient.
The incident had frightened him considerably. About a fortnight later he discussed the situation with Henry. Henry showed a lot of understanding. The question of hiding mistakes for fear of disciplinary action was discussed.

Example Four

In one hospital where Henry had worked it was usual practice for one member of staff to give out the drugs for one half of the ward and another nurse to continue with the second half. After having finished with his half, Henry handed over to a staff nurse to carry on with the rest of the ward. He had already checked out the tablets for one patient from the second half of the ward, signed for them as given, but left the cup on top of the trolley. The staff nurse checked out the tablets again and gave them to the patient. When she wanted to sign for them she saw Henry's signature. She was under the impression of having made a medication error. Only the next day she discussed the situation with Henry, who tried to reassure her. She was upset and felt that this had to be reported to the charge nurse. She blamed herself for having made an error.
The situation was discussed among the team and the drug-routine was changed. Drug-rounds were to be done by the same nurse throughout the whole ward.

Example Five

Henry had been told by a friend about a nurse who had been heavily disciplined because she had given the drug-cupboard keys to a doctor to prepare his own intravenous injections. Instead of water he mistakenly used Potassium Chloride to dilute the drugs. The patient suffered from severe shock. There were no consequences for the doctor.

Interview Eleven (Jane)

Jane is presently studying for a higher nursing degree. She is 32 years old and has qualified as a general nurse and a midwife in 1985 and 1987 respectively. She has worked as a staff midwife in the Lake District since 1987.

Example One

During an evening shift tablets of Paracetemol and of Brufen were given to the wrong patient by a student nurse who worked under Jane's supervision. The student acted as a 'runner' giving out the drugs previously checked by Jane. The patient did not wear an identification armband and the student omitted to verify her identity.
The patient was told about the mistake and reacted understandingly. The doctor was also informed and did not want the incident to be taken any further as he was going to prescribe these drugs for the patient anyway. The incident happened because 'Kardexes got muddled up' and many patients, being in the unit for several months did not wear identification-armbands. The situation was dealt with at hospital level first and was then passed on to the regional Health Authority. Statements had to be written and Jane was suspended from giving out medicines until the case was heard at regional level. A Union representative supported Jane through the hearing. The incident was noted in her files. The whole situation caused her a lot of distress.

Interview Twelve (Hilary)

Hilary is a 45 year old Scottish woman. She qualified as a nurse for the mentally handicapped in 1975 and worked in that field as a staff nurse for four years. She then did her general training and qualified as a general nurse in 1980. She is married and has three daughters, two of whom are training as nurses. Until 1989 she worked as a ward sister in an Ear, Nose an Throat department. Presently she studies part time for a higher degree in nursing.

Example One

About 11 years ago when Hilary was a pupil nurse and worked on night duty, she realised that two patients' night sedations were mixed up by the nurse in charge. The patients had changed beds. The charge nurse was not disturbed by the incident, whereas to Hilary it was the cause of much worry. She did not know then what effects the drugs had, and she was offered no explanation from the charge nurse either. She wanted to talk to someone about it, but that charge nurse did not deem this necessary.

Example Two
Hilary, when an enrolled nurse, questioned a prescribed dose of Prednisolone because it seemed too high. Even though the staff nurse in charge showed some reluctance at first, Hilary called the doctor to check the prescription. The doctor changed it as indeed she had made an error and the correct dosage was administered to the patient subsequently. Hilary's conscientiousness caused a good working relationship between herself and the staff nurse in charge.

Example Three
Hilary could prevent a medication error when she was a student nurse, training for the general register. She noticed how a staff nurse prepared to give a pre-meditation to the wrong patient. Even though all patients going for an ophthalmologic operation that morning, were to have the same drugs, it would have meant that this patient had his pre-medication too early. The nurse did not show any reaction at being corrected as the ward was very busy that morning.

5.3 SELF REPORTS

Self Report One
As a newly qualified staff nurse, the writer of this self report was in charge of a ward. Doing the drug-rounds with a student she directed the student to give Insulin to a patient. Both had gone through the correct process of checking. However, the student did not check the patient's armband to verify his identity and subsequently gave the Insulin to the wrong patient.
Doctor and nurse manager were informed. Statements were written. An RCN representative was involved at the hearing at hospital level. The writer was counselled and the incident recorded in her files.

Self Report Two
After 13 years of night duty the writer of this report had returned to work on day duty. On a busy surgical ward she gave the wrong pre-medication to a patient. The tablets were checked with a bank nurse

who did not know the routine well. The writer informed the anaesthetist and harm to the patient was prevented as he could adjust the anaesthetic.
Ward sister and nursing officer were informed, a statement had to be written and was kept in the writer's files for three months. The two nurses involved were counselled. The surgeon acknowledged the nurse's honesty.

Self Report Three

As a second year student the writer of this report was doing the drug-round with a staff nurse. He gave Warfarin to the wrong patient. A doctor was informed, but no further action was taken. The incident had distressed the writer greatly, as he had only recently come to Britain and felt still insecure in his new surroundings.

Self Report Four

About 20 years ago the writer, then a ward sister, was doing the drug-round alone. Instead of .01 mg. of Thyroxin she gave .1 mg. to a patient. The mistake was only noticed when she realised that there had been no Thyroxin .01 mg. on the trolley. Possibly, the patient had been given the larger dose for quite some time by various other nurses. Doctor was informed and he spoke to the patient. Apparently no harm had ensued. Statements from the sister, pharmacists and doctor were handed to the hospital matron. It was presumed that pharmacy had issued the wrong strength of Thyroxin. Sister was reprimanded by the matron. Shortly afterwards the drug-routine was changed. Two nurses were to check and give out the medicines.

Self Report Five,

Example One

While a second year student on a surgical ward on night duty the writer was checking out post-operative medications (Pethidine) with an agency nurse. Day staff discovered the next day that the patient should have had Pethilorfan because of respiratory discomfort. Doctor was informed, the mistake had no consequences for the patient.
The doctor understood that his handwriting could have been misread. The agency nurse had left for home after night duty was over, the student had to wait and was reprimanded by the assistant matron.

Example Two

When the writer was a newly qualified nurse she did not notice that two children in her ward had changed beds. The night duty situation in the ward was very busy. Two nurses were checking drugs. One child took the medicines intended for the other one. The respondent reported the incident to nursing administration and was called into the hospital again during the day. The consultant was informed, but did not worry as no harm had come to the child.

Self Report Six

This report was written by a German nurse who had worked in Germany and Great Britain. The incident happened about 20 years ago when the writer went back to Germany to work on an Intensive Care Unit that was attached to a medical ward.

While being observed by a male nurse she prepared the intravenous injections. She wanted to dissolve an Antibiotic with Sodium Chloride but mistakenly stretched her hand towards an ampoule with Natrium Citricum. The male nurse beside her made a comment and said "Do you want to kill the patient?" He seemed to gloat over the fact that he had caught her about to make a mistake. A mistake was prevented, but the nurse was strongly shaken and emotionally affected by the thought of what could have happened. The incident was never talked about.

5.4 UKCC DOCUMENTS

Document One (Nurse A.)

While a ward sister Nurse A. was doing the drug-round with a first year student. A patient was to have Salbutanol and Ipatropium via a nebulizer. Nurse A. checked out and prepared the drugs in a syringe, gave this to the student saying 'nebulizer'. The student injected the contents of the syringe intravenously into a venflon (an intravenous catheter). Nurse A. noticed the mistake and alarmed the student by crying 'no'. The relatives of the patient were at the bedside at the time. The nurses carried on with the drug-round. After the next patient had his tablets, Nurse A. explained the error to the student and the called a doctor and a clinical nurse specialist. The patient arrested and died quickly.

Statements were written at the time. A lot of publicity followed and two and a half years later the case was brought up to be dealt with by the UKCC Professional Conduct Committee. The nurse was found guilty of professional misconduct but her name was not removed from the register. The student carried on with her training.

Document Two (Nurse B.)

The nurse concerned has been a midwife since 1968. She worked as a midwifery sister on a labour ward and was in charge of a patient about to deliver. She felt that labour should be augmented by a Syntocinon infusion. She contacted a doctor and the infusion was authorised by telephone. A medical student commenced the infusion. Difficulties with the infusion pump arose which Nurse B. could not control and the patient received Syntocinon in a rapid flow for an unknown length of time. Another midwife was called to assist with the faulty infusion pump. She noticed the rapidly flowing Syntocinon and switched the infusion off. The foetal heart beat subsequently decelerated, medical assistance was called. Contractions commenced rapidly and delivery followed. The mother and child were well.

Notes written up by Nurse B. were found to be inadequate. At first she denied the fact that the patient had had a rapid flow of Syntocinon. As this was established according to the CTG-tracings, she admitted to it, saying that she did not know how the drip could have been switched on.

The disciplinary procedure was set in motion, Nurse B. was demoted to staff midwife grade and was only allowed to practice under the supervision of an experienced midwife, she was given a final warning at the time, and went into early retirement due to ill health nine months after the incident.

At the UKCC Professional Conduct Committee hearing two years later she was found guilty of professional misconduct and her name was removed from the register.

One problem that was identified during the disciplinary hearing was the fact that Syntocinon was added to the infusion before the drip was set up. But this was usual practice in the hospital.

Document Three (Nurse E. and Nurse S.)

Two part-time staff nurses, Nurse E. (a staff nurse since 1974) and Nurse W. were on night duty on a two bedded high dependency unit which was extremely busy the night in question. One patient was an 80 year old gentleman who had just undergone major surgery.

A doctor prescribed by telephone one gram of Digoxin for this patient, to be given via an intravenous infusion over 12 hours. Staff Nurse W., receiving the call was not willing to carry out this order unless it was put in writing. She questioned the dose. The doctor phoned back and confirmed the dose after consulting another doctor. Nurse W. and Nurse E. then calculated that they would need 20 Ampoules to make up one gram. This calculation was wrong. Had they calculated correctly, they would have arrived at 2000 ampoules and would have known that

the prescription could not be right. One gram would have been a lethal dose in any case. They asked the doctor to bring up some ampoules to make up the calculated 20. While doing so, the doctor wrote up the prescription. Nurse W. then went for her break and Sister S., part-time sister in charge (nursing since 1951) came to relieve her. She also brought up some ampoules to make up the 20 asked for. Sister S. checked the calculation, agreed on 20 Ampoules and helped Nurse E. to commence the infusion.
The patient arrested and died. The doctor had been on the unit throughout but the nurses found it difficult to communicate with her. It had been found that subsequently the prescription had been altered to one milligram of Digoxin; (as this was a matter concerning the doctors, this was not further addressed during the UKCC hearing).
An enquiry by the local health authority ended with a single stage final warning for Nurse E., she had to work on day duty for a short while and had to take part in an introduction and training programme before she went back on night duty. Meanwhile she had been promoted and worked as a full time sister on day duty in the unit. Nurse S. resigned from her job as a night sister following the incident, and has worked in a nursing home since. She had been involved in another drug error previously. At the UKCC Professional Conduct Committee hearing one and a half years later both nurses were found guilty of professional misconduct but their names were not removed from the register.

Document Four (Nurse C.)

A patient was brought into a psychiatric day hospital unit in a state of distress and suffering from myoclonic spasms. Nurse C. was in charge and worked together with a State Enrolled Nurse. It was an unusually busy morning. Doctor was contacted by the SEN and verbally ordered 5 mg. of Valium Elixir to be given from the patient's own supply. The doctor wanted to have lunch before he saw the patient. Nurse C. knew the woman to be an epileptic and feared she would get worse if not sedated properly; she administered 20 mg. of Valium Elixir. The patient settled and slept, Nurse C. checked on her every half hour. When the doctor came, Nurse C. asked him to write up 20 mg. of Valium for this patient retrospectively. He refused.
Nurse C. had qualified as a mental nurse in 1985. Since 1988 she had worked as a sister in the day hospital. After the incident she was dismissed following the local disciplinary procedures. The case was reported to the UKCC by her nursing managers.
She was charged with professional misconduct by the Professional Conduct Committee one and a half years later. She admitted to the

charge, which was confirmed during the hearing. Her name was not removed from the register.

Document Five (Nurse T.)

The nurse responsible for this sequence of events, Nurse T., was a sister on a busy medical ward. Together with a student nurse she checked out Morphine tablets 10 mg. and Tamoxifen 20 mg. for Mrs. O. at 8 am. The lady should have had the Tamoxifen at 6 am. and the Morphine at 8 am. Sister signed her Kardex and the DDA book (record for dangerous drugs) according to the prescription and not according to the time the drugs were actually given.

The student gave the tablets to the wrong patient Mrs. M., who was prescribed 40 mg. of Tamoxifen at 9 am. The student then continued the drug-round with her clinical teacher. When they came to Mrs. O., the student realised her mistake. The teacher informed Nurse T. who promised to sort things out. She notified Mrs. M.'s doctor, that the patient probably has had 10 mg. of Morphine which she was not supposed to have. Later on Nurse T. found a tablet on the office floor which she believed to be Morphine 10 mg., she discarded it and signed the register accordingly thinking that after all the patient did not have it. She informed the student that no error had occurred.

Nurse T. gave the next dose of Morphine 10 mg. to Mrs. O. at 2.30 pm. and got a staff nurse to sign for it as given at 6 pm. in order to comply with the prescription. Both patients had been diagnosed as having cancer of the spine and were known to suffer great pain. Nurse T. did not record any of the discrepancies on the patient's drug sheets or Kardexes. Thus Mrs. M. has probably had 20 mg. of Tamoxifen at 8 am. and Mrs. O. had only one dose of Morphine 10 mg. at 2.30 that day.

The staffing quality on the ward had been inadequate. Nurse T. had been a sister in that hospital for 7 years. A disciplinary hearing at hospital level ended with Nurse T. being dismissed. She appealed against the decision at board level and was offered reinstatement as a staff nurse. She declined this and eventually took up a sister's post in a home for the disabled. Her credits there were very good.

She was charged with professional misconduct by the UKCC Professional Conduct Committee. She admitted to being guilty of misconduct at the hearing three and a half years later. This was confirmed but her name was not removed from the register.

Document Six (Nurse P. and Nurse M.)

Nurse P. worked as a part time staff nurse on an eight bedded Coronary Care Unit on night duty. Nurse M. worked as a full time staff nurse there.

A 63 year old patient had been admitted that evening, who arrested on the unit, was resuscitated and was to be treated with intravenous Lignocaine subsequently. Two doctors who were not too familiar with that particular unit were on duty. A bad climate prevailed between medical and nursing staff. Apart from written orders there was not much communication.
The intravenous Lignocaine was written up as follows:

60 mls 10.30 - 11 pm.
120 mls 11.00 - 1 am.
240 mls 1.00 - 9 am.

As the infusion pump was working at millilitres per hour and as it had been usual to write up prescriptions in millilitres per hour, the nurses set the pump accordingly not realising that the doctor had meant the patient to have the stated quantities within the times written down and not throughout that time. The nurses were misled by the different way of writing this prescription. They did not convert it into millilitres per hour. In order to give the prescribed dose with this infusion pump it should have been set at:

120 mls for 1/2 hour (10.30 - 11.00 pm.)
60 mls for 2 hours (11.00 - 1 am.)
30 mls for 8 hours (1.00 - 9 am.)

Instead the patient got:

60 mls between 10.30 - 11 pm.
120 mls between 11.00 - 1 am.
240 mls between 1.00 - ...

This meant that the patient got only half the amount prescribed during the first thirty minutes, four times the amount between 11.00 pm., 1 am., and eight times the amount subsequently. The patient started to have convulsions at about 2.30 am., arrested and died.
Both nurses had a fair amount of experience in the CCU but had not done coronary care courses. Nurse P. did initially question the dosage on the prescription sheet but the doctor confirmed that he wanted it the way it was written, not realising that the nurses were going to misinterpret the prescription. The nurses were not aware of the fact that Lignocaine was given in decreasing doses. The doctors were not familiar with the infusion pump nor with the usual way of writing the doses on this ward. One doctor came at about 11.30 pm. to give an intravenous sedation to the patient. He did not notice that the speed of the intravenous Lignocaine was already too fast. The two nurses were

relieved by a nursing officer and a sister for their breaks, during short handovers no attention was drawn to the infusion.

The incident was followed up by the usual procedures, details of which are not recorded in the UKCC document. A hearing before the UKCC Professional Conduct Committee took place one and a half years later. It was decided that the facts did not constitute misconduct.

After the incident, in this hospital infusions given via an infusion pump were to be set up and controlled by doctors only. Nurses would be allowed to adjust the flowrate according to doctor's orders.

Index